Scepticism and Literature

Scepticism and Literature

An Essay on Pope, Hume,
Sterne, and Johnson

FRED PARKER

OXFORD
UNIVERSITY PRESS

*This book has been printed digitally and produced in a standard specification
in order to ensure its continuing availability*

OXFORD
UNIVERSITY PRESS

Great Clarendon Street, Oxford OX2 6DP

Oxford University Press is a department of the University of Oxford.
It furthers the University's objective of excellence in research, scholarship,
and education by publishing worldwide in

Oxford New York

Auckland   Cape Town Dar es Salaam   Hong Kong   Karachi
Kuala Lumpur Madrid Melbourne Mexico City   Nairobi
New Delhi Shanghai Taipei Toronto
With offices in
Argentina Austria Brazil Chile Czech Republic France Greece
Guatemala Hungary Italy Japan South Korea Poland Portugal
Singapore Switzerland Thailand Turkey Ukraine Vietnam

Oxford is a registered trade mark of Oxford University Press
in the UK and in certain other countries

Published in the United States
by Oxford University Press Inc., New York

ISBN 978-0-19-925318-0

For Jan

Acknowledgements

I AM grateful to Howard Erskine-Hill, Tamara Follini, David Hopkins, Tom Mansell, Jan Parker, and Felicity Rosslyn for reading earlier drafts of some or all of this material: it is a better book for their suggestions. I am also indebted to Stefan Collini, Susan Manning, Terry Moore, and the late Wil Sanders, who have provided stimulus and illumination in ways not to be pinned down in a footnote. And I thank my students at Clare for providing me with a splendid composite image of my ideal reader.

Contents

NOTE TO THE READER   viii

LIST OF ABBREVIATIONS   x

1. RATIONAL IGNORANCE AND SCEPTICAL
   THINKING   1

2. JUST SUPPOSING: LOCKE'S *ESSAY CONCERNING
   HUMAN UNDERSTANDING*   54

3. 'SWORN TO NO MASTER': POPE'S SCEPTICISM
   IN THE *EPISTLE TO BOLINGBROKE* AND *AN
   ESSAY ON MAN*   86

4. INNOCENCE AND SIMULATION IN THE
   SCEPTICISM OF HUME   138

5. *TRISTRAM SHANDY*: SINGULARITY AND THE
   SINGLE LIFE   190

6. JOHNSON'S CONCLUSIVENESS   232

SELECT BIBLIOGRAPHY AND FURTHER READING   282

INDEX   287

Note to the Reader

'SCEPTICISM', AS THE reader will discover, is not in this book used in a restricted or technical sense, but intended as a term of wide implication, that illuminates much that is valuable in eighteenth-century literature (and beyond). Therefore, although the book comes at this literature from a particular angle, it should also serve as a more general introduction to, and warm recommendation of, writing which those unfamiliar with it sometimes suppose to be unrewarding. There are separate chapters on Locke, Pope, Hume, Sterne, and Johnson; each can be read by itself, as a freestanding essay on a single author. I have not assumed that the reader already knows the material, and quote freely. At the same time, there is a broader, cumulative argument; this is partly about the eighteenth century, partly about living in (and writing out of) a condition of flux and irresolution, and partly about the relation between sceptical thought and literature. Although scepticism would seem to undermine the grounds of belief and action, in some of the best eighteenth-century literature a theoretically paralysing critique of reason, precept, and language went hand in hand with a vigorous intellectual, moral, and linguistic confidence. To realize philosophical scepticism *as literature* was effectively to transform it. This argument is outlined in the first chapter, and then more sharply focused through comparisons between my main authors, who can be seen more clearly in relation to (and, often, in dialogue with) one another. There are also sustained comparisons with Montaigne, who is a major presence in the book. The whole and the parts both have their interest; neither, I hope, has been subordinated to the other.

As far as I am aware, there exists no good general study of scepticism and eighteenth-century literature as such; discussion in this area has tended either to concentrate on single authors or to boil the literature down, more or less reductively, into the history of ideas. Distinguished exceptions, however, include the early chapters of A. D. Nuttall, *A Common Sky: Philosophy and the Literary*

Imagination (1974) and Leo Damrosch, *Fictions of Reality in the Age of Hume and Johnson* (1989); their arguments differ from mine, but the concerns of both books overlap with my own.

On a few occasions, details of spelling or punctuation in quotations which seemed likely to confuse a modern reader have been altered.

Abbreviations

Bolingbroke	*The Works of the late Right Honorable Henry St. John, Lord Viscount Bolingbroke*, ed. David Mallet, 5 vols. (London, 1754)
Boswell, *Life*	*Boswell's Life of Johnson. Together with Boswell's Journal of a Tour to the Hebrides and Johnson's Diary of a Journey into North Wales*, ed. G. B. Hill, rev. L. F. Powell, 6 vols. (Oxford, 1934–50)
Enquiries	David Hume, *Enquiries concerning Human Understanding and concerning the Principles of Morals*, ed. L. A. Selby-Bigge, 3rd ed. rev. P. H. Nidditch (Oxford, 1975)
Essay	John Locke, *An Essay concerning Human Understanding*, ed. Peter H. Nidditch (Oxford, 1975)
Johnson	*The Yale Edition of the Works of Samuel Johnson*, ed. John H. Middendorf *et al.* (New Haven and London, 1958–)
Johnson, *Lives*	Samuel Johnson, *Lives of the English Poets*, ed. G. B. Hill, 3 vols. (Oxford, 1905)
Montaigne	*Essays of Michael Seigneur de Montaigne*, trans. Charles Cotton, 2nd ed., 3 vols. (London, 1693)
Pope	Alexander Pope, *Poetical Works*, ed. Herbert Davis (Oxford, 1966)
Religion	David Hume, *The Natural History of Religion and Dialogues concerning Natural Religion*, ed. A. Wayne Colver and John Valdimir Price (Oxford, 1976)
Treatise	David Hume, *A Treatise of Human Nature*, ed. L. A. Selby-Bigge, 2nd ed. rev. P. H. Nidditch (Oxford, 1978)
Tristram Shandy	*The Florida Edition of the Works of Laurence Sterne. Volumes I–II: The Life and Opinions of Tristram Shandy, Gentleman*, ed. Melvyn New and Joan New (Gainesville, Fla., 1978)

Rational Ignorance and Sceptical Thinking

This is a book about literature in the eighteenth century, but I hope it may also seem timely at the start of the twenty-first. There is a sense in which we are all sceptics now. Any tolerably unpartisan overview of what goes on in the arts and humanities, and what has gone on over, say, the last forty years, reveals a clamorous plurality of approaches and priorities. It has become extraordinarily difficult to adopt any discourse as authoritative, as justifying one's procedures, rather than as merely providing a local idiom in which to speak, a *pro tem* framework within which work can seem to be done. That word 'discourse' is itself indicative. Like other current terms which press to be associated with the activity of thinking— 'model', 'paradigm', 'ideology', 'construction'—'discourse' speaks of a loss of intellectual innocence, of our modern sceptical hyper-alertness to thinking as a lens or filter or reconfiguring matrix, rather than a window onto the world. And colleagues or fellow-students—equally well-read, equally intelligent—are apt to be using lenses made up to quite different prescriptions, so that to glance across from one's own desk to see what others are doing can be to experience a certain giddiness. This giddiness is hardly allevi-ated by the reflection that such queasy moments are peculiarly responsive to the world we live in, the condition sometimes rather easily called postmodern, where the quantity and breadth of infor-mation available, the accelerating rate of cultural change, and the foregrounded role of historical and psychological conditioning, have reinforced the claims of pluralism and diversity to what can seem an unprecedented degree. Such a reflection does not help. The eternal verities may not be within reach, but thinking which forgoes all aspiration to truth seeks anxiously for another *raison d'être*. Intelligence will not happily resign its concern with fundamental ends and meanings, to accept a merely instrumental function.

For the malaise induced by this glance sideways, there can be two attempted remedies. One can return to the work in hand, and get one's head down—not in denial of what has been seen, but in response to it. After all, if understanding can be found only within some governing model or framework of thought, to be forever questioning the model is to make understanding impossible. Or one can stand up and walk about the room, looking at what is going on at many other workdesks, in pursuit of some less vulnerable, more globally adequate meta-understanding of the processes at work. The metaphor presents these as alternatives, and indeed they involve genuinely opposing tendencies—engagement on the one hand, critical detachment on the other—but if in practice they are mutually exclusive, they are likely each to prove unsatisfactory. To keep one's eyes on the page, head down, will not facilitate communication with those who see things differently; it encourages a rather stiff and inflexible posture, a mind emphatic as to the cogency of the local thesis, but uncertain—or defensive, or uninterested—as to its relation to wider concerns or its meaning for a wider audience. On the other hand, to be walking about the room looking over the work of others, whether exhilarated by the sense of one's own freedom, or dismayed and overwhelmed by the variousness revealed, may preclude the kind of serious engagement needed to give shape and life to any project. What is desirable is a synthesis, a way of incorporating the sceptical awareness of plurality and indeterminacy within the activity of positive inquiry and the articulation of strong perceptions, such as can at least hope for a more general endorsement. Hence the term 'sceptical thinking', which I use for this desirable quality of intelligence, is meant to suggest a certain unexpected co-existence: though imbued with scepticism, yet still thinking, and though thinking, yet still sceptical.

'Sceptical thinking' involves, then, a certain doubleness of stance. It is a practice, or a process, not an intellectual position, and where it advances positions it does so with a certain playfulness or irony, with a consciousness of their necessary provisionality or contingency: as if opening a dialogue. Indeed, actual dialogue may be its most natural habitat, as in some ideal university seminar, or in the practice (as we may imagine it) of Socrates in dialogue, from which the whole idea of academic education largely descends. But where university seminars fall below the ideal, and Socrates himself is no longer available, sceptical thinking can often be more effectively realized in writing and, in particular, in *literature*. The concept of the literary evades definition, of course, but it comes in indispensably here: for it is the literary artist who understands how, even in discursive writing, words can mean more than they say, and who best knows how to prevent the flow of intelligence from hardening into mere propositions. The sceptical thinker and the literary artist have, by this account, a certain natural affinity; if scepticism can lead to an opening up of the mind to what lies outside reason's scope, it is the imaginative writer who realizes and relishes this opening, finding pleasure in the play of intellect precisely while qualifying or modifying the kind of truth-claim that the intellect can make.

The American philosopher Richard Rorty has suggested that thinkers may be divided into two kinds, which he calls 'metaphysicians' and 'ironists'.[1] Metaphysicians believe that the truth is 'out there', rooted in the nature of things, in the reality of the world and of the self, and providing (in principle, whatever the difficulties in practice) the criteria by which the adequacy of our attempts to formulate it can be judged. When confronted with difference of opinion, the metaphysician looks to draw out significant principles of disagreement, errors to be purged, or problems to be argued through and solved in the drive towards truth. Ironists prefer a different account: that the truth is rather made than found, being a function of language, of those incommensurable formulations of moral value and way of seeing the world which Rorty describes as each culture's and each person's 'final vocabulary'. In difference of opinion the ironist sees the operation of different languages, which may challenge and supplant one another for a variety of contingent reasons, but not because one of them has more of the truth. For the ironist, fresh thinking is thus a matter of redescription rather than refutation, the juxtaposing of one 'final vocabulary' with another:

---

[1] See especially the first four chapters of Richard Rorty, *Contingency, Irony, and Solidarity* (Cambridge, 1989).

and whereas the metaphysician looks to the hard sciences, as traditionally understood, for a model of intellectual progress, the ironist
turns to literature, and its power to 'make it new' through
language, as the exemplary case of what thinking is.

Rorty's ironist has a good deal in common with my sketch of
the sceptical thinker, and to a large extent the one illuminates the
other. She (the gendering is Rorty's) is acutely aware of the situation of plurality which I described at the outset, and in response
has drawn conclusions which are as definite as the ironist stance
can allow: one outcome being an enlargement of the scope of literature, whose stories, visions, and persuasions fill the vacuum left
by the abdication of a compelling rationality. There are also differences. One is that my sceptical thinker is more likely than Rorty's
ironist to dwell on the *inadequacy* of the intellect, still
preserving—in a consciously unresolved tension—some notion of
that reality of things to which the intellect is inadequate. A related
point of difference, more immediately relevant here, has to do
with where Rorty places the metaphysician and the ironist in
history. In Rorty's account, the metaphysician dominates philosophical thought from Plato to Kant, in the tradition which looks
to distinguish appearance from reality, and seeks to establish
universal, ahistorical truths and laws. Little changed in this respect
when theology gave way to the Enlightenment project of the eighteenth century. Only in the nineteenth did the movements of
thought take place that were increasingly to facilitate and to
express the attitude of the ironist: the Romantic turn to subjectivity and imagination; German idealist philosophy; the work of
Nietzsche. This is a story with a strong plot, although for some
purposes it might be more helpful to think of the metaphysician
and the ironist as perpetually and recurrently in debate or
dialogue. Aspects of Rorty's formula for the ironist fit certain
traditions of classical rhetoric well enough, for example. But if one
had to name a century in which Rorty's metaphysician loses his
dominance and the ironist starts to look about her, there is a case
that Rorty begins too late: for the eighteenth century was not only
the period of the Enlightenment but also, and especially in Britain,
a pervasively sceptical age.

By opening with such a highly generalized description of sceptical thinking, I wanted to propose that the interest of this topic is
not confined to a single period. Radical scepticism is not the inven-

tion of the modern mind, and I hope to suggest that its strategies and implications, although perennial, have never been more interestingly explored than in the eighteenth century. This was a period when philosophy and literature were often on unusually friendly terms, and any line of demarcation between them sometimes disappeared altogether. Philosophy which felt the influence of Locke, or saw itself as involved in a more general civilizing enterprise, was reluctant to set itself apart as a specialism; and literature embraced discursive modes—biography, history, the essay, the epistle, the dialogue—at least as warmly as the modes of pure imagination, such as lyric or fiction, which more easily lend themselves to the notion of some fundamental dichotomy between poetry and philosophy, the imaginative artist and the penetrating thinker. That dichotomy is largely inactive in the eighteenth century. One mark of that is the scope granted to the literary category of *wit*, which at its finest is inseparably bound up with 'strength of thought', as Samuel Johnson put it, being 'at once natural and new'.[2] Such an account envisages the marriage of metaphysician and ironist. A high proportion of the finest eighteenth-century writing, in England as in France, is explicitly intellectual, exposing ideas to the transforming processes of literary realization and imbuing them with a new, subtle life, invisible in summary and resistant to abstraction, that easily evaporates in any history of thought. Where those ideas are themselves more or less explicitly touched by or concerned with scepticism, the thinker and the artist can come beautifully together.

That will best be shown when I come to look closely at specific works: Pope's *Essay on Man* and his Horatian epistle *To Bolingbroke*, Hume's *Enquiries* and *Dialogues concerning Natural Religion*, Sterne's *Tristram Shandy*, and Johnson's *Rasselas*. But those works do not stand alone; they come out of a wider culture of thought that may fairly be described as sceptical. Consider the entry in Johnson's *Dictionary* for 'Enthusiasm', which was, in eighteenth-century usage, a largely pejorative term.

ENTHUSIASM
1.   A vain belief of private revelation; a vain confidence of divine favour
     or communication.
          Enthusiasm is founded neither on reason nor on divine revelation,

---

[2] Johnson, *Lives*, i.19 f.

but rises from the conceits of a warmed or overweening brain.
Locke
2. Heat of imagination; violence of passion; confidence of opinion.

It is the inclusion of that last phrase that is striking. Johnson—who
is not, one would have thought, a man diffident in his own opinions—sees 'confidence of opinion' as an aspect of enthusiasm, and
classes it together with heat of imagination and violence of passion.
The religious 'enthusiast' is a deluded egotist who believes that
God has spoken to him directly; the man confident in his opinions
is hardly less liable to be suffering from the conceits of a warmed
or overweening brain.

The *Dictionary* entry records common usage, reflecting a
common assumption. Many eighteenth-century thinkers and writers in Britain shared an intellectual stance, a way of thinking, that
may broadly be called sceptical. This is not to minimize the differences between them; the scepticism of Pope is not that of Sterne,
the scepticism of Hume is in important respects opposed to that of
Johnson or of Burke. But they had all taken on board the fundamental lesson of Locke's *Essay concerning Human Understanding*:
that true knowledge must be grounded in actual experience, and
that this is a state of affairs which drastically restricts its scope and
reach:

> Whensoever we would proceed beyond these simple *Ideas*, we have from
> Sensation and Reflection, and dive farther into the Nature of Things, we
> fall presently into Darkness and Obscurity, Perplexedness and Difficulties;
> and can discover nothing farther, but our own Blindness and Ignorance.[3]

Hence they were all suspicious (or satirical) of confidence of opinion, they all emphasized the limitations of the intellect, the impossibility of arriving at rational certainty on the great questions of
human life. To suppose otherwise is the error of our natural human
vanity. Bolingbroke (Pope's 'guide, philosopher and friend' in the
Essay on Man) wrote in his *Letters or Essays* to Pope:

> Nothing can be more effectual than to go to the root of error, of that prim-
> itive error which encourages our curiosity, sustains our pride, fortifies our
> prejudices, and gives pretence to delusion. This primitive error consists in
> the high opinion we are apt to entertain of the human mind. . . . The less
> men know, the more they believe that they know.[4]

---

[3] *Essay*, II.xxiii.32: p. 314.   [4] Bolingbroke, iii.328, 330.

This displacement of the authority of human intellect is central to Pope's purposes in the *Essay on Man*: 'In Pride, in reas'ning Pride, our error lies.'[5] It is reasoning pride that produces 'confidence of opinion', a shallow knowingness that is absurdly unaware of the weakness of human reason. 'When this author presumes to speak of the universe, I would advise him a little to distrust his own faculties, however large and comprehensive.'[6] That is Johnson caustically reviewing the work of one Soame Jenyns, who had taken upon himself to justify the existence of evil within the providential order of the cosmos. Johnson attacked Jenyns' theory in two ways: he exposed some glaring logical contradictions and fallacies within the argument itself—using strong reasoning to overcome weak— but he also exposed Jenyns' reasoning *per se* to the test of experience. What Jenyns has to say about the compensations and side-benefits of poverty, for example, is all very logically argued, very reasonable and plausible on its own terms, *until one remembers what poverty is actually like.*

Life must be seen before it can be known. . . . The poor, indeed, are insensible of many little vexations, which sometimes embitter the possessions and pollute the enjoyments of the rich . . . but this happiness is like that of a malefactor who ceases to feel the cords that bind him when the pincers are tearing his flesh.[7]

Jenyns was an easy target; but the reference of theory to experience is, in this period, one of the fundamental strategies of the sceptical intelligence. 'Experience, which is constantly contradicting theory, is the great test of truth',[8] Johnson declared, making the characteristic assumption that experience will normally contradict, not corroborate, even the best hypotheses of the mind. Both his principal travel books—the fictional *Rasselas* and the *Journey to the Western Islands*—make much of the disparity between expectation and actuality; many of his essays advance some cogent general proposition which is then promptly modified under review. Burke invoked a similar principle in his polemic against those apologists for the French Revolution who believed one could impose an

---

    [5] *An Essay on Man*, I.123: Pope, p. 244.
    [6] Review of Soame Jenyns, *A Free Inquiry into the Nature and Origin of Evil* (London, 1757): *Samuel Johnson: Major Works*, ed. Donald Greene (Oxford, 2000), p. 531.
    [7] *Samuel Johnson*, ed. Greene, p. 527.
    [8] Boswell, *Life*, i.454 (July 1763).

abstract theory of rights, possessing all the truth that any such theory could claim, upon the complex circumstances of a real society:

These metaphysic rights entering into common life, like rays of light which pierce into a dense medium, are, by the laws of nature, refracted from their straight line. . . . The pretended rights of these theorists are all extremes; and in proportion as they are metaphysically true, they are morally and politically false.[9]

For a sceptical thinker, systematic rationalism is always suspect, at least when applied to human life, in matters moral and political, for it ignores all that Burke understands by 'refraction'. The progress of true intelligence is one in which, as Gibbon put it, 'the belief and knowledge of the child are superseded by the more rational ignorance of the man'.[10]

In calling this exercise of intelligence 'sceptical', I am using a term which most of these writers would have repudiated. In eighteenth-century usage 'sceptic' tends to have a more limited, and often pejorative, implication. The term is often used to recall the philosophical doctrine of Pyrrhonian scepticism (after the Greek philosopher Pyrrho), outrageous to common sense, which denies that the mind can attain to certain knowledge of anything whatsoever. (Sophisticated versions aspire simultaneously to doubt even the certainty of that denial.)[11] When Pope writes that man, although largely ignorant, still has 'too much knowledge for the Sceptic side',[12] it is of this extreme philosophical position that he is thinking. To embrace scepticism in this sense is generally regarded as a piece of mild philosophical lunacy, intellectual perversity, or mere (though, interestingly, modish) pretentiousness. Thus Johnson's portrait of Sim Scruple in the *Idler* is a piece of easy satire:

9 Edmund Burke, *Reflections on the Revolution in France*, ed. Conor Cruise O'Brien (Harmondsworth, 1968), pp. 152 f.

10 Edward Gibbon, *Memoirs of My Life*, ed. Georges A. Bonnard (London, 1966), p. 56.

11 Excellent studies of the history of philosophical scepticism are *The Skeptical Tradition*, ed. Myles Burnyeat (Berkeley and Los Angeles, 1983), and works by Richard H. Popkin: *The History of Scepticism from Erasmus to Spinoza* (Berkeley and Los Angeles, 1979) and *The High Road to Pyrrhonism* (San Diego, 1980). The last of these deals mainly with eighteenth-century thought.

12 *An Essay on Man*, ii.5: Pope, p. 250.

One of the greatest men of the society was Sim Scruple, who lives in a continual equipoise of doubt, and is a constant enemy to confidence and dogmatism. Sim's favourite topick of conversation is the narrowness of the human mind, the fallaciousness of our senses, the prevalence of early prejudice, and the uncertainty of appearances.[13]

And Hume describes Berkeley's arguments as 'merely sceptical' in that they *'admit of no answer and produce no conviction'*.[14] Although Hume himself does *entertain* a theoretical scepticism of this extreme and rigorous kind, as we shall see, he carefully differentiates it from the moderate or 'mitigated' version which he is recommending to his public.[15]

A second common implication of 'sceptic' in this period is specifically theological: one who doubts the truth of Christian revelation. In the seventeenth century scepticism had been a weapon of theological controversy between Catholic and Protestant; now, for the first time, there was a growing awareness, extending well beyond the circle of academic theology, that the truth of Christianity itself was susceptible of intelligent attack on rational grounds, or of displacement by a reasoned deism or 'natural religion' which had no use for Christian doctrine. The debate over the scope of human reason was profoundly bound up with the question of faith, as the defenders of Christianity struggled to determine whether reason was their friend or their foe. Berkeley's *Treatise concerning the Principles of Human Knowledge* was, its subtitle explained, an inquiry into *The Grounds of Scepticism, Atheism, and Irreligion*: the three overlapping terms represented a continuous spectrum of unbelief. The title of a work by Isaac Watts defines the area of debate in many works, and minds, of the time: *The Strength and the Weakness of Human Reason: or, The Important Question about the Sufficiency of Reason to Conduct Mankind to Religion and Future Happiness, Argued between an Inquiring Deist and a Christian Divine.* This conflict between the claims of deism and of Christianity could lead to a painful bewilderment; one of John Wesley's correspondents wrote to him as follows:

---

[13] *Johnson*, ii.259 (*Idler* 83).
[14] David Hume, *Enquiries*, p. 155 n.
[15] This is most clearly seen at the end of the *Enquiry concerning Human Understanding*, discussed in Chapter 4 below.

I have long laboured under a disease which comes the nearest to that which is named scepticism. I rejoice at one time in the belief, that the religion of my country is true; but how transient my joy! While my busy imagination ranges through nature, books, and men, I often drop into that horrible pit of Deism, and in vain bemoan my fall. The two main springs which alternately move my soul to these opposite opinions are, first: Can it be, that the great God of the boundless universe, containing many thousand better worlds than this, should become incarnate here, and die on a piece of wood? There I lose my belief of Christianity.

But on the other hand, I think, Well, let me examine the fitness of things which Deism boasts of. And certain it is I discern nothing but beauty and wisdom in the inanimate parts of the creation. But how is the animate side of nature? It shocks me with powerful cruelty and bleeding innocence. . . . Yet in Deism I can discern no reward for the one or punishment for the other. On this view of things the Castilian King might well say he could have directed God to amend His creation.[16]

For this writer, as surely for others, doubt as to the truth of Christianity was the gateway to a more radically sceptical uncertainty, an oscillation between 'opposite opinions'.

Although both the philosophical and the theological meaning of 'sceptic' are relevant—in particular, they can both be applied to Hume—neither can be identified with the quality of 'sceptical thinking' which is the subject of this study. Both refer to intellectual *positions* (on knowledge, on religion), or at most to an equipoise or oscillation between positions. Sceptical thinking, as I understand it, is something more dynamic and open-ended, a process. It is so because it responds to the expectation of almost inevitable slippage in a series of distinct but overlapping areas: between theory and experience, between the mind and the world, between language and its referents.

The most influential way of framing this expectation was provided by the philosopher John Locke. Locke's *Essay concerning Human Understanding*, published in 1690, did more than any other work to set the agenda for eighteenth-century thought. The *Essay* will be discussed in detail in the next chapter. But in brief summary, what Locke did was to ask *how* we know what we think we know, and to insist that this epistemological question be the foundation of all responsible inquiry. How does the mind build up

---

[16] *The Journal of the Rev John Wesley*, ed. Nehemiah Curnock, 8 vols. (1910), iv.141 f.; 2 Dec. 1755. The correspondent is identified by the editor as John Walsh.

its manifold ideas and cognitions from its sensory experience? Locke's own way of asking and answering that question foregrounded it as a question, an unexpectedly complex problem, and effectively drove a wedge between the mind and the world which no later thinker could ignore. Our ideas, according to Locke's persuasive analysis, are at best only obliquely and insecurely related to the realities which they offer to represent. The effect of this analysis was a kind of epistemological Fall, installing an angel with a flaming sword between the mind and the world, now no longer its natural home. Especially influential was Locke's focus on language, which he came to see as the heart of the problem: words are always liable to come loose from our actual ideas, and to project the mirage of ideas and knowledge which we do not in fact possess. This informs, for example, the kind of critique Johnson makes of Soame Jenyns: 'I do not mean to reproach this author for not knowing what is equally hidden from learning and from ignorance. The shame is to impose words for ideas upon ourselves or others. To imagine that we are going forward when we are only turning round.'[17] The shame is to impose words for ideas upon ourselves or others. The more completely the mind loses touch with real ideas, ideas which originate in actual experience of the world, the more busily and confidently it can produce its own opinions. Such is the common outcome of formal education, according to Pope's *Dunciad*; his sinister pedagogue, Dr Busby, explains:

> . . . Since Man from beast by Words is known,
> Words are Man's province, Words we teach alone.
> .　　.　　.　　.　　.　　.　　.
> We ply the Memory, we load the brain.
> Bind rebel Wit, and double chain on chain,
> Confine the thought, to exercise the breath;
> And keep them in the pale of Words till death.[18]

To use words like this is to have only the illusion of knowledge. The result is what Johnson called 'cant': the wordiness one falls into when one has lost one's soul to other men's formulations, to social convention, to intellectual fashion, to cliché of all kinds: the frictionless free-wheeling of the mind disengaged from the reality of

---

[17] *Samuel Johnson*, ed. Greene, p. 534.
[18] *The Dunciad*, IV.149–60: Pope, p. 557.

things. An example would be the philosopher who explains to Johnson's Rasselas what it means to live according to nature:

'When I find young men so humble and so docile,' said the philosopher, 'I can deny them no information which my studies have enabled me to afford. To live according to nature, is to act always with due regard to the fitness arising from the relations and qualities of causes and effects; to concur with the great and unchangeable scheme of human felicity; to co-operate with the general disposition and tendency of the present system of things.'

The prince soon found that this was one of the sages whom he should understand less as he heard him longer. He therefore bowed and was silent, and the philosopher, supposing him satisfied, and the rest vanquished, rose up and departed with the air of a man that had co-operated with the present system.[19]

But it is not only the fool and the charlatan whose language goes unendorsed by reality. The other philosopher that Rasselas encounters commands a much more substantial rhetoric: he showed, 'with great strength of sentiment, and variety of illustration', how reason should rule over passion and imagination, and how men might arm themselves with patience 'against the shafts of malice or misfortune'.[20] These words are not meaningless, and their tendency is one which Johnson would have approved. But when Rasselas, much edified, returns to the philosopher the next morning, he discovers him in a state of collapse: during the night his only daughter died of a fever.

'Have you then forgot the precepts,' said Rasselas, 'which you so powerfully enforced? Has wisdom no strength to arm the heart against calamity? Consider, that external things are naturally variable, but truth and reason are always the same.' 'What comfort,' said the mourner, 'can truth and reason afford me? of what effect are they now, but to tell me, that my daughter will not be restored?'

The prince, whose humanity would not suffer him to insult misery with reproof, went away convinced of the emptiness of rhetorical sound, and the inefficacy of polished periods and studied sentences.[21]

Perhaps the prince, who is always keen to be 'convinced', there swings too easily to another extreme: but it is this inevitable gap between even the best generalizing and meaning-giving structures

[19] *Johnson*, xvi. 88 f. (ch. 22).   [20] Ibid. 71, 73 (ch. 18).
[21] Ibid. 75 f. (ch. 18).

the mind can build through language, and the realities which lie beyond those structures, that sceptical thinking continually recognizes and works with.

NEGATIVITY

Such recognition tends to support the more modern, unphilosophical implication of 'sceptical': unsanguine, disillusioned. Not, in fact, given to 'enthusiasm' of any kind. Although in principle scepticism challenges the finality of any theory of life, pessimistic no less than optimistic, in practice its first effect is normally disconcerting or disillusioning. The explanatory structures the mind builds for and around itself are, naturally, likely to be affirmative or idealistic, or at the least to be usefully functional or comforting; scepticism routinely suggests that such formulations are unlikely to survive the encounter with experience. When Johnson writes, 'No place affords a more striking conviction of the vanity of human hopes than a publick library',[22] or Gibbon reflects that history is 'little more than the register of the crimes, follies and misfortunes of mankind',[23] these sentiments may not be formally expressed in the terms of philosophical scepticism—they are advanced as positive opinions, vigorously asserted—but they implicitly rebut more positive formulations of the significance and importance of intellectual achievement. In this respect they connect formal scepticism, whereby a theoretical position is found wanting, with the expression of a (in the looser sense) sceptical, disillusioned attitude of mind. This connection is a natural one: for scepticism questions man's pretensions to knowledge, and much of human dignity is vested in man's power to know, his status as a thinking being, and his ability to give an account of the significance of his life and the value of his achievements. The eighteenth-century reader must have thought it only fitting to learn of Pyrrho, the founder of scepticism, that 'no one was ever more completely persuaded . . . of the vanity of things':

---

[22] *Johnson*, iv.200 (*Rambler* 106).
[23] Edward Gibbon, *The History of the Decline and Fall of the Roman Empire*, ed. David Womersley, 3 vols. (Harmondsworth, 1994), i.102 (ch. 3).

He especially despised human nature, and he was forever repeating the words of Homer, where he compares men to leaves . . . he liked this parallel because it indicated the mortality of mankind and that inconstancy of their opinions, turning like leaves with every change of the wind. He greatly enjoyed other passages in Homer, where men are compared to birds and flies, and where their infirmities and childishness are described.[24]

The natural tendency of scepticism, then, would seem to be radically disillusioning and destabilizing. Of course, it could be used, and often was used, as a local tactical weapon, a way of breaking down support for one position in order to give breathing-space for another. An Enlightenment thinker with a positive, more or less rationalist programme, might play the sceptic with his adversaries. Or, on the other side of the religious divide, when Johnson demolished Soame Jenyns' pertly optimistic cosmology, this was, in part, to preserve orthodox Christian piety from contamination by such foolish rationalizations. But when the sceptical intelligence is once allowed free play, it readily invokes a more general negativity. Jenyns had suggested that the evils which afflict mankind may contribute to the greater good by giving pleasure to some higher order of beings, rather as the suffering of animals contributes, under some circumstances, to the pleasure of men. Johnson seized on this in unforgettable terms:

I cannot resist the temptation of contemplating this analogy, which I think he might have carried further very much to the advantage of his argument. He might have shown that these *hunters, whose game is man* have many sports analogous to our own. As we drown whelps and kittens, they amuse themselves now and then with sinking a ship, and stand round the fields of Blenheim, or the walls of Prague, as we encircle a cockpit. As we shoot a bird flying, they take a man in the midst of his business or pleasure, and knock him down with an apoplexy. Some of them, perhaps, are virtuosi, and delight in the operations of an asthma, as a human philosopher in the effects of the air pump. To swell a man with a tympany is as good sport as to blow a frog. Many a merry bout have these frolic beings at the vicissitudes of an ague, and good sport it is to see a man tumble with an epilepsy, and revive and tumble again, and all this he knows not why. As they are wiser and more powerful than we, they have more exquisite diversions; for we have no way of procuring any sport so brisk and so lasting as the paroxysms of the gout and stone, which undoubtedly must make high

---

[24] Pierre Bayle, *Historical and Critical Dictionary*, trans. Richard H. Popkin (Indianapolis, 1965), pp. 196, 208 f.

mirth, especially if the play be a little diversified with the blunders and puzzles of the blind and deaf.[25]

The rhetorical strategy here, perfectly adapted to scepticism, is that of the *reductio ad absurdum*, where an opponent's ideas are ironically 'carried further', allowed to unfold in logical abstraction to the point where the warping of experience (or credibility) away from theory becomes manifest. The human stupidity, the moral obscenity of Jenyns' analogy is mercilessly exposed. But what does this leave Johnson to affirm? The *reductio* is always a double-edged sword, when developed with the imaginative fullness that Johnson employs here: if one *were* to make rational inferences from the nature of the case, to inquire what kind of wise and powerful being would be gratified by human sickness and suffering, would the answer not indeed have to be something as disturbing as Johnson here allows himself to imagine? The aggression against Jenyns both masks and expresses an anger at the human condition—or at least, at *any* attempt to find the human condition justifiable. At one level, the implication is that one should abandon the attempt at a rational solution altogether; yet the alarming nature of what has been glimpsed in the process—a nightmare theology, a malignant deity—awakens the need for some kind of stabilizing account more urgently than before. Thus the tactical demolition of Jenyns threatens to go beyond its immediate target, to lead to a more fundamental sceptical impasse. Johnson writes as a Christian, but his argument at this point is surprisingly comparable with that put forward by the infidel Hume in his *Dialogues concerning Natural Religion*. In that work also, the religious traditionalist, Demea, calls in the help of the sceptic in order to see off the cause of rationalistic deism, but gets more than he bargained for. Philo develops this *reductio ad absurdum* of the deist's reasoned argument from design:

This World, for aught he knows, is very faulty and imperfect, compar'd to a superior Standard; and was only the first rude Essay of some Infant Deity, who afterwards abandon'd it, asham'd of his lame Performance: It is the Work only of some dependant, inferior Deity; and is the Object of Derision to his Superiors: It is the Production of Old-Age and Dotage in some superannuated Deity; and ever since his Death, has run on at Adventures, from the first Impulse and active Force, which it receiv'd from

---

[25] *Samuel Johnson*, ed. Greene, p. 535.

him—You justly give Signs of Horror, *Demea*, at these strange Suppositions: But these, and a thousand more of the same kind, are *Cleanthes*'s Suppositions, not mine. From the Moment the Attributes of the Deity are suppos'd finite, all these have Place. And I cannot, for my part, think, that so wild and unsettled a System of Theology is, in any respect, preferable to none at all.[26]

The sceptical speaker, Philo, does not mean to affirm these horrible possibilities, any more than Johnson does in the case of Jenyns; both formally lay them at their opponent's door ('these . . . are *Cleanthes*'s Suppositions, not mine'); yet it is Philo and Johnson who give imaginative substance to these dark visions, and invite us to entertain as rational what they simultaneously propose we should reject as intolerable. If this is stressful, Philo's sceptical alternative—no system of theology at all—scarcely offers greater comfort:

Look round this Universe. What an immense Profusion of Beings, animated and organiz'd, sensible and active! You admire this prodigious Variety and Fecundity. But inspect a little more narrowly these living Existences, the only Beings worth regarding. How hostile and destructive to each other! How insufficient all of them for their own Happiness! How contemptible or odious to the Spectator! The whole presents nothing but the Idea of a blind Nature, impregnated by a great vivifying Principle, and pouring forth from her Lap, without Discernment or parental Care, her maim'd and abortive Children.[27]

Such a great theological question as the cause of evil obviously throws the negativity of scepticism into peculiarly sharp relief. Scepticism did not attach itself only to religion, but the growing uncertainty about what Locke had called 'the reasonableness of Christianity', along with the swirling torrents of controversial writing which this generated, was one of its most potent sources, as well as its most striking manifestation. Gibbon's scepticism, for example, came partly from his experience of being converted in his youth from Protestantism to Catholicism, and then back again, and so becoming familiar with the strength of the negative arguments on both sides. As he pointed out, this kind of intellectual education was available to anyone who looked into the *Dictionnaire historique et critique* of Pierre Bayle. This was published in 1697, with important additions in the second edition of 1701; an English

---

[26] *Religion*, p. 194 (Part 5).   [27] Ibid. 241 (Part 11).

translation appeared in 1710, and was reprinted in 1734, at the same time as a second English translation that incorporated new material. It was a work highly influential on the intelligentsia in Britain as well as France; if Locke was one great source of eighteenth-century scepticism, Bayle was another. The term 'dictionary' is, however, misleading: Bayle's massive work is better described as a hugely learned and miscellaneous encyclopedia of thought, organized biographically, that displays a particular interest in theological and philosophical controversy. It is full of the sceptical play of argument and counter-argument. Even its format induces a kind of vertigo in the system-making mind. Articles generate a web of lengthy footnotes (with further footnotes of their own) in which the implications of a particular theoretical position are meticulously drawn into dialogue with the arguments that have been or that might be made against it. Gibbon rightly described it as the supreme textbook of modern scepticism:

In reviewing the controversies of the times, he turned against each other, the arguments of the disputants: successively wielding the arms of the Catholics and protestants, he proves that neither the way of authority, nor the way of examination can afford the multitude any test of Religious truth .... His critical Dictionary is a vast repository of facts and opinions; and he balances the *false* Religions in his sceptical scales, till the opposite quantities, (if I may use the language of Algebra) annihilate each other. The wonderful power, which he so boldly exercised of assembling doubts and objections had tempted him, jocosely to assume the title of the νεφεληγετα Ζευς, the cloud-compelling Jove; and in a conversation with the ingenious Abbé (afterwards Cardinal) de Polignac, he freely disclosed his universal Pyrrhonism. 'I am most truly (said Bayle) a protestant; for I protest indifferently against all Systems, and all Sects.'[28]

Although Bayle was a French Protestant refugee, writing in the safety of Holland, who always professed himself a believing Christian, Gibbon is right to stress the extraordinary, dizzying disinterestedness with which Bayle follows reason wherever it leads. In illustration, take his treatment of the origin of evil, as this arises from his article on the Manicheans. Of Manicheism, the heresy that there are two eternal principles of Good and Evil who make the universe their battleground, Bayle writes: 'It must be admitted that this false doctrine, much older than Manes, and incapable of being

---

[28] Gibbon, *Memoirs*, pp. 64 f.

maintained as soon as one accepts Scripture, in whole or in part, would be rather difficult to refute if maintained by pagan philosophers skilled in disputing.'[29] In a long footnote he sketches a debate between two pagan philosophers, one holding the Manichean hypothesis of two principles, the other maintaining that the universe is the product of a single divine principle. Bayle argues in some detail that the Manichean would be on much stronger ground when it came to giving a rational explanation of 'how it happens that man is wicked and so subject to pain and grief'.[30] 'The Manicheans, with a completely absurd and contradictory hypothesis, explain experiences a hundred times better than do the orthodox, with their supposition so just, so necessary, and so very true of an infinitely good and all-powerful first principle.'[31] No rational argument could be produced that would convince the Manichean that the hypothesis of the single principle was the correct one.

He would never be led back to the truth. Human reason is too feeble for this. It is a principle of destruction and not of edification. It is only proper for raising doubts, and for turning things on all sides in order to make disputes endless.[32]

In a complementary article ('Paulicians') Bayle turns to the actual arguments of the Church Fathers against the Manichean explanation of evil, and shows that their only strong argument was based on the appeal to Scripture, while their arguments that in principle 'it is not contrary to the nature of the good principle to permit the introduction of moral evil'[33] are open to the most damaging objections. And post-Reformation theology has only made matters worse: Bayle cites the disputes concerning predestination, 'in which Christians accuse one another of making God the author of sin or of depriving him of the government of the world'.[34] The dilemma is, for the rational-minded Christian, inescapable: if God permitted man freely to fall, he is culpably negligent, while if God predestined the fall, he is the author of sin. A modern Manichean familiar with this controversy would have even stronger rational arguments against orthodoxy. 'The disputes that have arisen in the West among Christians since the Reformation have so clearly shown that a man does not know what course to take if he wants to resolve the

---

[29] Bayle, *Dictionary*, p. 144.   [30] Ibid. 148.   [31] Ibid. 173.
[32] Ibid. 151.   [33] Ibid. 168.   [34] Ibid. 167.

difficulties about the origin of evil, that a Manichean would be much more formidable than previously; for he would refute each side by the others.'³⁵

In thus setting out the superior rationality of Manicheism as regards the origin of evil, Bayle is not commending it to his reader. Like Hume in the *Dialogues* and like Johnson on Jenyns, he is constructing a *reductio ad absurdum*, and like them, his fundamental point is the sceptical one, the insufficiency of reason. But Bayle differs from Hume or even Johnson in presenting a clear alternative to the sceptical impasse: the way of faith.

It is more useful than one would think to humiliate man's reason by showing him with what force the most foolish heresies, like those of the Manicheans, may play games with it in order to confuse the most fundamental truths. This ought to teach the Socinians, who want reason to be the rule of faith, that they are only throwing themselves onto a road to perplexity that is only fit to lead them step by step to denying everything, or doubting everything, and that they are laying themselves open to being beaten by the most abominable people. What must be done then? Man's understanding must be made a captive of faith and must submit to it.³⁶

In Hume, who also admired Bayle, such propositions would carry a subversive irony; Bayle's sincerity rests upon his ability to accept an absolute divorce between the realm of reason and the realm of faith. He reiterated this in the 'Clarifications' which he added, in response to criticism, to the second edition of the *Dictionary*:

One must necessarily choose between philosophy and the Gospel. If you do not want to believe anything but what is evident and in conformity with the common notions, choose philosophy and leave Christianity. If you are willing to believe the incomprehensible mysteries of religion, choose Christianity and leave philosophy.³⁷

What is extraordinary in Bayle—and made some of his readers suspect an ironic intention where none existed—is that he can assert this absolute incommensurability of reason and faith while being himself so committed to the exercise of reason. This is a precarious and intensely unstable stance, but not inherently inconsistent. It is because religious truths are mysteries that lie beyond the reach of reason, that nothing is sacred to Bayle as a reasoning philosopher. And if rational argument leads to scepticism and

³⁵ Ibid. 183.   ³⁶ Ibid. 186.   ³⁷ Ibid. 429.

perplexity, to the universal pyrrhonism which Gibbon found in Bayle, this can only facilitate the act of faith:

How great a chaos, and how great a torment for the human mind! It seems therefore that this unfortunate state is the most proper one of all for convincing us that our reason is a path that leads us astray since, when it displays itself with the greatest subtlety, it plunges us into such an abyss. The natural conclusion of this ought to be to renounce this guide and to implore the cause of all things to give us a better one. This is a great step toward the Christian religion.[38]

But it was not possible for eighteenth-century scepticism to follow Bayle in this. Even those who admired Bayle could not replicate his ability to stand, in 1697, astride the threshold of two worlds—reasoning as boldly as the freest thinker of the Enlightenment, while regarding Christian faith, in the manner of an earlier age, as an irreducible fact of life. When Gibbon discussed the rise of Christianity in the *Decline and Fall of the Roman Empire*, he observed, like Bayle, how scepticism may generate the conditions for faith, but he did so with an altogether different emphasis. The passage tacitly invites the reader to draw parallels between Imperial Rome and the eighteenth century:

The contagion of these sceptical writings [by Cicero and Lucian] had been diffused far beyond the number of their readers. The fashion of incredulity was communicated from the philosopher to the man of pleasure or business, from the noble to the plebeian, and from the master to the menial slave who waited at his table, and who eagerly listened to the freedom of his conversation . . . . The decline of ancient prejudice exposed a very numerous portion of human kind to the danger of a painful and comfortless situation. A state of scepticism and suspense may amuse a few inquisitive minds. But the practice of superstition is so congenial to the multitude, that if they are forcibly awakened, they still regret the loss of their pleasing vision . . . . So urgent on the vulgar is the necessity of believing, that the fall of any system of mythology will most probably be succeeded by the introduction of some other mode of superstition. Some deities of a more recent and fashionable cast might soon have occupied the deserted temples of Jupiter and Apollo, if, in the decisive moment, the wisdom of Providence had not interposed a genuine revelation, fitted to inspire the most rational esteem and conviction, whilst, at the same time,

---

[38] Bayle, *Dictionary*, p. 206. For a helpful discussion of the relation between scepticism and fideism in Bayle, see Oscar Kenshur, 'Pierre Bayle and the Structures of Doubt', in *Eighteenth-Century Studies* 21 (1987/8), 297–315.

it was adorned with all that could attract the curiosity, the wonder, and the veneration of the people. In their actual disposition, as many were almost disengaged from their artificial prejudices, but equally susceptible and desirous of a devout attachment; an object much less deserving would have been sufficient to fill the vacant place in their hearts, and to gratify the uncertain eagerness of their passions. Those who are inclined to pursue this reflection, instead of viewing with astonishment the rapid progress of Christianity, will perhaps be surprised that its success was not still more rapid and still more universal.[39]

Gibbon offers a secular, psychological explanation of the progress of Christianity which has nothing to do with its divine origin, and which coincides so suspiciously with the 'genuine revelation' sent by Providence as to contaminate it with irony. This irony recognizes a distinction within Gibbon's own readership between 'the multitude', who cannot live with scepticism and may therefore take Gibbon's phrases at their face value, and the select group of 'those who are inclined to pursue this reflection', who will recognize how Gibbon's analysis erodes the possibility of Christian belief. For both groups, scepticism and faith can no longer co-exist as they could for Bayle. But this implied divorce is not an entirely happy one. Even after we have picked up the ironies against Christianity, the viewpoint refuses to settle into that of a confident Enlightenment satire. The capacity of 'a few inquisitive minds' to be *amused*[40] by scepticism weighs distinctly light against such a resonant phrase as 'the danger of a painful and comfortless situation': credulity is normally an attractive target for satire, but it looks rather different when seen as the expression of metaphysical anxiety.[41] There is a terrific internal counterbalance in the passage: the more it is understood as an exposure of Christianity-as-superstition, the more it must also be understood as deploring the likely consequences of such exposure. To undermine superstition creates a vacuum which may well be filled by something worse. (Such as

---

[39] Gibbon, *Decline and Fall*, I.498 f. (ch. 15).

[40] 'AMUSE. To entertain with tranquillity; to fill with thoughts that engage the mind, without distracting it. To *divert* implies something more lively, and to *please*, something more important. It is therefore frequently taken in a sense bordering on contempt.' Johnson, *Dictionary*.

[41] This attitude to scepticism is already anticipated in Gibbon's early *Essai sur l'étude de la littérature* (London, 1761), p. 106: 'L'incertitude est pour nous un état forcé. L'esprit borné ne souroit se fixer dans cet équilibre dont se piquoit l'école de Pirrhon.'

the French Revolution, it turned out. Gibbon was to liken this to early Christianity, both being cases of deplorable 'innovation'; he applauded Burke's attack on the Revolution and said that in this cause he could willingly forgive him his reactionary 'superstition'.)[42] Straightforward irony relies on a sharp distinction between those who understand what is going on and those who can be imagined not to—in this passage, between the sceptical few and the credulous multitude—but the opening sentences on the trickle-down effect of sceptical philosophy suggest how this rhetorical distinction is blurred in the real world. The intellectual superiority of Gibbon's perspective is virtually conceded to be a function of his detachment as a non-participant, and what emerges is a more complex and sombre irony which seems, as elsewhere in Gibbon, to include within its shadow the superiority of the philosophical historian:

The rapid and perpetual transitions from the cottage to the throne, and from the throne to the grave, might have amused an indifferent philosopher; were it possible for a philosopher to remain indifferent amidst the general calamities of human kind.[43]

The instability there is political rather than religious, but again the perspective of an amused philosophical detachment is opposed to a more substantial sense of pain and distress.

Gibbon was an unbeliever, but for Johnson too, religious uncertainty could not generate that 'amused' indifference and tranquillity of mind which, according to the classical theory, was the whole point of scepticism. Classical writers—such as Cicero and Lucian—were able to argue about the gods with such good humour, he told Boswell, only 'because they were not in earnest as to religion. . . . Every man who attacks my belief, diminishes in some degree, my confidence in it, and therefore makes me uneasy; and I am angry with him who makes me uneasy'.[44] Johnson, like Gibbon, admired Bayle, but for Johnson too, Bayle's way with scepticism was not an option; the faith of an Anglican could not—unfortunately—be indifferent to rational argument.

---

[42] *The Letters of Edward Gibbon*, ed. J. E. Norton, 3 vols. (London, 1956), iii.216: to Lord Sheffield, 5 Feb. 1791.

[43] Gibbon, *Decline and Fall*, i.291 (ch. 10).

[44] Boswell, *Life*, iii.10 f. (April 1776).

If you join the Papists externally, they will not interrogate you strictly as
to your belief in their tenets. No reasoning Papist believes every article of
their faith. There is one side on which a good man might be persuaded to
embrace it. A good man, of a timorous disposition, in great doubt of his
acceptance with GOD, and pretty credulous, might be glad to be of a
church where there are so many helps to get to Heaven. I would be a Papist
if I could. I have fear enough; but an obstinate rationality prevents me.[45]

It was this 'obstinate rationality' that caused Johnson to seek more
evidence for an afterlife than revelation provided; that made him
angry, because uneasy, with those who attacked his faith. The
anger and the fear are, in some degree, peculiar to Johnson: but all
the sceptical thinkers I shall be concerned with could be described
as obstinately rational, committed to the process and practice of
reasoning even as it uncovers its own severe limitations.

THE RECOURSE TO NATURE: THE NECESSITY OF IRONY

Sceptical thinking in this period is not concerned only with theology. Religious anxiety was simply the most conspicuous manifestation of the radically unsettling question, as old as Socrates, but
bound to emerge with increasing urgency as theological certainties
fell away: if knowledge is uncertain, if argument can always be met
by counter-argument, or found to fall short of experience, or seen
as an expression of the mind's subjectivity, can we ever hope to
know how to live, to *ground* our living on some sanction or principle which gives it meaning? Or are we merely—as far as we can ever
hope to tell—the creatures of arbitrary impulse and blind contingency? Johnson's Rasselas did not succeed, and could never have
succeeded, in his search for information that would permit him to
make a rational 'choice of life'; nor could he find the role-model he
sought, the man wise enough to tell or show him how to live.
' "What then is to be done?" said Rasselas; "the more we enquire,
the less we can resolve." ' So the book ends with a 'conclusion, in
which nothing is concluded'.[46] That was the result of consulting
experience, surveying the world around. Hume reached a similar
impasse by a process of close reasoning. In the first book of his
Treatise of Human Nature he demonstrates that our knowledge of

[45] Ibid. iv.289 (June 1784).   [46] *Johnson*, xvi.99 (ch. 22), 175 (ch. 49).

causality is an illusion, that the existence of an external world is insecure, that the cause of even our own thoughts and actions—that which we call the 'self'—is unknown to us. The world of our experience is held together by nothing more than custom and imagination. This being so, Hume asks, what follows? How, in that case, ought we to live? In the final section, simply yet also precariously entitled 'Conclusion of this book', he sets out the alternatives. Should we try to live by a severely rational scepticism that is so corrosive that it condemns all our common-sense knowledge of the world as illusion? Or should we abandon rationality, and risk opening the floodgates to every impulse of the subjective imagination?

This question is very difficult, and reduces us to a very dangerous dilemma, whichever way we answer it. For if we assent to every trivial suggestion of the fancy; beside that these suggestions are often contrary to each other; they lead us into such errors, absurdities, and obscurities, that we must at last become asham'd of our credulity. . . . But on the other hand, if the consideration of these instances makes us take a resolution to reject all the trivial suggestions of the fancy, and adhere to the understanding, that is, to the general and more establish'd properties of the imagination; even this resolution, if steadily executed, wou'd be dangerous, and attended with the most fatal consequences. For I have already shewn, that the understanding, when it acts alone, and according to its most general principles, entirely subverts itself, and leaves not the lowest degree of evidence in any proposition, either in philosophy or common life. . . . We have, therefore, no choice left, but betwixt a false reason and none at all.[47]

This would seem to be a philosophically desperate state of affairs.

But when Socrates reduced his interlocutors to the same condition of intellectual helplessness in which he professed to find himself, it was with an implication—ironically suggested, elusive to scrutiny, impossible to demonstrate in a court of law—that something valuable was happening in this seemingly destructive process. There is a comparable implication in this passage of Hume. The sense of intellectual crisis is genuine: it comes out of a sequence of sustained and rigorous argument, and it recalls the nervous debility which afflicted Hume for some years, which he described to a physician as 'the Disease of the Learned' and attributed to his

---

[47] *Treatise*, pp. 267 f.

philosophical studies.[48] But in the *Treatise* he presents this 'dangerous dilemma' to his reader almost with the flourish of an escape-artist displaying the strength of his locks and chains. It is true that, for these eighteenth-century writers, faith did not offer itself as the escape from scepticism, or rather as (in both senses) its end, as it had done in the fideism of Bayle—or, differently, in the experience of mystics, with whose dark night of the soul Hume had remarkably compared his own cloud of unknowing.[49] But there was available to them a somewhat parallel move. Instead of faith, they could invoke 'nature'. In the *Abstract* in which Hume summarized the leading thoughts of the *Treatise*, he wrote, 'Philosophy wou'd render us entirely *Pyrrhonian*, were not nature too strong for it.'[50] To see what he meant by this, we can return to the passage in the conclusion to the first book, in which the sceptical impasse reaches its crisis:

We have, therefore, no choice left but betwixt a false reason and none at all. For my part, I know not what ought to be done in the present case. .... The *intense* view of these manifold contradictions and imperfections in human reason has so wrought upon me, and heated my brain, that I am ready to reject all belief and reasoning, and can look upon no opinion even as more probable or likely than another. Where am I, or what? From what causes do I derive my existence, and to what condition shall I return? Whose favour shall I court, and whose anger must I dread? What beings surround me? and on whom have I any influence, or who have any influence on me? I am confounded with all these questions, and begin to fancy myself in the most deplorable condition imaginable, inviron'd with the deepest darkness, and utterly depriv'd of the use of every member and faculty.

Most fortunately it happens, that since reason is incapable of dispelling these clouds, nature herself suffices to that purpose, and cures me of this philosophical melancholy and delirium, either by relaxing this bent of mind, or by some avocation, and lively impression of my senses, which obliterate all these chimeras. I dine, I play a game of back-gammon, I converse, and am merry with my friends; and when after three or four hour's amusement, I wou'd return to these speculations, they appear so cold, and strain'd, and ridiculous, that I cannot find in my heart to enter into them any farther.

---

[48] *The Letters of David Hume*, ed. J. Y. T. Greig, 2 vols. (Oxford, 1932), i.14 (March or April 1734).
[49] Ibid. i.17 (March or April 1734).
[50] *Treatise*, p. 657.

Here then I find myself absolutely and necessarily determin'd to live, and talk, and act like other people in the common affairs of life.[51]

And Hume goes on to acquiesce in the necessity of yielding to what he calls 'the current of nature', his disposition of the moment. If indeed he returns, after a while, to his philosophical speculations, this can only be because the mood so takes him, 'more from the returns of a serious good-humour'd disposition, than from the force of reason and conviction'. For his interest in philosophy is not itself a rational matter, but rather a matter of 'sentiments' (a term that merges opinions with feelings) which 'spring up naturally in my present disposition'.[52]

This movement from sceptical impasse to the current of nature is a very remarkable one. It describes a kind of paradigm shift, whereby the intellectual dilemma is not at all addressed in its own terms but is simply abandoned, displaced by the arrival of a truth of a quite different kind. The shift is from intellect to experience, from Hume as philosopher to Hume as man—a man who dines, has a social life, is subject to mood swings; it is not only described, but enacted in the prose, which moves from a disinterested harvesting of the fruit of reflection into a first-person present-tense subjectivity which offers to register the immediate flux of impulse and emotion. This shift also involves remembering the body ('some . . . lively impression of my senses'); it means a rediscovery of the realm of instinct, a more fundamental way of being in the world than the intellect can provide, which makes possible the relaxation of the intellectual will-to-resolution. At the same time, no grand claim is being made for the realm of nature. Hume's personification of Nature as a force is felt as barely more than whimsy; 'nature herself' is scarcely more than the contingencies of the quotidian, the diversions and distractions of social pastime. Crucial to the effect of the passage is the disparity between the seriousness of the sceptical impasse, as felt from within, and the triviality of the cure. If the cure is not felt as wholly trivial, that is not because of some philistine exaltation of the pleasures of dinner and backgammon over the life of the mind. It is because the cure cannot be altogether

[51] *Treatise*, pp. 268 f.
[52] Ibid. 269–71. On the shift in the connotation of 'sentiment' from 'principle' to 'feeling', see Michael Bell, *The Sentiment of Reality: Truth of Feeling in the European Novel* (London, 1983), pp. 2–7, 15–59.

separated from what precedes it. For if yielding to the current of nature represents, at one level, the collapse of Hume's philosophical enterprise (for his philosophizing achieves nothing: outside his study, he will live and talk and act just like other people), it is also, at another, its truly philosophical outcome. Its value depends on the scepticism which it can be said to evade, yet which it can also be said to preserve and, moreover, to transform into a way of living: for Hume's radical scepticism authorizes such evasion, authorizes its own overthrow, as it could authorize nothing else.

In a later chapter I shall try to relate that passage to Hume's other writing, and to develop an argument specifically about Hume. For the present I want to work with a broader generalization: that the movement there brought into sharp focus informs some of the most interesting works of eighteenth-century literature; it lies at the heart of those works' vitality, and speaks of a common enterprise, that can be traced across works formally quite unlike. Compare, for example, the quotation given above from Hume with this paragraph from *Tristram Shandy*, which has as much claim as any to lie at the centre of that most eccentric book. Tristram has committed a small blunder in the course of writing out a fair copy of his autobiography, is vexed, and feels the need to relieve his feelings:

Instantly I snatch'd off my wig, and threw it perpendicularly, with all imaginable violence, up to the top of the room—indeed I caught it as it fell—but there was an end of the matter; nor do I think anything else in *Nature*, would have given such immediate ease: She, dear Goddess, by an instantaneous impulse, in all *provoking cases*, determines us to a sally of this or that member—or else she thrusts us into this or that place, or posture of body, we know not why—But mark, madam, we live amongst riddles and mysteries—the most obvious things, which come in our way, have dark sides, which the quickest sight cannot penetrate into; and even the clearest and most exalted understandings amongst us find ourselves puzzled and at a loss in almost every cranny of nature's works; so that this, like a thousand other things, falls out for us in a way, which tho' we cannot reason upon it,—yet we find the good of it, may it please your reverences and your worships—and that's enough for us.[53]

Somewhat as in Hume, the sceptical condition of being 'puzzled and at a loss' is juxtaposed to a realm of natural instinct which

<hr/>

[53] *Tristram Shandy*, iv. ch. 17: p. 350.

brings relief. The relief—as in Hume—is not at all a matter of resolving the sceptical impasse; indeed, it exemplifies and reinforces it, being itself opaque to rational understanding. It implies, not any solution of the 'riddles and mysteries' of life, but a way of 'living amongst' them; it comes through a shift between paradigms, from a state of mental abstraction (Tristram immersed in the world of his autobiography) to a sudden recollection of physical surroundings and bodily impulse (Tristram writing out the pages of his book). This is not unlike the shift from Hume expounding philosophical argument to Hume writing about his reactions to his arguments. And as with Hume yielding to 'the current of nature', the shift in Sterne is marked by a new sense of passivity to a larger force: Nature 'determines us' and 'thrusts us', things 'come in our way' and 'fall out for us'. This force is felt as benign, even providential: Hume's 'most fortunately it happens' is more emphatically restated in Tristram's description of Nature as 'dear Goddess'.

This idea of Nature as a force which makes good the deficiencies of reason, and which scepticism both uncovers and is rescued by, is in some respects most clearly theorized by Edmund Burke in his *Reflections on the Revolution in France*. But here the contrast with the passages already quoted will be as significant as the parallel. Burke is defending, against French rationalist critique, the British prejudice in favour of what is traditional and long-inherited:

This policy appears to me to be the result of profound reflection; or rather the happy effect of following nature, which is wisdom without reflection, and above it. . . . Through the same plan of a conformity to nature in our artificial institutions, and by calling in the aid of her unerring and powerful instincts, to fortify the fallible and feeble contrivances of our reason, we have derived several other, and those no small benefits, from considering our liberties in the light of an inheritance. . . . We procure reverence to our civil institutions on the principle upon which nature teaches us to revere individual men; on account of their age; and on account of those from whom they are descended. All your sophisters cannot produce anything better adapted to preserve a rational and manly freedom than the course that we have pursued, who have chosen our nature rather than our speculations, our breasts rather than our inventions, for the great conservatories and magazines of our rights and privileges.[54]

54 Burke, *Reflections*, pp. 119, 121.

In some ways, this could stand as a manifesto for the quality of sceptical thinking which is the subject of this book. Reason is, by itself, 'fallible and feeble'; recourse must be had to 'following nature', to 'the aid of her unerring and powerful instincts'; 'our speculations' stand virtually opposed to 'our nature', which must be chosen in preference to them. Such a summary might equally be drawn from the Hume or the Sterne. But what puts Burke outside the tradition of sceptical thinking as I wish to describe it, is that he writes with none of their playfulness or irony. His language is not willing to give itself away as language: it asserts a rhetoric of power, and constitutes a claim on reality. 'Nature' is invoked as a real, quasi-metaphysical entity, the potential focus of ideological attack and defence. To accuse Burke of being *fanciful* in thus invoking Nature (as his political opponent Tom Paine was in fact to accuse him) would be an attempt to do him real damage: whereas the fanciful quality of the personification of Nature in Hume or in Sterne is already and openly part of their meaning. The image of Hume playing backgammon, or Tristram throwing his wig into the air, is given with perfect consciousness of how incongruously slender a basis this offers for a philosophy of life. But Burke, as Johnson remarked, possessed all the mental powers to an extraordinary degree, *except only wit*.[55] Burke has no use for irony because he does not stand in two places at once: having first made 'nature' as inclusive a concept as possible, his prose insists on the choice between the realm of 'nature' and that of 'speculations', rather than moving between them.[56] If, in this passage as in others, he *theorizes* the sceptical turn to nature with peculiar clarity, this is partly because he sees it, despite himself, from the outside.

That is to say: the situation in which 'sceptical thinking' becomes possible is one that can be fully realized only through the

---

[55] 'We talked of Mr Burke.—Dr. Johnson said, he had great variety of knowledge, store of imagery, copiousness of language.—*Robertson*. "He has wit too."—*Johnson*. "No, sir; he never succeeds there. 'Tis low; 'tis conceit. I used to say, Burke never once made a good joke. What I most envy Burke for, is, his being constantly the same.' Boswell, *Life*, v.32 (Aug. 1773).

[56] Of course, this is a point about the occasion of the *Reflections* as well as about its author: a political emergency is a bad moment for irony. Still, it is an indication of Burke's natural vehemence of mind that his first substantial work, the *Vindication of Natural Society* (1756), was an irony so powerfully sustained that he had to add a preface to the second edition explaining that the work was indeed an irony.

play of irony. It cannot be expressed as an intellectual position, a completed thought; it cannot be registered as a simple item within the history of ideas, or translated into a moral exhortation. Without irony it dwindles into the empty rhetoric of the vain philosopher in *Rasselas*:

> The way to be happy is to live according to nature, in obedience to that universal and unalterable law with which every heart is originally impressed . . . . Other men may amuse themselves with subtle definitions, or intricate ratiocination. Let them learn to be wise by easier means: let them observe the hind of the forest, and the linnet of the grove: let them consider the life of animals, whose motions are regulated by instinct; they obey their guide and are happy. Let us therefore, at length, cease to dispute, and learn to live.[57]

Although thought may be the problem, thought is not simply to be put aside in that way. Irony recognizes the paradox on which sceptical thinking rests: broadly, the paradox that scepticism generates understanding. A theoretically paralysing critique of the pretensions of reason, precept, and language goes hand in hand with a marked intellectual, moral, and linguistic confidence, and this naturally calls out a certain reflexive irony. Thus Johnson maintains that 'definition is, indeed, not the province of man',[58] while at the same time composing the *Dictionary*. Hume offers the reasoned argument that no reasoned argument can have a moral effect, with the evident intention of writing as a moralist. Sterne writes a novel in which successful communication through language seems all but impossible, yet which relies to an extraordinary degree on the rapport between author and reader. Pope's *Essay on Man* castigates the folly of man's attempt to understand his place in the cosmos, as part of Pope's larger understanding of man's place in the cosmos.

This last point is nicely underlined by an observation Johnson makes on the *Essay* in his *Life of Pope*:

> The subsequent editions of the first Epistle exhibited two memorable corrections. At first, the poet and his friend
> > 'Expatiate freely o'er this scene of man,
> > A mighty maze *of walks without a plan*.'
> For which he wrote afterwards

---

[57] *Johnson*, xvi.85–7 (ch. 22).   [58] Ibid. iv.300 (*Rambler* 125).

'A mighty maze, *but not without a plan*':
for, if there were no plan, it was in vain to describe or to trace the maze.
The other alteration was of these lines:
'And spite of pride, *and in thy reason's spite*,
One truth is clear, whatever is, is right';
but having afterwards discovered, or been shewn, that the *truth* which
subsisted *in spite of reason* could not be very *clear*, he substituted
'And spite of pride, *in erring reason's spite*.'
To such oversights will the most vigorous mind be liable when it is
employed at once upon argument and poetry.[59]

On a narrow view, there is no resisting Johnson's logic: but the
irony Johnson turns against Pope's poem is not really so alien to
Pope's own way of seeing within his poem. The proposition that
life is a maze without a plan is in fact, in the *Essay*, strangely
compatible with its formal opposite, that life is a maze 'not without a plan'; hence Pope's insertion of 'not' makes surprisingly little
difference, the one insight flips so easily into the other. Both these
'oversights' in the first edition speak of Pope's willingness to entertain the paradox that scepticism generates knowledge, that a
certain kind of truth might be all the more clear for existing 'in
spite of reason'. The revisions he made in later editions tidy up the
logic locally, but the fundamental paradox remains at the heart of
the poem. One might say that Pope, writing as a poet, sees a
pattern in the maze in spite of the logic of his scepticism: but it
would be more accurate to say that he is never more truly sceptical
than when 'employed at once upon argument and poetry', since it
is precisely the characteristic of sceptical thinking to bring reasoned
argument into relation with that whole field of fully complex
human experiencing of which 'poetry' stands as both symbol and
manifestation. Pope's 'Whatever is, is right' may have the form of
a proposition in a reasoned argument, but when reasoned argument is seen in a sceptical light it becomes, instead, the report of an
experience, an experience not unlike that suggested by Hume and
by Sterne: in which rational inquiry, through the very process by
which it establishes its own inadequacy, finds itself yielding to the
current of nature, and finds in that yielding a paradoxical sense of
rightness. To speak of a play of irony in the *Essay on Man* is to see
how it might be a poem which turns 'at once upon argument and

59 Johnson, *Lives*, iii.162.

poetry', not as trying to ride two horses at once, but as realizing a way of thinking that dissolves the strong dichotomy between argument and 'poetry' which rationality proposes.

MONTAIGNE

Later chapters will look in detail at some of the writers—Pope, Hume, Sterne, and Johnson—in whose work this turn through scepticism to nature is central, and will also attend to the significant differences between them; at this stage I am trying only to identify certain general characteristics, to sketch a template which will suggest the coherence of the topic. But it may be possible to fill out that sketch a little by introducing the work which provided later writers with the most accomplished and influential model of sceptical thinking: the *Essais* of Michel de Montaigne.

The viewpoint of the *Essais* cannot easily be summarized. It is part of the essays' meaning that they portray a mind in movement, so that the vitality of Montaigne's scepticism is communicated at least as much through the manner of his writing as through his explicit declarations. But the long central essay entitled 'Apology for Raimond Sebond' offers a convenient starting-point, being almost a manifesto, in which Montaigne urges the negative aspect of scepticism with great vigour and unusual single-mindedness. In this essay he developed and disseminated the traditional topics of scepticism while adding his own crushing emphasis on the weakness of human reason and the absurd presumption of reasoning man. The classical arguments concerning the senses' power to deceive or overrule reason are reinforced with a tremendous battery of other considerations. Our powers of mind are in many respects not fundamentally different from those of other animals. Intellectuality promotes melancholy, and ignorance is preferable. Opinions, laws, and customs are irredeemably diverse, and often plainly dependent on the accidents of culture and geography: 'What Truth is it that these Mountains impale, and keep it from the World beyond them?'[60] This is true even of religion, which we 'receive . . . after our own fashion by our own hands';[61] theology is hopelessly contaminated by man's inability to conceive of the

---

[60] Montaigne, ii.409.   [61] Ibid. 177.

divine except in human terms. 'What can be more Vain than to imagine to guess at Almighty God by our Analogies and Conjectures? To direct and govern him and the World, by our *Capacities* and our *Laws?*'[62] On such a fundamental question as the nature of the soul, learned opinion is desperately and ludicrously diverse. Diverse phenomena support diverse explanations; any principle of selection between them can only be arbitrary; and in any case, any phenomenon can be interpreted or moralized in opposite senses: "Tis a Pot with two Ears, that a man may take by the Right or Left.'[63] Not only are the objects of our cognition in continuous flux, so is the subjectivity that seeks to grasp them:

Finally, there is no constant Existence, neither of the Objects Being, nor our own: Both we and our Judgments, and all mortal things, are evermore incessantly running and rolling, and consequently, nothing certain can be established from the one to the other, both the judging and the judged being in a continual Motion and Mutation: We have no communication with *Being*, by reason that all human Nature is always in the midst, betwixt being Born and Dying, giving but an obscure apparence and shadow, a weak and uncertain Opinion of it self. And if peradventure you fix your thought to apprehend your Being, it would be but like grasping Water, for the more you clutch your hand to squeeze and hold what is in its own nature flowing, so much more you lose of what you would grasp and hold.[64]

Our judgements are thus inescapably parochial, unstable, and subjective.

The 'Apology' ends with a brief, almost perfunctory invocation of divine truth as that which lies beyond all human understanding. This, however, is uncharacteristic. Far more pervasive in the *Essais* is the paradoxical movement by which such seemingly destructive scepticism accompanies, or liberates, access to 'nature'; it is this that makes Montaigne not only a source of negative scepticism, along with Locke's destabilizing epistemology and Bayle's arsenal of arguments and counter-arguments, but also a model of sceptical thinking in its more dynamic and enabling aspect.

In truth we are all of us, insensibly in this Error, an Error of a very great Train, and very pernicious Consequence. But whoever shall represent to his Fancy, as in a Picture, that great Image of our Mother Nature, portrayed in her full Majesty and Lustre, whoever in her Face shall read so

[62] Ibid. 294. [63] Ibid. 413. [64] Ibid. 446.

general and so constant a Variety . . . that man alone is able to value things according to their true Estimate and Grandeur.[65]

We are 'all of us' stranded in the subjectivity of error; yet our ability to glimpse what it would be to apprehend nature 'in her full majesty and lustre', means that we find ourselves in two places at once: both insensibly in error, and, through the scepticism that raises that state of error into consciousness, obliquely in touch with the truth of things. Through the destruction of all claims to a general, normative knowledge, the arch-sceptic can nevertheless invoke the idea of nature, or of living naturally, as a kind of normative understanding from which we can at least realize our divergence, and so which we can, in a manner, possess.

There are many ways of placing the emphasis when reading Montaigne; mine is, inevitably, a selective interpretation. (One reason for thinking it a good one is that passages which affirm and exhibit this naturalness of being come more frequently and more impressively in the final book of the *Essais*, as unfolding more and more fully the potentialities of the sceptical stance.) The reading I am proposing here does, however, echo how Montaigne was read at the start of the eighteenth century, by at least one intelligent reader. In the 'Dialogue of the Dead' which Matthew Prior constructed between Montaigne and Locke, Locke is dry, cautious, moderate, and logical, while Montaigne is all Gascon exuberance and provocative inconsequentiality: yet it is Locke who stands accused of a way of thinking that leads to a sceptical cul-de-sac. His emphasis on epistemology has had the effect of confining him within the self; his analysis of the internal workings of the mind has necessarily cut him off from the realities of life and action. He is one of those philosophers who 'think with too much Subtilty to be pleased with what is natural'.[66] Prior was not alone among early readers in remarking how easily Locke's empiricism ran into scep-

---

[65] Montaigne, i.238 (ch. 25).

[66] *The Literary Works of Matthew Prior*, ed. H. Bunker Wright and Monroe K. Spears, 2 vols. (Oxford, 1959), i.623. The phrase is lifted from La Bruyère, as quoted in the 'Vindication of *Montaigne*'s Essays' prefixed to the 1711 fourth edition of Cotton's translation, p. 13: 'Two writers, says he, (meaning *La Mothe le Vayer* and *Malbranche*) have condemn'd *Montaigne* . . . . One of 'em thinks too little to taste such an Author, who thinks a great deal; and the other thinks too subtily to be pleas'd with what is natural. This, I believe, is the general Character of *Montaigne*'s Enemies.'

ticism, as we shall see in the next chapter. But what is significant is his choice of Montaigne as the opponent of Lockean scepticism and solipsism, despite the fact that the *Essais* appeared to promote a scepticism far more extreme than could easily be derived from Locke, and presented themselves very much as the outpouring of a highly personal subjectivity. Notwithstanding, Prior's Montaigne consistently speaks as possessing that access to realities which Lockean empiricism can never securely establish:

> Lock. I take the Liberty to tell you that the Glass I looked into, was a fair true Mirour, and rightly placed.
> Montaigne. Let the Glass be of what Figure You please, if You presented nothing before it but Your own Dear Person what could you See but that flattered the Foppery of Youth, and at last Shewed only the Decays and wrinkles of Age.
> Lock. And pray, Sir, inform us a little into what Glass did You look?
> Montaigne. Into the great Miror of the World, where I saw the Universal face of Nature, and the Images of all Objects that the Eye can possibly take in.[67]

Whereas Locke looks into a mirror and sees only the self, Montaigne looks into the mirror of the self in such a way that it becomes 'the great Mirour of the World', something which can show him 'the Universal face of Nature'.

This seems a paradoxical image: how can the subjective become the universal? But Prior is here sensitive to something at the heart of the *Essais*. Because Montaigne, as sceptic, finds objective knowledge so problematic, he turns to what remains: his subjectivity. Hence the *Essais* come increasingly to take the form of internal reflection, setting out the flow of Montaigne's consciousness from topic to topic, along with his consciousness that that is the case:

> The World looks always opposite, I turn my sight inwards, there fix and employ it: Every one looks before him, *I* look into my self, I have no other business but my self, I am eternally meditating upon my self, controul and taste my self; other mens Thoughts are ever wand'ring abroad, if they set themselves to thinking, they are still going forward,
>
> *Nemo in sese tentat descendere.*
>
> No man attempts to dive into himself.
> for my part, I circulate in my self.[68]

---

[67] Prior, *Works*, i.626.   [68] Montaigne, ii.533 f. (ch. 17).

The emphasis on movement and process is significant; this turn to self-knowledge discovers only the slipperiness of its task, for there can be no question of the kind of self-knowledge that might rest in knowledge of the self as a definite entity. 'Man (in good earnest) is a Marvellous vain, fickle, and unstable Subject',[69] and this inconstancy applies not only to the species but also to the individual. 'While we would make one continued thing of all this succession of passion, we deceive our selves.'[70] Montaigne's project of self-discovery is therefore necessarily an endless process, a matter of uncovering the workings of his mind in all their arbitrariness and inconsequentiality. He may have hoped at the beginning that this would have some corrective function:

When I lately retired my self to my own House, with a Resolution, as much as possibly I could, to avoid all manner of Concern in Affairs, and to spend in privacy and repose the little remainder of time I have to Live: I fancied I could not more oblige my mind than to suffer it at full leisure to entertain and divert it self, which I now hoped it might the better be entrusted to do, as being by Time and Observation become more settled and mature; but I find,

> —*Variam semper dant otia mentem.*
> —Even in the most retir'd Estate
> Leisure it self does various Thoughts create.

that, quite contrary, it is like a Horse that has broke from his Rider, who voluntarily runs into a much more violent Career than any Horseman would put him to, and creates me so many *Chimaeras* and fantastick Monsters one upon another, without Order or Design, that, the better at leisure to contemplate their Strangeness and Absurdity, I have begun to commit them to Writing, hoping in time to make them asham'd of themselves.[71]

But this was a vain hope; so far from making his mind ashamed of itself, Montaigne developed a form of writing that allowed uninhibited expression to all its vagaries. An essay by Montaigne is characteristically a free and open-ended series of reflections, connected to one another by paths of association which are never clearly signposted, spontaneously unfolding without any apparent 'Order or Design'. This enacts the sceptical vision in at least two ways. Firstly, the aspiration to intellectual control is largely abandoned as illusory. In reading any of the later essays one is never

[69] Montaigne. i.6 (ch. 1).   [70] Ibid. 371 (ch. 37).   [71] Ibid. 43 f. (ch. 8).

entirely sure where the argument is going or whether it has arrived, what is the centre and what the digression. Secondly, all Montaigne's assertions and arguments appear in this context not as truth propositions, but as mental phenomena, aspects of his psychological self-disclosure:

These also are but my own particular Opinions and Fancies, and I deliver them for no other, but only, what I my self believe, and not for what is to be believ'd. Neither have I any other end in this Writing, but only to discover my self, who also shall peradventure be another thing to morrow, if I chance to meet any Book, or Friend, to convince me in the mean time. I have no Authority to be believ'd, neither do I desire it being too conscious of my own inerudition to be able to instruct others.[72]

In what I say, I warrant no other certainty, but that 'tis what I had then in my Thought. Tumultuous and wavering Thought. All I say is by way of discourse, and nothing by way of Advice.[73]

There is more to this than a defence against the censor. By present-ing all his opinions as saturated in subjectivity, Montaigne appar-ently disclaims any access to general norms, any ability to speak prescriptively, 'by way of advice'. His 'way of discourse'—a tumul-tuous and wavering discourse—expresses and enacts his intellec-tual helplessness, expressing his confinement within the subjectivity of the self. 'Could my Soul once take footing, I would not essay, but resolve; but it is always learning and making trial.'[74] Yet in the very next sentence he goes straight into his famous apology for dwelling so much upon himself: 'Every Man carries the entire form of human Condition'.[75] It is this kind of movement which under-lies Prior's suggestion that Montaigne looked into his mirror and saw the world. It is as though, precisely by realizing so richly and fully the 'floating' nature of experience, the fact that the soul can never take secure footing in a fixed truth outside itself, Montaigne has reached a larger insight into the nature of things, the form of human condition.

The formula for this very characteristic emphasis can be found at the beginning of that same essay: *Les autres forment l'homme; je le recite.* In Cotton's translation—'Others form *Man*, I only report him'[76]—the word 'only' concedes too much. It is true that Montaigne has nothing to teach or prescribe, he is only a witness,

---

72 Ibid. 218 (ch. 25).   73 Ibid. iii.411 (ch. 11).
74 Ibid. 27 (ch. 2).   75 Ibid.   76 Ibid. 26 (ch. 2).

and a witness only to the vagaries of his mind and being. Yet 'je le recite' involves a more positive claim than 'I only report him'. The act of self-witnessing alters what is witnessed;[77] by reciting or rehearsing himself in his writing, Montaigne adds the dimension of consciousness. The intellectual helplessness which means that Montaigne can only live as he lives, when 'recited' with the special consciousness of the *essai*, becomes a kind of resourcefulness. This is nowhere better shown than in the great final essay, 'Of Experience'. In that essay, contemplating his bouts of illness and his decline into old age, Montaigne rejects the prescriptions of medicine as hopelessly involved in the foolishness of all attempts to legislate for the human condition. He turns instead to the knowledge, such as it is, yielded by self-experience merely, and offers an extended and highly circumstantial account of the likings and practices by which he lives, and by which he endures both old age and the agonies of kidney-stones. The circumstantial nature of this recital is an expression of Montaigne's scepticism: in defiance of all attempts to subsume his individual case under the general rules of art, to render it an intelligible object for diagnosis and therapy, his own 'regimen' in illness is the product of accident and idiosyncrasy, consciously without rationale, simply what he likes to do and how he happens to live. This falling back onto the mere contingencies of the personal, as the abandonment of all prescription, is, however, itself a prescription, for what it leads to is a powerfully inward, and authoritatively generalizing, realization of the state of health, health in the largest sense, even if grasped largely through divergence from it:

'Tis an absolute, and as it were, a Divine Perfection, for a Man to know how loyally to enjoy his Being: We seek other conditions, by reason we do not understand the use of our own; and go out of our selves, because we know not how there to reside. 'Tis to much purpose to go upon stilts, for, when upon stilts, we must yet walk upon our Legs: And when seated upon the most elevated Throne in the World, we are but seated upon our Breech. The fairest Lives, in my opinion, are those which regularly accommodate themselves to the common and human model: but without miracle, and without extravagance.[78]

[77] 'I have no more made my Book than my Book has made me. 'Tis a Book consubstantial with the Author.' Montaigne, ii.543 (ch. 18).
[78] Ibid. iii.558 (ch. 13). The movement of thought in this essay is more fully discussed in Chapter 5.

The fairest life of all, for Montaigne, was that of Socrates, who comes into this essay, as into others, as the great model of how to live. What Montaigne emphasizes in Socrates, with a selective, eclectic emphasis that reflects his own achievement, is the co-existence of the radical sceptic in philosophy—who is 'eternally upon Questions and stirring up Disputes, never determining, never satisfying: and professes to have no other Science but that of opposing himself'[79]—with the man who knows how to live according to nature, 'how loyally to enjoy his Being':

Nor is there anything more remarkable in *Socrates*, than that, old as he was, he found time to make himself be instructed in dancing and playing upon Instruments, and thought it time well spent; who never the less has been seen in an *Exstacy* standing upon his feet a whole day and a night together in the presence of all the *Grecian* Army, surpriz'd and ravish'd with some profound Thought. He was the first, who amongst so many valiant men of the Army, ran to the relief of *Alcibiades* . . . But was that man oblig'd to drink to him by any Rule of Civility? he was also that Man of the Army to whom the advantage [in drinking] remain'd. And he never refus'd to play at *Cob-nut*, nor to ride the *Hobby-horse* with the Boyes, and it became him well; for all Actions, says *Philosophy*, equally become and equally honour a wise man. We have enough wherewith all to do it, and we ought never to be weary of representing the *Image* of this great Man in all the patterns and forms of Perfection. There are very few Examples of Life full and pure.[80]

Alexander conquered the world, but Montaigne regards Socrates as the more impressive figure, in that he knew how to 'carry on human Life conformable to its natural Condition'.[81] This can be seen not only in how he lived and died but also in how he spoke:

Socrates makes his Soul move a natural and common motion. *A country peasant said this, a Woman said that*; he has never any thing in his Mouth, but *Carters, Joiners, Cobblers*, and *Masons*. These are inductions and similitudes drawn from the most common and known Actions of Men, every one understands them. . . . By these common and natural *Springs*, by these vulgar and ordinary *Fancies*, without being mov'd or making any bustle in the Business, he set up, not only the most regular, but the most high and vigorous *Beliefs, Actions*, and *Manners* that ever were. . . . He has done human Nature a great kindness in shewing it how much it can do of it self. We are all of us richer than we think we are; but we are taught

[79] Montaigne, ii.288 (ch. 12).   [80] Ibid. iii.547 f. (ch. 13).
[81] Ibid. 35 (ch. 2).

to borrow and to beg, and brought up more to make use of what is another's than our own.[82]

Later in the essay Montaigne quotes, by way of example, part of Socrates' speech at his trial, and comments:

Is not this an innocent childish pleading of an unimaginable loftiness . . . equally admirable, both in simplicity and vehemence? Really, it is much more easy to speak like *Aristotle* and to live like *Caesar*, than to speak and live as *Socrates* did. There lies the extream degree of perfection and difficulty: Art cannot reach it.[83]

This is a most uncommon commonness, an extraordinary ordinariness. What makes such naturalness so thrilling to Montaigne is, of course, that it comes from Socrates, the master of masters, and is charged with consciousness and intelligence in the highest degree. Naturalness thus charged with consciousness is always liable to involve a certain special play of irony. The passage from Socrates which Montaigne quotes comes from the speech he made to his judges after his conviction but before his sentencing, in which he proposed, as the alternative to the death sentence, that he should be maintained at the common expense as a public benefactor: this immensely provocative act was a piece of artless simplicity only in a very special sense of those terms, and for Montaigne to describe it as 'an innocent childish pleading' is to press the paradox of Socrates' ironical straightforwardness with a certain ironical, though not disingenuous, simplicity of his own. Socratic naturalness is not artless, but beyond art. Thus in another essay, where Montaigne is discussing ethics, he begins by opposing an involuntary, instinctive disposition of goodness, such as his own temperamental dislike of all forms of cruelty, to the 'nobler' practice of true virtue, which involves the positive exercise of the will in resisting temptation, overcoming inclination, and choosing the better course. But this dichotomy will not account for Socrates, to whom virtue came naturally: 'I am come thus far at my ease; but here it comes into my head, that the Soul of *Socrates*, the most perfect that ever came to my knowledge, should, by this Rule, be of very little Recommendation.'[84] And so Montaigne posits a third, most rare category: in Socrates there must have been a fusion, an interpene-

---

[82] Montaigne, iii. 418–21 (ch. 12).   [83] Ibid. 449, 451 (ch. 12).
[84] Ibid. ii. 146 (ch. 11).

tration, of will and instinct: 'so perfect a Habitude to Vertue, that it was turn'd to a Complexion. It is no more a laborious Vertue, nor the precepts of Reason, to maintain which, the Soul is so wracked; but the very essence of [his soul, its] natural and ordinary Habit.'[85] Socrates stands as the rare and supreme example of a life lived *naturally*. His is the unique example of a high virtue which yet involves no element of suppression, no setting of the will against any pleasure or natural impulse.

The quality Montaigne saw in Socrates was something he enacted in his own manner of writing. Just as Montaigne the moralist does not offer to 'form man', so Montaigne the essayist seems hardly to form his writings, but simply to set down, without order or design, whatever comes to him. Yet this openness and apparent passivity are charged with self-consciousness; naivety and self-consciousness spiral around one another. Montaigne himself makes the association with Socrates in one of his apologies for his digressiveness:

... This medley is a little from my Subject. I go out of my way; but 'tis rather upon the account of licence than oversight. My Fancies follow one another, but sometimes at a great distance; and look towards one another, but 'tis with an oblique glance. I have read a *Dialogue* of *Plato*, of such a motley and fantastick Composition, as had the beginning of *Love*, and all the rest to the end of *Rhetorick*. They stick not at these Variations, and have a marvellous Grace in letting themselves be carried away at the pleasure of the Wind; or at least to seem as if they were. ... A little Folly is tolerable in him that will not be guilty of too much, says both the Precepts; and more, the Examples of our Masters.[86]

This is something like Hume's yielding himself to 'the current of nature', as I have described it: the relaxation of the anxious will-to-significance opens consciousness to the larger forces that move and carry us, and render foolish our conscious purposes. But there is more to this 'marvellous grace' than simply letting oneself go. The qualification—'or at least to seem as if they were'—hints at a certain play of irony, suggests the paradoxical resourcefulness or wisdom at the heart of (yet not cancelling or displacing) Socrates' intellectual helplessness, his 'folly'. The dialogue of Plato that Montaigne is thinking of is the *Phaedrus*, in which Socrates professes himself possessed by a local deity—'carried away at the

<hr/>

[85] Ibid. 149 (ch. 11).   [86] Ibid. iii.349 (ch. 9).

pleasure of the wind', so to speak—to produce a second speech on love which contradicts the sentiments he has just uttered in his first. At some level we feel that he is clearly playing games with his interlocutor, even while he is also truly, at some level, possessed and carried away. This play of irony is essential to the 'marvellous grace' to which Montaigne refers; it is transmitted in his own writing by his handling—his virtual invention—of the *essai*, where a radical scepticism generates a form of writing that knows, like Socrates, to 'stick not at these variations':

I cannot fix my Object, 'tis always tottering and reeling by a natural Giddiness. I take it as it is at the instant I consider of it. I do not paint its Being, I paint its Passage; not a passing from one Age to another, or, as the People say, from seven to seven Years; but from Day to Day, from Minute to Minute. I must accommodate my *History* to the Hour: I may presently change, not only by Fortune, but also by Intention: 'Tis a counterpart of various and changeable Accidents, and irresolute Imaginations, and, as it falls out, sometimes contrary: Whether it be that I am then another self, or that I take Subjects by other Circumstances and Considerations; so it is that I may peradventure contradict: But, as *Demades* said, I never contradict the Truth. Could my Soul once take footing, I would not essay, but resolve; but it is always learning and making trial.[87]

This famous description of 'essaying' identifies the situation of the sceptic with a certain manner of expression; it points to the sense in which Montaigne was an influential source and model, not just for the negative arguments of radical scepticism, but also for that more affirmative activity of 'sceptical thinking' which requires literary realization. It is through Montaigne that 'essay' enters the English language, with its multiple meaning of a piece of writing, an attempt, and (as in 'assay') a testing: and for a long time both the term and the practice retained something of the original sceptical charge and significance. This was sustained by the continuing popularity of the *Essais*. Even after Montaigne fell out of favour in France, around the 1670s, he continued to be well known in England, both in English translation and in the French original. The fine translation by Charles Cotton, from which I quote in this study, went through ten editions and reprintings between 1685 and 1776; the French text edited by Pierre Coste, the Huguenot translator of Locke, was published in London in 1724 and re-issued

---

[87] Montaigne, iii. 26 f. (ch. 2).

seven times between 1727 and 1771.[88] In this period the *Essais* were more widely read in England than in France, and one element in this popularity was the perception that Montaigne was meat too strong for the refinement of contemporary French taste. Halifax, Cotton's dedicatee, congratulated the translator 'for doing him more right than his country will afford him':

> To transplant and make him *Ours*, is not only a Valuable *Acquisition* to us, but a Just *Censure* of the Critical *Impertinence* of those *French Scribblers* who have taken pains to make little *Cavils* and *Exceptions*, to lessen the Reputation of this great *Man*, whom Nature hath made too big to Confine himself to the Exactness of a Studied Stile. He let his *Mind* have his full *Flight*, and sheweth by a generous kind of *Negligence* that he did not Write for Praise, but to give to the World a true Picture of himself and of Mankind.[89]

Stylistic condemnation of this 'generous kind of negligence' was reinforced in France by disapproval of Montaigne's egotism, his shamelessness, his frankness-cum-obscenity, his unsound philosophizing, his 'pagan' equanimity about death and his casualness with religion: he inspires a nonchalance about salvation, wrote Pascal, *'without fear and without repentance'*.[90] Theological anxiety at the tendency of his scepticism caused the *Essais* to be placed on the Papal Index of prohibited reading in 1676, and after that they were for a long time unpublishable in France except in simpli-

---

[88] There was indirect influence too, through Charron's *De la sagesse*, also translated into English. Charron was a follower of Montaigne's, and his work is virtually a Montaigne anthology, in which the *Essais* are purged of their subjectivity and re-organized into something resembling a coherent system of thought. Although this did damage to the original, by implying that the essence of Montaigne's thinking could be abstracted from the manner of the writing, it also sent the helpful signal that Montaignean scepticism is not merely idiosyncratic, nor wholly destructive, nor fundamentally incoherent. Through Charron Montaigne's thoughts gained a still wider circulation, and were made more immediately accessible.

[89] *The Works of George Savile Marquis of Halifax*, ed. Mark N. Brown, 3 vols. (Oxford, 1989), iii.23.

[90] *Pascal's Pensées*, trans. Martin Turnell (London, 1962), p. 410: no. 936, Lafuma numbering; no. 63, Brunschvicg numbering. Nos. 62–5 (Brunschvicg), or nos. 48, 758, 935, 936 (Lafuma), of the *Pensées* give, with the utmost conciseness and penetration, many of the principal charges to be brought against Montaigne, although for Pascal himself these criticisms were only one element in a deep engagement characterized by a complex ambivalence. 'It is not in Montaigne, but in myself, that I find everything that I see there' (p. 343).

fied selections.[91] These, however, were precisely matters that could enhance Montaigne's appeal for English readers, happy to observe their distance from the excesses of French rationalism, French intolerance, French neo-classicism, and French regularity. 'An Author who talks freely of every thing, is not suitable to the Temper of a servile Nation that has lost all sense of Liberty', declared the 'Vindication of *Montaigne*'s Essays' first prefixed to the 1711 edition of Cotton's translation.[92] Montaigne was seen as a questionable *model*, to be sure, and an extreme case: but an extreme case of qualities in themselves desirable. If he was often praised with some note of qualification or apology—as his readers dissociated themselves from his profession of foolishness—he was rarely cited without some kind of praise.[93] He was certainly widely read, and, I believe, deeply influential. Dryden praised him as 'wise Montaigne', frequently drew on him, and claimed his 'rambling' manner as a model;[94] Pope admired him, as we shall see; Fielding spoke of 'my favorite Montagne', who 'of all men, except only *Aristotle*, seems best to have understood Human Nature';[95] Sterne acknowledged that he knew him as well as the

---

[91] See Dudley M. Marchi, *Montaigne among the Moderns: Receptions of the Essais* (Providence, RI and Oxford, 1994), pp. 39–53.

[92] Montaigne, *Essays*, trans. Cotton, 3 vols., 4th ed., 3 vols. (London, 1711), i.13.

[93] e.g. Addison on Montaigne's literary egotism: 'This lively old *Gascon* has woven all his bodily Infirmities into his Works, and after having spoken of the Faults or Virtues of any other Man, immediately publishes to the World how it stands with himself in that Particular. Had he kept his own Counsel he might have passed for a much better Man, tho' perhaps he would not have been so diverting an Author.' (*The Spectator*, ed. Donald F. Bond, 5 vols. (Oxford, 1965), iv.520: no. 562) In that essay Addison remarks that the indictment of '*Egotism*' in literature comes from the 'Gentlemen of *Port-Royal*'; his slightly patronizing but also distinctly favourable account of Montaigne's egotism can be compared with Pascal's much more astringent comment in *Pensées* no. 62/48 (Brunschvicg/Lafuma).

[94] He is 'the wise Montaigne' in the Preface to *Don Sebastian* (*Of Dramatic Poesy and other critical essays*, ed. George Watson, 2 vols. (London, 1962), ii.50). In the preface to the *Fables* Dryden wrote that 'the nature of a preface is rambling, never wholly out of the way, nor in it. This I have learned from the practice of honest Montaigne' (ibid., ii.278). Other passages in Dryden where Montaigne is a strong presence include the dedication prefixed to *Aureng-Zebe* and the translations from Lucretius.

[95] To James Harris, 29 Sept. 1741, in *The Correspondence of Henry and Sarah Fielding*, ed. Martin C. Battestin and Clive T. Probyn (Oxford, 1993), p. 18; *An Enquiry into the Causes of the late Increase of Robbers*, ed. M. R. Zirker (Oxford, 1988), p. 170. For some other references by Fielding to Montaigne, see the *Correspondence*, pp. 20 f., fn. 15.

prayer book;[96] Johnson wrote that the 'vivacity' of his writing had 'reconciled mankind' to the absence of method in modern essays, and compared the freedom of his prose to the 'lightness and agility' of classical lyric;[97] writers as various as Cibber and Gibbon used him as a point of departure for their autobiographies.[98] Of course, this does not mean that he was always read as I have been reading him here, as a sceptic whose scepticism breaks the mind open to 'nature': but Prior's dialogue shows how he could, at least, be read in that way. And as well as working directly upon its readership, the scepticism of the *Essais* exerted an indirect influence through the genre of the essay. Addison distinguished between two kinds of paper which he published in *The Spectator*:

There are some which are written with Regularity and Method, and others that run out into the Wildness of those Compositions, which go by the name of *Essays*. As for the first, I have the whole Scheme of the Discourse in my Mind, before I set Pen to Paper. In the other kind of Writing, it is sufficient that I have several Thoughts on a Subject, without troubling myself to range them in such order, that they may seem to grow out of one another, and be disposed under the proper Heads. *Seneca* and *Montaigne* are Patterns for Writing in this last Kind.[99]

This opposition of 'the regularity of a Set Discourse' to 'the Looseness and Freedom of an Essay',[100] as Addison phrases it elsewhere, was a commonplace.[101] This does not mean that all essays were written in a manner that recalled Montaigne; from the beginning Bacon's *Essays* offered an alternative model that was impersonal, aphoristic, authoritative, brief, and to the point. Yet in many of the essays that claim that title, as well as in some that do not,

[96] *Letters of Laurence Sterne*, ed. L. P. Curtis (Oxford, 1935), p. 122.

[97] *Johnson*, v.77 (*Rambler* 158).

[98] In Cibber's *An Apology for the Life of Mr Colley Cibber* (London, 1740), Montaigne is a strong presence in the first chapter, and cited by name in the fifteenth, as a model for Cibber's cheerful confession of his foolishness and vanity. For Gibbon and Montaigne, see Charles Dédéyan, *Montaigne chez ses amis anglosaxons*, 2 vols. (Paris, 1944), ch. 7, pp. 59–76.

[99] *The Spectator*, ed. Donald F. Bond, 5 vols. (Oxford, 1965), iv.185 f.: no. 476.

[100] Ibid. ii.465: no. 249.

[101] Thus in Johnson's *Dictionary* the 'essay' is twice set against *systematic* discussion; the two quotations together may be taken to express a certain ambivalence in Johnson himself: 'Now we deal much in essays, and unreasonably despise *systematical* learning; whereas our fathers had a just value for regularity and systems. *Watts* . . . I treat of the usefulness of writing books of essay, in comparison of that of writing *systematically*. *Boyle*'.

Montaigne's presence is written into the genre. In writings as diverse as Dryden's engagingly first-person critical prefaces, Cowley's free prose meditations, William Temple's genteel disquisitions, Addison's decorous reflections on morality and manners, and Johnson's organized combats between arguments pro and con, there is an implicit understanding that an essay is not a set treatise but a work of literary creation, that it expresses the presence of the thinking self within the process of thinking, rather than an accumulation of thought or thoughts, and that it can thereby deal with a kind of truth too subtle or too evasive to be accessible to direct rational inquiry or impersonal philosophical discourse. This understanding is the legacy of Montaigne, and it is subscribed to in the titles of Pope's *An Essay on Man* and Hume's *Philosophical Essays concerning Human Understanding*;[102] even, it can be argued, in Locke's *An Essay concerning Human Understanding*;[103] and certainly in the digressive, spontaneous, *essayistical* manner in which Tristram Shandy sets down his life and opinions.[104]

SCEPTICISM AND SOCIETY

To connect eighteenth-century essay-ing with the *Essais* of Montaigne in this way may seem to overlook one important difference between them. This has to do with the much higher degree of social consciousness in eighteenth-century writing. To put it simply (too simply): where Montaigne turns to the self, the eighteenth-century essayist plays to the public. It is not that Montaigne's play of consciousness is *private*; even where his material seems most personal, he is clearly setting down his reflections in order to communicate them, with an expectation of being read; but one does not feel that that activity of self-reflection is itself a social act, or that the essaying self is primarily a social being. Something similar might be said of Thomas Browne, in the seventeenth century,

---

[102] The title under which *An Enquiry concerning Human Understanding* was first published.

[103] See Rosalie Colie, 'The Essayist in his *Essay*', in *John Locke: Problems and Perspectives*, ed. John W. Yolton (Cambridge, 1969), pp. 234–61.

[104] The affinity between Montaigne and Sterne was registered by Byron when he wrote of *Don Juan*, 'I mean it for a poetical T Shandy—or Montaigne's Essays with a story for a hinge.' *Byron's Letters and Journals*, ed. Leslie A. Marchand, 12 vols. (1973–82), x.150.

who sometimes recalls Montaigne's special quality of conscious *naiveté*, or William Hazlitt, at the start of the nineteenth, who can achieve something of the same effect of a spontaneous personal thinking presence: but in the thoroughly socialized literary culture of the eighteenth century none of Montaigne's admirers emulates his naked directness of self-presentation. For one fundamental characteristic of eighteenth-century literature is that so much of it is self-consciously public discourse. It refers itself to (without necessarily observing) canons of politeness and propriety, it expects to be read and discussed within one or more quite closely defined public spheres, and it regularly appeals to what might be called the social skills of its readers, who are invited to be alert to implication as well as statement, to a coded, allusive language of gesture and tone. In its consciousness of artifice, it mirrors the artificiality of social exchange and public language, which is necessarily and always a construction, but in eighteenth-century culture was felt as such with peculiar acuteness.

Such a medium might seem ill-adapted to transmit Montaigne's emphasis on the natural, as we find it both in the free spontaneity of his manner and in his praise of a plain, instinctive, simple way of living (ancient Sparta, the American 'cannibals', the French peasantry) above the alienated forms of civilized life and sophisticated thought. From this point of view, it would seem to be Jean-Jacques Rousseau, rather than any of the British writers under discussion, who is Montaigne's true eighteenth-century heir. Although Rousseau does not dwell on the topics of scepticism, he is the enemy of rationalism and of civilized society, and an acute analyst of how those things lead to estrangement from the truth of one's own experience. That is the great sceptical doctrine taught in the *Discourses*, which see intellectual culture and civilized society as twin forces of corruption, and in *Emile*, Rousseau's thought-experiment in an ideal education, in which the young Emile is to be exposed only to facts, not ideas; he is to grow and develop only in response to a world of objective necessities, with *Robinson Crusoe* as his only permitted reading. In the *Confessions* and, still more, in *Reveries of the Solitary Walker*, the emphasis on the natural expresses itself in the project of writing the self, undertaken with an authenticity that directly recalls the example of Montaigne, and indeed offers to outdo it:

My enterprise is like Montaigne's, but my motive is entirely different, for he wrote his essays only for others to read, whereas I am writing down my reveries for myself alone. If, as I hope, I retain the same disposition of mind in my extreme old age, when the time of my departure draws near, I shall recall in reading them the pleasure I have in writing them and by thus reviving times past I shall as it were double the space of my existence. In spite of men I shall still enjoy the charms of company, and in my decrepitude I shall live with my earlier self as I might with a younger friend.[105]

It is this condition of solitary reverie, Rousseau tells us, that confers on him a godlike self-sufficiency, allowing him to enter into the state of natural bliss which is 'the simple feeling of existence, a feeling that fills our soul entirely'.[106] Such was his condition during the few magical weeks he spent on the small island of Saint-Pierre, walking and idling and drifting in a boat, which he describes in the Fifth Walk of the *Reveries*. This alone is true happiness, and liberation from the realm of relativity and change; Rousseau summarizes Montaigne's vision of the fluidity of things in order to show how he can pass beyond it:

Everything is in constant flux on this earth. Nothing keeps the same unchanging shape, and our affections, being attached to things outside us, necessarily change and pass away as they do. . . . But if there is a state where the soul can find a resting-place secure enough to establish itself and concentrate its entire being there . . . as long as this state lasts, we can call ourselves happy . . . . Such is the state which I often experienced on the Island of Saint-Pierre in my solitary reveries.[107]

---

[105] Jean-Jacques Rousseau, *Reveries of the Solitary Walker*, trans. Peter France (Harmondsworth, 1979), pp. 33 f. Another crucial difference between Rousseau and Montaigne lies in Rousseau's estimate of human nature. He wrote of his *Confessions*: 'I decided to make it a work unique and unparallelled in its truthfulness, so that for once at least the world might behold a man as he was within. I had always been amused at Montaigne's false ingenuousness, and at his pretence of confessing his faults while taking good care only to admit to likeable ones; whereas I, who believe, and always have believed, that I am on the whole the best of men, felt that there is no human heart, however pure, that does not conceal some odious vice.' (*The Confessions of Jean-Jacques Rousseau*, trans. J. M. Cohen (Harmondsworth, 1953), pp. 478 f.) It was not for nothing that Rousseau grew up in the city of Calvin. 'False ingenuousness' translates 'la fausse naiveté de Montaigne', but the essence of the ironic quality of Montaigne's writing—the dimension of *consciousness*—is that his voice is neither ingenuous nor faux-naif: a third term is required.

[106] Rousseau, *Reveries*, p. 88.

[107] Ibid.

Montaigne never makes this kind of claim for himself. 'Could my Soul once take footing, I would not essay, but resolve; but it is always learning and making trial.' The naturalness of being which Rousseau either possesses absolutely, or experiences as absolute loss, is in Montaigne realized *through* scepticism, *through* the activity of the alienated mind, an activity of thinking that, although profoundly sceptical about its own outcomes, never claims that it can set itself aside: 'We are all of us richer than we think we are; but we are taught to borrow and to beg, and brought up more to make use of what is another's than our own.'[108] Rousseau subscribed to every word of that; but what he could not follow was Montaigne's way of being in both places at once, both rich in our participation in nature and thinking ourselves poor (and so, being poor) in our acculturated alienation from it: both understanding and foolish (and therefore most foolish): 'We are, I know not how, double in our selves, which is the cause that what we believe we do not believe, and cannot disengage our selves from what we condemn.'[109] Rousseau, by contrast, always seeks to disengage himself from what he condemns; he does not move, as does Montaigne, from 'I' to 'we'. The opposition between sincerity and society, the natural and the civilized, is regularly presented by Rousseau as absolute. 'Forced to combat either nature or society, you must make your choice between the man and the citizen, you cannot train both.'[110] Hence Rousseau does not write with the play of irony that is alive to multiple viewpoints; and hence, almost as a corollary of this, his emphasis on the solitary self.

If Rousseau, then, develops certain aspects of Montaigne's thinking very strongly in one direction (which an English reader might think of as ultra-Wordsworthian), he does so at the cost of others. Like his great enemy Burke, he represents a tendency of mind that *precludes* sceptical thinking, for all that both he and Burke, in their very different ways, could claim to affirm the natural against the rational. As opposed to the line of development

---

[108] *Montaigne*, iii.421 (ch. 12).
[109] Ibid. ii.473 (ch. 16).
[110] *Emile*, trans. Barbara Foxley (London, 1911), p. 7. The final section of *Emile* is the exception that proves the rule: when, after many delays, Rousseau finally attempts to introduce his naturally brought up protégé into the real world of personal relationships, intellectual interests, and political responsibilities, the effect is embarrassingly awkward and unconvincing.

from Montaigne which culminates in the *reverie*, the dimension of social consciousness implicit in the eighteenth-century *essay* mode is at least equally responsive to the scepticism of the *Essais*, and far more hospitable to the quality of sceptical thinking which I am seeking to describe. Literature written in this mode may be described as habitually bordering upon the ironic: in its consciousness of its public condition, it works with conventions and surfaces while knowing them to be such. Such an ironic mode need not imply scepticism, but they dovetail together with peculiar felicity. The traditional recourse of scepticism, when reason comes to the end of its tether, is to conventional belief, to the custom of the country. This notion of a saving recourse to custom was immensely deepened and intensified by the argument, readily inferred from Locke, that an enlightened philosophy deals only with the appearances of things. Hume developed this into the explicit argument that it is not reason but custom that holds together our experience of the world, albeit sometimes at so deep a level that it functions as a powerful force of nature or instinct. The end of Hume's crisis of belief, as we have seen, is that he finds himself 'absolutely and necessarily determined to live, and talk, and act like other people in the common affairs of life'. A certain irony is intrinsic to this situation, which requires the sceptic to live by conventions while knowing them to be without rational foundation, to live on the surface—since *depth* is inaccessible or unreal—with a consciousness that nevertheless redeems that living from superficiality. The praxis of scepticism thus maps readily onto the art of living in society, and onto the habitually self-conscious or ironic employment of public modes of discourse.

One consequence of this doubling of the sceptical and the social is to invest the idea of 'nature' with a peculiar subtlety. When sceptical thinking appeals from the paralysis of reason to the current of nature, it welcomes the paradoxical alignment of the natural with the social, with the product of convention, consensus, and construction. One sees here again how the sceptical approach to 'nature' cannot be articulated—cannot exist—without a certain literary play of irony. It is a plausible speculation that this quality of irony draws on the idealized ambience of a distinctively eighteenth-century social institution: the 'club' or 'salon', and the practice of intellectual exchange that could be imagined as taking place there. In an essay written near the start of the century, Shaftesbury describes to his addressee a discussion at which he was present, and explains why he is inclined to celebrate rather than condemn its inconclusiveness:

A great many fine schemes, it is true, were destroyed; many grave reasonings, overturned; but, this being done without offence to the parties concerned and with improvement to the good humour of the company, it set the appetite the keener to such conversations. And I am persuaded that, had Reason herself been to judge of her own interest, she would have thought she received more advantage in the main from that easy and familiar way than from the usual stiff adherence to a particular opinion.

But perhaps you may still be in the same humour of not believing me in earnest. You may continue to tell me I affect to be paradoxical in commending a conversation as advantageous to reason which ended in such a total uncertainty of what reason had seemingly so well established.

To this, I answer that, according to the notion I have of reason, neither the written treatises of the learned nor the set discourses of the eloquent are able of themselves to teach the use of it. It is the habit alone of reasoning which can make a reasoner. And men can never be better invited to the habit than when they find pleasure in it. A freedom of raillery, a liberty in decent language to question anything, and an allowance of unravelling or refuting any argument without offence to the arguer, are the only terms which can render such speculative conversations any way agreeable.[111]

Such a passage epitomizes the sceptical-social ideal almost too neatly. If Shaftesbury there suggests one of the great lost strengths of eighteenth-century culture, he does so in a tone that may simultaneously trigger a certain disquiet. One cannot tell from this passage alone—and in fact one cannot tell even after reading the whole of Shaftesbury—just how strong an ideal is represented by that emphasis on 'the good humour of the company' and on speculative conversations which are always 'agreeable'. Could there be just a whiff of effeteness about this? or, to put it another way, is Shaftesbury's ideal overly dependent on a select, privileged ethos, a free-thinking aristocratic circle quite exclusively drawn, that becomes, in the course of the eighteenth century, harder and harder to sustain as an ideal of the public sphere, as more urgent and clamorous voices gain admission to the sphere of 'speculative conversation'? Johnson's famous 'Club' has much in common with the mores Shaftesbury describes, but it also seems to have been a rougher and more heterogenous affair, frequently touching the

[111] Anthony Ashley Cooper, Third Earl of Shaftesbury, *Characteristics of Men, Manners, Opinions, Times*, ed. Lawrence E. Klein (Cambridge, 1999), p. 33.

boundaries of 'offence'. To take the ideal of sceptical thinking seriously, one needs to feel that the social circle in which it thrives can
accommodate the kind of serious concern, the depth of potential
negativity, sketched earlier in this chapter.

That is to say: it would need to survive the kind of critique that
one might associate with Swift. Consider the following passage
from the 'Digression concerning Madness' in *A Tale of a Tub*, in
which Swift's unreliable narrator is expounding the advantages of
irrationalism and insanity. The main argument of this chapter is
there treated with a casual, yet searching intensity. Swift summarizes the bankruptcy of rational inquiry with a brilliance all the
more impressive in that it does not itself make claim to be a
reasoned position; he even sketches a version of the sceptical 'solution' to the impasse—a willingness to live by appearances rather
than searching after fundamentals; but in so far as he anticipates
similar sentiments in Hume or in Sterne, he does so as a pre-
emptive strike:

In the Proportion that Credulity is a more peaceful Possession of the Mind,
than Curiosity, so far preferable is that Wisdom, which converses about the
Surface, to that pretended Philosophy which enters into the Depth of Things,
and then comes gravely back with Informations and Discoveries, that in the
inside they are good for nothing . . . . Whatever Philosopher or Projector can
find out an Art to solder and patch up the Flaws and Imperfections of
Nature, will deserve much better of Mankind, and teach us a more useful
Science, than that so much in present Esteem, of widening and exposing
them (like him who held *Anatomy* to be the ultimate End of *Physick*.) And
he whose Fortunes and Dispositions have placed him in a convenient Station
to enjoy the Fruits of this noble Art; He that can with *Epicurus* content his
Ideas with the *Films* and *Images* that fly off upon his Senses from the
Superficies of Things; Such a Man truly wise, creams off Nature, leaving the
Sour and the Dregs for Philosophy and Reason to lap up. This is the sublime
and refined Point of Felicity, called, *the Possession of being well deceived*;
The Serene Peaceful State of being a Fool among Knaves.
    But to return to *Madness* . . .[112]

Swift, like the other sceptical thinkers I have been discussing, is at
once committed to the exercise of the rational intelligence and
deeply sceptical of its claims, formulations, and conclusions. But

---

[112] Jonathan Swift, *A Tale of a Tub*, ed. Herbert Davis (Oxford, 1939; repr.
1965), pp. 109 f.

Swift's ironies leave the reader with nowhere to stand. The sceptic's insistence that the findings of 'Philosophy and Reason' are futile and destructive is vigorously aired, and obliquely confirmed by the sense of bamboozling paradox associated with the intellectual brilliance of the writing ('Look! This is all that cleverness amounts to!'), yet the alternative—'that Wisdom, which converses about the Surface'—is mooted only to be unforgettably demolished. Such irony does not accommodate the conventional, but cuts it adrift; it opposes surfaces to depths, without connecting them. Another way of putting this would be that the irony, although unmistakably present, is peculiarly hard to perform or *voice*: is the overt tone of the final sentence, for example, closer to the rhapsodic or the sarcastic? One's difficulty in answering such a question illustrates the divide that Swift maintains between the critical intelligence that animates his satire and the public, social forms of its expression. Here as often elsewhere, Swift seems to stand in relation to the emerging high culture of the eighteenth century—the culture of wit, good humour, raillery, politeness, reasonableness, the culture, in a word, of accommodation—in the role of accuser. Are all such accommodations not, at bottom, forms of complacency and self-deception? After all, it is precisely Swift's awareness of the social dimension ('a Fool *among* Knaves') that gives his critique its cutting edge. Or is it, notwithstanding, possible to see the eighteenth-century turn from sceptical crisis to backgammon and dinner-parties as 'truly wise'?

Exploring that question will be the project of later chapters, which consider specific works by Pope, Hume, Sterne, and Johnson. In this chapter I hope simply to have given some outline of the overall subject and to have begun to suggest its interest. In summary: by 'sceptical thinking' in the eighteenth century is meant a reasoned emphasis on the severe limitations of rationality, such as radically undermines the grounds of belief and action, which nevertheless generates a surprising confidence of assertion, often described in terms of 'following nature'. Its intellectual sources include Locke, Bayle, and especially Montaigne, who is an influential model as well as a source. It depends for its realization upon a certain play of irony which flourishes in a space at once imaginative and social; the limits and perimeter of that space can be thought of as marked, at three separate boundaries, by salient tendencies in the writing of Burke, Rousseau, and Swift.

2

Just Supposing: Locke's *Essay concerning Human Understanding*

This study is primarily concerned with writers—Pope, Hume, Sterne, Johnson—whose engagement with scepticism issued in the kind of imaginative literary creation which I have marked with the term, 'sceptical thinking'. Locke is not such a writer, and the reader whose interest is in imaginative literature only may wish to skip to the following chapters, which do not directly depend on what follows here. But Locke's *Essay concerning Human Understanding* does have a place in the larger story. Published in 1690, the *Essay* had an immense and pervasive influence on eighteenth-century thought, comparable to that of Freud in the twentieth century; Locke provided the dominant way of modelling the working of the mind, even for those who disagreed with some aspect of his theory or who had themselves never read him.[1] This is not to imply that sceptical thinking was simply the product of the Lockean theory. Locke's *Essay*—like the writings of Bayle, who was cited in the opening chapter alongside Locke as contributing to a climate of scepticism—is perhaps as much manifestation as cause of that climate, which should not in any case be thought of as restricted to the eighteenth century; the *Essais* of Montaigne, published a century earlier than Locke's *Essay*, may well have been a more vital influence and inspiration. But what is true is that the Lockean model of the mind provided the eighteenth century with many of its basic assumptions and starting-points, and presented sceptical

[1] Sill a valuable study is Kenneth Maclean, *John Locke and English Literature of the Eighteenth Century* (Princeton, 1936; reissued New York, 1962).

thinking with a particular stimulus to further development. This stimulus arose from the indeterminate relation with scepticism in which Locke's *Essay* stands, and it is this fruitful indeterminacy which I want to bring out in this chapter.

The first way in which radical scepticism appears in the *Essay* is as the danger which Locke's project exists to oppose and to banish. In a passage near the start, he sets out what he hopes to achieve:

I shall imagine I have not wholly misemploy'd my self in the Thoughts I shall have on this Occasion, if, in this Historical, plain Method, I can give any Account of the Ways, whereby our Understandings come to attain those Notions of Things we have, and can set down any Measures of the Certainty of our Knowledge, or the Grounds of those Perswasions, which are to be found amongst Men, so various, different, and wholly contradictory; and yet asserted some where or other with such Assurance, and Confidence, that he that shall take a view of the Opinions of Mankind, observe their Opposition, and at the same time, consider the Fondness, and Devotion wherewith they are embrac'd; the Resolution, and Eagerness, wherewith they are maintain'd, may perhaps have Reason to suspect, That either there is no such thing as Truth at all; or that Mankind hath no sufficient Means to attain a certain Knowledge of it.[2]

Writing towards the end of a century of intense ideological conflict, Locke sees scepticism as an entirely plausible inference from the plurality of contradictory opinions running loose in the world. His remedy is to concentrate on *how* the mind comes by its opinions; he thus makes epistemology the basis of all philosophical inquiry. Locke's fundamental doctrine is that the mind, as far as cognition and thought-content are concerned, brings nothing with it, no self-evident truths or innate principles of reason. The understanding is a *camera oscura*, or '*dark Room*'. All our ideas come to us from outside, as sensory impressions, and all our thinking is constituted by—and ultimately limited to—these sense impressions and the new ideas which the mind builds up by combining and comparing them.

External and internal Sensation, are the only passages that I can find, of Knowledge, to the Understanding. These alone, as far as I can discover, are the Windows by which light is let into this *dark Room*. For, methinks, the *Understanding* is not much unlike a Closet wholly shut from light, with

[2] John Locke, *An Essay concerning Human Understanding*, ed. Peter H. Nidditch (Oxford, 1975), I.i.2: p. 44.

only some little openings left, to let in external visible Resemblances, or *Ideas* of things without.[3]

Locke gives much space to explaining how the towering edifice of human understanding and discourse is built up on these simple foundations: but, he always comes back to insisting, it is on these foundations that it must rest. To be real, our knowledge can never go beyond our experience, and can only ever be of our experience. It is only when language, in particular, leads us astray, and we suppose that we can reach beyond experience to have knowledge of the essential nature of things, that we fall into confusion and contradiction. This principle, when fully grasped and assimilated, will, Locke believes, promote a solid, consensual knowledge, by enabling us to distinguish between forms of understanding which are securely grounded and those areas of dispute which turn on questions that are ultimately unanswerable or meaningless. We shall have a way of steering between the Scylla of 'enthusiasm', in all its destabilizing plurality, and the Charybdis of 'perfect Scepticism'.[4]

Locke thus does not propose to do away with scepticism altogether, but rather to confine it to its proper realm. His aim in the *Essay* is the clear demarcation of a boundary between those areas where the understanding can get proper purchase, and those areas of inquiry which are necessarily and permanently dark, and where the understanding's proper task is to grasp that here it has nothing to do. The result of this project will be to set limits to the scope of human understanding—'to prevail with the busy Mind of Man, to be more cautious in meddling with things exceeding its Comprehension'[5]—but also to establish its clear, solid, uncontrovertible grounds within its proper sphere. 'We shall not have much Reason to complain of the narrowness of our Minds, if we will but employ them about what may be of use to us; for of that they are very capable.'[6] Locke did not see the sceptical strain in his epistemology as radically subversive of human certainties—at any rate, of such certainties as human beings need. 'The infinite wise

---

[3] *Essay*, II.xi.17: pp. 162 f. Or in Blake's hostile, implacably anti-sceptical paraphrase in *The Marriage of Heaven and Hell*: 'Man has closed himself up, till he sees all things through narrow chinks of his cavern.' *The Poems of William Blake*, ed. W. H. Stevenson and David V. Erdman (London, 1971), p. 114.

[4] *Essay*, I.i.7: p. 47.   [5] Ibid. 4: pp. 44 f.

[6] Ibid. 5: pp. 45 f.

Contriver of us, and all things about us, hath fitted our Senses, Faculties, and Organs, to the conveniences of Life, and the Business we have to do here.'[7] What good would it be, he asks, if a man's powers of perception were vastly enhanced, 'if such an acute Sight would not serve to conduct him to the Market and Exchange'.[8] Such an association of limited knowledge with humanly useful knowledge is one of the foundation stones of eighteenth-century thought. It is closely echoed in Pope's *Essay on Man*, for example, and reappears in Candide's famous deferral of metaphysical speculations in favour of more immediate priorities: *Il faut cultiver notre jardin.* What is held out here—the possibility of simply outgrowing our existential anxieties, our hunger for metaphysical sanction, and settling down to the more substantially useful work of cultivating the garden of civil society or domestic life—was a deeply congenial idea. Locke's *Essay* was valued so highly because it contributed directly to the dominant intellectual concern with drawing an accurate boundary-line between what we can and cannot understand, or, in Locke's own image, establishing 'the Horizon . . . which sets the Bounds between the enlightend and dark Parts of Things'.[9] Bolingbroke, for example, met Leibniz's censure of Locke as 'a superficial philosopher' head on:

To speak the truth, tho it may seem a paradox, our knowledge on many subjects, and particularly on those which we intend here [theology and ethics], must be superficial to be real. This is the condition of humanity. We are placed, as it were, in an intellectual twilight, where we can discover but few things clearly, and none intirely.[10]

Locke's own way of making this assertion supports Bolingbroke's general account of him, yet also sounds a more complicated note:

Whensoever we would proceed beyond these simple *Ideas*, we have from Sensation and Reflection, and dive farther into the Nature of Things, we fall presently into Darkness and Obscurity, Perplexedness and Difficulties; and can discover nothing farther, but our own Blindness and Ignorance.[11]

What we experience when we seek a ground to our experience is, necessarily, a 'fall . . . into Darkness': at such moments Locke seems to allow such darkness a disturbing reality of its own.

To acknowledge the potency of scepticism within its own sphere

[7] Ibid. II.xxiii.12: p. 302. [8] Ibid. 303. [9] Ibid. I.i.7: p. 47.
[10] Bolingbroke, iii.329. [11] *Essay*, II.xxiii.32: p. 314.

need not in principle detract from Locke's explicit programme: the
depth of the surrounding 'Darkness and Obscurity' defines the
circle of the light. However, Locke could not in practice distinguish
light from darkness as sharply as that programme suggests. His
own positive arguments contribute to the twilight of which
Bolingbroke speaks; they can themselves be seen to generate, when
their implications are fully developed, the kind of paradoxes and
uncertainties associated with scepticism. At the most fundamental
level, this is because of the ambiguity involved in any appeal to
experience. From one point of view, what is grounded in experience can be seen as the ineluctably real and self-evident, the infallible touchstone for what reason theorizes or tradition hands down.
But from another point of view, what is grounded in experience is
necessarily saturated in subjectivity. When Locke emphasizes the
dimension of experience he sees it as a *medium*, composed of
'ideas' whose relation to their archetypes is not straightforward,
and which therefore separates (at least as much as connects) the self
which seeks knowledge, from the world which is to be known. As
his biographer Maurice Cranston puts it,

> The human predicament, according to Locke's account of it, is like that of a
> man permanently imprisoned in a sort of diving bell, receiving some signals
> from without and some from within his apparatus, but having no means of
> knowing which, if any, of these signals come from outside; or of testing their
> authenticity when he thinks they do come from outside. He cannot therefore
> have any definite knowledge whatever of the external world.
>
> Locke, it must in fairness be said, sees this last difficulty himself, and he
> admits he does not know how to answer it.[12]

This uncertainty in Locke is vigorously exposed in the work of
both Berkeley and Hume, who accepted Locke's empiricist
premises, only to show how these implied the most radically
disabling scepticism—from which an escape could be found only in
Berkeley's divinely supported immaterialism, or, even more equiv-
ocally, in Hume's recourse to dinner, backgammon, and 'common
sense'. Thus in Berkeley's *Three Dialogues*, the Lockean Hylas,
who begins by ascribing the bugaboo term of 'sceptic' to his opponent, is driven by Philonous to accept that the term is much more
fitting to his own position. According to your (Lockean) opinion,
says Philonous,

[12] Maurice Cranston, *John Locke: A Biography* (Oxford, 1957), p. 269.

the ideas we perceive by our senses are not real things, but images, or copies of them. Our knowledge therefore is no farther real, than as our ideas are the true representations of those originals. But as these supposed originals are in themselves unknown, it is impossible to know how far our ideas resemble them; or whether they resemble them at all. We cannot therefore be sure we have any real knowledge. Farther, as our ideas are perpetually varied, without any change in the supposed real things, it necessarily follows they cannot all be true copies of them: or if some are, and others are not, it is impossible to distinguish the former from the latter. And this plunges us yet deeper in uncertainty. Again, when we consider the point, we cannot conceive how any idea, or anything like an idea, should have an absolute existence out of a mind: nor consequently, according to you, how there should be any real thing in Nature. The result of all which is, that we are thrown into the most hopeless and abandoned *scepticism*.[13]

Nor did it require the brilliance of a Berkeley or a Hume to perceive this tendency in Locke's thought. Several of his early readers felt that by basing everything on experience and 'the way of ideas', Locke's approach dispensed with more than it could make good. John Norris, Locke's first critic, objected: 'I very much wonder that our Author professing . . . to discourse of Truth in general . . . should yet confine his Discourse to Truth of Words and Truth of Thoughts without the least mention of Objective Truth. Which indeed is the Principal Kind of Truth.'[14] Henry Lee was so struck by the sceptical tendency of Locke's *Essay* that he thought fit to title his chapter-by-chapter commentary *Anti-Scepticism*; in this he 'sought to prove (1) that "Our Knowledge is of something else, besides of our own Ideas"; (2) that if it is only of our own ideas, knowledge is entirely useless; and (3) that such a definition as Locke gives "involves us in endless Scepticism or Doubtfulness of the Truth of all Propositions whatever".'[15] Swift seized upon a controversialist's use of Lockean terminology as a mark of obscurantism:

[13] *The Works of George Berkeley, Bishop of Cloyne*, ed. A. A. Luce amd T. E. Jessop, 9 vols. (London, 1948–57; repr. 1964), ii.246.

[14] John Norris, *Cursory Reflections upon a Book Call'd, An Essay Concerning Human Understanding* (London, 1690), p. 38.

[15] Quoted in John W. Yolton, *John Locke and the Way of Ideas* (Oxford, 1956), p. 101. Pages 98–114 document other similar responses, and the book as a whole gives a full and helpful discussion of how the *Essay* was received by its early readers.

He telleth us . . . *It will be necessary to shew what is contained in the Idea of Government.* Now, it is to be understood that this refined Way of Speaking was introduced by Mr *Locke*: After whom the Author limpeth as fast as he was able. All the former Philosophers in the World, from the Age of *Socrates* to ours, would have ignorantly put the Question, *Quid est Imperium?* [What is government?] But now it seemeth we must vary our Phrase; and since our modern Improvement of Human Understanding, instead of desiring a Philosopher to describe or define a Mouse-trap, or tell me what it is; I must gravely ask, what is contained in the Idea of a Mouse-trap? But then to observe how deeply this new Way of putting Questions to a Man's Self, maketh him enter into the Nature of Things . . .[16]

Swift's sarcasm extends by implication beyond his immediate target to Locke's *Essay*, 'our modern Improvement of Human Understanding'. It is true that the early critics of Locke were often speaking from their own *parti pris*, and may have felt threatened by the broadly anti-authoritarian cast of Locke's empiricism; moreover, the issue was complicated by the suspicion of a dangerous deistical tendency, if not indeed a hidden agenda, in his philosophy—so that the sceptic in epistemology was frequently blurred together with the sceptic as to Christian revelation and underminer of the Church. This suspicion was fed by *The Reasonableness of Christianity* (not acknowledged by Locke, but widely recognized as his), and the way in which Locke's attitudes were taken up by openly deistical or heterodox writers. Thus Toland's *Christianity Not Mysterious* was a subversively rationalistic work that invoked Locke as its intellectual godfather,[17] and Swift, in the passage quoted above, was replying to an attack on high-Church orthodoxy. But even if Locke's early critical readers were writing out of their own concerns and alarms, they were also responding to many passages written by Locke himself, which repeatedly emphasize the dimension of negativity and uncertainty in the new positive philosophy. When Swift sardonically remarks how little Lockean philosophical method, 'this new Way of putting Questions to a Man's Self', helps one 'enter into the Nature of Things', he is only echo-

[16] 'Remarks upon a Book, intitled *The Rights of the Christian Church*', in Jonathan Swift, *Bickerstaff Papers and Pamphlets on the Church*, ed. Herbert Davis (Oxford, 1940), p. 80.
[17] See the section 'Locke and Toland' in Leslie Stephen, *History of English Thought in the Eighteenth Century*, 3rd ed., with a preface by Crane Brinton, 2 vols. (London, 1962), i.78–100. It was Toland's self-description as a follower of Locke that first brought the big guns of Stillingfleet to bear on the *Essay*.

ing what is written in the *Essay*: 'Whensoever we would proceed beyond these simple *Ideas*, . . . and dive farther into the Nature of Things, we fall presently into Darkness and Obscurity.'[18]

If Lockean empiricism is built on the edge of a crumbling cliff, Berkeley and Swift are hardly more conscious of that fact than is Locke himself. Although he presents empiricism as the antagonist of scepticism, his empiricism is itself deeply involved with scepticism, as his early readers protested, and as he is himself strikingly willing to recognize, in a number of passages whose relation to his positive project of clarification and enlightenment is far from self-evident. The *Essay concerning Human Understanding* offered itself as a vaccination against scepticism, but it was a vaccine which carried some risk of transmitting the condition in active and perhaps virulent form.

*   *   *

In illustration of what has been said so far, let me now offer a summary of some of the main arguments of the *Essay*, indicating just how far Locke is prepared to drive his epistemological wedge between the mind and the reality of things, and how comparatively tentative and precarious are the bridges which he builds across the divide. He begins, in the first of the *Essay's* four books, by dispatching the doctrine of 'innate notions'. If we were born with innate ideas, he argues, these would be universally known and assented to: which is very evidently not the case: 'But alas, amongst *Children*, *Ideots*, *Savages*, and the grosly *Illiterate*, what general Maxims are to be found? What universal Principles of Knowledge? Their Notions are few and narrow, borrowed only from those Objects, they have had most to do with'.[19] In support of this position, Locke sets up as anthropologist, citing the diversity of cultural practices sanctioned by different societies and situations; thus we hear of the sexual license enjoyed by Islamic saints, of the total suspension of moral principle in an army sacking a town, of atheist peoples, of nations that eat their enemies, or their parents, or their children. 'There is scarce that Principle of Morality to be named, or *Rule* of *Vertue* to be thought on (those only excepted, that are absolutely necessary to hold Society together, which commonly too are neglected betwixt distinct Societies) which is

---

[18] *Essay*, II.xxiii.32: p. 314.   [19] Ibid. I.ii.27: p. 64.

not, somewhere or other, *slighted* and condemned by the general Fashion of *whole Societies* of Men.'[20] Locke is not afraid to draw the inference that human notions of vice and virtue depend on social convention, on 'Custom, a greater power than Nature'[21]— although at the same time he endeavours to set a limit to the relativism of this by preserving the idea of a 'Law of Nature' as, though not innate, yet 'something that we being ignorant of may attain to the knowledge of, by the use and due application of our natural Faculties'.[22]

By getting rid of innate ideas, Locke clears the way for the empiricism set out in the remainder of the *Essay*. All our knowledge of whatever kind is derived from, and reducible to, experience, from the impression of 'simple ideas' on the mind (hard, yellow, warm etc.) and the mind's operations on and responses to those ideas. It follows that our immediate knowledge is not of the objective world but of our own ideas. This is a potentially serious restriction, since most of the ideas left in our minds by objects are not of 'primary qualities'—solidity, extension, figure—which, Locke supposes, do bear resemblance to the real constitution of the things which give us those ideas (an object which feels solid is inherently solid), but of 'secondary qualities', such as colour, which exist only relative to the subject (an object which looks yellow is not inherently yellow). This opens a large gap between the cognitive mind and the world which it seeks to know:

To discover the nature of our *Ideas* the better, and to discourse of them intelligibly, it will be convenient to distinguish them, as they are *Ideas* or Perceptions in our Minds; and as they are modifications of matter in the Bodies that cause such Perceptions in us: that so we *may not* think (as perhaps usually is done) that they are exactly the Images and *Resemblances* of something inherent in the subject.[23]

Gold appears yellow to us, but we are absolutely in the dark as to how its inherent atomic constitution produces that effect. For our knowledge is not (or barely) at all of the substance, but only of its 'accidents', its effects or qualities as they appear in human experience. We may say in casual speech that we know gold is yellow, heavy, fusible etc., but what our experience actually gives us knowledge of is a conjunction of certain secondary qualities of

[20] *Essay*, I. iii.10: p. 72. [21] Ibid. 25: p. 82.
[22] Ibid. 13: p. 75. [23] Ibid. II.viii.7: p. 134.

yellowness, heaviness, and fusibility, which come together in the *je ne sais quoi* that we call 'gold'. Our idea, 'gold', is simply the knot which holds these sensory ideas together and which remarks their conjunction; but beyond this, when we talk of gold we have, strictly speaking, no idea what it is that we are talking about. And this is true of all our ideas of substances:

If any one should be asked, what is the subject wherein Colour or Weight inheres, he would have nothing to say, but the solid extended parts: And if he were demanded, what is it, that that Solidity and Extension inhere in, he would not be in a much better case, than the *Indian* before mentioned; who, saying that the World was supported by a great Elephant, was asked, what the Elephant rested on; to which his answer was, a great Tortoise: But being again pressed to know what gave support to the broad-back'd Tortoise, replied, something, he knew not what. And thus here, as in all other cases, where we use Words without having clear and distinct *Ideas*, we talk like Children; who, being questioned, what such a thing is, which they know not, readily give this satisfactory answer, That it is *something*; which in truth signifies no more, when so used, either by Children or Men, but that they know not what; and that the thing they pretend to know, and talk of, is what they have no distinct *Idea* of at all, and so are perfectly ignorant of it, and in the dark.[24]

The way to improve our knowledge of things is, therefore, experimentally, through careful observation of the phenomena—although experiment and observation can take us only a very little way towards certain general knowledge or (in this strict sense) 'science'.[25] 'Our Knowledge in all these Enquiries, reaches very little farther than our Experience.'[26] This was not unlike Newton's view; but it is noticeable how Locke, here as elsewhere, plays on the sceptical theme, dwelling less on the real advances to be obtained from experimental inquiry than on the radical limitations which it imposes on our knowledge of 'Being':

The Things that, as far as our Observation reaches, we constantly find to proceed regularly, we may conclude, do act by a Law set them; but yet by a Law, that we know not: whereby, though Causes work steadily, and Effects constantly flow from them, yet their *Connexions* and *Dependancies* being not discoverable in our *Ideas*, we can have but an experimental Knowledge of them. From all which 'tis easy to perceive,

[24] Ibid. xxiii.2: pp. 295 f.   [25] Ibid. IV.xii.9-10: pp. 644 f.
[26] Ibid. iii.14: p. 546.

what a darkness we are involved in, how little 'tis of Being, and the things that are, that we are capable to know.[27]

A further consequence of Locke's epistemology is that the terms we use for species, too, are thoroughly misleading in their apparent solidity of reference. We may have experimental knowledge of the particular behaviour of particular men, but 'Man', like 'gold', is merely our gesture towards a *je ne sais quoi*—in this case, the unknown common ground in which we may suppose that John, Peter, and Henry all participate. Locke often appears to accept that we cannot help but suppose the existence of some such common ground: but supposition, he always insists, is not knowledge. If we wish to give 'Man' any precise meaning, we must employ it as what Locke calls a 'mixed mode', that is, an idea freely put together by the mind for its own purposes, and quite independent of any real archetype in nature. 'General Natures are nothing but abstract *Ideas*'; '*General and Universal*, belong not to the real existence of Things; but *are the Inventions and Creatures of the Understanding*, made by it for its own use, *and concern only Signs*, whether Words, or *Ideas*.'[28] The dispute, say, over whether an embryo or a foetus at a particular stage of development is or is not human,[29] turns not on the essential nature of humanity, but on the definition of terms. The content of the word 'Man' depends on how one cares to define 'man', not on what man really is.

This is a position that might seem to have disturbing implication, if one still hankers to engage with what man really is—as we shall see, it disturbed Edward Stillingfleet, Locke's most vigorous early critic—but it encourages Locke in a more positive speculation about the importance of language. His great dream is that most if not all the intellectual debates which divide mankind may be, when rightly understood, matters of semantics rather than substance:

The multiplication and obstinacy of Disputes, which has so laid waste the intellectual World, is owing to nothing more, than to this ill use of Words. For though it be generally believed, that there is great diversity of Opinions in the Volumes and Variety of Controversies, the World is distracted with;

[27] *Essay*, IV.iii.29: p. 560.
[28] Ibid. III.iii.9: p. 412; Ibid. 11: p. 414.
[29] Locke touches on this at III.x.22, although his more common example is that of a changeling i.e. a child so mentally handicapped or physically deformed as to raise a question as to whether they belong to the human species.

yet the most I can find, that the contending learned Men of different Parties do, in their Arguings one with another, is, that they speak different Languages. For I am apt to imagine, that when any of them quitting Terms, think upon Things, and know what they think, they think all the same: Though perhaps, what they would have, be different.[30]

This sensitivity to the role of language was a crucial part of the *Essay*; no aspect of the work was more powerfully influential than the Third Book, 'Of Words'. To recall a point already made in the previous chapter: when Johnson wrote of the shame of imposing words for ideas, when Gibbon made fun of the early Christian theological disputes over the exact nature of the Trinity; when Hume suggested that disputes about free-will might be verbal rather than real; or when Pope spoke in the *Dunciad* of the power of education to imprison the mind within the pale of words, they were all drawing upon Locke's classic account of the vice of using language not securely anchored in experience.

One may observe, in all Languages, certain Words, that if they be examined, will be found, in their first Original, and their appropriated Use, not to stand for any clear and distinct *Ideas*. These, for the most part, the several *Sects* of Philosophy and Religion have introduced. For their Authors, or Promoters, either affecting something singular, and out of the way of common apprehensions, or to support some strange Opinions, or cover some Weakness of their Hypothesis, seldom fail to coin new Words, and such as, when they come to be examined, may justly be called *insignificant Terms*. . . .

   Others there be, who . . . familiarly *use Words*, which the Propriety of Language has affixed to very important *Ideas, without any distinct meaning* at all. *Wisdom, Glory, Grace*, etc. are Words frequent enough in every Man's Mouth; but if a great many of those who use them, should be asked, what they mean by them? they would be at a stand, and not know what to answer.[31]

This treacherousness of language is due not only to its abuse by the sophistical and the idle, but also by its inherent and ineradicable tendency to mislead: hence the virtual impossibility of overcoming it altogether. Our possession of the names of substances and species, for example, is very liable to delude us into supposing that in using those words we know something of the realities to which they refer—a fallacy which Locke devotes a large proportion of the

---

[30] *Essay*, III.x.22: p. 504.   [31] Ibid. 2–3: pp. 490 f.

Essay to detecting and exposing. Underlying this mistake of confusing words with things is the deeper but virtually universal fallacy of supposing that words can stand directly for things; properly speaking, Locke insists, language refers not outward to the world of things, of objective reality, but inward, to the realm of individual, subjective consciousness. '*Words in their proper or immediate Signification, stand for nothing, but the* Ideas *in the Mind of him that uses them.*'[32] Words are, in the first place, mirrors, not windows, in the mind; the treacherousness of language lies in the tenuousness of the relation between our ideas and the world, and the extreme difficulty of establishing how much the idea which a particular word calls up in my mind has in common with the idea which it calls up in someone else's.

Locke gives a great deal more time and energy to these propositions about how language leads us astray, than to prescribing good practice. After two powerful chapters analysing the imperfection and the abuse of words, the chapter which follows, proposing remedies, seems distinctly thin. Men should use only words for which they have determinate ideas which they can, at will, decompound into their constituent clear and distinct simple ideas; and where the signification of these words is not supported by common usage, they should communicate their meaning by 'showing' (for simple ideas), 'defining' (for mixed modes), and a combination of showing, defining, and experimental investigation (for names of substances)—a suggestion which leads to the utopian desideratum of a Dictionary of all the sensible qualities of things. These remedies come from the clinical, analytic impulse in Locke, from the seeker after clarity and precise denotation who declared all figurative language to be an abuse of language's proper function. It is a position which anyone who values imaginative literature will find reductive. One thinks by contrast of Johnson's classic account of the vitality of language, and the consequent impossibility of precise definition, in the Preface to the *Dictionary*:

While our language is yet living, and variable by the caprice of every one that speaks it, these words are hourly shifting their relations, and can no more be ascertained in a dictionary than a grove, in the agitation of a storm, can be accurately delineated from its picture in the water. . . . Such

[32] *Essay*, III.ii.2: p. 405.

is the exuberance of signification which many words have obtained that it was scarcely possible to collect all their senses.[33]

This impossibility of 'ascertaining' meaning is not simply to be regretted; throughout the Preface Johnson associates it with the fluidity of all that is 'living', and with the larger movements of the world—'the revolutions of the sky, or intumescence of the tide'.[34] The resistance presented to the mind's impulse to demarcate and to fix, is salutary. 'All will be better understood as [words] are considered in greater variety of structures and relations.'[35] Or, for a more complicated contrast with Locke, one might recall the linguistic philosophers Gulliver meets in the Academy of Lagado. Some of these have abolished all words but nouns, while others have dispensed with words altogether, and hold conversations by the more truly philosophical means of showing one another objects (which they carry round for the purpose in a sack). In one sense Swift is there entirely Lockean in satirizing the notion that words stand directly and immediately for things; but at another level the satire offers a kind of *reductio ad absurdum* of Locke's mistrust of language, an image of the sterility of communication if altogether purged of the subjective and metaphorical dimension that language brings. Many of Swift's hardly-human narrators are impeccable Lockeans in their precisely referential use of words, their implicit elevation of judgement over wit, and their avoidance or incomprehension of metaphor. (There is a strong ambivalence in Swift here: the man who wrote the unironic *Proposal for Correcting, Improving and Ascertaining the English Tongue* was powerfully attracted to as well as repelled by such non-human cleanliness of discourse, and in many of his ironic works the extraordinary co-presence of an extreme stylistic austerity and the most mischievously multiple play of irony functions to allow full expression to both these contrary impulses.)

In fact, as I have said, Locke's chapter on remedies comes almost as an afterthought. His main concern in Book III, 'Of Words', is that we should understand the slipperiness of language, the frequently misleading, inadequate or downright illusory character of its claim to make direct reference to the real external world. The

[33] *Samuel Johnson: The Major Works*, ed. Donald Greene (Oxford, 2000), pp. 316 f.
[34] Ibid. 325. [35] Ibid. 317.

reader emerges impressed with the need for better standards of linguistic hygiene, certainly, but this new critical alertness to the vocabularies of mystification readily bleeds into a more general scepticism, fed by Locke's suspicion that all intellectual disputes may, at bottom, turn on matters of semantics rather than substance, and by Locke's insistence that the immediate reference of language is inward, to the ideas of the user. As we have already seen, these ideas bear a problematic relation to the world of external realities. Hence, in Prior's dialogue of the dead between Locke and Montaigne, Locke stands accused of a wilful solipsism, and his defence that the *Essay* promotes self-knowledge is held to be no defence at all:

Really who ever writes in Folio should convince people that he knows something besides himself, else few would read his Book, except his very particular Friends. . . . Your Mind was given You for the Conduct of your Life, not meerly for Your own Speculation; nor should it be imployed only upon it self, but upon other things.[36]

Where the mind is thus employed upon itself, communication becomes inconceivable. 'You, and Your understanding are the *Personae Dramatis*, and the whole amounts to no more than a Dialogue between John and Lock.'[37] After a very funny burlesque—anticipating passages in *Tristram Shandy*—featuring the difficulties that Locke's servant John may have in communicating the new philosophy to Margaret the kitchen-maid without being misunderstood as talking bawdy, Prior's Montaigne concludes that the *Essay concerning Human Understanding* may have meaning only for Locke himself, and be quite unable to communicate Locke's ideas to others:

probably neither Robin, John, Margrate You or I, or any other five Persons alive have either the same Idea's of the same thing, or the same way of Expressing them. . . . there may be as much difference between your Conceptions and mine, as there is between your Band and my Ruff. If so it may happen I say, that if no Mans Ideas be perfectly the same Locks Human Understanding may be fit only for the Meditation of Lock himself.[38]

[36] *The Literary Works of Matthew Prior*, ed. H. Bunker Wright and Monroe K. Spears, 2 vols. (Oxford, 1959), i.623 f.
[37] Ibid. 620.   [38] Ibid. 639.

This critique is nicely amplified by the way Prior's use of the dialogue-form plays up the incommensurable differences between one mind and another. Locke and Montaigne never do come to an understanding in the course of their conversation, or even properly engage with the other's view.

Although comically expressed, this plays on an authentically Lockean area of concern. In the tower of experience to which Locke confines us, words are discovered to be not windows but mirrors, and ideas are not windows either (apart from simple sensory impressions, and of these, only primary qualities come to us through clear plane glass) but wall-paintings, created not according to any simply mimetic scheme of art. Experience, under this analysis, is beginning to seem more potentially private, subjective, and incommensurable with that of others, than might have been supposed. How substantial can the knowledge be which is available to us in such a tower? Locke himself raises this question directly in the fourth and final book, 'Of Knowledge and Opinion'. After defining knowledge as the perceived agreement or disagreement of one of our ideas with another, Locke imagines a vigorous protest from his reader:

I Doubt not but my Reader, by this time, may be apt to think, that I have been all this while only building a Castle in the Air; and be ready to say to me, To what purpose all this stir? Knowledge, say you, is only the perception of the agreement or disagreement of our own *Ideas*: but who knows what those *Ideas* may be? Is there any thing so extravagant, as the Imaginations of Men's Brains? Where is the Head that has no *Chimeras* in it? Or if there be a sober and wise Man, what difference will there be, by your Rules, between his Knowledge, and that of the most extravagant Fancy in the World? They both have their *Ideas*, and perceive their agreement and disagreement one with another. If there be any difference between them, the advantage will be on the warm-headed Man's side, as having the more *Ideas*, and the more lively. And so, by your Rules, he will be the more knowing. If it be true, that all Knowledge lies only in the perception of the agreement or disagreement of our own *Ideas*, the Visions of an Enthusiast, and the Reasonings of a sober Man, will be equally certain. 'Tis no matter how Things are: so a Man observe but the agreement of his own Imaginations, and talk conformably, it is all Truth, all Certainty. Such Castles in the Air, will be as strong Holds of Truth, as the Demonstrations of *Euclid*. That an Harpy is not a Centaur, is by this way as certain knowledge, and as much a Truth, as that a Square is not a Circle. But *of what use is all this* fine *Knowledge of Men's own Imaginations*, to a Man that enquires after the reality of Things? It matters not what Men's Fancies are, 'tis the Knowledge of things that is only to be prized: 'tis this alone gives a value to our Reasonings, and preference to one Man's Knowledge over another's, that it is of Things as they really are, and not of Dreams and Fancies.[39]

It was rather splendid of Locke to give such strong expression to this hostile voice; passages like these in the *Essay* may well have prompted the unease that they were intended to pre-empt. Locke felt, however, that he could answer such objections through his account of moral knowledge, which has a special status that places it beyond the reach of scepticism. Moral knowledge, he explains, can claim a certainty denied to the sphere of natural philosophy, entangled as this is in the disjunction between primary and secondary qualities, the inaccessibility of substance, and the unreality of species. This is because moral knowledge employs 'mixed modes', which are not drawn from the impenetrable world of phenomena but freely defined and put together by the mind; hence in the sphere of morality we can attain to demonstrably certain general knowledge, rather as we can in mathematics. From this Locke feels encouraged to infer that morality, not natural philosophy, is our proper concern. After so much illusory understanding has been sluiced away, what we are left with at the bottom of Locke's sieve is, after all, something which justifies our search: the solid gold of moral knowledge.

It remains a question, however, whether this gold can be exchanged for anything worth having. For Locke's firm distinction between experience of the world and the sphere of moral knowledge leaves a worrying gap. We would seem to have reliable knowledge of a general kind concerning only such ideas as are altogether independent of real existence. Would this really satisfy the indignant questioner that Locke imagines, who was hoping to enquire 'after the reality of Things'? Or is our escape from subjectivism into the realm of abstract moral propositions—morality-as-mathematics—something of a hollow achievement? Once again, Locke sees this objection coming, although he believes he can answer it:

The Truth and Certainty of *moral* Discourses abstracts from the Lives of Men, and the Existence of those Vertues in the World, whereof they treat:

---

[39] *Essay*, IV.iv.1: pp. 562 f.

Nor are *Tully*'s Offices less true, because there is no Body in the World that exactly practises his Rules, and lives up to that pattern of a vertuous Man, which he has given us, and which existed no where, when he writ, but in *Idea*. If it be true in Speculation, *i.e.* in *Idea*, that *Murther deserves Death*, it will also be true in Reality of any Action that exists conformable to that *Idea* of *Murther*.[40]

For an empiricist, this is an extraordinary turnaround against the primacy of particular experience, as Bolingbroke was later to point out when he discussed the passage:

Shall we believe that men were lawgivers and moralists, before they were spectators of the actions of one another? . . . Our ideas are fantastic, and our knowledge imaginary, when the former are framed without a sufficient conformity to existence. . . . The mind must be constantly intent to frame its ideas and notions after that great original, nature; for tho these ideas and notions are properly and usefully framed by the mind, that they may serve as architypes by which we reason, and according to which we judge, yet must all the parts of them be taken from nature, and no otherwise put together than nature warrants.[41]

On this point of moral knowledge Locke lacked the courage of his empirical convictions, according to Bolingbroke, who offers to help empiricism over its last inhibitions into a full consistency. And although he underestimates the degree to which Locke needs this theory of morality-as-mathematics in order to keep scepticism at bay, his essential point about the moral uselessness of purely analytic propositions, has considerable force. For, to take up Locke's own example that murder deserves death, how could our possession of this abstract certainty 'in *Idea*' help us to tell whether a particular act of killing was murder or manslaughter (say), or whether a particular act of euthanasia was or was not 'murder', given Locke's reiterated polemic against taking the names of species for real essences of things? This polemic makes the gap between mental categories and particular events extraordinarily difficult to leap. General ideas have no existence in nature, Locke insisted. Berkeley was to push this a stage further with the argument that abstract general ideas have no existence even in the mind; our terms may be general, but our ideas are always only of

[40] Ibid. 8: p. 566.
[41] Bolingbroke, iii.496 f., 413.

particulars.[42] But even on Locke's view, it is not quite as plain as he wishes it to be that Cicero's true propositions about the perfectly virtuous man are entirely unlike true propositions about harpies and centaurs. Bishop Stillingfleet, Locke's formidable early critic, registered a similar protest; like the deist Bolingbroke, he refers Locke to nature, although in a more exalted sense: 'However the *abstract Ideas* are the work of the Mind; yet they are not meer Creatures of the Mind. . . . The *general Idea* is not made from the simple *Ideas* by the meer Act of the Mind abstracting from Circumstances, but from *Reason* and Consideration of the true Nature of Things.'[43] Yet consideration of the true nature of things is just what Locke's empiricism renders problematic. One can understand why Shaftesbury, despite (or perhaps because of) the experience of having Locke as his personal tutor, could not believe in Lockean philosophy as a foundation for ethics. ''Twas Mr Locke that struck at all fundamentals, threw all order and virtue out of the world and made the very idea of these . . . unnatural and without foundation in our minds.'[44]

A further objection to the suggestion that Book IV somehow puts the imp of scepticism back in its bottle, lies—as Shaftesbury suggests—in the absence of any ethical *ground* to Lockean moral knowledge. In Book II good and evil were defined with unflinching empiricism as 'nothing but Pleasure or Pain, or that which occasions, or procures Pleasure or Pain to us. *Morally Good and Evil* then, is only the Conformity or Disagreement of our voluntary Actions to some Law, whereby Good or Evil is drawn on us, from the Will and Power of the Law-maker.'[45] These laws are of three kinds, divine, civil, and the 'Law of *Opinion* or *Reputation*', which—Locke again unflinchingly accepts—determines what is virtue and what is vice.[46] As the last two of these laws are plainly subject to the contingencies of custom, and as moreover human desires for earthly happiness come in such diverse and subjective

[42] See the 'Introduction' to *A Treatise concerning the Principles of Human Knowledge*: Berkeley, *Works*, ii.25-40.

[43] Edward Stillingfleet, *A Discourse in Vindication of the Doctrine of the Trinity* (1697), repr. as vol. 4 of *The Philosophy of Edward Stillingfleet: Including his Replies to John Locke*, ed. G. A. J. Rogers, 6 vols. (Bristol, 2000), pp. 257 f.

[44] *The Life, Unpublished Letters, and Philosophical Regimen of Anthony Ashley Cooper, Earl of Shaftesbury*, ed. B. Rand (London, 1900), p. 403.

[45] *Essay*, II.xxviii.5: p. 351.

[46] Ibid. 7: p. 352.

forms as to fall under the principle *de gustibus non est disputandum*, there is no arguing over matters of taste,[47] the only anchorage for Lockean morality lies in the prospect of infinite reward or punishment in the afterlife.[48] Locke does indeed assert that 'the *Idea* of a supreme Being, infinite in Power, Goodness, and Wisdom' is sufficient in itself, when attentively considered, to 'place *Morality amongst the Sciences capable of Demonstration*,'[49] but this begs the question of whether the idea of such a Being corresponds to any reality, rather than being like the idea of a harpy or a centaur. In a separate, later chapter Locke maintains that the existence of God is demonstrably certain, as the Creator in whom the Creation necessarily has its origin, but this in itself does not reach further than one of the more impersonal versions of Deism, and does nothing to support the inclusion of infinite *goodness* in Locke's earlier account of 'the *Idea* of a supreme Being'. Both deist and Christian could reasonably query how Locke, as an empiricist, comes by this idea. Bolingbroke remarked that we have, from the evidence of the creation, much clearer ideas of divine wisdom than of divine goodness, and in Isaac Watts' philosophical dialogue between a deist and a divine, the deist is quickly brought to abandon 'the goodness of God' as a tenable inference from the phenomena.[50] Locke himself argues that we get to the idea of divine power and wisdom by extrapolating from our experience of our own limited power and intelligence, multiplying what we find in ourselves, so to speak, by infinity,[51] but he does not press the same argument in respect of goodness, and with reason: our moral goodness is for Locke dependent on the idea of our subjection to a lawgiver, but to base *divine* goodness on dependency on a law-giver, as if God were susceptible to punishment and reward, would be absurd. The gap between *Idea* and reality thus remains open, and Locke's suggestion that it is bridged by moral knowledge seems to be something of a fudge; it is not clear how Locke could answer Thomas Burnet's intelligently troublesome questions:

---

[47] Ibid. xxi.54–5: pp. 268–70.   [48] Ibid. II.xxi.70: pp. 281 f.
[49] Ibid. IV.iii.18: p. 549.
[50] Bolingbroke, v.335; Isaac Watts, *The Strength and Weakness of Human Reason: or, The Important Question about the Sufficiency of Reason to Conduct Mankind to Religion and Future Happiness*, 2nd ed. (London, 1737), pp. 47 f.
[51] *Essay*, II.xxiii.33: p. 314, and IV.x.1–6: pp. 619–21.

You allow, I think, moral good and evil to be such antecedently to all human laws; but you understand them to be such (if I understand you right) by the divine law. To know your mind farther, give me leave to ask: what is the reason or ground of that divine law, whether the arbitrary will of God, the good of men, or the intrinsic nature of the things themselves? If I knew upon which of these three grounds you would build your demonstration of morality, I could make better judgement of it. You seem to resolve all into the will and power of the law-maker. But has the will of a law-maker no rule to go by? And is not that which is a rule to His will a rule also to ours, and indeed the original rule?[52]

These are large questions, which press Locke towards the kind of metaphysical assertion that he did not want to make. His brief and irritable reply to Burnet merely asserts the primacy of gospel revelation—without replying to Burnet's inquiry as to why, on Locke's principles, we should believe that Scripture gives us revelation—and attacks Burnet for raising doubts and problems which may admit of no answer. 'If anyone finds that there be many questions that my principles will not resolve, he will do the world more service to lay down such principles as will resolve them than to quarrel with my ignorance, which I readily acknowledge.'[53] In private correspondence with a friend at Oxford, he responded to similar pressure by backtracking on the question of demonstrability, and insisting on the strictly limited scope of the *Essay*:

Will nothing then passe with you in Religion or Morality but what you can demonstrate? . . . I did not designe here to treat of the grounds of true morality which is necessary to true and perfect happinesse; and 'thad been impertinent if I had so designed: my businesse was only to shew whence men had moral Ideas and what they were.

The simple fact of 'some mens bare supposition of such a [divine] law whether true or false', was, he explained, all that his project required.[54] This firmly, or obstinately, restates Locke's more characteristic stance in the *Essay*: he limits his inquiry to the circle of experience, observes the gap that exists between the mind and the nature of things, and declines to go further—despite the prompt-

[52] *Remarks on John Locke by Thomas Burnet: with Locke's Replies*, ed. George Watson (Doncaster, 1989), p. 25.

[53] Ibid., 35.

[54] To James Tyrrell, 4 Aug. 1690; *Correspondence of John Locke*, ed. E. S. de Beer, 8 vols. (Oxford, 1976–89), iv.111–13.

ings of readers keen to resolve the tensions his arguments have created.

*   *   *

There is a particularly clear example of this in Locke's account of substance and the controversies which it generated. Locke maintained that the mind could have no idea of substance as such, without, however, positively denying its existence. This generated a demand for clarification, in one direction or another, and became the focus of an extensive debate.[55] Stillingfleet argued that on Locke's empirical principles 'substance' could not be justified at all, being a wholly un-empirical hypothesis of reason: this was such an unsatisfactory state of affairs as to discredit the premises which supported it. 'So that the most men may come to in this way of *Idea's* is, That it is possible it may be so, and it is possible it may not; but that it is impossible for us *from our Ideas*, to determine either way. And is not this an admirable Way to bring us to a certainty of Reason?'[56] Isaac Watts took an opposite tack. A broadly sympathetic commentator, he thanked Locke for exploding the delusion that we can have knowledge of the substance which underlies the empirical qualities of objects, but still wished that Locke had not left behind the notion of substance as a real unknown being—a position which opened the door to the materialist hypothesis that this fundamental unknown ground might be the same for physical and spiritual phenomena alike.[57] That anxiety went to the heart of what made Locke's scepticism on substance so alarming: its applicability, not only to external objects, but also to the internal subject, the self. The real nature of the experiencing self is as dark to Locke, as radically hidden from experiential knowledge, as the objective world which occasions its experience; speaking of our idea of God, he remarks, in casual parenthesis, that

---

[55] So much so that in the third chapter of *Joseph Andrews* the essence of matter has been a topic for energetic discussion by Parson Adams and Mrs Slipslop.

[56] Stillingfleet, *A Discourse in Vindication of the Doctrine of the Trinity*, p. 243. 'Without having to wait until Berkeley and Hume pushed Locke's theory to its logical conclusion, Stillingfleet perceived that a kind of scepticism was already involved. ... Locke's world was reduced to Hume's at the very outset, without any further intellectual development being involved.' R. H. Popkin, 'The Philosophy of Bishop Stillingfleet', *Journal of the History of Philosophy* 9 (1971), 303–19: p. 316.

[57] Isaac Watts, *Philosophical Essays on Various Subjects . . . With some Remarks on Mr Locke's Essay on the Human Understanding* (London, 1733), Essay II: 'Of Substance', pp. 47–54.

we cannot of course know God's real essence, 'not knowing the
real Essence of a Peble, or a Fly, or of our own selves'.[58] Locke
sounds entirely cool about this, but the alarming import of such a
doctrine was highlighted for his readers by two related speculations, which proved to be among the most controversial passages
of the entire *Essay*. At IV.iii.6, as an example of the kind of inquiry
which is beyond the scope of reason to determine, Locke gives the
question of whether or not matter might be capable of thought:

> We have the *Ideas* of *Matter* and *Thinking*, but possibly shall never be able
> to know, whether any mere material Being thinks, or no; it being impossi-
> ble for us, by the contemplation of our own *Ideas*, without revelation, to
> discover, whether Omnipotency has not given to some Systems of Matter
> fitly disposed, a power to perceive and think, or else joined and fixed to
> Matter so disposed, a thinking immaterial Substance ... since we know
> not wherein Thinking consists.[59]

It was generally held that the strongest logical argument for the
immortality of the soul depended upon its immateriality; by admit-
ting the possibility that the unknown substance or basis of thought
could be material (a possibility which cannot be refuted, since,
although we think, and know that we think, 'we know not wherein
Thinking consists'), Locke seemed to endanger the whole structure
of Christian belief. 'We can have no certainty upon these
Principles, whether we have any *Spiritual Substance* within us or
not', Stillingfleet protested.[60] The other related speculation
provoked no less comment. If the essence of my thinking self is
utterly unknown to me, wholly inaccessible to experience, then
how am I justified in regarding myself today as in some sense
continuous with the person that I was last week, or last year? What
is the principle which guarantees personal identity? Locke gave the
only reply which his empiricism could permit: consciousness.

> As far as any intelligent Being can repeat the *Idea* of any past Action with
> the same consciousness it had of it at first, and with the same conscious-
> ness it has of any present Action; so far it is the same *personal self*. For it
> is by the consciousness it has of its present Thoughts and Actions, that it
> is *self* to it *self* now, and so will be the same *self* as far as the same
> consciousness can extend to Actions past or to come.[61]

[58] *Essay*, II.xxiii.35: p. 315.   [59] Ibid. IV.iii.6: pp. 540 f.
[60] Stillingfleet, *A Discourse in Vindication of the Doctrine of the Trinity*, p. 242.
[61] *Essay*, II.xxvii.10: p. 336. For one aspect of the literary take on this idea, see

This bristles with difficulties, as Locke was aware. It is by no means clear what is meant by 'the same consciousness'; and Locke's concession that a man when drunk is not the same person as when sober generated some hair-raising possibilities with regard to moral responsibility. We cannot justly be punished for our vices, or rewarded for our virtues, it would seem, if drunkenness or madness or senility have wiped away our consciousness of them as ours; Isaac Watts objected that if a madman is conscious of having had Plato for his pupil, and believes himself to be 'the same Person with *Socrates*', it is not clear, on Locke's principles, how he can be answered.[62] Joseph Butler too thought that Locke had been 'hasty' on this point, and pointed to the alarming use which free-thinkers could make of such a doctrine:

Some of those hasty Observations have been carried to a strange Length by Others; whose Notion when traced and examined to the bottom, amounts, I think, to this: That Personality is not a permanent, but a transient thing: That it lives and dies, begins and ends continually: That no one can any more remain one and the same Person two Moments together, than two successive Moments can be one and the same Moment . . . And from hence it must follow, that it is a Fallacy upon Ourselves, to charge our present Selves with any thing we did, or to imagine our present Selves interested in any thing which befell us yesterday; or that our present Self will be interested in what will befall us to morrow: since our present Self is not, in Reality, the same with the Self of yesterday, but another like Self or Person coming in its Room, and mistaken for it; to which another Self will succeed to morrow.[63]

Under such circumstances, justice becomes unworkable, perhaps inconceivable. Locke had indeed allowed that human laws were unavoidably unjust when they punished the sober man for the actions of the drunk; but divine justice, he supposed, would order things better.[64] But it is not easy to see how. Having exonerated the sober consciousness, will God then condemn the drunken as a distinct entity? How many consciousnesses will each of us produce

Christopher Fox, *Locke and the Scriblerians: Identity and Consciousness in Early Eighteenth-Century Britain* (Berkeley and Los Angeles, 1988).

[62] Watts, *Philosophical Essays*, p. 299.

[63] Joseph Butler, 'Of Personal Identity', Appendix 1 to *The Analogy of Religion Natural and Revealed to the Constitution and Course of Nature* (London, 1736), p. 305.

[64] *Essay*, II.xxvii.22: pp. 343 f.

for separate judgement at the last day?[65] Christian eschatology
seems irretrievably damaged by this, as does any idea of ultimate
personal accountability. From Locke's location of self in the activity of consciousness, it is only a small step, as Butler could see, to
the entirely disintegrative scepticism shortly to be expressed by
Hume:

> For my part, when I enter most intimately into what I call *myself*, I always
> stumble on some particular perception or other, of heat or cold, light or
> shade, love or hatred, pain or pleasure. I never can catch *myself* at any time
> without a perception, and never can observe any thing but the perception.
> When my perceptions are removed for any time, as by sound sleep; so long
> am I insensible of *myself*, and may truly be said not to exist.[66]

It follows that mankind 'are nothing but a bundle or collection of
different perceptions, which succeed each other with an inconceivable rapidity, and are in a perpetual flux and movement'.[67]
Although Butler was writing just before Hume, such alarming
consequences of Locke's reasoning were perfectly apparent to him;
in an effort to block them, he argued that personal identity is not
constituted by consciousness, only *recognized* by consciousness.
The radical alternative, as ever, was Berkeley's: if identity is constituted by consciousness, then, for identity to be stable, it must be
God's consciousness that is doing the constituting.

*　*　*

Such controversies have a representative significance. Butler was
like other critics or revisers of Locke in implying that Locke had
developed empiricism to a point of crucial instability, where it had
to either go on, into a confessed scepticism which would—
surely?—discredit itself, or go back, and anchor mental experience
more reliably in something beyond itself. For the only alternative
to such an anchored or modified empiricism seemed to be the radical scepticism that was to be expressed in the philosophy of Hume.
In some key passages, Hume seems simply to be highlighting the
implications of what is already there in Locke.

All those sublime Thoughts, which towre above the Clouds, and reach as
high as Heaven it self, take their Rise and Footing here: In all that great

---

[65] For expressions of this concern delivered from the eighteenth-century pulpit,
see Fox, *Locke and the Scriblerians*, p. 70.
[66] *Treatise*, p. 252.　　　　　　　　　　　　　　　　　[67] Ibid.

Extent wherein the mind wanders, in those remote Speculations, it may seem to be elevated with, it stirs not one jot beyond those *Ideas*, which *Sense* or *Reflection*, have offered for its Contemplation.[68] [Locke]

Now since nothing is ever present to the mind but perceptions, and since all ideas are deriv'd from something antecedently present to the mind: it follows, that 'tis impossible for us so much as to conceive or form an idea of any thing specifically different from ideas and impressions. Let us fix our attention out of ourselves as much as possible: Let us chace our imagination to the heavens, or to the utmost limits of the universe; we never really advance a step beyond ourselves, nor can conceive any kind of existence, but those perceptions, which have appear'd in that narrow compass. This is the universe of the imagination, nor have we any idea but what is there produc'd.[69] [Hume]

Hume is there doing no more than repeating the fundamental tenet of Locke's empiricism, but with phrasing that carries a subversive implication which was, at most, latent in Locke. Such passages bear out the anxiety Stillingfleet expressed at the end of his answer to Locke's first reply to his criticisms:

Before I conclude my self, I must take notice of your *Conclusion*, viz. *That you must content your self with this condemned way of Ideas, and despair of ever attaining any knowledge by any other than that, or farther than that will lead me to it.* Which is in effect to say, that you see no way to avoid *Scepticism* but this: but my great Prejudice against it is, that it leads to *Scepticism*.[70]

In certain respects, Stillingfleet was a prophet; Locke's *Essay* did indeed stimulate that scepticism against which it was intended to be a vaccination. Locke's early critics may have worked out the sceptical implication of his arguments largely as a *reductio ad absurdum*, a warning that, in one area or another, against Christian orthodoxy or against common sense, he was going too far: but the *reductio*, as easily happens, acquired a cogency of its own, until in the work of Hume the implications of Lockean empiricism seemed to render both Christian orthodoxy and common sense wholly irrational.

However, Locke's *Essay* also stimulated sceptical thinking in a

[68] *Essay*, II.i.24: p. 118.
[69] *Treatise*, pp. 67 f.
[70] *The Bishop of Worcester's Answer to Mr Locke's Letter* (1697), reprinted in vol. 5 of *The Philosophy of Edward Stillingfleet*, p. 125.

rather different sense, one closer to the heart of this study. It did so
through a kind of reticence, that declined to work empiricism
through to the kind of subversive conclusions that its critics alleged
or anticipated. To the ultimatum that it provoked—qualify your
empiricism or embrace scepticism altogether—the *Essay* offered a
somewhat inscrutable resistance. On the one hand Locke insisted
that our knowledge reaches little further than the circle of our
ideas, and that the relation of those ideas to substantial archetypes
is entirely unknown, or tenuous in the extreme. For example, when
Stillingfleet demanded to know whether, despite Locke's arguments
in the *Essay*, he did not possess 'according to true reason . . . a clear
idea of man; not of Peter, James, or John, but of a man as such',
Locke replied with an intelligent if exasperating sidestep:

This, I think, nobody denies: nor can any body deny it, who will not say,
that the general abstract idea which he has in his mind of a sort or species
of animals that he calls man, ought not to have that general name man
applied to it: for that is all (as I humbly conceive) which these words of
your lordship here amount to.[71]

Stillingfleet asks, 'Do I not have an idea of *man*?' and Locke replies,
'Yes, certainly you have an *idea*, "man" (which is all that your
question can mean).' Stillingfleet lays claim to a knowledge that
reaches beyond the mind's hall of mirrors, and Locke shows him
his claim reflected in a mirror. Stillingfleet alleges that there is a
point of substance at issue between them; Locke replies with
semantics, and the implication that Stillingfleet, with his finally
meaningless belief that language can somehow reach to 'man as
such', has mistaken Locke's meaning, or mistakes his own.[72]
   On the other hand, Locke was clearly not writing as the destabilizing sceptic or closet infidel that some of his early readers feared
him to be. He presents himself as a friend to morality; he accepts
Christian revelation; he never writes as though he doubts the existence of a substantial world outside the hall of mirrors, or a spiri-

---

[71] *A Letter to the Right Reverend Edward, Lord Bishop of Worcester: The
Works of John Locke*, 9th ed., 9 vols. (London, 1794), reprinted with introduction
by John W. Yolton (London, 1997), iii. 24.
[72] One can see, even from this small example, how the controversy between them
might run and run. There were three separate attacks by Stillingfleet, with charges
increasing in seriousness; and three replies by Locke, of increasing length. The
exchanges were ended only by Stillingfleet's death; the issues gained wider currency
through extracts footnoted in editions of the *Essay* after 1700.

tual substance beneath the flow of consciousness. Several times in the final book he refers, most un-empirically, to the superior intelligence of angels, as a way of expressing the supposition that a more adequate knowledge of things is there even if it is not there for us.[73] The point he makes again and again to Stillingfleet is that he is dealing with our understanding of things and its limitations, not with things themselves, about which few inferences, positive or negative, can be drawn from his philosophy. Thus he writes to Stillingfleet, within just a few pages of the quotation given above,

I ground not the being, but the idea of substance, on our accustoming ourselves to suppose some substratum; for it is of the idea alone I speak there [in the *Essay*], and not of the being of substance. And having everywhere affirmed and built upon it, that a man is a substance; I cannot be supposed to question or doubt of the being of substance, till I can question or doubt of my own being.[74]

The role of *supposing* here is an interesting one. Although not a term on which Locke appears to place any weight, it quietly represents an activity of mind which his philosophy makes, almost unwittingly, extremely important. Substance (literally, Locke reminds us, '*standing under*'),[75] is something of which experience gives us no distinct idea, and which we therefore *suppose* (literally: place under). Substance is supposition; the *Essay* is very clear about this:

Not imagining how these simple *Ideas* can subsist by themselves, we accustom our selves, to suppose some *Substratum*, wherein they do subsist, and from which they do result, which therefore we call *Substance*.

So that if any one will examine himself concerning his *Notion of pure Substance in general*, he will find he has no other *Idea* of it at all, but only a Supposition of he knows not what support of such Qualities, which are capable of producing simple *Ideas* in us.[76]

Supposition is what lies beyond experience, and outside knowledge. As an empirical philosopher, Locke often seems to be warning us against it: in the passage from which I am quoting, he says

---

[73] *Essay*, IV.iii.6, 23, 27: pp. 543, 554, 557f; IV.xi.12: p. 637; IV.xvi.12: p. 666; IV.xvii.14: p. 683.
[74] *A Letter to the Right Reverend Edward, Lord Bishop of Worcester*: *Works* iii.18.
[75] *Essay*, II.xxiii.2: p. 296.
[76] Ibid. 1–2: p. 295.

that it is 'by inadvertency' that we consider substance 'as one simple *Idea*, which indeed is a complication of many *Ideas* together'.[77] But he also goes on to say that although spiritual substance is—just like bodily substance—a supposition, this is no reason to 'conclude its non-Existence'.[78] Similarly with morality: strict empiricism must make our knowledge of divine law problematic, but Locke still discusses how the idea of a divine law operates on human conduct, because, as he defended himself to his Oxford friend, it was 'men's bare supposition of such a law, whether true or false' that supported his argument. And in the passage to Stillingfleet quoted above, it is Locke's act of supposing that has given him the idea that 'man is a substance', which he has 'every-where affirmed and built on'. This affirming and building is not based on *knowledge* about being (we have not left the tower of the mind), but on a kind of supposing or (with only a slight pun) under-standing which enables practice, and draws a certain validation from that enabling. Although Locke will not say that he knows that substance exists, he 'cannot be supposed to question or doubt' it.

Equally interesting is that last use of 'supposing'. Instead of telling his readers what he thinks, Locke speaks of what he can or cannot be supposed to think, of what readers may suppose lies beneath his words. 'Supposing' here is a term for how one has to think when one thinks what is in someone else's mind; it recognizes the obliquity of meaning and communication. As with the supposition of substance, here, too, supposing is empirically illegitimate, but practically indispensable. In the third book of the *Essay*, on language, Locke explains that men 'speak of Species of Things, as supposing them made by Nature, and distinguished by real Essences', because without this illegitimate supposition, the names of substances, referring as they do only to the conjunctions of those qualities which the speaker happens to perceive, would be understood to '*have different Significations, as used by different Men*'. This, Locke says with a certain dry understatement, 'would very much cumber the use of Language'.[79] The thought active here is that language, as an instrument of communication, depends upon unwarrantable suppositions; it gets its fullest expression in one other remarkable passage:

---

[77] *Essay*, II.xxiii.1: p. 295.   [78] Ibid. 5: p. 298.
[79] Ibid. III.vi.48 f.: pp. 469 f.

But though Words, as they are used by Men, can properly and immediately signify nothing but the *Ideas*, that are in the Mind of the Speaker; yet they in their Thoughts give them a secret reference to two other things.

First, they suppose their Words to be Marks of the Ideas *in the Minds also of other Men, with whom they communicate*: For else they should talk in vain, and could not be understood, if the Sounds they applied to one *Idea*, were such, as by the Hearer, were applied to another, which is to speak two Languages. . . .

Secondly, Because *Men* would not be thought to talk *barely* of their own Imaginations, but of Things as really they are; therefore they *often suppose their Words to stand also for the reality of Things*. . . . Though give me leave here to say, that it is a perverting the use of Words, and brings unavoidable Obscurity and Confusion into their Signification, whenever we make them stand for any thing, but those *Ideas* we have in our own Minds.[80]

Words, 'properly and immediately', signify nothing but ideas in the mind of the speaker. Locke's whole argument in Book III is that to suppose otherwise is to impose upon ourselves, to abuse language, and to give ourselves up to 'unavoidable Obscurity and Confusion', to that whole lamentable state of intellectual discourse of which the *Essay* represents the diagnosis. Yet this passage recognizes that if we did not tacitly suppose otherwise in our actual linguistic practice, by that 'secret reference' of our words to illegitimate objects— namely, the world, and other people—we should be all but autistic, trapped within the hall of mirrors of our private subjectivities, talking, in a private language, of 'barely our own imaginations', like some hilarious-desperate non-exchange between the characters in *Tristram Shandy*. Instead, we do indeed suppose in our practice that we can successfully communicate with one another, and understand the world, through language. If it is the irrationality of such supposition or 'secret reference' which causes all our problems, it is also this irrationality which, apparently, saves us. Our use of language operates by a kind of act of faith—unjustifiable by Locke's criteria elsewhere, when he says that faith should only be granted 'upon good Reason'[81]—but which we can hardly help but make. To be alerted to this dimension of 'secret reference' is not to relinquish such practice, but rather to become more aware of the element of provisional fiction, of *supposing*, which holds our world together; for the optimal functioning of language depends on our

[80] Ibid. ii.4 f.: pp. 406 f.   [81] Ibid. IV.xvii.24: p. 687.

both remembering and forgetting the irrationality of the supposition on which it is built.

The crucial role of such 'supposing' or 'secret reference' suggests the importance of imagination in the activity of understanding; it points toward the special power of imaginative literature, and away from Locke's own manner of writing and his explicit desiderata with regard to language. One can almost hear a door closing at the end of the passage quoted above, as Locke's normal priorities re-establish themselves: 'Though give me leave here to say, that it is a perverting the use of Words, and brings unavoidable Obscurity and Confusion into their Signification, whenever we make them stand for any thing, but those *Ideas* we have in our own Minds.' In its dominant tendency, Locke's thought allows no value to 'supposing', and discusses it only to explain how we get into the muddles that we do. Yet in many respects it is the link which holds together the destructive and constructive aspects of his epistemology, and makes sense of his refusal to play down either implication, or to subordinate one to the other. What I have called Locke's reticence forced his more thoughtful successors to rediscover this link for themselves, or to develop their own equivalents for it. This was the only way of assimilating the strong double implication of the *Essay*: that the 'way of ideas' infects our knowledge and language-use with radical uncertainties; *and* that this same 'way of ideas' is ultimately salutary and tonic, doing much to liberate us from or compensate us for the uncertainties which it creates or discovers. Locke's own attempts at theorizing how this might be did not convince many of his early readers, who felt, with some justification, that they raised more problems than they solved. But as the status and influence of the *Essay* grew and grew, and the way of ideas became an axiomatic principle rather than a disputable theory, the next generation and the wider audience were more willing to play down or edit out those problems. Influential here was the lead given by *The Spectator* in mediating Locke's thought: at least a dozen papers make substantial reference to aspects of the *Essay*, adopting Locke as a kind of house philosopher, a penetrating but also constructive thinker whom Mr Spectator is delighted to recommend to a wider acquaintance. Without falsifying the positions he cites from the *Essay*, Addison smoothly gears them to urbane or edifying reflection, often with an emphasis on divine providence. One striking example is the paper in which Locke's doctrine of secondary qualities is presented as a manifestation of God's goodness, in that God has so arranged the Creation that the drab world of 'Objects themselves' plays as a delightful *son et lumière* illusion in our imaginations. 'Our Souls are at present delightfully lost and bewildered in a pleasing Delusion, and we walk about like the Enchanted Hero in a Romance.'[82] If it seems ironic that Locke, of all people, should be enlisted to support this pleasure in imagination, it may also be seen as ironically appropriate. What Locke offered the eighteenth century, over and above the detail of his specific arguments, was a paradoxical but pervasive intuition: the intuition of the constructive, salutary potential of a radically sceptical epistemology. It was this inconsistency or open-endedness in the *Essay*, this hint of an unsolved riddle, that was the fruitful, stimulating legacy. For the 'sceptical thinkers' of this study, the riddle was to be solved through literary expression: a way of thinking which takes an altogether uncredulous delight in the activity of supposing.

---

[82] *The Spectator*, ed. Donald F. Bond, 5 vols. (Oxford, 1965), iii.546: no. 413. Positions taken explicitly from Locke's *Essay* appear in nos. 62, 94, 110, 121, 291, 373, 387, 413, 519, 531, 578. The writer is almost always Addison.

3

'Sworn to no Master': Pope's Scepticism in the *Epistle to Bolingbroke* and *An Essay on Man*

Scepticism and inconsistency go together; each promotes the other. One specific point of apparent inconsistency in Pope will provide the framework for this chapter: it concerns Pope's attitude to intellectual discipleship. *An Essay on Man* was dedicated to Henry St John Lord Bolingbroke, and in an extended address at the end of the poem Pope pays warm tribute to Bolingbroke as his 'guide, philosopher and friend', the 'master of the poet, and the song'. Four years later Pope once more addressed a poem—his Horatian imitation, *The First Epistle of the First Book of Horace*—to Bolingbroke, who is again invoked as a moral teacher and ideal; in this poem, however, Pope speaks of himself as 'sworn to no Master', and appears less than confident of Bolingbroke's power to teach him to live well.

I would like to discuss these two poems in relation to one another, and in their relation also to Bolingbroke's own philosophical writing, which draws one particular sceptical thread from the bundle of possibilities offered by Locke. This will allow me to say something about the specific issue of Pope's intellectual relationship to Bolingbroke in the *Essay on Man*, and how the warmth of Pope's tribute may be reconciled with the differences that exist between his thinking and Bolingbroke's. However, the real interest of this question about Pope and Bolingbroke lies in the larger topic which it focuses. If the idea of intellectual discipleship suggests an unsceptical commitment to some distinctive and clearly defined intellectual position, to understand Pope's attitude here may be to see something about *how* positions are held in the *Essay on Man*, and about how the ideas in play in that poem may be related to qualities in Pope's poetry more generally.

An Essay on Man lends itself naturally to such a discussion because of its slippery status as a philosophical poem. That is to say, it is not versified philosophy (although it can, unrewardingly, be read as such), but something else: a work in which Pope shows himself deeply interested in certain ideas that may well be called philosophical, but equally intent on realizing those ideas in an idiom that recognizes their saturation in the dimension of experience, where understanding is a movement of mind plotted through time, and depends upon an irreducible compound of thought, feeling, and imagination.[1] If one needs to speak at all of a structure of abstract thought 'behind' *An Essay on Man* (which may be ultimately as inappropriate as, in Locke's view, to inquire into the substance behind any set of phenomena), this forces the recognition that in the course of achieving expression such thought has been taken across a transforming boundary. Somewhat as in Montaigne's more philosophical essays, Hume's philosophical dialogues, or Johnson's philosophical fable *Rasselas*, Pope's philosophical poetry declines the purity of abstraction, but insists on the incarnation of thought as experience, in a way that flows from the exercise of an essentially sceptical intelligence.

What Pope's sceptical intelligence most characteristically recognizes is diversity and flux, a flux which includes the observing mind as well as the material for observation. A systematic philosophy should be stable and logically self-consistent, and those seeking to derive a systematic philosophy from the *Essay* have always been able to produce from it contradictory positions—most obviously, in its attitudes toward knowledge, and toward religion. The poem appears to tell us both that we can, and that we cannot, know that whatever is, is right; and where the Swiss professor of logic Crousaz uncovered a work of anti-Christian fatalism, Warburton, with an about equally plausible amount of forcing interpretation, was able to extract an orthodox theology perfectly compatible with

---

[1] For an eloquent case against thinking of literature and moral philosophy as properly separate and discrete kinds of discourse, see Martha C. Nussbaum, *Love's Knowledge: Essays on Philosophy and Literature* (Oxford, 1990).

Christianity. But what can be extrapolated as contradiction at the level of theory may be, in experience, many different things: an eclectic flexibility, a dynamic tension, a Keatsian negative capability, or a taste for paradox, as well as, of course, a simple intellectual incoherence or confusion.

There are choices for the reader here. In his study of the poem, A. D. Nuttall speaks of 'the tension between the *Essay* as a system and the *Essay* as a miscellany', by which 'Pope himself felt torn', and suggests that Pope's friendliest readers have been those who allow themselves to set the poem's philosophical claims aside and read it as a work of casual 'Horatian irregularity', without pressing the cruel question of how its various assertions hang together, and whether they are true.[2] This, he implies, is a well-meaning condescension which finally diminishes the poem; his own study pays Pope-as-philosopher the compliment of taking the *Essay on Man* seriously as a work of systematic thought—by which criterion he finds it frequently incoherent, question-begging, and unpersuasive. Given his premises, Nuttall makes a strong case. I shall want, on the whole, to resist it, by appealing to the notion of philosophical poetry outlined above, and the scepticism which informs it, a scepticism which licenses an almost metaphorical use of philosophical ideas to express an underlying, non-rational intuition. This is to resist Nuttall's either/or: the *Essay* is neither a mere miscellany, nor a system of thought, but a work of sceptical thinking. Yet this is an argument which can itself easily be overstated. Like a photographic double exposure, the *Essay on Man* presents both a would-be philosophical system and a work of sceptical thinking, and my argument is really an attempt to bring the second into focus, where Pope's poetic energies are most deeply engaged, without denying the existence of the first. For Pope himself was not perfectly clear

[2] A. D. Nuttall, *Pope's 'Essay on Man'* (London, 1984), p. 185. Nuttall's preference is vigorously challenged by Harry M. Solomon in *The Rape of the Text: Reading and Misreading Pope's Essay on Man* (Tuscaloosa, Ala. and London, 1993). Solomon places Pope in a tradition of Academic or Ciceronian scepticism; failure to understand this has caused 'logocentric' critics (such as Nuttall) to misread and decry the *Essay* as a piece of botched or contradictory philosophy. This approach has much in common with my own, although Solomon's category of Academic scepticism is very broad, and defined primarily through its denial of 'logocentricity', rather than through any positive intuition that it makes possible. Ironically, it is Solomon's pro-sceptical argument that is conducted in the more doctrinaire and single-minded spirit, while Nuttall's pro-rationalist reading is often good at conveying the variousness and subtlety of the poem.

about what he was doing in the *Essay*. With some part of his mind he hoped that he could enjoy the freedom of the sceptic without forgoing the claim of the system-maker. In his introduction to the *Essay*, he wrote, 'If I could flatter myself that this Essay has any merit, it is in steering betwixt the extremes of doctrines seemingly opposite . . . and in forming a *temperate* yet not *inconsistent*, and a *short* yet not *imperfect* system of Ethics.'[3] In the first part of that quotation Pope understands that the merit of his poem does not lie in any doctrine that it appears to espouse. 'Doctrines' run to extremes, and appear to exclude and oppose other doctrines; Pope suggests that he is not setting out such a doctrine at all, as a philosopher might, but 'steering betwixt' opposites, a strategy appropriate to the *Essay*'s vision of the interconnectedness of the creation. Pope's poetry habitually works with oppositions and polarities, in ways that simultaneously arrest and acknowledge the multifariousness of things. Yet fully to register such multifariousness may pull the mind into logical inconsistencies, and this is something which Pope here hastens to deny, in the phrase '*temperate* yet not *inconsistent*': a 'perfect system of ethics' would seem to preclude inconsistency. When Pope read Warburton's rationalizing defence of the *Essay*, which rendered it unproblematically consistent with orthodox Christianity, his gratitude was revealing: 'You have made my System as clear as I ought to have done & could not . . . . I know I meant just what you explain, but I did not explain my own meaning so well as you.'[4] No poet, if truly a poet, should concede so much to any commentator. The author of the *Dunciad* knew that well enough. But Pope had thought of the *Essay on Man* as a 'system of Ethics', and was glad to believe that a systematic body of thought could be extracted from his poem, even while—with one part of his mind—he knew that his poem was no such thing.

Pope sometimes knew himself best in the mask of Horace. His philosophical inconsistency, and the difficulty of achieving any consistent evaluation of it, is the main subject of the Horatian *Epistle to Bolingbroke* (as it came to be known). 'Sworn to no Master, of no Sect am I' is how Pope there describes himself, in a

---

[3] Pope, *Poetical Works*, ed. Herbert Davis (Oxford 1966), p. 239.
[4] To Warburton, 11 April 1739: *The Correspondence of Alexander Pope*, ed. George Sherburn, 5 vols. (Oxford, 1956), iv.171.

line which renders Horace's *nullius addictus iurare in verba magistri*. As an intellectual ideal, this condition of being sworn to no master has a range of possible implications. When Bolingbroke himself quotes Horace's line in his philosophical writing, he finds that it speaks of 'the reasonable liberty of embracing truth wherever [one] found it'.[5] Such an interpretation places an enlightenment emphasis on reason and liberty, on the mind's activity of intellectual self-determination when set free from 'the chains of philosophical bigotry'.[6] But to be sworn to no master can have a quite different connotation: that of being unable to rest in any one intellectual position, because so sceptically open to the claims of other ways of thinking. If this is indeed an intellectual ideal, rather than the statement of a more or less deplorable fact about the fickleness of the mind, its value must lie in its embrace of the fluidity of mental process: something imaged more readily as a passivity to larger forces, than as an act of self-determination.

It is in this way that Pope interprets the line, as the context shows:

> But ask not, to what Doctors I apply?
> Sworn to no Master, of no Sect am I:
> As drives the storm, at any door I knock:
> And house with Montagne now, or now with Locke.
> Sometimes a Patriot, active in debate,
> Mix with the World, and battle for the State,
> Free as young Lyttleton, her cause pursue,
> Still true to Virtue, and as warm as true:
> Sometimes with Aristippus, or St. Paul,
> Indulge my candor, and grow all to all;
> Back to my native Moderation slide,
> And win my way by yielding to the tide.   (23–34)[7]

Pope began the poem by declaring that he is now to devote himself, in the evening of his days, to the life-values that truly matter; in this passage his inconstancy, or mobility of mind, seems more like the fruit of this new wisdom, than the weakness which means he will never achieve it. Pope's variousness certainly goes further, and deeper, than Horace's:

---

[5] Bolingbroke, iv.393.   [6] Ibid.
[7] Pope's poetry is quoted from: Pope, *Poetical Works*, ed. Herbert Davis (Oxford, 1966).

> nullius addictus iurare in verba magistri,
> quo me cumque rapit tempestas, deferor hospes.
> nunc agilis fio et mersor civilibus undis,
> virtutis verae custos rigidusque satelles:
> nunc in Aristippi furtim praecepta relabor
> et mihi res, non me rebus, subiungere conor.

'I am not bound over to swear as any master dictates; wherever the storm drives me, I turn in for comfort. Now I become all action, and plunge into the tide of civil life, stern champion and follower of true Virtue; now I slip back stealthily into the rules of Aristippus, and would bend the world to myself, not myself to the world.'[8]

Horace moves with easy poise between symmetrical, binary alternatives. Pope as patriot battling for the state corresponds well enough to the first of these, but the second subdivides further into 'Aristippus, or St. Paul', who stand for two very different ways of 'indulging one's candour'. These might themselves be significant alternatives, but 'or' in this line casually runs them together with a giddying nonchalance, as though Pope in this vein is so fluidly 'all to all' that he can scarcely pause to distinguish the philosopher of hedonism from the Christian moralist. 'Yielding to the tide', he wins his way, through a sliding back from militant virtue, which, although vigorously asserted, then breaks like a wave into a more fundamental fluidity and variousness. There is a real sense of being given up to larger forces that one doesn't feel in Horace, whose nominal passivity turns into an active resourcefulness, either in the one way (all action in the tide of civil life) or in the other (bending the world to himself). By ending with a yielding to the tide, Pope, by contrast, returns to the earlier image of being driven before the storm:

> As drives the storm, at any door I knock:
> And house with Montagne now, or now with Locke.

It is worth dwelling on that juxtaposition of Montaigne and Locke, for which there is no equivalent in the Latin. Warburton, Pope's literary executor and editor, gives a potentially misleading note:

---

[8] Horace, *Satires, Epistles and Ars Poetica: with an English Translation by H. Rushton Fairclough* (Cambridge, Mass. and London, 1978), pp. 251–3.

i.e. Chuse either an *active* or a *contemplative* life, as is most fitted to the season and circumstances.—For he regarded these Writers as the best Schools to form a man for the world; or to give him a knowledge of himself: *Montagne* excelling in his observations on social and civil life; and *Locke*, in developing the faculties, and explaining the operations of the human mind.[9]

'Active' and 'contemplative' seem odd terms with which to distinguish Montaigne and Locke; Warburton may be too tidy-minded here, trying to assimilate the pairing both to the symmetrical categories in the Latin, and to the religious resonance that Pope introduces into his version of the whole poem. The association of worldly knowledge with Montaigne, and self-knowledge with Locke, does, however, echo the claims that they make for themselves in Matthew Prior's 'Dialogue between Mr John Lock and Seigneur de Montaigne', which Pope's pairing surely recalls. Pope read Prior's *Dialogues of the Dead* in manuscript and thought them 'very good'; that between Locke and Montaigne he described as being 'on a most regular and a very loose way of thinking'.[10] That opposition between 'regular' and 'loose' thinking is a helpful way of understanding Pope's line. It is certainly in those terms that Prior opposes his two thinkers. Montaigne is all 'voluble impetuosity' in his criticisms, but Locke, the sober reasoner, remains unperturbed:

> Lock. So that You, the loosest of Writers, have no great respect for my close way of Reasoning.
> Montaigne. Really, Mr Lock, I should flatter You, if I said I had. One may read your Book over as the Irish Man eat Whipt Cream, and when they asked him what he had been doing, he said he had been tasting a great Nothing. All the while you wrote you were only thinking that You thought; You, and Your understanding are the *Personae Dramatis*, and the whole amounts to no more than a Dialogue between John and Lock.
> > As I walk'd by my Self
> > I talked to my Self,
> > And my Self said unto me.
> You seem, in my poor apprehension, to go to and fro upon a

⁹ *The Works of Alexander Pope*, ed. Warburton, 9 vols. (London, 1751), iv.102 n.

¹⁰ Joseph Spence, *Observations, Anecdotes and Characters of Books and Men: Collected from Conversation*, ed. James M. Osborn, 2 vols. (Oxford, 1966), i.92.

Philosophical Swing like a Child upon a wooden Horse always in
motion but without any Progress, and to Act as if a Man instead of
Practising his Trade should spend all his Life in Naming his Tools.
Lock. *Pian Piano*, good Seigneur, one must be able to Name one's
Tools before one Learns the use of them, But, if a Man does not leap
Hedge and Ditch, in your Opinion, he stands stock stil. I begin,
continue, and always keep close to my subject, the Human
Understanding.
Montaigne. That's the very thing I object to, I think you keep so close
to your subject, that You have spoilt your Book.[11]

It is Locke's close way of reasoning that has spoiled his book,
according to Montaigne: 'close' brings together the idea of tightly
coherent, consequential reasoning with the idea of confinement
and limitation. Montaigne, by contrast, ranges widely. This allows
Locke to accuse Montaigne of compiling a mere patchwork of
thoughts from the ancients, which he contrasts with the originality
of his own work, but for Montaigne this is another proof of
Locke's confinement within his own mind. Locke has spun his
work out of his own thoughts as does

a Spider out of her own Bowels; and yet a Cobweb is good for Nothing
else that I know of but to catch flies, and Stanch cut Thumbs. I am so far
from concealing what you seem to call Thefts that I glory in them. I have
made other Mens thoughts my own, and given them to the World in
greater Beauty than I received them from their Authors. Let me be
Compared to a Bee, who takes Something from every Flower and Shrub,
and by that various Labour collects one of the greatest Ingredients of
Human health, and the very Emblem of Plenty.[12]

Such 'Plenty' is precisely what Montaigne feels he has to offer, and

[11] *The Literary Works of Matthew Prior*, ed. H. Bunker Wright and Monroe K.
Spears, 2 vols. (Oxford, 1959), i.621 f.
[12] Prior, *Works*, i.632. This opposition of bee and spider is, appropriately and
wittily, itself an ostentatious 'theft' from Swift's allegory in the *Battle of the Books*.
Prior may have been recalling Locke's claim that his doctrines were 'spun barely out
of my own thoughts, reflecting, as well as I could, on my own mind, and the ideas
I had there; and were not, that I know, derived from any other original', to which
Stillingfleet retorted that 'those who *write out of their own Thoughts* do it with as
much Ease and Pleasure as a Spider spins his Web' (*The Works of John Locke*, 9th
ed., 9 vols. (London, 1794; repr. London, 1997), iii.49; *The Bishop of Worcester's
Answer to Mr Locke's Second Letter* (1698), p. 4, reprinted in vol. 5 of *The
Philosophy of Edward Stillingfleet Including his Replies to John Locke*, ed. G. A. J.
Rogers, 6 vols. (Bristol, 2000)). The bee as gatherer of other men's thoughts is an
image gathered from Montaigne's actual *Essais* (Montaigne, i.225 (ch. 25)).

what his 'looseness' as a thinker allows him to realize and to communicate. Accordingly, when he offers Locke a sample of his thinking, his speech runs into page upon page of pithy observations—faithfully collected by Prior from the actual *Essais*—on the most diverse aspects of human nature and human life, all piled up in a wonderful disconnected heap. With a dizzying abruptness that accurately caricatures the effect of the *Essais*, Montaigne's account ranges from the profound to the banal, and from the commonplace to the radical, across a myriad of topics: the power of custom, the value of pleasure, the concerns of government, how to die, solitude, princes . . .

> . . . Would You have any more, Mr Lock, Mort de ma Vie, Why You are fast asleep! Man.
>
> Lock. I might continue so 'till to morrow Morning, and when I wake I might find You stil walking up Stairs in Buskins. Ay, Sir, and all this, and fifty times more of fifty sorts, all jumbled all Pindaric, All Lucrecius' his World. One Chapter is of Friendship; the next of Nine and Twenty Songs of Boetius; One of Moderation; the next of Canibals. From the use of Clothing away we Scud to a Character of Cato Junior, and from remarks upon Virgil to a Dissertation concerning Coaches. This leaf is upon Experience, turn it but over, you are upon Phisionomy and among lame People. Here is the Resemblance that Children have to their Fathers, and there a Defence of Seneca and Plutarch; In short no Man ever dreamt so wildly as You have writ, without the least regard to Method. . . .
>
> Montaigne. Method! our life is too short for it. . . . Method in the Sense You mean it, is the thing I contemn; Tis poor, 'tis little: I put my thoughts down, just as they occurred to me. Could I have better Method than that which the course of my life gave me, and the order of things as they presented themselves to my view. How would You have had me range them. Is it not the variety it self that pleases while it instructs.[13]

Prior's dialogue is a comic work, not a contribution to the history of philosophy, and none of Montaigne's assertions seriously engage with the logic of Locke's arguments in the *Essay*; logic, Montaigne confesses, is something he doesn't much care for, and he breaks off the conversation at just the moment when Locke is about to get down to technicalities. Nothing in the dialogue impugns Locke's *Essay* on its own terms, as a work of reasoned argument. But those

---

[13] Prior, *Works*, i.629 f.

terms are themselves opened up to challenge. Simply by exposing
the idea of methodical, reasoned argument to the sense of variety
and plenty generated by Montaigne's 'loose' thinking, Prior calls
into question the relation of any reasoned, 'philosophical' position
to the fertile multiplicities of experience: the comedy of his dialogue
lightly presses the question of how Locke's philosophy—any
philosophy—is to be *lived*.

That question might be said to be central to the sceptical thinking explored in this study. It is certainly at the heart of Pope's
poem, with its explicit concern with whether any philosophical
'master' can teach Pope to be wise. When Pope invokes Montaigne
in this connection he, like Prior, is surely invoking a congenial
spirit. We know that Pope had a long-standing enthusiasm for
Montaigne's *Essais*, which he first read in his youth, and knew
well. Inside the back cover of his copy of Cotton's translation he
wrote: 'This is (in my Opinion) the very best Book for Information
of Manners, that has been writ. This Author says nothing but what
every one feels at the Heart. Whoever deny it, are not more Wise
than Montaigne, but less honest.'[14] There are many aspects of
Montaigne's writing that must have appealed to Pope, which
Maynard Mack has conveniently summarized in his biography; but
Montaigne's 'chief contribution' to his eighteenth-century readers,
Mack says well, 'was to render vivid and irrefutable, as most of the
classical poets had done, the sub- and nonrational dimensions of
human personality'.[15] Pope praised Montaigne for his honesty: a
large part of that honesty concerned the inconstancy of the mind.
Montaigne held man to be 'a Marvellous vain, fickle, and unstable
Subject',[16] for whom no stable intellectual position was possible.
The portrait of his own mind that he painted in the *Essais* was

a counterpart of various and changeable Accidents, and irresolute
Imaginations, and, as it falls out, sometimes contrary: Whether it be that I
am then another self, or that I take Subjects by other Circumstances and
Considerations; so it is that I may peradventure contradict: But, as
Demades said, I never contradict the Truth. Could my Soul once take foot-

[14] Maynard Mack, *Collected in Himself: Essays Critical, Biographical, and
Bibliographical on Pope and some of his Contemporaries* (London and Toronto,
1982), p. 431.
[15] Maynard Mack, *Alexander Pope: A Life* (New Haven and London, 1985), p.
84.
[16] Montaigne, i.6 (ch. 1).

ing, I would not essay, but resolve; but it is always learning and making trial.[17]

He offered his restless love of travelling as a case in point:

I know very well, that to take it by the Letter, this pleasure of travelling is a Testimony of Uneasiness and irresolution, and also those two are our governing and predominating qualities. Yes, I do confess they are: I see nothing, not so much as in a dream, and in a wish, whereon I could set up my rest: Variety only, and the possession of diversity, can satisfy me, if any thing can.[18]

Thus when Pope illustrates his own variousness by speaking of himself as housing 'with Montaigne now, or now with Locke', the name of Montaigne has a certain priority. It was Montaigne himself that could say, 'He, that I am reading, seems always to have the most Force, and I find that every one has reason, tho' they contradict one another.'[19] It is because Pope houses from time to time with Montaigne that he can move so freely between ethical stances seemingly incompatible, from civic virtue to Aristippus to St Paul.

But if Pope houses with Montaigne, he also houses with Locke, who does put forward a distinct intellectual position, and who (in Prior's dialogue) regards Montaignean variety as mere confusion. For all Pope's affinities with Montaigne, it would be wrong to minimize Pope's passion for intellectual clarity, resolution, and synthesis. For several years in the 1730s, Pope intended—with one part of his mind, at least, for he never wholly committed himself to the project—that the *Essay on Man* should be merely the gateway to a single and still more ambitious work, a series of interrelated ethical epistles or 'system of ethics', in which the analysis of human nature in the *Essay* would stand as the foundation for further epistles on such matters as the use of riches, the inconsistencies of character, the knowledge and characters of men, the characters of women, the limits of reason, the use of pleasure, the principles of civil and ecclesiastical polity, and the function of education.[20] The four separate works we know as the *Epistles to Several Persons*, together with the passages on education and on reason in Book IV

---

[17] Montaigne iii.27 (ch. 2).   [18] Ibid. 336 f. (ch. 9).
[19] Ibid. ii.393 (ch. 12).
[20] See Miriam Leranbaum, *Alexander Pope's 'Opus Magnum' 1729–1744* (Oxford, 1977), esp. ch. 1.

of the *Dunciad*, are likely to be, at some level, the remnants of this great unfinished project. It is true that Pope declined, finally, to carry this project through; yet even to have entertained it as seriously as he did marks a clear difference between himself and Montaigne. It may therefore be significant that whenever Montaigne appears in the moral poetry Pope wrote in the 1730s, he appears as one of a pair:

> . . . say Montagne, or more sage Charron![21]
>
> I love to pour out all myself, as plain
> As downright SHIPPEN, or as old Montagne[22]
>
> And house with Montagne now, or now with Locke.[23]

On each occasion, the balancing figure stands for a position, or a way of thinking, more clearcut and logically coherent than Montaigne's. Charron was a follower of Montaigne's who purged Montaigne's thinking of its subjective form and reduced the 'looseness' of the *Essais* into something resembling a systematic treatise. This was entitled *De la sagesse*: hence Pope's 'more sage'— although the word is on a knife-edge, since in English it easily becomes a vulnerably precious term ('sage historians!',[24] within fifty lines, is openly mocking). Shippen was an outspoken MP of proclaimed Jacobite sympathies who had nailed his political colours to the mast: as well as the explicit parallel with Montaigne's frankness of expression, there is also a contrast with the Montaigne who claimed that he was, politically, a guelf to the ghibellines and a ghibelline to the guelfs (an originally Horatian claim which Pope himself echoed just a few lines later in the same epistle: 'Tories call me Whig, and Whigs a Tory').[25] And Locke too is paired with Montaigne as both a similar and a contrasting figure. They are both thinkers and moralists, both concerned to limit the pretensions of human knowledge and to ground knowledge in experience: yet Locke's empiricism is a painstakingly worked out philosophical argument that strikingly contrasts with the nonconsequential, essayistic character of Montaigne's sceptical appeal to experience. These pairings, then, suggest a certain ambivalence

---

[21] *Epistle to Cobham*, l. 87: Pope, p. 286.
[22] *Epistle to Fortescue*, l. 51-2: Pope, p. 342.
[23] *Epistle to Bolingbroke*, l. 26: Pope, p. 351.
[24] *Epistle to Cobham*, l. 133: Pope, p. 287.
[25] Montaigne, iii.431 (ch. 12). *Epistle to Fortescue*, l. 68: Pope, p. 343.

or tension. It may speak of a Montaignean fluidity that Pope's authorities or role-models should come in pairs, as alternatives, but the pairings chosen also suggest Pope's need for a greater seriousness, a more definite intellectual commitment, than can be met by the loose essayist alone.

This tension is, in a general way, central to all Pope's poetry in the 1730s, where the serious and *engagé* moralist, whose poetry is devoted to a cause or principle or truth, is continually collaborating, or colluding, or competing with another voice, more casual, more elusively ironic, perhaps more disinterestedly creative, more inclined simply to delight in its own nature and being. In the *Epistle to Bolingbroke*, this tension is brought into the sharpest focus, as the ease of the Horatian original is immediately tested by the choice of Bolingbroke as addressee. Under suspicion of treason, Bolingbroke had returned from exile to become the intellectual leader of the opposition to Walpole; for Pope to address this poem to him, in the place of Horace's Maecenas, was an act of pointed political commitment, the act, perhaps, of a patriot battling for the state—a Shippen rather than a Montaigne. It is true that Bolingbroke is addressed as a philosophical moralist rather than a statesman, in a poem that desiderates a philosophical retirement from the hurly-burly, and there may be in this a hint from Pope to Bolingbroke as to how his genius would be best employed. Even so: Pope's claim that he is sworn to no master (be it confession or boast), and that he houses indifferently with Locke and Montaigne, acquires a sharper point when delivered to Bolingbroke, the intellectual role-model addressed in the *Essay on Man* as 'master of the poet, and the song', who (we shall see) was proud to acknowledge Locke as his own master in matters of moral philosophy.

The poem begins with a strong expression of the need for the self-determination with which, at the end, Bolingbroke will be associated. Pope, like Horace, represents himself as being at a turning-point in his life. He has outgrown the trivial distractions and diversions of his life hitherto—specifically, the life of a successful poet in the public eye—and he recognizes that it is now, at last, time to grow serious.

> Farewell then Verse, and Love, and ev'ry Toy,
> The rhymes and rattles of the Man or Boy;
> What right, what true, what fit we justly call,
> Let this be all my care—for this is All.   (17–20)

It is time for Pope to devote himself *totally*—'All' is the emphatic word—to what is right and true; it is time to work out the values of a true moral philosophy, and to live by them: an urgently needed wisdom, which 'ev'ry day will want, and most, the last'. As Dante in the dark wood at thirty-five, so Pope, writing to Bolingbroke at the age of forty-nine, in what he calls the Sabbath of his days.

But to a sceptical thinker, it is not possible to make 'the choice of life', as Johnson's Rasselas calls it, in any such clearcut way. Dante had Virgil and then Beatrice to guide him, but Pope, as we have seen, finds himself moving from one moral authority to another, as diverse and seemingly incompatible as may be: the initial impulse to dedicate himself to one supreme principle dissipates itself, or relaxes, into the image of Pope yielding to the tide. This opening mirrors, structurally, the body of the poem. The central section satirizes the modern obsession with money-making and the shallow mutability of modern life, and does so with moral energy and purpose: but the vigorous, committed voice of the satirical moralist, 'still true to virtue', cannot be indefinitely sustained, and gives way at the end to the return of Pope's rueful reflection on his own personal inconsistency, imaged once more as a tidal ebb and flow that returns helplessly upon itself:

> You laugh, half Beau, half Sloven if I stand,
> My wig all powder, and all snuff my band;
> You laugh, if coat and breeches strangely vary,
> White gloves, and linen worthy Lady Mary!
> But when no Prelate's Lawn with hair-shirt lin'd,
> Is half so incoherent as my Mind,
> When (each opinion with the next at strife,
> One ebb and flow of follies all my life)
> I plant, root up; I build, and then confound;
> Turn round to square, and square again to round;
> You never change one muscle of your face,
> You think this Madness but a common case . . .
>
> .   .   .   .
> Is this my Guide, Philosopher, and Friend?   (161–77)

Pope's inconsistency is much more fully realized than Horace's: for, in this passage as well as elsewhere in the poem, Pope is *both* more frivolous *and* more serious than his Latin original. He is more frivolous in, for example, the jibes at contemporaries: Lady Mary Montagu's slovenliness, for example, or the earlier archness of

'Public too long, ah let me hide my Age! | See modest Cibber now
has left the Stage' (5–6). At the same time, Pope is more serious in
the suggestions of a kind of *ars moriendi* or art of dying, gather-
ing together some wisdom in preparation for, specifically, Pope's
last day (Horace has *mox*, 'soon, some day'). The undertone of
religious seriousness is sustained in 'no Prelate's Lawn with hair-
shirt lin'd', or the Scriptural echo in 'I plant, root up; I build, and
then confound.' This relates the vacillating poet to God's true
prophet Jeremiah, but with a ruefully ironic sense of difference:
'See, I have this day set thee over the nations and over the kingdoms, to root out, and to pull down, and to destroy, and to throw
down, to build, and to plant.'[26] No such prophetic certainty of
conviction is available to Pope. But as the sceptical pluralism
evoked at the beginning of the epistle threatens to become a
disabling, ludicrous helplessness, a state of conviction seems all
the more strongly desirable. And so the poem turns to
Bolingbroke, the 'guide, philosopher, and friend' of the *Essay on
Man*, as the man with the best claim to possess such internal
coherence and freedom; perhaps Bolingbroke can reform Pope,
and deliver him altogether from the ebb and flow? The question is
asked with some intensity.

> Is this my Guide, Philosopher, and Friend?
> This, he who loves me, and who ought to mend?
> Who ought to make me (what he can, or none,)
> That Man divine whom Wisdom calls her own;
> Great without Title, without Fortune bless'd;
> Rich ev'n when plunder'd, honour'd while oppress'd;
> Lov'd without youth, and follow'd without pow'r;
> At home, tho' exil'd; free, tho' in the Tower:
> In short, that reas'ning, high, immortal Thing,
> Just less than Jove, and much above a King,
> Nay, half in heav'n—except (what's mighty odd)
> A Fit of Vapours clouds this Demi-god.   (177–88)

There is nothing arch or knowing about the anti-climax at the end;
it takes nothing away from the reality of the aspiration, which is
much more powerfully voiced in the final ten lines of Pope than in
the corresponding three lines of Horace:

[26] Jeremiah, 1:10.

Ad summam: sapiens uno minor est Iove, dives,
liber, honoratus, pulcher, rex denique regum,
praecipue sanus, nisi cum pituita molesta est.

'To sum up: the wise man is less than Jove alone. He is rich, free,
honoured, beautiful, nay a king of kings; above all, sound—save when
troubled by the 'flu'!'[27]

In Horace's brief coda the general advantages of wisdom are lightly
given, in a cursory, self-possessed summary that runs wittily into
conscious exaggeration; at the end Horace and Maecenas enjoy a
joke together against what is unrealistic in the ideal of the stoic
sage. Pope's portrait of a truly magnanimous mind, single in itself,
heroically superior to circumstance and fortune, is much more
strongly felt, and not at all willing to give itself away as unrealistic.
Although the portrait is a general one, which opens out beyond
Bolingbroke, its elements are rooted in reality: several of its terms
invite application to Bolingbroke as political victim and former
exile, still denied his seat in the House of Lords, while other
elements can be referred to other friends of Pope, such as Oxford
and Atterbury, who had indeed been committed to the Tower.
Because of this, the anti-climax at the end is felt as a real change of
tone and direction. The intrusion of Pope's 'Fit of Vapours'—an
ailment of mind as well as body[28]—does not so much detonate a
prepared irony ('Demi-god' cannot be reduced to a sarcasm) as
enact a real fluidity of attitude. As Pope remembers the inconstancy
of man, the poem itself shifts tack, and we see that Pope cannot
house permanently with Bolingbroke, any more than with Locke.
Flux supervenes upon the aspiration to single-mindedness, and the
fit of vapours that abruptly derails Pope's poem casts its shadow on
Bolingbroke's power—the power of the moral philosopher—to
redeem Pope from a life lived at random, in which a fit of vapours
may always deflect what the will determines.

How are we to read this powerfully open ending? What Pope
gives us is plainly something more substantial than the worldling's
easy tolerance of moral shortcoming, but Frank Stack may go too
far in the other direction when he writes, in his excellent study of

---

[27] Horace, *Satires, Epistles and Ars Poetica: with an English Translation by H.
Rushton Fairclough* (Cambridge, Mass. and London, 1978), pp. 258–9.
[28] 'Diseases caused by flatulence, or by diseased nerves; hypochondriacal
maladies; melancholy; spleen' (Johnson's *Dictionary*, under VAPOURS).

Pope and Horace, that Pope ends 'on a note of anguished personal failure'.[29] This is to identify Pope entirely with his defeated desire for single-mindedness and for the wisdom which would confer supremacy over circumstance. For Brean Hammond, the failure expressed at the end of the poem is not so much Pope's as Bolingbroke's. The real uncertainties we hear in this epistle, he argues, reflect Pope's growing disenchantment with the Bolingbroke who inspired the writing of the *Essay on Man*, a disenchantment which was to lead to Pope's transfer of affiliation from Bolingbroke to Warburton (who was shortly to defend the *Essay* against charges of irreligion), i.e. from one philosophical mentor to another.[30] Although these readings differ from one another, they both assume that the failure of the philosopher-teacher to bring Pope into the state of wisdom, so that he may become and remain 'that reas'ning, high, immortal Thing', is presented as something absolutely to be regretted, and Pope's inconsistency or mutability as absolutely to be deplored. Against both those readings, I want to suggest that what we have at the end does not feel altogether like failure. By ending so strikingly on the note of sceptical openness, the poem succeeds in identifying, at least to some degree, with those larger movements of flux which make mischief with the impulse to rational, philosophical self-determination. The voice which reproaches Bolingbroke cannot stand for the whole consciousness of the poem, for Bolingbroke is reproached for tolerating in Pope that incoherence or instability which the poem acknowledges, at the end, to be an all but inescapable fact of life. Perhaps, then, Bolingbroke's tolerance of Pope's mutability—'You think this Madness but a common case'—is not so entirely misguided after all.

It might be helpful to draw an analogy with those dialogues of

---

[29] Frank Stack, *Pope and Horace: Studies in Imitation* (Cambridge, 1985), p. 273. Jacob Fuchs also finds the poem 'a confession of defeat', primarily political defeat: Jacob Fuchs, *Reading Pope's Imitations of Horace* (London and Toronto, 1989), p. 129.

[30] Brean Hammond, *Pope and Bolingbroke: A Study of Friendship and Influence* (Columbia, NY, 1984), pp. 110–25. Although my argument differs from Hammond's, there is much in his book that I have found helpful: not least his general emphasis on Pope's profound admiration for Bolingbroke, and his insistence that Pope's relationship with Bolingbroke really matters in the *Epistle*. As a matter of biography, Hammond may be right about Pope's changing attitude to Bolingbroke: but I cannot hear it in the poetry.

Plato (*Protagoras, Meno*) in which Socrates inquires whether virtue can be taught. The discussion ends only in paradox and uncertainty; Socrates, like Pope here, claims to fall short of the wisdom or knowledge he is seeking. The dialogues record a philosophical failure, then; unless Socrates' uncovering of failure is itself a kind of teaching, rather as it was Socrates' conscious ignorance that made him, according to the oracle, the wisest man in Athens. This insight depends, however, on maintaining an open-ended play of irony, a genuine doubleness of perspective, whereby confusion or ignorance seems to be *also* a form of understanding; if the irony were resolved, so that ignorance seemed to be *really* understanding (or a mask for understanding), the effect would disappear. If something of this Socratic irony animates the end of Pope's poem, then one might feel that the paradox from earlier in the poem is still active, and that Pope, by acknowledging the genuine failure of philosophy, is winning his way by yielding to the tide.

*   *   *

To support that reading of the *Epistle to Bolingbroke*, and to appreciate its full significance, I hope to identify a similar movement in the *Essay on Man*, where the double attitude toward philosophy in the *Epistle* is first theorized and worked out. Most obviously, Pope's philosophical poem strives to meet the need for a stable overview, a total philosophy of life rendered coherent and intelligible: yet it is also in the *Essay on Man* that Pope most explicitly offers to connect scepticism—an insistence on the weakness and inadequacy of human reason—with the value of yielding to the tide. That value is signalled with the formula, 'Whatever is, is right'.

The poems are most obviously linked in that both invoke Bolingbroke as Pope's philosophical and moral teacher. The *Epistle* opens with lines to Bolingbroke that were first drafted as part of the *Essay on Man* project, being originally intended for a projected epistle on the 'Limits of Reason';[31] and it concludes with the appeal to Bolingbroke that explicitly recalls his role in the *Essay* as 'guide, philosopher, and friend'. That Bolingbroke should redeem Pope from his inconsistencies, is Pope's own, unHoratian emphasis: Maecenas was Horace's patron, but not his guide in philosophy,

---

[31] See Leranbaum, *Pope's 'Opus Magnum'* p. 25. For Pope's shifting intentions to include with the *Essay* an epistle on the limits of reason, see esp. pp. 24–30.

and there is no suggestion in the Latin that the addressee 'ought to mend' the inconsistent poet. However, if the *Epistle* doubts whether Bolingbroke will in fact be able to teach Pope wisdom, it also recalls and warmly restates the admiration expressed in the *Essay on Man*. There, interestingly, Bolingbroke's wisdom is explicitly associated with 'various nature', as though the essence of what he offers Pope is a proper mobility or fluidity of self:

> Come then, my Friend, my Genius, come along,
> Oh master of the poet, and the song!
> And while the Muse now stoops, or now ascends,
> To Man's low passions, or their glorious ends,
> Teach me, like thee, in various nature wise,
> To fall with dignity, with temper rise;
> Form'd by thy converse, happily to steer
> From grave to gay, from lively to severe;
> Correct with spirit, eloquent with ease,
> Intent to reason, or polite to please.
> Oh! while along the stream of Time thy name
> Expanded flies, and gathers all its fame,
> Say, shall my little bark attendant sail,
> Pursue the triumph, and partake the gale?
> When statesmen, heroes, kings, in dust repose,
> Whose sons shall blush their fathers were thy foes,
> Shall then this verse to future age pretend
> Thou wert my guide, philosopher, and friend?
> That urg'd by thee, I turn'd the tuneful art
> From sounds to things, from fancy to the heart;
> For Wit's false mirror held up Nature's light;
> Shew'd erring Pride, WHATEVER IS, IS RIGHT.
> (IV.373–94)[32]

The passage marries the notions of intellectual fluidity and intellectual discipleship which reappear as dichotomies in the *Epistle*. It is, however, not necessary to infer that Pope has grown disen-

---

[32] The first half of this compliment (down to 'polite to please') was originally intended to lead into the great opening of the second epistle, with its representation of man as a being who unstably 'hangs between' contrary extremes. Bolingbroke's versatility would thus have appeared even more clearly as a kind of wisdom about the human condition itself. See Alexander Pope, *An Essay on Man: Reproductions of the Manuscripts in the Pierpoint Morgan Library and the Houghton Library with the Printed Text of the Original Edition*, ed. Maynard Mack (Oxford, 1962): Pierpoint Morgan Library MS, Epistle II p. 1 and Houghton Library MS, p. 15.

chanted with Bolingbroke in the meantime, if we suppose that Pope in the *Epistle* is not so much distancing himself specifically from Bolingbroke, as reflecting on the insufficiency of *any* single-minded, closely reasoned philosophy or philosophical master (even the admirable philosophy of the admirable Bolingbroke) to turn us into self-determining moral beings. That stance, I want to argue, is already to be found in the *Essay on Man*, and informs much of the best writing in the poem. But what complicates the situation—for us, and surely for Pope—are the elements in Bolingbroke's philosophical thought which could allow Pope to feel that he shared that sceptical stance with Bolingbroke himself. That Pope should have felt this is perfectly intelligible, as I shall show: yet to compare Bolingbroke's philosophical writing with the *Essay on Man* is to become aware of the difference between philosophy as a body of abstract thought and philosophy which cannot be adequately set out in conceptual terms but can only be grasped experientially, or 'essayed'—a difference especially teasing when the explicit tendency of the philosophy itself is to subordinate reason to experience. It is to return to the dichotomy of Locke and Montaigne.

I should begin by summarizing Bolingbroke's moral philosophy. This is preserved in a work entitled the *Letters or Essays addressed to Alexander Pope, Esq.*, which consists of four long essays, followed by a series of 'Fragments or Minutes of Essays' on closely connected themes. It was published only after the deaths of both Pope and Bolingbroke, when its deism made it briefly notorious. A lengthy work which overflows two folios, it is presented as Bolingbroke's more fully elaborated record of views he was expressing in philosophical conversations with Pope around the time that Pope was composing his philosophical poem. Bolingbroke apologizes from time to time for the loose, conversational form of these *Letters or Essays*, but in fact they are conversational only in their occasional use of the second person, and loose only in their repetitiveness;[33] in other respects they read as a treatise with a logically consequential argument, supported by a wealth of scholarly reference: so that they are less 'essayistic' even than the *Essay* composed by Locke, let alone any essay by Montaigne. Although addressed to Pope, and represented as a record and continuation of conversation, there is nothing dialogic about them:

[33] For the contrary view, see Hammond, *Pope and Bolingbroke*, pp. 16–23.

Pope's contributions to the discussion are not mentioned, so the impression made is of Bolingbroke somewhat relentlessly expounding his ideas, if not quite as master to pupil, then to a passive, but presumably receptive, listener. We know from other evidence that philosophical conversations did indeed take place between them, and that Bolingbroke wrote a document of several pages (which has not survived) designed to help Pope with the argument of the *Essay*. However, the *Letters or Essays* as we have them were clearly written, or at least revised, some years after the *Essay on Man*, so that their exact relation to Pope's poem is not at all straightforward, and any argument about detailed influence must be highly problematic. At any point where the *Letters* and the *Essay* coincide, Bolingbroke may have influenced Pope, or Pope Bolingbroke, or the two men may have worked out their ideas in partnership. What can be said, however, is that the *Letters or Essays* give a full and coherent account of Bolingbroke's philosophical thought; that Bolingbroke shared some of this, at least, with Pope; and that Pope was sufficiently impressed with what he heard to write the tributes that he did.

Bolingbroke's main positions are plain enough. The first essay has the title, 'Concerning the Nature, Extent, and Reality of Human Knowledge', and it is through epistemology that Bolingbroke lays the foundations for all that follows. For this Bolingbroke draws largely and gratefully upon Locke, 'that great author . . . my master, for such I am proud to own him'.[34] The great achievement of Locke, Bolingbroke argues, is to have shown how utterly our knowledge is limited to the realm of experiment and observation; any attempt to go beyond this realm, to reason, for example, *a priori* about the nature of things in themselves, is empty metaphysics. 'Metaphysics' is always, in Bolingbroke, a derogatory term: the whole thrust of the *Letters* is the polemic against idealism and the insidious ways in which it has infected our thinking. Even the great Locke has not perfectly succeeded in cutting all his links with idealist assumptions, and in two ways Bolingbroke goes further than Locke in seeking to bind our knowledge to the actual. Firstly, he has learnt from Berkeley to question the reality—the reality in the mind, that is—of abstract general ideas. Triangularity, or humanity, are useful terms with which to

[34] Bolingbroke, v.16, 18.

refer to sets of particulars that have features in common, but we have no idea of triangularity or humanity per se.[35] Secondly, he does not care for Locke's concession that the mind can put together 'mixed modes' freely, independently of sense-experience, and that a kind of substantial knowledge can result from this. This, it will be recalled, was an important matter for Locke because it guaranteed the objectivity of our moral knowledge; Bolingbroke sees the vulnerability of this part of Locke's argument without recognizing its importance, and feels able to sweep it away in the name of common sense.[36]

This might seem to open the door to the radical scepticism, the intellectual helplessness or *aporia*, which is a powerful latent tendency in Lockean philosophy. Bolingbroke certainly speaks with some vigour about the limitations of the intellect, and the prideful folly of supposing that we can penetrate into the reason of things. But he is a true Lockean also in asserting the adequacy of the intellect to the purposes of human life, and the thrust of the *Letters* is not, finally, sceptical but positivist. The scepticism that Bolingbroke develops out of Locke is a tool, rather than the element and medium of his thinking, as it was in Montaigne. The tool is mainly used for destruction. Bolingbroke takes Locke's critique of substance and— as Locke himself had done, but without Locke's disinterestedness— focuses it on propositions about the soul and about spiritual substance. Such propositions are exposed as empty metaphysics, mere words without meaning. Bolingbroke follows Locke in maintaining that nothing can be said about the essential principle that makes us the thinking beings that we find ourselves to be, while hinting much more broadly than Locke that there would be nothing absurd, or even improbable, in supposing thought to arise from modifications of matter, and consciousness to be a function of physiology. The theory which divides man into soul and body explains nothing, cannot appeal convincingly to experience, and creates endless unnecessary difficulties in explaining how soul and body interact; in particular, it founders on the question of man's relation to the animal kingdom, since all the available hypotheses (that animal and human souls are the same; that there are different kinds of soul; that animals are automata) lead to conclusions outrageous to common sense. Yet the assumption that we are souls in bodies is

[35] Ibid. iii.432–8, v.16–29.   [36] Ibid. iii.406–17, 493–8.

an insidiously attractive one, since it feeds human pride: it fosters, and is fostered by, the impious delusion that man, as a spiritual being, partakes in some sense of the divine.[37]

This false way of thinking, the 'philosophical delirium'[38] which purports to deal with spiritual or ideal realities that have no basis in observation and experiment, largely derives from Plato, 'the father of philosophical lying',[39] who is cast as the arch-villain in Bolingbroke's history of philosophy. Socrates and Plato rejected the true path of scientific experiment and inquiry, and, disastrously, promoted instead the inquiry into the real essences of things.[40] This essentially platonizing, metaphysical cast of mind has dominated, and vitiated, the whole Western philosophical tradition—until first Bacon and then Locke began the work of returning mankind to their senses. Above all, it permeates the whole of theology. Beginning with St Paul, Christian theologians have corrupted and sophisticated the simple truths of the gospel out of all recognition. All discourse on the mysteries of religion is mystification, exploiting the weakness of the multitude for the sake of priestly pride and priestly power.

The real truths of natural religion, according to Bolingbroke, are plain and simple. Given the evidence of organization and design in the creation around us, no man can rationally doubt the existence of God, a First Cause of stupendous intelligence and wisdom, of whom we should think with due reverence. That is all, however, that we can know of God. We can have no further knowledge of his nature: in particular, no knowledge of his moral attributes. Our ideas of goodness and justice have meaning in relation to humanity, but they are not eternal verities, and there is no reason to suppose that God's goodness and justice should be intelligible in human terms: to think so is the fundamental error of the pride which supposes man to be the end of creation, rather than one part of the larger whole. For Bolingbroke, this argument sweeps away the whole problem of evil, along with arguments for the necessity of an afterlife in which divine justice will be realized.[41] Such theo-

---

[37] Bolingbroke, iii.525–61.   [38] Ibid. 379, again at iii.442.
[39] Ibid. iv.148, iii.
[40] Ibid. 111–59. Bolingbroke reads Plato by the light of the neoplatonist Ficino, 'to whose exposition of PLATO's meaning there can be no objection made' (iv.149 f.).
[41] Ibid. v.310–38 (fragments XLI–XLIII).

logical attempts to rationalize the ways of God in human terms are, in fact, dangerous to the cause of true religion, since they are always liable to generate arguments for atheism; one of Bolingbroke's favourite strategies is to put divines and atheists in the same camp, with his own experience-led philosophy resisting the presumptuous way of thinking common to both.

It is still possible, however, to live by an ethics which one can think of as divinely sanctioned. We can know the will of God only as it is revealed in the creation; man has been created with a principle of self-love that impels him to seek his own happiness, and a tendency to sociability and benevolence that promotes the happiness of those around him; this is the law of nature, and to live in accordance with the law of nature is to live in conformity with the will of God as revealed through the way in which we are constituted. In so far as Christ's teaching of benevolence accords with this, the gospels can be thought of as God's 'republication' of the law of nature, but the truth of Christ's teaching is authorized by our understanding of the law of nature, rather than by its alleged status as the word of God. Bolingbroke's deism is willing to tolerate the profession of Christianity, in this carefully limited sense, and he speaks of himself, without obvious irony, as a friend to gospel Christianity (always distinguished from the institutionalized teaching of the church), but this is an entirely secularized and subordinated Christianity, stripped of all special authority (there is a highly sceptical discussion of the doctrine of Incarnation, for example), which can at best do no more than illustrate the truths of natural religion and natural law.[42] (Bolingbroke passes very lightly over the actual record of Christ's teaching.)

This brief summary will have suggested a number of points at which the *Letters* coincide with *An Essay on Man*. It is not difficult to imagine how, in the conversations between the two men associated with the writing of the poem, Pope could feel that he shared with Bolingbroke a conviction about the value and tendency of a proper intellectual scepticism. Bolingbroke's philosophy, as set out in the *Letters*, is grounded in the assertion of an ultra-Lockean

---

[42] Ibid. iv.316: 'Christianity, as it stands in the gospel, contains not only a complete but a very plain system of religion; it is in truth the system of natural religion, and such it might have continued to the unspeakable advantage of mankind, if it had been propagated with the same simplicity with which it was originally taught by CHRIST himself.'

empiricism which drastically restricts the scope of human reason; this is what distinguishes his deism from the more intellectually assertive versions of Toland and of Tindal, satirized by Pope in the *Dunciad*. A parallel scepticism can readily be seen as the motor of the *Essay on Man*, with its vigorous attack on the pretensions of reason—strictly, 'reas'ning pride'—to pronounce upon the ordering of the universe. For Pope as for Bolingbroke, the proper use of reason is a moral, not merely an intellectual matter: the sceptical stance sets itself against the egotism that puts self at the centre, and then presumes to judge the cosmos from that perspective. One could even feel that Bolingbroke leaves some, albeit marginal, space for Christianity. And Pope might certainly feel that he shared with Bolingbroke a common understanding of how scepticism could be functional, could open the door to the affirmation of a life lived according to nature.

But then we come to a fork in the road. Bolingbroke's philosophy is built on scepticism, in the sense that it continually recurs to the drastic limitations on human knowledge, but it is not sceptical in its manner or its affiliations. In his outline history of philosophy, Bolingbroke passes dismissively over Academic scepticism as incapable of inspiring conviction.[43] He deplores the attempts of Sextus Empiricus and Montaigne to show, from the diversity of custom and practice, 'that there is no such thing as a fixed immutable law of nature, which obliges all men at all times alike'.[44] And it is no great compliment when he applies to the Eclectic sect Horace's line about being sworn to no master, '*Nullius addicti jurare in verba magistri*': this was all very well insofar as they 'delivered themselves from the chains of philosophical bigotry', but in fact their absurd mixing of classical with Christian thought merely gave 'farther occasion to the heathen converts to corrupt christianity'.[45] So much, one might suppose, for Pope indulging his candour with a mixed diet of Aristippus and St Paul, or indeed for his original intention of beginning the *Essay on Man* with an 'address to our Saviour, imitated from Lucretius' compliment to Epicurus' in the passionately anti-religious *De Rerum Natura*.[46] Such startlingly fluid thinking would run quite counter to Bolingbroke's single-minded clarity of position. The authority he claims for his own

---

[43] Bolingbroke, iv.144 f.   [44] Ibid. v.101.
[45] Ibid. iv.393.   [46] Spence, *Anecdotes*, i.135.

views is, after all, the authority of reason, now purged, thanks to
Locke, of its delusions. Hence, for example, he speaks of resignation to the ways of God—that is, to the way things are—as a rational determination. Pope can sound like that too. 'To reason right is
to submit', he maintains in the first epistle.[47] But it would be much
less true of Pope than of Bolingbroke to say that an enlightened
rationality, a piece of clear-headed thinking, is offered as the
mind's proper goal and resting-place.[48]

This can be clearly seen in their different attitudes to unreasonableness. In Bolingbroke the unreasonableness of those who
complain against providence, or would judge the ways of God by
human standards, is largely felt as the unreasonableness of other
people—delirious philosophers, overweening theologians, and
machinating priests. These malcontent groups hardly feature in the
Essay on Man: the unreasonableness against which the poem
protests is recognized as profoundly human. The characteristic
quality of sceptical thinking, as discussed in previous chapters,
makes itself felt: Pope seems to be in two places at once. He may
begin by sounding as if he can scold the attitude of complaint into
feeling ashamed of itself:

> Presumptuous Man! the reason wouldst thou find,
> Why form'd so weak, so little, and so blind?
> First, if thou canst, the harder reason guess,
> Why form'd no weaker, blinder, and no less!   (I.35–8)

But the schoolteacherly sarcasm of this turns into a more complex,
more troubled antagonism that acknowledges the energy and the
universality of the impulse being opposed:

> Go, wiser thou! and in thy scale of sense
> Weigh thy Opinion against Providence
>
> .   .   .   .
>
> Snatch from his hand the balance and the rod,
> Re-judge his justice, be the GOD of GOD!
> In Pride, in reas'ning Pride, our error lies;
> All quit their sphere, and rush into the skies.

[47] *Essay on Man*, i.164; Pope, p. 245.
[48] For two contrary views, both insisting on the intellectual kinship between
Bolingbroke and Pope in the *Essay on Man*, see Hammond (*Pope and Bolingbroke*)
who aligns Pope with Bolingbroke the rational philosopher, and Solomon (*Rape of
the Text*) who aligns Bolingbroke with Pope the Ciceronian or Academic Sceptic.

Pride still is aiming at the blest abodes,
Men would be Angels, Angels would be Gods.   (I.113–26)

The bliss of Man (could Pride that blessing find)
Is not to think or act beyond mankind.   (I.189–90)

The first epistle of the *Essay on Man* is, quite consciously, a
complaint against complaint: from which comes its vitality. The
paradox which complicates the moral message is, of course, that
the impulse to move beyond the conditions set, to 'quit one's
sphere', is itself a defining characteristic of mankind. This is a paradox with deep attractions for Pope, as Johnson recognized in char-
acterizing the 'genius' which counterbalances Pope's 'good sense':

... Pope had likewise genius; a mind active, ambitious, and adventurous,
always investigating, always aspiring; in its widest searches still longing to go
forward, in its highest flights still wishing to be higher; always imagining
something greater than it knows, always endeavouring more than it can do.[49]

Such aspiration is treated from various angles in Pope's earlier
poetry: in the sympathetic but suicidal 'ambition' of his
Unfortunate Lady, and in his Eloisa's passionate, unappeasable
imaginings of a fulfilment that is now both impossible and forbid-
den. In his translation of the *Iliad*, the profoundly human anger of
Achilles against the human condition is set against the necessity of
acquiescence in the way things are—crystallized in the assertion
Pope gave to Zeus: 'What *is*, that *ought* to be.'[50] The comic version
of this in *The Rape of the Lock* is Belinda's spleen against
constraints which are imposed upon her, as Clarissa fruitlessly
points out, by both her situation as a woman in society, and the
fact of her mortality. The solace that Pope finally offers Belinda,
like the solace that Eloisa finally imagines for herself, is that of
poetry, and much of Pope's poetry can be read in terms of the
attempt to find an imaginative resolution of the need for actuality
to be other than it is.

In the *Essay on Man* the paradox is given its clearest, most
generalized expression. The proper study of mankind should rest in
man, yet man is a creature whose restlessness of mind is intrinsic to
his being:

⁴⁹ Johnson, *Lives*, iii.217
⁵⁰ *The Twickenham Edition of the Poems of Alexander Pope*, vol. vii: *The Iliad
of Homer*, ed. Maynard Mack (London and New Haven, 1967), p. 122: Book I, l.
731.

> Placed on this isthmus of a middle state,
> A being darkly wise, and rudely great:
> With too much knowledge for the Sceptic side,
> With too much weakness for the Stoic's pride,
> He hangs between; in doubt to act, or rest,
> In doubt to deem himself a God, or Beast;
> In doubt his Mind or Body to prefer;
> Born but to die, and reas'ning but to err;
> Alike in ignorance, his reason such,
> Whether he thinks too little, or too much:
> Chaos of Thought and Passion, all confus'd;
> Still by himself abus'd, or disabus'd;
> Created half to rise, and half to fall;
> Great lord of all things, yet a prey to all;
> Sole judge of Truth, in endless Error hurl'd:
> The glory, jest, and riddle of the world!   (II.3–18)

This famous passage is itself in movement. It oscillates between being a judicious, balanced view of a being in a 'middle state', and a satirical depiction of something closer to a 'vile Antithesis'.[51] The recognition of positive elements in the mix ('or disabus'd', 'Created half to rise') comes to teeter on the edge of outright sarcasm ('Great lord of all things', 'Sole judge of truth'); and in the final line any notion of a balance between opposites is thrown into jeopardy as the binary dualisms culminate in a triad: 'glory, jest, and riddle'. The dynamic instability of the human creature communicates itself to the poetry, which thus acknowledges itself as implicated in what it describes. Inconsistency is radical, is intrinsic. A stable platform of rational thought from which to reassess the situation, is simply not available. For Pope, the resolution of the tension involved in being human could only be a vision that speaks to a fundamentally non-rational creature, who 'reasons but to err'. And it could only be a vision that accommodates inconsistency: a *concordia discors*, a principle basic to the composition of Popean verse, but in this poem pressed into something like metaphysical status.

This may be the best way to come at Pope's affirmation of the ultimate harmony and rightness of things:

---

[51] Pope's description of Sporus in the *Epistle to Arbuthnot*, l. 325: Pope, p. 337.

> All Nature is but Art, unknown to thee;
> All Chance, Direction, which thou canst not see;
> All Discord, Harmony, not understood;
> All partial Evil, universal Good:
> And, spite of Pride, in erring Reason's spite,
> One truth is clear, 'Whatever is, is RIGHT.'   (I.289–94)

Here is that effect of 'double exposure' which I spoke of earlier. Is this the conclusion of a reasoned argument, or the expression of an intuition which reason can only find paradoxical? Surely it is both; surely, also, it is more rewarding, and more fully integrated in the poem as a whole, when taken as the latter. Whatever the would-be philosopher in Pope may have hoped, this passage does not play well as the conclusion to a philosophical argument. As a rational argument, it appears to depend on the doctrine sometimes known as 'the great chain of being', according to which the condition of humanity occupies its necessary, and therefore necessarily right, place in the plenitude of the divine creation. This is a doctrine with a substantial intellectual history:[52] but it would be strange to find Pope seriously embracing it, and not only because it is hardly the world-view one would expect from the scathing satirist of the 1730s. More particularly, for someone so sceptical about the power of 'erring Reason', the existence of the great chain of being seems an awful lot to know. To be intellectually respectable, the theory of the great chain of being depends on certain *a priori* arguments about what follows axiomatically from the nature of God and the conditions of creation—just the kind of 'high Priori' reasoning that Pope was to satirise in the fourth book of the *Dunciad* (and Bolingbroke offers to demolish in the *Letters*). In the *Essay on Man* Pope invokes such an argument only briefly and hypothetically, with a significant 'if':

> Of Systems possible, if 'tis confest,
> That Wisdom infinite must form the best,
> Where all must full or not coherent be,
> And all that rises, rise in due degree ...   (I.43–6)

> And if each system in gradation roll,
> Alike essential to th'amazing whole ...   (I.247–8)

[52] See A. O. Lovejoy, *The Great Chain of Being: A Study in the History of an Idea* (Cambridge, Mass., 1936).

As many commentators have pointed out, such reasoning is hardly compatible with the firmly empirical stance which is much more fundamental to the poem, and with its attack on 'reasoning pride': 'Say first, of God above, or Man below, | What can we reason, but from what we know?' (I.17 f.). It would be a fatal mistake to allow this kind of sceptical empiricism anywhere near the affirmation that whatever is, is right, if this is being offered as a philosophically serious claim. Any suggestion that such a claim rests on arguments *a posteriori*, grounded in experience, is of course desperately vulnerable. Such a suggestion was normally the tactic of those wishing to destroy metaphysical optimism—as Johnson does in reviewing Jenyns, or Voltaire in his poem on the Lisbon earthquake and in *Candide*. It is therefore interesting to note that Voltaire, the great antagonist of metaphysical optimism, had no problem with *An Essay on Man*; in his *Philosophical Letters* he described it as 'the most beautiful didactic poem and the most usefull and sublime that has ever been written in any language'.[53]

Nor does it seem likely that Pope has run inadvertently into this paradox by following Bolingbroke, who is much more consistent and more carefully rational in his empiricism. Bolingbroke speaks in general terms of the intelligence and power of the Supreme Being as manifested in his creation, but he lays no emphasis on the plenitude of creation. One of the few passages where he does touch on the idea is offered, rather defensively, as a gloss on Pope: in a footnote he defends Pope's line as a rational extrapolation from the theism grounded in observation:

The proposition is not advanced as an argument to prove the existence of God, nor as a profession of faith, 'un acte de foi.' I presume Mr POPE meant it as a reasonable consequence of what he supposed already proved, and that when design and wisdom were so evidently marked in all the works of God which are objects of human observation and knowledge, it became his creatures to conclude that the same wisdom and design were employed in the whole, tho human observation and knowledge cannot reach to the whole . . . . It is a truth which no man should be ashamed to own, and which every rational creature should be ashamed to contradict.[54]

Bolingbroke saves some kind of logical consistency for Pope by justifying 'whatever is, is right', as a theoretical inference. It is a

[53] *Pope: The Critical Heritage*, ed. John Barnard (London and Boston, 1973), p. 421.   [54] Bolingbroke, iv.258 n.

piece of right reasoning by analogy,[55] 'which every rational creature should be ashamed to contradict'—and here one is reminded
of how, despite all Bolingbroke's tactical scepticism, he is at
bottom a rationalist. But Pope, more fundamentally the sceptic,
makes his affirmation *in spite of reason*, 'in erring reason's spite'.
He does not sound like someone making a rational inference, but
as though he is speaking from a more immediate understanding or
intuition; the forms of rational argument are used partly to generate the sense of reason coming to the end of its figurative tether,
producing the paradoxes and contradictions in which lies the hope
of further insight. The second-person address allows a complex
effect: 'All Nature is but Art, unknown to thee', where 'thee' flick-
ers between including all mankind in its unavoidable ignorance of
the divine pattern, and referring to the presumptuous, wrong-
headed reasoner repeatedly berated in the first epistle, than whom
Pope would seem to know better. The harmonious ordering of the
universe is, it seems, both unintelligible and intelligible. Protest at
the way things are is presumptuous, because we have no knowledge of the workings of the universe; and it is mistaken, because we
know the universe works harmoniously. The first epistle of the
Essay oscillates within this contradiction. The line in the opening
passage, in which Pope describes 'this scene of Man' as 'A mighty
maze! but not without a plan' stood in the first edition (as Johnson
pointed out): 'A mighty maze! of walks without a plan'[56] and
something of the nonchalance with which Pope felt able to substi-
tute the one, logically contradictory phrase for the other is retained
throughout the whole poem, where the unintelligibility of things
lies very close to—can almost be felt to turn into—its opposite.
'Whatever is, is right' is Pope's (philosophically incautious, but also
cannily unphilosophical) expression of the sense of rightness—an
experience, not an inference—that his scepticism delivers. The
metaphysical idea is used expressively; any claim that it delivers a
rigorous philosophical truth is mitigated twice over, first by the
unrigorous genre in which it finds itself—an informal epistle, an
essay, and a poem—and second, by the scepticism which underwrites such choice of genre, with the implication that all philo-

---

[55] Bolingbroke is driven to this, defensively; he does not normally care for reasoning by analogy on metaphysical or theological topics.
[56] *The Twickenham Edition of the Poems of Alexander Pope*, vol. iii.i: *An Essay
on Man*, ed. Maynard Mack (London, 1950), p. 11.

sophical ideas are, in any case, liable to be nothing more (or less) than rationalizations of what we believe upon instinct, or feel upon our pulses.

*   *   *

This reading becomes more persuasive when it is seen that a similar movement can be traced in the second and third epistles of the *Essay*, whose subject-matter is apparently quite distinct. In those epistles, the affirmations of passion and of instinct express broadly the same experience as the affirmation of metaphysical rightness in the first epistle: scepticism leads to, and terminates in, the intuition of a benign disposing power distinct from and beyond the scope of reason, yet with which the reasoning consciousness can associate itself.

To begin with passion. The second epistle of the *Essay* sets out Pope's model of individual psychology, which is centred on the dynamic of passion, and gives rise to his theory of a ruling passion. That theory was most fully developed in the *Epistle to Cobham: Of the Knowledge and Characters of Men*, which was written at the same time that Pope was working on the *Essay on Man*, and was originally intended to be part of the larger work to which the *Essay* was to be the introduction. But the ruling passion is only the secondary subject of this *Epistle*; its main subject is scepticism, and the first two-thirds of the epistle constitute the most sustained expression of radical scepticism in all of Pope. The subject of this scepticism is knowledge of the self, or the idea that an individual has an intelligible character which underlies and illuminates behaviour. The fourth and final epistle of the *Essay on Man* finished with the reflection that 'all our Knowledge is, OURSELVES TO KNOW', with the seeming implication that such knowledge, although excluding a great deal, is in itself something solid and substantial. However, that epistle was, at one stage, to have been followed by a fifth, on the 'Inconsistencys of Character',[57] and this seems to have become the *Epistle to Cobham*. For some 175 lines, the *Epistle* applies the most thoroughgoing scepticism to the notion that the self—in particular, the individual's 'principle of action'—can ever be securely known. Merely to quote part of the opening synopsis shows how intensely problematic Pope makes this enterprise:

---

[57] Leranbaum, *Pope's 'Opus Magnum'* p. 20.

That it is not sufficient for this knowledge to consider Man in the Abstract: Books *will not serve the purpose, nor yet our own* Experience *singly. General maxims, unless they be formed upon both, will be but notional. Some Peculiarity in every man, characteristic to himself, yet varying from himself. Difficulties arising from our own Passions, Fancies, Faculties, &c. The shortness of Life, to observe in, and the uncertainty of the* Principles *of action in men, to observe by. Our own Principle of action often hid from ourselves. Some few Characters plain, but in general confounded, dissembled, or inconsistent. The same man utterly different in different places and seasons. Unimaginable weaknesses in the greatest. Nothing constant and certain but* God *and* Nature. *No judging of the* Motives *from the actions; the same actions proceeding from contrary* Motives, *and the same* Motives *influencing contrary actions.*

That scepticism is expressed in the poem itself with the greatest energy; we know that Pope associated the poem with his reading in Montaigne,[58] and nowhere is Pope's affinity with Montaigne more apparent. Each individual differs from the next, so that no general laws can be confidently applied; there must be at least as many sorts of mind as the '300 sorts of Moss observed by Naturalists'.[59] But what matters more, the individual also 'varies from himself'; the mind is in a condition of continuous rapid flux:

> Our depths who fathoms, or our shallows finds,
> Quick whirls, and shifting eddies, of our minds?
> On human actions reason tho' you can,
> It may be Reason, but it is not Man:
> His Principle of action once explore,
> That instant 'tis his Principle no more.
> Like following life thro' creatures you dissect,
> You lose it in the moment you detect.   (23–30)

Not only is the object of our would-be knowledge in perpetual flux, but our attempts at knowledge are shot through with all the distortions of subjectivity:

> Yet more; the diff'rence is as great between
> The optics seeing, as the objects seen.
> All Manners take a tincture from our own;
> Or come discolour'd thro' our Passions shown.

---

[58] Spence, *Anecdotes*, i.142 and ii.709. The first essay in Montaigne's second book, 'Of the Inconstancy of our Actions', is singled out for special mention.
[59] Pope's footnote to l. 18.

> Or Fancy's beam enlarges, multiplies,
> Contracts, inverts, and gives ten thousand dyes.   (31–6)

Knowledge of one's own motives is hardly easier than knowledge of others', especially if our determining motives are not the rational choices we like to suppose, but as contingent, arbitrary and irrational as the stuff of dreams:

> Nor will Life's stream for Observation stay,
> It hurries all too fast to mark their way:
> In vain sedate reflections we would make,
> When half our knowledge we must snatch, not take.
> Oft, in the Passions' wild rotation tost,
> Our spring of action to ourselves is lost:
> Tir'd, not determin'd, to the last we yield,
> And what comes then is master of the field.
> As the last image of that troubled heap,
> When Sense subsides, and Fancy sports in sleep,
> (Tho' past the recollection of the thought)
> Becomes the stuff of which our dream is wrought;
> Something, as dim to our internal view,
> Is thus perhaps the cause of all we do.   (37–50)

After 173 lines of such formidable critique, comes a turning-point, and a solution. But after what has gone before, this solution, which occupies the final third of the poem, seems absurdly inadequate:

> Search then the RULING PASSION: There, alone,
> The Wild are constant, and the Cunning known;
> The Fool consistent, and the False sincere;
> Priests, Princes, Women, no dissemblers here.
> This clue once found, unravels all the rest.   (174–8)

And Pope goes on to give some examples: Wharton's love of praise, Caesar's ambition, Narcissa's vanity, Cobham's patriotism—vigorous simplifications excellent for the purposes of the satirist, but that hardly address the scepticism explored in the body of the poem, which so powerfully rules out any attempt to reduce individual behaviour to a single key. The switch from scepticism to knowledge in the epistle is so abrupt that it could itself stand as a case of the bewildering inconsistency that makes understanding of the self so difficult ('Alas! in truth the man but chang'd his mind').[60] And Pope's theory of the ruling passion is in itself even less philosophically persuasive than his exposition of the great chain of being. In both cases, the switch from scepticism to knowledge does not work well if read as a problem stated then solved: the statement of the problem being far more compelling than the solution. It can better be understood as a way of recognizing and expressing the confidence inherent in the passages of scepticism, a confidence that can be felt in the energy of the writing, the palpable pleasure found in the evocation of flux and multiplicity. Reason's awareness of its own drastic limitations is not simply negative, for it corresponds to the discovery of that which, in its fluidity and movement, lies beyond reason's grasp: 'Life's stream', let us call it, after Pope. And although it may seem illogical—it is illogical—for Pope to translate this sense of flux and multiplicity into a concept of something fixed and single, the 'ruling passion', as a cognitive object that reason can apprehend, the crucial thing about the ruling passion is its non-rational character: it is a given, prior to rational or moral considerations, a determining force which reason must acknowledge, and can modify only in clearly subordinate ways.

A comparable intuition, perhaps more cautiously expressed, can be traced in the second epistle of the *Essay*, where the motive power of all human behaviour is located in the passions—ultimately, modes of self-love—and man's passionate pursuit of real or seeming goods; vice and virtue are mutations of the same fundamental passions. In the hands of some moralists—a Hobbes, a La Rochefoucauld, a Mandeville, perhaps a Swift—such an account led to cynical or severely disillusioned conclusions, but Pope's vision is affirmative, in ways that depend less on *reasons* (Providence turning individuals' passions to the good of the whole; an aesthetic pleasure in *concordia discors*) than on the feeling for the richness and energy and diversity of the flow of life. Reason, without motive power itself, has a strictly subordinate role:

> The rising tempest puts in act the soul,
> Parts it may ravage, but preserves the whole.
> On life's vast ocean diversely we sail,
> Reason the card, but Passion is the gale;

[60] *Epistle to Cobham*, l. 127: Pope, p. 287.

Nor God alone in the still calm we find,
He mounts the storm, and walks upon the wind.

(II.105-10)

It is for reason to 'keep to Nature's road'. At the start of the epistle this is compatible with a deliberative, restraining, instrumental
function; but the role of Reason shrinks markedly when Pope
introduces the idea of the ruling passion:

> Nature its mother, Habit is its nurse;
> Wit, Spirit, Faculties, but make it worse;
> Reason itself but gives it edge and pow'r;
> As Heav'ns blest beam turns vinegar more sowr;
> We, wretched subjects tho' to lawful sway,
> In this weak queen, some fav'rite still obey.
> Ah! if she lend not arms, as well as rules,
> What can she more than tell us we are fools?
> Teach us to mourn our Nature, not to mend,
> A sharp accuser, but a helpless friend!
> Or from a judge turn pleader, to persuade
> The choice we make, or justify it made;
> Proud of an easy conquest all along,
> She but removes weak passions for the strong. (II.145-58)

That sense of passion's natural supremacy remains, even when
Pope is trying to retrieve some ground for reason:

> Yes, Nature's road must ever be prefer'd;
> Reason is here no guide, but still a guard:
> 'Tis hers to rectify, not overthrow,
> And treat this passion more as friend than foe:
> A mightier Pow'r the strong direction sends,
> And sev'ral Men impels to sev'ral ends.
> Like varying winds, by other passions tost,
> This drives them constant to a certain coast.
> Let pow'r or knowledge, gold or glory, please,
> Or (oft more strong than all) the love of ease;
> Thro' life 'tis follow'd, ev'n at life's expence;
> The merchant's toil, the sage's indolence,
> The monk's humility, the hero's pride,
> All, all alike, find Reason on their side. (II.161-74)

If this is a reasoned account of the way men live, what more,
indeed, can reason do than tell us we are fools? The satirical poten-
tiality of this is subsumed into a larger acceptance. And towards

the end of the epistle Pope rises to a sublimely acquiescent vision of the subjective, non-rational comforts inspired by self-love and the ruling passion:

> Whate'er the Passion, knowledge, fame, or pelf,
> Not one will change his neighbor with himself.
> The learn'd is happy nature to explore,
> The fool is happy that he knows no more;
> The rich is happy in the plenty giv'n,
> The poor contents him with the care of Heav'n.
> See the blind beggar dance, the cripple sing,
> The sot a hero, lunatic a king;
> The starving chemist in his golden views
> Supremely blest, the poet in his Muse.   (II.261–70)

Here we have another evocation of 'Life's stream'. Some of these forms of happiness look much more vulnerable to rational objection than others, yet they are all allowed as equally real in their subjectivity; reason registers a distinction between, for example, the 'learned' who explores nature and the lunatic who thinks himself a king, but reason has no authority to pronounce on the validity of their experience. The poet's vision, too, is included. Pope's self-references are always masterly, but the effect here is particularly fine, as the poet's perspective which remarks irrationality as universal is confessed to be itself part of the picture, and the celebration of general happiness to be the effect, not of reason, but of the poet's own passion-inspired vision, his own 'golden views'. The tone of 'supremely blest' is exquisite: the possibility of irony is fully felt (reason is active) yet the sense of blessing is real (for reason can never press a claim against reality). With a certain ironic awareness, a necessary element of detachment, the observing consciousness nevertheless acknowledges its own participation in life's larger processes. *A mightier power the strong direction sends*: while the act of recognition and acquiescence belongs, still, to the conscious, reasoning mind.

A similar insight is realized in the third epistle, where it is couched in terms of the relation between reason and instinct—specifically, the instinct of animals. The relation of man to the animals was a naturally fertile area for scepticism. The traditional ground of human distinction, that man is a reasoning animal, no longer seemed so meaningful or so secure; Addison remarked how

'Sceptical Men' liked to blur the distinction between animals and reasoning humans.[61] A long section of Montaigne's 'Apology for Raimond Sebond' had compared men and animals, disputing sometimes the reality and sometimes the advantageousness of the attributes alleged to be specific to humanity. Bayle set the implausibility of the Cartesian hypothesis that animals are automata against the dangerous implications for religion of the Aristotelian view that animals have souls.[62] Locke's analysis of the human understanding seemed to many readers to discuss processes not fundamentally different in kind from what one might suppose to take place in the minds of the higher animals.[63] Hume explicitly endorsed and reinforced this, proposing a continuum between animal and human understanding by redescribing human reasoning as habit and as instinct.[64] And Bolingbroke, as we have seen, made the relation of animal and human a crucial part of his argument against the soul/body distinction in the first of the *Letters*. He there supposes a difference in degree, rather than in kind, between animal faculties and human: the fact of human superiority is indisputable, but its ground is impossible to categorize with any clarity.

Pope, however, begins quite differently, making the orthodox distinction between Instinct and Reason as the defining attributes of the animals and of man. Instinct is in many respects the preferable: directly instilled by the Creator, it never fails or errs, unlike reason, and it brings together knowledge and action as one. 'Reason raise o'er Instinct as you can, | In this 'tis God directs, in that 'tis Man.' (III.97–8) This, although strikingly expressed, is not an original thought; the Twickenham editor cites a number of parallels.[65] One of these is 'The Logicians Refuted', an anonymous poem attributed both to Swift and to Goldsmith, in which the poet debunks human pretensions to reason by reference to the moral superiority of the animals:

[61] *The Spectator*, ed. Donald F. Bond, 5 vols. (Oxford, 1965), i.491: no. 120.
[62] Under 'Rorarius'; see Pierre Bayle, *Historical and Critical Dictionary: Selections*, ed. Richard H. Popkin (Indianapolis, 1965), pp. 213–45.
[63] See Kenneth MacLean, *John Locke and English Literature of the Eighteenth Century* (New York, 1962: reissued edition), pp. 68–81.
[64] See 'Of the Reason of Animals', in *Enquiries*, pp. 103–8.
[65] Others could be added e.g. Somerville, in *The Chase*: 'that Instinct, which unerring guides | The brutal race, which mimics reason's lore, | And oft transcends: Heaven-taught' (ii.2–4), or Brooke's description in *Universal Beauty* of the migration of birds (vi.367–83), which echoes or anticipates Pope.

Logicians have but ill defined
As rational, the human kind;
Reason, they say, belongs to man,
But let them prove it if they can.

.   .   .   .   .

[I] must in spite of them maintain
That man and all his ways are vain;
And that this boasted lord of nature
Is both a weak and erring creature;
That instinct is a surer guide
Than reason-boasting mortals' pride;
And that brute beasts are far before 'em,
Deus est anima brutorum.
Whoever knew an honest brute
At law his neighbour prosecute,
Bring action for assault and battery,
Or friend beguile with lies and flattery?[66]

These are certainly Swiftian sentiments, although Swift could work such material into much less straightforward forms. In *Gulliver's Travels* the presentation of truly rational animals—the Houhynhmns—leaves the situation of humanity acutely problematic. And Swift's *Modest Proposal* also plays on uncertainties in this area: the proposed equation of children's flesh with animal flesh creates a horrified recoil, but the most immediate ground of distinction between animal and human that presents itself is the impeccable rationality of the proposer. But there is nowhere in Swift the smallest spark of sympathy for what Pope proposes: that the proper task of Reason is not to strike out on its own line, but to imitate the action of instinct. This intuition is embodied in Pope's sketch of a state of nature in which 'Man walk'd with beast, joint tenant of the shade',[67] a golden age in which the arts of civilization could be modelled on the animal kingdom:

See him from Nature rising slow to Art!
To copy Instinct then was Reason's part;
Thus then to Man the voice of Nature spake—
'Go, from the Creatures thy instructions take:

---

[66] *The Poems of Thomas Gray, William Collins, Oliver Goldsmith*, ed. Roger Lonsdale (London, 1969), pp. 765 f.
[67] *Essay on Man*, iii.152: Pope, p. 263.

> Learn from the birds what food the thickets yield;
> Learn from the beasts the physic of the field;
> Thy arts of building from the bee receive;
> Learn of the mole to plow, the worm to weave;
> Learn of the little Nautilus to sail,
> Spread the thin oar, and catch the driving gale.
> Here too all forms of social union find,
> And hence let Reason, late, instruct Mankind
>
> .   .   .   .
>
> And for those Arts mere Instinct could afford,
> Be crown'd as Monarchs, or as Gods ador'd.'   (III.169–98)

Such social harmony was destroyed by historical forces of super-stition and tyranny, but it remains the model for the enlightened 'Poet or Patriot' to restore; the ideal is a society built on 'the Faith and Moral, Nature gave before'.[68]

As a set of ideas, this may not seem particularly penetrating: Pope has little to say, for example, on what makes such 'natural society' so difficult to achieve or sustain. Nor is this convincing, or meant to be convincing, as a realistic analysis of the prehistoric origins of society. But these philosophical deficiencies go hand in hand with a different kind of excellence. Writing in the *Treatise of Human Nature* on the origins of justice and the social virtues, David Hume argued that more could be learnt from poets' acknowledged fictions of the 'golden age' than from hard-headed philosophical accounts of a pre-social 'state of nature' filled with 'war, violence, and injustice':

However philosophers may have been bewilder'd in those speculations, poets have been guided more infallibly, by a certain taste or common instinct, which in most kinds of reasoning goes farther than any of that art and philosophy, with which we have been yet acquainted.[69]

It is not certain that Hume, who is said to have presented a hand-corrected copy of the *Treatise* to Pope,[70] was thinking here of the *Essay on Man*, but that possibility is suggested by his choice of the word 'instinct' and his elevation of instinct in this context above conventional philosophical reasoning. What Pope is doing, as Hume would seem to have recognized, is giving more or less rational form

---

[68] Ibid. 285 f.: Pope, p. 266.   [69] *Treatise*, pp. 493 f.
[70] Solomon, *The Rape of the Text*, p. 132.

(propositions about the historical origins of society) to an essentially instinctive or intuitive apprehension of 'Nature' as underlying human culture and society. That is to say: just as Nature underlies culture and society, so Pope's instinctive apprehension underlies and guides the forms of rational articulation which he finds for it. The poetry itself is a case of Reason copying Instinct, enacting the principle which, in this epistle, it also describes. From this point of view, the real achievement of the epistle is to be found in those passages where Pope vividly renders, and celebrates, the life of instinct in the voice of reason:

> Who taught the nations of the field and wood
> To shun their poison, and to chuse their food?
> Prescient, the tides or tempests to withstand,
> Build on the wave, or arch beneath the sand?
> Who made the spider parallels design,
> Sure as De-moivre, without rule or line?
> Who bid the stork, Columbus-like, explore
> Heav'ns not his own, and worlds unknown before?
> Who calls the council, states the certain day,
> Who forms the phalanx, and who points the way?
>
> (III.99–108)

The best of human culture imitates the instinctive activity of the natural world, according to Pope in this epistle, which stresses both the separateness and the interdependence of the human and the animal creation. In this passage, contemplating the wonders of that instinctive activity from the human side of the reason/instinct divide, he cannot but apprehend those wonders in specifically human terms, which, even as they are uttered, acknowledge their own falling short. The questions begin as expressions of the inquisitive human reason, and then break like waves (the repetition is crucial to the effect) into being expressions of understanding, for which the exact terms of the solution or 'answer' (God; Nature; no-one) have become redundant. Just as animals don't need teachers or leaders, so the poet imitates and shares in some of that instinctive understanding, as his questions turn into exclamations of delight. To compare Pope's questions with Blake's—

> Tiger, tiger, burning bright
> In the forests of the night,

What immortal hand or eye
Could frame thy fearful symmetry?[71]

—is to be surprised by how much the passages have in common,
despite Blake's irrationalism: yet Pope surpasses Blake in managing
to build imaginative connections between the life of reason and the
life of instinct while maintaining (as Blake also maintains) both
their mutual alienness, and the supremacy of instinct.[72]

*   *   *

In all these areas of the *Essay on Man*, Pope may well have been
housing with Montaigne. In the footnotes in the Twickenham
edition, Montaigne is cited no fewer than thirty-two times (almost
always in connection with the first three epistles: the fourth epistle
is a different matter).[73] The attack on anthropocentrism pursued in
the first epistle is the great theme of the Apology for Sebond, and
Pope later brings this attack on human presumption together with
reference to the animal kingdom in a way that strongly recalls
Montaigne:

[71] *The Poems of William Blake*, ed. W. H. Stevenson and David V. Erdman
(London, 1971), p. 214.
[72] It should be noted that the relation of reason and instinct implied here is quite
different from that announced in the first epistle. There also, Pope imagines instinc-
tual life with extraordinary acuteness: 'The spider's touch, how exquisitely fine! |
Feels at each thread, and lives along the line.' (217–18). But Pope is there committed to the theory of a hierarchical scale of being, which betrays him into this clumsy
and unconvincing finish: 'Without this just gradation, could they be | Subjected
these to those, or all to thee? | The pow'rs of all subdu'd by thee alone, | Is not thy
Reason all these pow'rs in one?' (229–32). This attitude is scarcely compatible with
the stance of the third epistle—a further reminder of Pope's carelessness about intellectual consistency, although in this case the inconsistency marks an incoherence
rather than a sceptical doubleness or openness.
[73] In the fourth epistle, on happiness, Pope loses the sceptical thread. The epistle
abandons the central emphasis on the inadequacies of reason, lacks any equivalent
to passion or instinct as a strong disposing natural force, and struggles to find arguments that support 'whatever is, is right', which is now understood as a seriously
held doctrine identifying virtue and happiness, of which Pope feels obliged to give a
persuasive defence. Because the epistle is conducted in this way, its contradictions
and question-begging irritate, and are *properly* open to intelligently hostile analysis
(as in A. D. Nuttall, *Pope's 'Essay on Man'* (London, 1984), pp. 128–74). The best
passages are written as satire. Pope is not, in any case, the poet of happiness. There
is some external evidence that the fourth epistle was composed somewhat separately
from the first three.

> While Man exclaims, 'See all things for my use!'
> 'See man for mine!' replies a pamper'd goose.   (III.45-6)

For why may not a *Goose* say thus . . . I am the Darling of Nature? Is it not Man that treats, lodges and serves me?[74]

Many of the pages in Montaigne's 'Apology' devoted to the life of animals, in comic mockery of human rationality, chime with Pope's account of instinct in the third epistle.[75] In the *Epistle to Cobham*, Pope's sceptical analysis of the difficulty of fixing the individual character as an object of knowledge, is known to have been inspired by Montaigne, who gets explicit acknowledgement in the text: 'What made (say Montagne, or more sage Charron!) | Otho a warrior, Cromwell a buffoon?' (87-8) Montaigne, better than anyone, understands the elusiveness of the self. In the *Essay on Man*, Pope's contrasting of scientific inquiry with the elusiveness of self-knowledge is entirely in Montaigne's spirit:

> Could he, whose rules the rapid Comet bind,
> Describe or fix one movement of his Mind?   (II.35-6)

Those People, who ride astride on the *Epicycle* of *Mercury*, who see so far into the Heavens . . . do not know, how that moves which they themselves move nor how to give us a Description of the Springs they themselves govern and make use of.[76]

Pope's discussion of the positive function of vices and passions in the total economy of the psyche has parallels in Montaigne, and possible sources in the *Essais* have been adduced even for Pope's theory of the ruling passion, one of the more obviously original parts of the *Essay*.[77]

---

74 Montaigne, ii.329 (ch. 12).

75 In the *Twickenham* edition, pp. 101 n. and 108 n., Mack gives two striking parallels. To attribute animal acts to instinct is to understand 'Nature, with a maternal Sweetness, to accompany and lead them, as it were, by the hand, . . . whilst she leaves us to Chance and Fortune, . . . so that their brutish Stupidity surpasses, in all conveniences, all that our Divine Intelligence can do.' On man walking with beast, 'Plato, in his Picture of the Golden Age under *Saturn*, reckons, amongst the chief Advantages, that a Man then had, his communication with Beasts, of whom inquiring and informing himself, he knew the true Qualities and differences of them all, by which he acquired a very perfect Intelligence and Prudence, and led his Life more happily, than we could do' (Montaigne, ii.195; ii.190).

76 Montaigne, ii.496 f. (ch. 17).

77 For vices and virtues, see esp. *Twickenham*, p. 76 n. Mack supposes that the theory of the ruling passion may be indebted to Montaigne's description of a 'forme maistresse' in the soul (*Twickenham*, p. xxxvi), and at p. 70 n. Mack quotes from

Another significant parallel, if not influence, between Pope and Montaigne concerns the 'looseness' or 'inconsistency' of their thinking with regard to religion. In the 'Apology for Raimond Sebond', Montaigne offers a nominal defence of natural theology (that is, the drawing of inferences about God from the evidence of the natural world), overlays this with a crushing scepticism as to the power of the intellect to attain knowledge of the divine, and yet finishes with a brief affirmation of Christianity—or, if not quite that, still a reminder that nothing that has been said need cut against Christianity:

What a vile and abject thing, says [Seneca], is Man, if he do not raise himself above Humanity! 'Tis a good word, and a profitable desire, but withal absurd; For to make the handle bigger than the Hand, and the Cubit longer than the Arm, and to hope to stride further than our Legs can reach, is both impossible and monstrous; or that Man should rise above himself and Humanity: for he cannot see but with his Eyes, nor seize but with his Power. He shall be exalted, if God will lend him his extraordinary hand; he shall exalt himself, by abandoning and renouncing his own proper means, and by suffering himself to be rais'd and elevated by means purely Celestial; It belongs to our Christian Faith, and not to the Stoical Vertue, to pretend to that Divine and miraculous Metamorphosis.[78]

This curiously understated conclusion reads neither like the passionate, all-or-nothing fideism of a Pascal, nor like the pointed irony of an Enlightenment satirist. It may have been simply a way of mollifying the censor. But it also permits a more interesting reading, whereby scepticism refuses (true to its nature) to resolve its relation to religious belief; instead, it admits the possible co-existence of such faith, which no longer offers to dominate the whole of experience from any privileged position of authority, but is still not excluded from its place at table. Something similar can be said of Pope, and the seeming inconsistency between the scepticism of the Essay, the deism of the Essay, and Pope's own Catholicism. An Essay on Man mixes a good deal of natural theology with a good deal of scepticism about the power of reason, in ways that some contemporaries found directly threatening to Christianity. Yet we

i.368, where Montaigne relates the standard theory of a predominant humour in the body to a predominant motion in the soul: 'So, though the Soul have in it divers motions to give it Agitation; yet must there of necessity be one to over-rule all the rest'.

[78] Montaigne, ii.450 f. (ch. 12).

know that Pope himself did not regard the *Essay* as a positively unChristian poem: he at one point intended to include within it an invocation to Christ, and next to 'Whatever is, is RIGHT' he wrote on the manuscript the marginal gloss, 'Thy Will be done, in Earth as it is in Heaven'.[79] It is impossible to define the relation of that gloss to the text—whether to say that the gloss shows the conclusion of the epistle (even in Pope's intention) to be Christian in spirit, or to say (as Bolingbroke would have said) that all that is valuable in Christian belief can be rewritten as deism. The quotation from Scripture simply sits alongside the philosophical conclusion, rather as Scriptural allusion is present within the published text, neither decisively re-orienting the overt argument and the broadly paganizing ethos of the poem, nor yet assimilated by them. Pope, we may remember, claimed that he could house with Aristippus and St Paul. To some temperaments, such sceptical openness is simply incompatible with Christian belief; the classic statement here is Luther's, against Erasmus. 'A man must delight in assertions or he will be no Christian. . . . The Holy Spirit is no Skeptic, and it is not doubts or mere opinions that he has written on our hearts.'[80] Erasmus, however, thought it possible to be a sceptical Christian, and so, it may be, did both Pope and Montaigne.

But more important than the question of specific parallels and debts is the more general affinity between the two writers. In Montaigne's *Essais*, scepticism about the power of human reason leads to an affirmation of the way things are—of 'whatever is', of nature—as something lying beyond and beneath the active intellect, which the intellect knows only through its alienation from it, yet which it can in some sort copy or trace. In the *Essay on Man*, the cosmology of 'whatever is, is right', and the modellings of reason's relation to passion and to instinct, work primarily as ways of theorizing and expressing a similar intuition.

In expressing this intuition, Pope need not have felt that he was opposing the main principles of Bolingbroke's thought. This offers a coherent theory linking intellectual scepticism with an acquies-

[79] Pope, *An Essay on Man: Reproductions of the Manuscripts*, p. xiv and Pierpoint Morgan Library MS, Epistle I, leaf 6 recto.

[80] *Luther and Erasmus: Free Will and Salvation*, ed. E. G. Rupp and P. S. Watson (Philadelphia, 1969), pp. 105, 109.

cence in the way of nature, which could, in broad outline, be seen as theorizing the movement of experience to be found in Montaigne. In the introductory address to Pope, Bolingbroke is happy to quote Montaigne with approval:

The private interests of many, the prejudices, affections, and passions of all ... put a sort of bias on the mind, which makes it decline from the strait course ... till men lose sight of primitive and real nature, and have no other guide but custom, a second and a false nature. ... From hence it happens, that the most civilised nations are often guilty of injustice and cruelty, which the least civilised would abhor, and that many of the most absurd opinions and doctrines, which have been imposed in the dark ages of ignorance, continue to be the opinions, and doctrines of ages enlightened by philosophy and learning. If I was a philosopher, says MONTAIGNE, I would naturalise art, instead of artilising nature. The expression is odd, but the sense is good.[81]

And Bolingbroke is happy to quote Montaigne, along with Locke, on the severely limited scope of human reason: 'Nothing can be truer ... than what MONTAIGNE has said, "les extremitez de notre perquisition tombent toutes en eblouissement." '[82] But Bolingbroke's endorsement of Montaigne only goes so far. He dissents from his scepticism when it becomes too radical, preferring the less subjective and more systematic Charron, and for one passage in the 'Apology for Sebond' Montaigne is ranked with the detested Plato as 'another prose-poet':

MONTAGNE, another prose-poet, deals with man as divines deal with God, and having drawn down human nature as low as he could, he raises that of some other animals so high, that he ascribes a sense of religion to elephants, and represents them deep in meditation and contemplation before the rising sun, and attentive at certain hours of the day to perform certain acts of devotion. He took this from PLINY.[83]

Two points are worth making about this, both of which have relevance for Pope and for the difference between Pope and Bolingbroke. The first is that Bolingbroke regularly uses 'poet' as a term of abuse for Plato, and for all the pedlars of empty metaphysics who derive from him. They give us 'mere poetry in a philosophical dress: and, I think, you must admit that Plato,

---

[81] Bolingbroke, iii.315.   [82] Ibid. 390; see also ibid. 354.
[83] Ibid. v.324 f.

Malebranche, and a good friend of ours [i.e. Berkeley], to instance
in none of inferior note, are as truly poets as Homer and you'. This
reference to 'mere poetry' runs counter to the view that poetry and
philosophy spring from a single root—Edward Young, for example, held that 'in the first ages, Philosophy and Poetry were the
same thing'[84]—and reverses the emphasis that Bolingbroke could
have found in Montaigne: 'Certainly *Philosophy* is no other than a
falsified *Poesie*. From whence do the Ancient Writers extract their
Authorities, but from the *Poets*? And the first of them were *Poets*
themselves, and writ accordingly. *Plato* is but a *Poet* unripened.'[85]
But Bolingbroke meant it as no compliment to a philosopher to call
him a poet: 'Allusion, allegory, metaphor, and every part of figurative style is the poet's language. Figments of imagination are his
subject. The philosopher may sometimes employ the former
cautiously, and under much controul: the latter never. Reason must
be his guide, and truth alone his subject.'[86] This sharp (and
perfectly Lockean) dichotomy between poetry and philosophy is
tactlessly urged upon a writer engaged, as was Pope, in philosophical poetry. Whenever Bolingbroke recalls in the *Letters* that he is
talking philosophy to a poet, his tone is genially condescending; he
clearly did not suppose that the poetic or literary expression of
thought could radically transform the thought being expressed, still
less that literary expression might be thought *essential* to the best
practice of philosophy.

    The second point is a related one. Bolingbroke seems deaf to the
playfulness in Montaigne's prose, the irony that regularly attaches
itself to the notion of what constitutes evidence or makes a proposition cogent. Montaigne does not worry about the scientific plau-
sibility of his anecdotes, it is enough that they illustrate his point;
indeed he is happy to highlight their status as anecdotes, whose
truth may very well be called in question. 'For the Tales I borrow,
I charge upon the Consciences of those from whom I have them'.[87]
This deafness or insensitivity in Bolingbroke also appears in his
other frequent term of abuse for Plato: when he is not calling him
a poet, he suggests, with an uncertain sarcasm, that Plato must
have been writing *in jest*. 'I do not believe that PLATO was an

---

[84] Edward Young, *Love of Fame: The Universal Passion*, 5th ed. (1752), A2
verso.
[85] Montaigne, ii.336 (ch. 12).   [86] Bolingbroke, iv.147.
[87] Montaigne, i.139 (ch. 20).

enthusiast, in any other sense than you poets affect to appear such, when you call for inspiration and boast of the divine fury: and I could sooner persuade my self that he was never in earnest, than that he was always so.'[88] Bolingbroke may in fact have owed this suggestion to Montaigne, but if so he understands something very different by it. At one point in the 'Apology for Sebond', Montaigne suggests—himself perhaps half-seriously—that even high Platonism, the theory of Forms, is touched by the irony of Socrates, of which he is a passionate admirer; for Montaigne, one might almost say, irony as Socrates employs it is the only approach to truth.[89] But for Bolingbroke, to suggest that Plato was not in earnest is another way of dismissing his philosophizing as negligible. Just as one deals either in 'figments of imagination', or in 'truth alone', so one is either in earnest or in jest: these dichotomies are fixed, not fluid. Bolingbroke cannot see how a certain kind of irony might be, for a sceptical thinker and literary artist, the very expression of intelligence, the intelligence that recognizes how any thought is both a reaching after truth and a moment in the flow of experience. This blankness about irony touches his own work; the *Letters or Essays* is clearly a polemic against everything his contemporaries understood by Christianity, but when he professes himself a friend to true Christianity, his writing is curiously toneless and irony-free. At such moments he is using language according to what might be called the official protocol of Locke, where all that a word can stand for is an idea in the mind of the person who uses it, with no admission of consciousness that it might signify differently in other minds. (It is interesting how prominently the idea of irony figures in some of the attacks on the *Letters or Essays*: as though Bolingbroke's antagonists were drawing attention to a quality of intelligence conspicuously missing in his work.)[90]

---

[88] Bolingbroke, iv.143.   [89] See Montaigne ii.288–93 (ch. 12).

[90] When Johnson instances IRONY in the *Dictionary*, it is Bolingbroke of whom, polemically, he thinks: 'as when we say, Bolingbroke was a holy man'. Burke's *Vindication of Natural Society* (1756), purporting to do for the idea of society what Bolingbroke had done for religion, is a sustained irony. And Fielding, in his 'Fragment of a Comment', ironically suggests that as Bolingbroke is so full of contradictions about religion, he must have been writing as an ironist. 'We doubt not but to make it appear as a fact beyond all contest, that his lordship was in jest through the whole work which we have undertaken to examine. If an inflamed zealot should, in his warmth, compare such jesting to his in the Psalmist; or, if a cooler disposition should ask, how it was possible to jest with matters of such

There is, therefore, a fine appropriateness, at the end of the
Epistle to Bolingbroke, in the irony which deflects the appeal to be
raised into a state of single-minded, reasoning autonomy. The truly
philo-sophical poet, who loves the wisdom he does not possess,
sees further than the unironic philosopher, and speaks in a tone in
which jest and earnest are inseparably fused.

> Is this my Guide, Philosopher, and Friend?
> This, he who loves me, and who ought to mend?
> Who ought to make me (what he can, or none,)
> That Man divine whom Wisdom calls her own;
> Great without Title, without Fortune bless'd;
> Rich ev'n when plunder'd, honour'd while oppress'd;
> Lov'd without youth, and follow'd without pow'r;
> At home, tho' exil'd; free, tho' in the Tower:
> In short, that reas'ning, high, immortal Thing,
> Just less than Jove, and much above a King,
> Nay, half in heav'n—except (what's mighty odd)
> A Fit of Vapours clouds this Demi-god.   (177–88)

As Montaigne wrote, 'while we would make one continued thing
of all this succession of passion, we deceive our selves'.[91]
Inconsistency will always supervene, as it supervenes here at the
end, reminding us of the inconsistency which is one main theme of
the poem throughout (and to which the only viable exception
seems to be the obsessive, dehumanized desire for 'Wealth and
Place').[92] There is no other option; behind the formal necessity for
Pope to follow Horace at the end, lies the deeper necessity of
following the fluidity of 'Life's stream':

importance? I confess I have no defence against the accusation, nor can give any
satisfactory answer to the question. To this, indeed, I could say, and it is all that I
could say, that my lord Bolingbroke was a great genius, sent into the world for great
and astonishing purposes. That the ends, as well as means of action in such person-
ages, are above the comprehension of the vulgar. That his life was one scene of the
Wonderful throughout. That, as the temporal happiness, the civil liberties and properties of Europe, were the game of his earliest youth, there could be no sport so
adequate to the entertainment of his advanced age, as the eternal and final happiness of all mankind.' *Complete Works of Henry Fielding*, 16 vols. (repr. New York,
1967), xvi.314.

   [91] Montaigne, i.371 (ch. 37).
   [92] *To Lord Bolingbroke*, l. 104: Pope, p. 353.

Others form *Man*, I only report him, and represent a particular one, ill-fashion'd enough; and whom, if I had to model anew, I should certainly make him something else than what he is: But that's past re-calling.[93]

Les autres forment l'homme; je le recite. And Montaigne's act of self-recital alters what is witnessed; by 'reciting' or rehearsing himself in his writing, Montaigne embraces the reality of his condition in a way that transforms the impression of helplessness. What, similarly, makes Pope's poem something other than an expression of mere helplessness—the psychological equivalent of the fatalism with which the *Essay on Man* was charged—is the play of an ironic self-consciousness, readily felt in that final parenthesis ('what's mighty odd'), but present throughout (for example, in the poem's self-aware relation to the Latin, or in the felt mediation between personal feeling and public statement). That play of consciousness stands in relation to the flow of sentiments rather as 'Reason' stands to 'Passion' or to 'Instinct' according to the models proposed in the *Essay on Man*. But what is theorized in the *Essay*, and expressed in certain passages that seem to depend upon those theoretical models, is in the *Epistle* fully and effortlessly realized, without any further need for philosophical scaffolding or support.

The achievement of the *Epistle to Bolingbroke* is present also, to a lesser or greater extent, in much of Pope's writing in the 1730s. Rather as the somewhat doctrinaire scepticism of Montaigne's 'Apology' may have been necessary to release the extraordinarily free and relaxed manner of the essays that followed, so the structures of thought that Pope worked out to his own satisfaction in the first three epistles of the *Essay on Man*, resulted in—or supported, at least—his 'pouring himself out as plain . . . as old Montaigne' in the writing that followed. One mark of the special sceptical consciousness in Montaigne, which required the invention of the essay for its expression, is the way that Montaigne's thinking never offers to step outside the flow of experience onto some platform of objective knowledge, but remains within what Pope calls the stream of life. Hence whatever Montaigne is thinking about in the *Essais*, his thinking is always the representation of a mind in motion, a form of (increasingly conscious) self-portraiture, where the portrait is necessarily always in process, never concluded. There is something parallel in

[93] Montaigne, iii.26 (ch. 2).

the passages of quasi-autobiographical self-representation which are such a marked feature of Pope's writing in the 1730s. Even where Pope has a model for this in Horace, he regularly goes beyond Horace in the effect of unfiltered revelation; the Pope who shares with us that 'Content with little, I can piddle here | On broccoli and mutton, round the year'[94] recalls Montaigne as much as Horace. But the effect is not confined to the passages of autobiographical *content*; it is there also in the idiom of remarkable directness which Pope can now command:

> Shut, shut the door, good John! fatigu'd I said,
> Tye up the knocker, say I'm sick, I'm dead.
> The Dog-star rages! nay 'tis past a doubt,
> All Bedlam, or Parnassus, is let out . . .[95]

> Pictures like these, dear Madam, to design,
> Asks no firm hand, and no unerring line;
> Some wand'ring touches, some reflected light,
> Some flying stroke alone can hit 'em right . . .[96]

This is part of a more general sense of spontaneous utterance, which in itself operates as a form of self-presentation, where the sense of a living self has less to do with Pope's biographical history than the subjective flow of immediate opinion, sentiment, and feeling. It is the poetry of the mind in process. Pope's sentiments may be strongly felt, but there is no possibility of transcendence: they are within the flow, not outside it, and their truth to life's stream is guaranteed by their variousness and mobility. *Whatever is, is right.* This is a literary effect, not a philosophical position, and a sufficiently rare achievement in literature: but in Pope's best passages it is so effortlessly realized, and so much a matter of manner rather than content, that it almost escapes notice. And of course with Pope there is always more to attend to: when Pope pours himself out, there is often an ethical strategy at work, always an artistic one: and always a rhetorical consciousness of audience. Sometimes the naturalness can seem too consciously a trope, a device serving other artistic or ethical ends: Pope took such 'great delight in artifice', Johnson observed, that 'he hardly drank tea without a strat-

---

[94] *The Second Satire of the Second Book of Horace Imitated: To Mr Bethel*, l. 137–8: Pope, p. 349.
[95] *Epistle to Dr Arbuthnot*, ll. 1–4: Pope, p. 328.
[96] *Epistle to a Lady*, ll. 151–4: Pope, p. 295.

agem'.[97] (This is the opposite of Montaigne, where the effect of arbitrary or random outpouring can be only too convincing.) But in Pope's more relaxed passages the impression is irresistible of a consciousness which copies and embraces, not without some play of irony, a more instinctual life. Johnson wrote in his *Life of Pope* that 'the *Imitations of Horace* seem to have been written as relaxations of his genius',[98] and although this was not meant entirely as a compliment, the phrase points up a quality of Pope's writing in the 1730s that Montaigne would have valued highly:

Yielding and facility, do methinks wonderfully honour, and best become a strong and generous Soul.[99]

At these moments in Pope's poetry, the impression of design seems impossible to differentiate from the way things pour out: which is, after all, the core of what Pope wanted to convey in *An Essay on Man*.

[97] Johnson, *Lives*, iii.200.   [98] Ibid. 246.
[99] Montaigne, iii.546 (ch. 13).

4

Innocence and Simulation in the Scepticism of Hume

Nothing, therefore, can be more innocent . . . than this doctrine.

David Hume is widely agreed to be the central figure of modern philosophical scepticism, as well as perhaps the most important of all British philosophers. He took empiricism to one kind of logical extreme, he developed from it certain sceptical paradoxes which were the immediate stimulus for the work of Kant, and his arguments about the basis of our knowledge, and of our moral life, have exercised professional philosophers from his day to our own. He did not, however, regard himself as a professional philosopher so much as a man driven by the 'passion for literature, which has been the ruling passion of my life', as he says in his brief autobiography.[1] Most of the hard reasoning which underlies his thought is worked through in the early *Treatise of Human Nature*, but after this failed to achieve a readership Hume devoted himself for more than a decade to more obviously accessible, essayistic writings, and came to think these superior to the *Treatise*, whose arguments they sometimes repeat, popularize, or silently presuppose. This shift is significant of more than just Hume's desire for recognition; it bears on the relation between philosophizing and living. 'Axioms in philosophy are not axioms until they are proved upon our pulses',[2] wrote Keats; Hume has some stringent reasons for thinking that arguments in philosophy are *only* arguments in philosophy unless and until their relation to experience finds expression. This relation

[1] David Hume, *Essays Moral, Political, and Literary*, ed. Eugene F. Miller (Indianapolis, 1985), pp. xxxii f.
[2] *The Letters of John Keats*, ed. Maurice Buxton Forman, 4th ed. (Oxford, 1952), p. 141; to Reynolds, 3 May 1818.

cannot be straightforward, since a cardinal element in Hume's scepticism is that reasoning, including sceptical reasoning, has no direct influence upon behaviour and belief, which is an effect rather of feeling and imagination. What Hume's arguments mean, what they amount to, depends upon how they strike the imagination, what they feel like in experience. Thus Hume's concern to make his scepticism *accessible*—which may seem an essentially 'literary' ambition, a matter of tone and style and rhetorical presentation— is equally the attempt to establish the connection between sceptical theory and practical experience, to address the problem as he thus expressed it:

For here is the chief and most confounding objection to *excessive* scepticism, that no durable good can ever result from it; while it remains in its full force and vigour. We need only ask such a sceptic, *What his meaning is? And what he proposes by all these curious researches?* He is immediately at a loss, and knows not what to answer.[3]

The more essayistic writings that came after the *Treatise* were successful in making Hume's name, both in Britain and abroad. No one thought of him as merely a man of 'curious researches', a disinterested spinner of sceptical paradoxes which had no tendency beyond themselves. But opinion divided sharply as to whether that tendency was pernicious, or radiantly benign. He became an intensely controversial figure. Adam Smith wrote in a famous letter of tribute published on Hume's death: 'Upon the whole, I have always considered him, both in his lifetime and since his death, as approaching as nearly to the idea of a perfectly wise and virtuous man, as perhaps the nature of human frailty will permit.'[4] That judgement was shared by the salons of Paris society, which accorded Hume something close to hero-worship during the two years he spent there. His works were read as those of 'le bon David', as he was generally known among his friends. But most of England thought of him under another name, that of 'the great Infidel', a sceptic whose work was subversive not only of Christian doctrine but of all principles for living whatsoever. Johnson was

---

[3] David Hume, *Enquiries concerning Human Understanding and concerning the Principles of Morals*, ed. L. A. Selby-Bigge, 3rd ed. rev. P. H. Nidditch (Oxford, 1975), p. 159 f.
[4] 'Letter from Adam Smith, LL.D. to William Strahan, Esq.', in Hume, *Essays*, ed. Miller, p. xlix.

one of those who regarded Hume's philosophical writing as poisonous; this anecdote from Walter Scott gives some idea of the conflicting feelings which the name of Hume could arouse:

> Mr Boswell has chosen to omit, for reasons which will be presently obvious, that Johnson and Adam Smith met at Glasgow . . . Smith, leaving the party where he had met Johnson, happened to come to another where . . . knowing that Smith had been in Johnson's society, they were anxious to know what had passed, and the more so as Dr Smith's temper seemed much ruffled. At first Smith would only answer, 'He's a brute—he's a brute'; but, on closer examination, it appeared that Johnson no sooner saw Smith than he attacked him for some point of his famous letter on the death of Hume. Smith vindicated the truth of his statement. 'What did Johnson say?' was the universal inquiry. 'Why, he said,' replied Smith, with the deepest impression of resentment, 'he said, *you lie!*' 'And what did you reply?' 'I said, you are a son of a——!' On such terms did these two great moralists meet and part, and such was the classical dialogue between two great teachers of philosophy.[5]

Such violent division of opinion can be partly explained in terms of Hume's reputation as antagonist to Christianity. But it goes beyond that, for it reflects a doubleness that lies at the heart of Hume's work, which puts forward the paradoxical eighteenth-century conjunction of scepticism and confidence in perhaps its sharpest form. The characteristic movement of Hume's thought is twofold: a corrosive scepticism that undermines the foundations of all our structures of belief, and an endorsement of the unsanctioned life lived according to custom, sentiment, and inclination. Interpreting Hume thus means striking a delicate balance. Let the emphasis fall one way and you have a dangerous subversive, whose discoveries do away with just about everything that human beings live by; let the emphasis fall differently and he becomes a solid, almost bland, defender of the natural feelings of mankind. Hume unmistakably plays to both lines of interpretation, with tantalizing suggestion of an underlying poise that accommodates both, and is larger than either.[6]

---

    [5] James Boswell, *Life of Samuel Johnson*, ed. John Wilson Croker, 5 vols. (London, 1831), iii.65n.
    [6] For a good account of Hume that recognizes this doubleness, see David Simpson, 'Hume's Intimate Voices and the Method of Dialogue', in *Texas Studies in Literature and Language*, 21/i (1979), pp. 68–92. In the dialogic qualities of Hume's writing and the difficulties which these present to interpretation, Simpson

This can be illustrated, to begin with, from the *Treatise*, his earliest and most intellectually ambitious work. The destabilizing, seemingly destructive movement in his thought sets out from the empiricism of Locke, which Hume tips over the edge of the sceptical abyss on which it was teetering. The Lockean 'way of ideas' is stripped of its residual claims to anchorage in an external reality and redescribed in coolly alarmist mode:

Nothing is ever present to the mind but perceptions. ... Let us fix our attention out of ourselves as much as possible: Let us chace our imagination to the heavens, or to the utmost limits of the universe; we never really advance a step beyond ourselves, nor can conceive any kind of existence, but those perceptions, which have appear'd in that narrow compass. This is the universe of the imagination, nor have we any idea but what is there produced.[7]

One key element in this is Hume's analysis of causality. Suppose I see a billiard ball strike a second ball, which then rolls forward. I naturally say to myself that I know the movement of the second ball was caused by the impact, but in fact, as a strict empiricist, I know nothing of the kind. My experience went no further than the perception of one event, the impact, followed by a second, the other ball in motion; no element of causation is apparent to me, only the conjunction of two events. Because I have experience of many similar conjunctions, what Hume calls 'constant conjunctions', my mind readily associates the two events together and, moving easily from one to the other, marks this felt easiness of association with the notion of cause-and-effect. But this notion

is inclined to find a strategic subversiveness, 'a philosophical method organized to disrupt the hopeful notions of clarity, distinction, and consensus which the public face of the rationalist tradition might seem to require' (p. 68), while I tend rather to look for an underlying poise. But Simpson's discussion is subtler and more various than that quotation suggests. Also worth comparing with my own account is the rich discussion by John J. Richetti in *Philosophical Writing: Locke, Berkeley, Hume* (Cambridge, Mass., and London, 1983): 'Hume's writing takes place, it seems to me, within the following paradox: on the one hand, he sought to write for the discerning public who formed the ideal republic of letters and he aspired to establish an easy clarity around the traditional philosophic problems; on the other hand, he uncovered and relentlessly articulated in the *Treatise* an epistemological and moral world of turbulent uncertainty where the common sense and humanist continuities supporting the republic of letters are canceled or at best rendered arbitrary and imperiled.' (pp. 189 f.)

[7] David Hume, *A Treatise of Human Nature*, ed. L. A. Selby-Bigge, 2nd ed. rev. P. H. Nidditch (Oxford, 1978), p. 67 f.

relates only to a feeling in the mind of a percipient; it does not involve access to anything about the nature of billiard balls or any rationale behind the laws of motion. It is the effect of custom, not a piece of cognition. And the fact that if I watch one ball moving towards another I expect that the second ball will move, is likewise a matter of habitual association of ideas: having experienced many comparable conjunctions in the past, my mind readily calls up the idea of the second ball moving after impact, and the special vividness of this idea I mark with the term 'belief'. But such beliefs—which hold our world together—depend only upon habit and custom; they have no basis at all in reason. 'If we believe, that fire warms, or water refreshes, 'tis only because it costs us too much pains to think otherwise.'[8]

In the first book of the *Treatise*, Hume develops this epistemological scepticism to an extreme. Our belief in the continuous existence of an external world is exposed as without rational foundation. The notion of personal identity, a continuous self 'behind' the flux of perceptions and associations that constitute experience, is likewise untenable, since such a self is never known to experience.[9] Custom and imagination give the law by which we live: to accept this is to surrender to all the freaks and whimsies of subjectivity; yet to seek to live by reason is to entangle oneself in paradox, since reason 'entirely subverts itself, and leaves not the lowest degree of evidence in any proposition, either in philosophy or common life'. We are reduced to 'a very dangerous dilemma', with the intolerable choice 'betwixt a false reason and none at all'.[10] The rigour with which Hume pursues these topics opens out into an existential distress. For the questions which he has deprived himself of the power to answer are not merely those of the academic philosopher, but express what seems to be a fundamental human need for sanction. By the end of the first book the matter has come to a crisis, and Hume begins 'to fancy myself in the most deplorable condition imaginable, inviron'd with the deepest darkness, and utterly depriv'd of the use of every member and faculty'.[11] To recognize this experience as the effect of 'fancy' is in

[8] Hume, *A Treatise of Human Nature*, 270.

[9] 'What we call a *mind*, is nothing but a heap or collection of different perceptions, united together by certain relations, and suppos'd, tho' falsely, to be endow'd with a perfect simplicity and identity' (*Treatise*, p. 207).

[10] Ibid. 267 f.   [11] Ibid. 268 f.

no way to place or control it, since the claim that fancy should yield to judgement has been irrevocably given up. But then comes the remarkable turn in the argument—or rather, in the narrative— which I have already quoted in the opening chapter as epitomizing the movement of sceptical thinking:

> Most fortunately it happens, that since reason is incapable of dispelling these clouds, nature herself suffices to that purpose, and cures me of this philosophical melancholy and delirium, either by relaxing this bent of mind, or by some avocation, and lively impression of my senses, which obliterate all these chimeras. I dine, I play a game of back-gammon, I converse, and am merry with my friends; and when after three or four hours' amusement, I wou'd return to these speculations, they appear so cold, and strain'd, and ridiculous, that I cannot find in my heart to enter into them any farther.
>
> Here then I find myself absolutely and necessarily determin'd to live, and talk, and act like other people in the common affairs of life.[12]

The 'very dangerous dilemma' is not resolved, but neglected; the chain of sceptical reasoning which, in the moment of philosophical intensity, seemed so disturbingly subversive, proves in practice to have little power to hold our attention or affect our behaviour. Theory is cured, or simply abandoned, by experience; the philosopher relaxes, or gives up; as the current of nature takes its course, we are returned to the flow of contingent impression and inclination from which the impulse to philosophy, and the desire to align our lives with some absolute sanction outside ourselves, struggled so absurdly to emerge. The corrosive and destabilizing scepticism of inquiry into the basis of things, gives way to a kind of affirmation of, or at least acquiescence in, the way things are.

This 'turn'—from sceptical crisis to 'the common affairs of life'—is central to what Hume is about. It is most sharply and dramatically presented in the conclusion of the first book of the *Treatise* from which I have been quoting, although there are several parallel passages earlier:

> 'Tis happy, therefore, that nature breaks the force of all sceptical arguments in time, and keeps them from having any considerable influence on the understanding. Were we to trust entirely to their self-destruction, that can never take place, 'till they have first subverted all conviction, and have totally destroy'd human reason.[13]

---

[12] Ibid. 269.   [13] Ibid. 187.

This sceptical doubt, both with respect to reason and the senses, is a malady, which can never be radically cur'd, but must return upon us every moment, however we may chace it away, and sometimes may seem entirely free from it. 'Tis impossible upon any system to defend either our understanding or senses; and we but expose them farther when we endeavour to justify them in that manner. As the sceptical doubt arises naturally from a profound and intense reflection on those subjects, it always encreases, the farther we carry our reflections, whether in opposition or conformity to it. Carelessness and in-attention alone can afford us any remedy. For this reason I rely entirely upon them; and take it for granted, whatever may be the reader's opinion at this present moment, that an hour hence he will be persuaded there is both an external and internal world.[14]

This movement—between the destabilizing realm of philosophical reflection and the reassuring realm of 'nature' and common sense— underlies not only the shape of the *Treatise* itself, in which epistemological scepticism is followed by discussion of the passions and the moral sentiments, but also the shape of Hume's literary career, as he moved from the abstruse philosophizing of the *Treatise* to appear as essayist and, finally, historian. It is also reflected in the way that he repeatedly offers his philosophizing as subversive in theory but innocuously conservative in practice. He regularly demolishes the rational foundations on which the edifice of morality, or religion, or political conviction was supposed to stand, then assures us that it stands well enough without them. His analysis of the source of allegiance to government, for example, elegantly unpicks the contract theory on which the right of government was widely supposed to depend; this is part of his larger argument that justice itself is what he calls an artificial virtue, not a moral absolute but a human invention, a useful convention, grounded in the common perception of the public interest. The Hanoverians' claim on allegiance, therefore, is based not on anything so ethically imposing as contract theory or natural law, but on merely pragmatic considerations: the social disorder which revolution would entail. Yet this is as strong a claim as can be had:

Having found that *natural*, as well as *civil* justice, derives its origin from human conventions, we shall quickly perceive, how fruitless it is to resolve the one into the other, and seek, in the laws of nature, a stronger foundation for our political duties than interest, and human conventions.[15]

---

[14] *Treatise*, 218.   [15] Ibid. 543.

Hume's analysis of morality does something similar. In the third book of the *Treatise*, he reduces all moral judgements to matters of sentiment, feelings of pleasure or uneasiness in the percipient which cannot themselves be said to be good or rational or true but are simply facts of our experience behind which we cannot go. This, as Hume is careful to point out, could be seen as radically destructive of established ways of thinking about morality:

In every system of morality, which I have hitherto met with, I have always remark'd, that the author proceeds for some time in the ordinary way of reasoning, and establishes the being of a God, or makes observations concerning human affairs; when of a sudden I am surpriz'd to find, that instead of the usual copulations of propositions, *is*, and *is not*, I meet with no proposition that is not connected with an *ought*, or an *ought not*. This change is imperceptible; but is, however, of the last consequence. For as this *ought*, or *ought not*, expresses some new relation or affirmation, 'tis necessary that it shou'd be observ'd and explain'd; and at the same time that a reason should be given, for what seems altogether inconceivable, how this new relation can be a deduction from others, which are entirely different from it. But as authors do not commonly use this precaution, I shall presume to recommend it to the readers; and am persuaded, that this small attention wou'd subvert all the vulgar systems of morality, and let us see, that the distinction of vice and virtue is not founded merely on the relations of objects, nor is perceiv'd by reason.[16]

Moral judgements have no better claim to give us access to a realm of verities, to offer us some metaphysical ground beneath our feet, than any other element of our experience. But then comes the movement of reassurance: subversive though this analysis may be of moral theory, it cannot have any effect on moral practice, which, being a matter of feeling or sentiment, is immune to any amount of sceptical reasoning concerning its foundation:

Vice and virtue, therefore, may be compar'd to sounds, colours, heat and cold, which, according to modern philosophy, are not qualities in objects, but perceptions in the mind: And this discovery in morals, like that other in physics, is to be regarded as a considerable achievement of the speculative sciences; tho', like that too, it has little or no influence on practice. Nothing can be more real, or concern us more, than our own sentiments of pleasure and uneasiness; and if these be favourable to virtue, and unfavourable to vice, no more can be requisite to the regulation of our conduct and behaviour.[17]

---

[16] Ibid. 469 f.   [17] Ibid. 469.

Indeed, when it comes to practical morality Hume drily observes that he is the most harmlessly conservative of thinkers, since according to him whatever we think of as virtuous is, by that very fact, virtuous; 'there is just so much vice or virtue in any character, as every one places in it, and . . . 'tis impossible in this particular we can ever be mistaken'.[18]

By suggesting that Hume makes that last observation 'drily', I wish to raise the question of the tone in which this profession of innocence is made. It might be called ironic, though not if irony implies saying one thing but meaning the opposite. Hume means just what he says: but he also communicates a surplus, in the consciousness with which he turns from subversive theory to conformist common-sense practice. In the passages just quoted, it is the sceptical theorist who supplies the insight that our moral sentiments can never be said to be mistaken, since they are subjective feelings rather than objective cognitions. But the insight is then *pitched* in terms which invoke the realm of common sense, where we naturally and inevitably fall into the illusion that our moral sentiments refer to vice and virtue, rather than constitute vice and virtue. In the realm of common sense, the tautology that 'there is just so much vice or virtue in any character, as every one places in it' feels like a genuine reassurance. However, this move to reassurance is not performed without a certain consciousness. There is something almost disingenuous, a momentary bantering of the reader, when the arch-sceptic tells us that 'it is impossible in this particular we can ever be mistaken', since the word 'impossible' reminds us that, by the same reasoning, it is equally impossible that we can ever be *right*. Our moral judgements can never be justified. They simply *are*, part of the constitution of our nature by which we cannot help but build our sense of the world—just as, when we dine or converse with others, 'nature' restores to us our sense of a solid, causally intelligible external world, groundless though philosophy has shown this to be.

Here is another example of Hume's 'dry' tone in the *Treatise*. In the second book he develops the argument that reason, whose function is simply to compare one idea with another, can never by itself supply a motive for action. In the vocabulary of unphilosophical common sense we may speak of conflicts between reason

[18] *Treatise*, 547.

and passion, but inaccurately, since in truth what influences the will, what moves us to act, can only be passion (although there are calm passions as well as violent ones). The implications of this demotion of reason are, for the most part, worked through soberly and unsensationally enough. But Hume also chooses to offer this soundbite summary:

We speak not strictly and philosophically when we talk of the combat of passion and of reason. Reason is, and ought only to be the slave of the passions, and can never pretend to any other office than to serve and obey them.[19]

'This opinion,' Hume urbanely grants, 'may appear somewhat extraordinary'.[20] That combination of urbanity and sensationalism makes the effect; 'the slave of the passions' is a startlingly emotive phrase drawn from the register of scandalized common sense, yet genuinely offered as an example of what it would be to speak 'strictly and philosophically'. By allowing the discourses of philosophy and common sense to run into one another here, Hume is teasing the reader, trailing his coat for a moment in the pose of the morally outrageous free-thinker, while holding out the prospect that this startling paradox will terminate, after all, not too far from the conventional pieties. What this flash of irony permits, remarkably, is just that elision of 'is' into 'ought' which Hume himself declares to be philosophically illegitimate. 'Reason is, and ought only to be the slave of the passions': within the philosophical frame of reference, the 'ought' is a conscious *non sequitur*, whose logical illegitimacy is underlined by its shock-value as a moral proposition. We cannot take it to be installing a ground of absolute moral obligation. Hume, we perceive, is momentarily invoking the frame of reference of common sense, where 'ought' is the unimpeachable marker of feeling, not cognition. The feeling—a logical *non sequitur*, but an experiential reality—is one of approval, of assent to the way things are. Whatever is, is right; as in Pope, whose metaphor of passion as ruler may have given rise to Hume's metaphor of reason as slave, the recognition of the sovereignty of passion yields an unexpected assurance. And this is effected, once

[19] Ibid. 415. The slave image develops the metaphor in Pope's 'ruling passion', a phrase which Hume borrows elsewhere; his general account of the primacy of passion is close to Pope's in *An Essay on Man*.
[20] *Treatise*, p. 415.

more, by the stylistic poise that offers simultaneous access to the perspective of the sceptic and the perspective of common sense.

Much modern commentary on Hume recognizes this double aspect to Hume's thought—one modern study is subtitled *Common-Sense Moralist, Sceptical Metaphysician*—and is exercised by the relation between the two movements in his thought.[21] Commentators working within the discipline of philosophy, who are properly concerned with the logical *implications* of Hume's arguments, naturally tend to be impatient of doubleness.[22] If we call the juxtaposition in Hume of destructive philosophizing and conserving common sense ironic, commentary of this kind naturally seeks to establish the upshot of such irony, its point of termination, thus drawing out the philosophical implications in non-ironic form. This can be done by drawing a line of clear demarcation between the scepticism and the common sense as properly operating within different fields; the only connection

---

[21] David Fate Norton, *David Hume: Common-Sense Moralist, Sceptical Metaphysician* (Princeton, 1982). The issue is well stated by Galen Strawson, writing about one specific aspect of Hume's thought. 'If we are to accept the beliefs in objects and causes, this must mean either that common life in some way trumps philosophy, or that philosophy and common life somehow work together, with philosophy not completely subverting but rather correcting or merely weakening the common life beliefs.' (*The Secret Connexion: Causation, Realism and David Hume* (Oxford, 1989), p. 1.) The phrasing of 'If we are to accept' hankers for that dimension of final justification which it is Hume's distinction to do without.

[22] Recent attempts to establish Hume as a 'sceptical realist'—that is, a thinker who affirms (or, accepts, or at least, does not deny, for the precise term is revealingly difficult to settle) the reality of an external world of objects and causes, even while he denies that that reality can ever be known in its essential nature—are responsive to Hume's doubleness, although they often seem to respond to it, unsceptically enough, by seeking to resolve it into a philosophically stable position. See *The New Hume Debate*, ed. Rupert Read and Kenneth A. Rickman (London, 2000). The cogency of the arguments in that volume pro and con the 'new Hume' nicely illustrate the difficulty of adding together the sceptical and the affirmative or naturalist aspects of Hume's thinking in a single sum. Two contributors who do recognize this difficulty as something other than a problem which technical analysis can solve, are Edward Craig, 'Hume on causality: projectivist *and* realist?' (pp. 113–21), and Anne Jaap Jacobson, 'From cognitive science to a post-Cartesian text: what did Hume really say?' (pp. 156–66). Craig helpfully figures Hume as construing his commentators' inquiries into his true position as an inquiry into what he would think *were he to switch his imagination off*; and Jacobson discerns three distinct personas or perspectives in play in the first *Enquiry*, so that 'no simple quoting of the texts can determine "what Hume really thought" about causality', and adds a sharp footnote: 'I have very considerable reservations about filling out a philosophical position and then calling it Hume's because it provides the "best explanation" of why Hume says what he says' (p. 164; p. 166, fn. 14).

between them then becomes the simply functional one, that scepticism as to metaphysical absolutes and certainties demonstrable by reason simply clears the board for the appeal to experience and common sense. Or the doubleness can be undone by resolving the irony on one side or the other. In the recent *Cambridge Companion to Hume*, for example, one contributor presents Hume's rational scepticism as clearly subordinate to his constructive, psychological or naturalistic analysis of how, if not rationally, the mind notwithstanding comes by its firm beliefs about morality and about the external world.

Hume's recommendation is to replace endless and fruitless 'cogitating,' in an attempt to give a philosophical justification of our beliefs, with an attempt to find a scientific explanation of their origin. . . . It is to give up being a 'metaphysician' and to become a scientist—an 'anatomist'—of the mind, of human nature.[23]

On this reading, Hume's irony cuts only against reason's self-defeating quest for principles of justification. But in an equally cogent essay in the same volume, we are invited to see essentially the same 'double movement' of Hume's scepticism in a quite different light:

First, *reasoning* shows us that our belief in an external world is not based on sound argument, for no such sound argument on this matter exists, and, second, when *empirical investigation* lays bare the actual mechanisms that lead us to embrace this belief, we are immediately struck by their inadequacy.[24]

On this reading, our hunger for rational justification is mocked, not assuaged, by the shallow complacencies of experience.

Both these propositions seem to me true, of different passages to different degrees. Therefore, both can be generalized beyond a certain point only by becoming highly selective in their emphasis, and by making the assumption that one can discuss Hume's 'position' (or positions) as something abstracted from the immediate texture of his writing. This runs the risk of treating his manner as a kind of rhetorical packaging, which needs to be undone in order

[23] John Biro, 'Hume's New Science of the Mind', in *The Cambridge Companion to Hume*, ed. David Fate Norton (Cambridge, 1993), pp. 44 f.
[24] Robert Fogelin, 'Hume's Scepticism', in *The Cambridge Companion to Hume*, p. 93.

to get at the substance of his thought—an approach which is open to the standard empiricist objections to the quest after 'substance' as a quest for an unreality never met with in experience. Instead, one can take the doubleness of his emphasis, and the way in which that doubleness is, at moments, evoked or played on in the manner of his writing, as precisely the point: that point being, how one *connects* the negations of the sceptical intelligence with the assurances of common sense. How is one to reconcile living 'like other people in the common affairs of life' with the knowledge that the security which accompanies such living is, from the perspective of strict reason, a grotesque illusion, or a surface stretched over an abyss? How does one live the unsanctioned life?

Such a question cannot be answered with a proposition or an argument, but only with a manner: see, this is how I do it. Ultimately, this implies a style not just of writing but of living, and there seems little doubt that in the eyes of his friends, Hume's personal manner constituted a most impressive answer to the question of how a sceptic lives his scepticism. Laurence Sterne said of Hume, 'it is this amiable turn to his character, that has given more consequence and force to his scepticism, than all the arguments of his sophistry.'[25] That amiability was undisturbed even by the approach of death, and Hume's manner in his last days was regarded by those who witnessed it as a crucial event in the interpretation of his thought. The central account is Adam Smith's, in the obituary letter:

Upon his return to Edinburgh, though he found himself much weaker, yet his cheerfulness never abated, and he continued to divert himself, as usual, with correcting his own works for a new edition, with reading books of amusement, with the conversation of his friends; and, sometimes in the evening, with a party at his favourite game of whist. His cheerfulness was so great, and his conversation and amusements run so much in their usual strain, that, notwithstanding all bad symptoms, many people could not believe he was dying. . . . He said that . . . when he was reading a few days before, Lucian's Dialogues of the Dead, among all the excuses which are alleged to Charon for not entering readily into his boat, he could not find one that fitted him; he had no house to finish, he had no daughter to provide for, he had no enemies upon whom he wished to revenge himself. . . . He then diverted himself with inventing several jocular excuses, which he supposed he might make to Charon, and with imagining the very surly

[25] *Letters of Laurence Sterne*, ed. L. P. Curtis (Oxford, 1935), p. 218.

answers which it might suit the character of Charon to return to them. 'Upon further consideration,' said he, 'I thought I might say to him, Good Charon, I have been correcting my works for a new edition. Allow me a little time, that I may see how the Public receives the alterations.' But Charon would answer, 'When you have seen the effect of these, you will be for making other alterations. There will be no end of such excuses; so, honest friend, please step into the boat.' But I might still urge, 'Have a little patience, good Charon, I have been endeavouring to open the eyes of the Public. If I live a few years longer, I may have the satisfaction of seeing the downfal of some of the prevailing systems of superstition.' But Charon would then lose all temper and decency. 'You loitering rogue, that will not happen these many hundred years. Do you fancy I will grant you a lease for so long a term? Get into the boat this instant, you lazy loitering rogue.'[26]

To which can be added Boswell's vivid record of his visit to Hume's deathbed:

I had a strong curiosity to be satisfied if he persisted in disbelieving a future state even when he had death before his eyes. I was persuaded from what he now said, and from his manner of saying it, that he did persist. I asked him if it was not possible that there might be a future state. He answered it was possible that a piece of coal put upon the fire would not burn; and he added that it was a most unreasonable fancy that we should exist for ever. . . . I asked him if the thought of annihilation never gave him any uneasiness. He said not the least; no more than the thought that he had not been, as Lucretius observes. 'Well,' said I, 'Mr Hume, I hope to triumph over you when I meet you in a future state; and remember you are not to pretend that you was joking with all this infidelity.' 'No, no,' said he. 'But I shall have been so long there before you come that it will be nothing new.'[27]

The same teasing display of *sang froid* in the face of mortality can be found in the brief autobiography Hume wrote shortly before his death, and required to be prefixed to his works.

What counts for us now, of course, is not how Hume lived and died, but how he wrote: specifically, how finely his manner of writing accommodates the ironic condition of human life that his scepticism revealed to him. A searching test would be to ask how far

---

[26] 'Letter from Adam Smith, LL.D. to William Strahan, Esq.', in Hume, *Essays*, ed. Miller, pp. xliv–xlvi.

[27] *Boswell in Extremes 1776–1778*, ed. Charles M. Weis and Frederick A. Pottle (London, 1971), pp. 11 f.

Hume's manner can survive comparison with the scathing irony of Swift in the following passage from *A Tale of a Tub*. The passage has already been quoted at the end of the first chapter, as a clairvoyant, pre-emptive attack on eighteenth-century complacencies which threatens to identify the constructive aspect of sceptical thinking as mere foppery. It so precisely anticipates the Humean 'turn' from sceptical inquiry to backgammon, dinner-parties, and 'natural beliefs' that I quote it again here:

In the Proportion that Credulity is a more peaceful Possession of the Mind, than Curiosity, so far preferable is that Wisdom, which converses about the Surface, to that pretended Philosophy which enters into the Depth of Things, and then comes gravely back with Informations and Discoveries, that in the inside they are good for nothing . . . . Whatever Philosopher or Projector can find out an Art to solder and patch up the Flaws and Imperfections of Nature, will deserve much better of Mankind, and teach us a more useful Science, than that so much in present Esteem, of widening and exposing them (like him who held *Anatomy* to be the ultimate End of *Physick*.) And he whose Fortunes and Dispositions have placed him in a convenient Station to enjoy the Fruits of this noble Art; He that can with *Epicurus* content his Ideas with the *Films* and *Images* that fly off upon his Senses from the *Superficies* of Things; Such a Man truly wise, creams off Nature, leaving the Sour and the Dregs for Philosophy and Reason to lap up. This is the sublime and refined Point of Felicity, called, *the Possession of being well deceived*; The Serene Peaceful State of being a Fool among Knaves.[28]

It is true that Swift was not there thinking specifically of philosophical scepticism. But scepticism, as Hume developed and practised it, similarly asserts the self-entangling impotence of rational inquiry which would enter 'into the depth of things', and deliberately turns to what is in some sense 'the superficies', the realm of appearances as stabilized by custom and convention, and the approval of society. In the *Enquiry concerning the Principles of Morals*, Hume wrote:

Though the philosophical truth of any proposition by no means depends on its tendency to promote the interests of society; yet a man has but a bad grace, who delivers a theory, however true, which he must confess, leads to a practice dangerous and pernicious. Why rake into those corners of nature which spread a nuisance all around? Why dig up the pestilence from

---

[28] Jonathan Swift, *A Tale of a Tub*, ed. Herbert Davis (Oxford, 1939: repr. 1965), pp. 109 f.

the pit in which it is buried? The ingenuity of your researches may be admired, but your systems will be detested; and mankind will agree, if they cannot refute them, to sink them, at least, in eternal silence and oblivion. Truths which are *pernicious* to society, if any such there be, will yield to errors which are salutary and *advantageous.*[29]

Hume might be said to be advocating and practising that 'noble art' of being pleased which Swift's satire condemns as culpably superficial, even though he knows quite as well as Swift how shallowly the roots of that attitude reach into the reason of things. Is this consciousness enough to protect him from the Swiftian accusation, to undo Swift's irony and make of this attitude a kind of wisdom? Or might it only blacken the case against him, as more knave than fool?

*   *   *

To look more closely at the quality of this special consciousness in Hume, let me return to the conclusion to Book One of the *Treatise*. At the beginning of its final section, Hume recapitulates the 'dangerous dilemma' to which his scepticism has brought him: to hold to the conclusions of the reason is to be sucked into an endlessly regressive spiral of uncertainty, but to abandon reason altogether is to abandon oneself to all the illusions of an unaccountable and credulous imagination. Hume presses the question of what his scepticism is good for, of how, given this situation, life ought to go on: 'The question is, how far we ought to yield to these illusions.'[30] Hume presents this question as unanswerable, as requiring an intolerable choice between absurdities; he can only, helplessly, retreat from 'ought' to 'is', to the recognition of what in fact is the case:

We have, therefore, no choice left but betwixt a false reason and none at all. For my part, I know not what ought to be done in the present case. I can only observe what is commonly done; which is, that this difficulty is seldom or never thought of; and even where it has once been present to the mind, is quickly forgot, and leaves but a small impression behind it.[31]

It is part of this retreat from speculation to actuality that 'we' becomes 'I'. As reason breaks down, nothing is left to Hume—like Montaigne—but his subjectivity, so that the only option left him is

[29] *Enquiries*, p. 279.   [30] *Treatise*, p. 267.   [31] Ibid. 268.

to express and record what are merely his 'fancies', his own personal and shifting 'humour' or inclination, and helplessly to follow where this leads. 'For my part, I know not what ought to be done' introduces a shift from an analytic, generalizing mode to what poses as the immediate registration of the flux of personal experience; we no longer seem to be reading a treatise, but instead a kind of dramatic monologue: 'But what have I here said, that reflections very refin'd and metaphysical have little or no influence upon us? This opinion I can scarce forbear retracting, and condemning from my present feeling and experience.'[32] A truly dynamic, reflexive scepticism can never stabilize itself, for it continually remembers that any philosophical 'position' exists only in a human mind, a mind which is, as Montaigne put it, *ondoyant*, various and fluctuating, inextricably involved with contingency and change; Hume's helplessness to do other than follow, through all apparent contradictions, his 'present feeling and experience' parallels Pope's conscious inconsistency in the *Epistle to Bolingbroke*, and would be taken to a comic extreme by Sterne in *Tristram Shandy*.[33] Here, submission to the present moment leads Hume into the crucial 'turn' already quoted, when he is rescued from his 'philosophical melancholy and delirium' not by reason but by such things as a good dinner, a game of backgammon, and the company of friends. In consequence, Hume reflects, 'I find myself absolutely and necessarily determin'd to live, and talk, and act like other people in the common affairs of life.'[34] Notice the ghost of an ambiguity in 'determined'. The main meaning is the philosophical one, as in 'determinism'; Hume *necessarily* lives like other people

---

[32] *Treatise*, p. 268
[33] There are several other examples in the *Treatise*, e.g. at p. 217: 'But to be ingenuous, I feel myself *at present* of a quite contrary sentiment . . .' [Hume's own italics]. George Horne, Bishop of Norwich, was not unperceptive in caricaturing Hume as a thinker of *Shandean* fluctuation and caprice. 'I could indeed wish, if it were possible, to have a scheme of thought, which would bear contemplating, at any time of the day; because, otherwise, a person must be at the expence of maintaining a brace of these metaphysical Hobby-Horses, one to mount in the morning, and the other in the afternoon. . . . In the Postscript to this Letter, a view will be taken of the HUMIAN system, taken exactly as it appeared to it's author at six o'clock in the evening.' *A Letter to Adam Smith Esq. LL.D. on the Life, Death and Philosophy of his Friend David Hume Esq.* (Oxford, 1777), pp. 7 f. and n.; quoted in *Philosophical Dialogues: Plato, Hume, Wittgenstein*, ed. Timothy Smiley, Proceedings of the British Academy, 85 (Oxford, 1995), p. 42 n.
[34] *Treatise*, p. 269.

in the common affairs of life, he has no choice, he is driven by what he is about to call 'the current of nature', just as in the semi-dramatic mode of this passage he represents his thoughts not as something over which he has any control, but as driven by 'present feeling and experience'. But, 'to be determined', in common usage—as used, in fact, 'in the common affairs of life'—has an almost opposite meaning: it implies the exercise of the will, the act of principled choice, in a situation where the question, 'What *ought* I to do?', is not an absurd or meaningless one. Accordingly, it is to this question that Hume now returns: if he must, in the end, 'yield to the current of nature', must rejoin the unenlightened, instinctual flow of life, then why should he torment himself in the service of such vain and impotent philosophy at all? Why not embrace what he calls the 'indolence' of drifting on the current of nature?

Notwithstanding that my natural propensity, and the course of my animal spirits and passions reduce me to this indolent belief in the general maxims of the world, I still feel such remains of my former disposition, that I am ready to throw all my books and papers into the fire, and resolve never more to renounce the pleasures of life for the sake of reasoning and philosophy. For these are my sentiments in that splenetic humour, which governs me at present. I may, nay I must yield to the current of nature, in submitting to my senses and understanding; and in this blind submission I shew most perfectly my sceptical disposition and principles. But does it follow, that I must strive against the current of nature, which leads me to indolence and pleasure; that I must seclude myself, in some measure, from the commerce and society of men, which is so agreeable; and that I must torture my brain with subtilities and sophistries, at the very time that I cannot satisfy myself concerning the reasonableness of so painful an application, nor have any tolerable prospect of arriving by its means at truth and certainty. Under what obligation do I lie of making such an abuse of time? And to what end can it serve either for the service of mankind, or for my own private interest?[35]

This internal debate is seriously meant. In the semi-dramatic work-ing of the passage, Hume allows us to feel the will to significance, the need for sanction, in real struggle against the current of nature, able neither to challenge the blind contingency of life nor to accept it. Yet the 'splenetic humour, which governs me at present' is, at the same time, indulged with a self-consciousness that verges on the

---

[35] Ibid. 269 f.

comic, or at least suggests a limit to the influence of such spleen.
(One might compare Pope's poetic resolutions to forsake poetry.)
If Hume elsewhere banters his readers, he seems here almost to be
bantering himself; he is both inside and outside his sentiments, one
feels, and it is this fluidity of consciousness which makes possible
his reply:

> These are the sentiments of my spleen and indolence; and indeed I must
> confess, that philosophy has nothing to oppose to them, and expects a
> victory more from the returns of a serious good-humour'd disposition,
> than from the force of reason and conviction. In all the incidents of life we
> ought still to preserve our scepticism. If we believe, that fire warms, or
> water refreshes, 'tis only because it costs us too much pains to think other-
> wise. Nay, if we are philosophers, it ought only to be upon sceptical prin-
> ciples, and from an inclination, which we feel to the employing ourselves
> after that manner. Where reason is lively, and mixes itself with some
> propensity, it ought to be assented to. Where it does not, it never can have
> any title to operate upon us.[36]

We have arrived at a resolution of Hume's dilemma. This has not
been achieved through any rational argument; the current of
nature—'disposition', 'inclination'—still holds sway. But this no
longer feels like a matter of 'blind submission', of coercion from
without, but rather something in which the sceptical intelligence
can participate. The mode is never wholly dramatic: if these quasi-
confessional passages give us the sceptical crisis from within, we
are made simultaneously aware of a cool observing consciousness
that enacts the possibility of 'preserving one's scepticism' even
while one's feelings carry one along. The rhetorical poise of the
entire passage holds open the possibility that the current of nature
which necessarily carries Hume along might also represent a movement freely assented to by a self outside that current, something
which not only 'is' but 'ought to be'. This elision of 'is' into 'ought'
marks the moment at which the two realms of intellectual reflection and natural feeling are felt to co-exist, rather than to be mutually exclusive:

> In all the incidents of life we ought still to preserve our scepticism.

> Where reason is lively, and mixes itself with some propensity, it ought to
> be assented to.

[36] *Treatise*, p. 270.

This meticulous equanimity represents both the triumph of philosophy over nature (since we thereby preserve our scepticism in the incidents of life) and the collapse of philosophy into nature (since this stance merely records 'the returns of a serious good-humoured disposition').

Perhaps the key element in this is the relaxation of the will. 'Indolence', here as elsewhere in Hume, is associated with a kind of wisdom. This is supported by the explicit argument later in the *Treatise* that the actions of the will are not free but arise from necessity. The argument flows from the account of necessary causation already established. By this account, necessary causation—even in a physical event, like one billiard-ball striking another—is (as far as we can ever know) never in fact a property of the event, out there in the physical world, but always a feeling in the mind of the spectator of the event, who has witnessed many similar events in the past and is thereby habituated to connect an idea of the impact with an idea of the second ball in movement. This habituation is what necessity means. Mental events are no different; there, too, any movement of the will is regularly connected in the mind of a spectator with the idea of a motive, or influencing passion: such connection is necessity. The actions of the will may feel free to the agent, Hume acknowledges, but they look determined to the percipient, which is just the same as saying that they are determined.

We may imagine we feel a liberty within ourselves; but a spectator can commonly infer our actions from our motives and character; and even where he cannot, he concludes in general, that he might, were he perfectly acquainted with every circumstance of our situation and temper, and the most secret springs of our complexion and disposition. Now this is the very essence of necessity, according to the foregoing doctrine.[37]

To hold that the will is subject to necessity, in this sense, is a doctrine which Hume insists makes no difference to practice, however radical its contribution to philosophical thought. Firstly, where the doctrine really bites is on the nature of necessary causation, not the nature of volition; if anyone should be startled it is the physicist, not the moralist. Secondly, Hume is merely giving a clear formulation of everyone's common-sense understanding of human

[37] Ibid. 408 f.

motivation; if we really believed the will were free, acts of volition would appear to us as matter of pure chance, and the notion of responsibility would collapse—which is patently not the case. And thirdly, the anxiety that this doctrine will somehow undermine morality, since if our volitions are necessitated they cannot justly attract sentiments of moral approval or disapproval, will not hold water: moral sentiments are impervious to such considerations, being grounded wholly in our apprehension of what qualities are useful or agreeable to oneself or others.

However, even if this account of the will does not in itself affect practical morality, it does throw light on Hume's escape from the 'dangerous dilemma' of scepticism as set out in the *Treatise*. The sense of dangerous dilemma rests upon the illusion of a free choice to be made. But what to the agent in the present moment feels like an intolerable dilemma, looks to the spectator like no such thing, since to the spectator however the will settles is how it had to settle. When Hume described the mind as 'a kind of theatre, where several perceptions successively make their appearance',[38] his metaphor pulls away from the strict logic of his argument by suggesting an audience watching the perceptions on the stage. What that metaphor of the theatre momentarily suggests is more assuredly conveyed by the poise or self-consciousness with which Hume writes, and which is especially marked at the moment of sceptical crisis. This permits a kind of self-spectatorship that releases Hume from the stress of choice into the saving flow of 'disposition', and reveals the moment of dilemma to be a freeze-frame abstraction from the moving current of events. Hume thus conjures out of the reduction to subjectivity something unexpectedly positive. What lies at the heart of this achievement is the proper relation of reflective consciousness to what may be called the current of nature.

This is something like Montaigne, whose manner of writing in the *Essais* expresses a comparable self-awareness: the movements of his mind appear to him as caprices or events with a life of their own, rather than as deliberations with which his whole consciousness can be identified. Hence the importance of spontaneity in Montaigne, the gesture of setting down his reflections as they come to him in the present moment, being both what he thinks and what he *happens* to think, which Hume echoes at crucial moments of the

---

[38] *Treatise*, p. 253.

Treatise. In Montaigne, this conscious spontaneity is underwritten by a lively sceptical sense of intellectual limitation, of the foolishness of trying to impose one's will on the stuff of life: general laws are unreliable, the linkage of cause and effect is impenetrable, and deliberation has absurdly little to do with outcomes, whether on the battlefield, in medical treatment, or in bed. In writing as in everything else, trying for a premeditated end is unwise, even counter-productive:

I know experimentally, a Disposition so impatient of a tedious and elaborate Premeditation, that if it do not go frankly and gayly to work, can perform nothing to purpose . . . . The solicitude of doing well, and a certain striving and contending of a mind too far strain'd, and over-bent upon its Undertaking, breaks, and hinders it self, like Water, that by force of its own pressing violence and abundance, cannot find a ready issue through the neck of a Bottle, or a narrow Sluice . . . I am always worst in my own possession, and when wholly at my own dispose. Accident has more title to any thing that comes from me, than I; Occasion, Company, and even the very rising and falling of my own Voice, extract more from my Fancy, than I can find when I examine and employ it by my self.[39]

The spontaneity of the writing discovers a positive value in this relaxation of the will, this openness to contingency; for Montaigne as for Hume, the reflective consciousness does well to align itself with a deeper current of nature, which is felt as positively benign. There is, however, an important difference between them in this respect: the greater role Hume gives to society and social convention. When Montaigne wishes to assert the bedrock of human nature, that which lies beneath the restless caprices of the conscious intellect, he does so in various ways: through appeal to the pains and pleasures of the body, through the precious image of 'Life full and pure' that he finds in the figure of Socrates or in the anecdotes recorded by his beloved Plutarch, or through the depth and comprehensiveness of his self-portrait, which shows how 'every Man carries the entire form of human Condition'.[40] He reaches the universal through the exploration of his own individuality, in solitude; it is part of their meaning that the *Essais* were written in a room in a tower, by a man retired from public life, with books as his most vital companions, his one profoundly intimate relationship

---

[39] Montaigne, i.56 f. (ch. 10).   [40] Ibid. iii.548 (ch. 13); iii.27 (ch. 2).

a thing of the past.[41] For Hume, by contrast, man, as a solitary individual, 'is altogether insufficient to support himself', and he writes with striking force of the pleasure of acquaintance and company:

> The mind . . . naturally seeks after foreign objects, which may produce a lively sensation, and agitate the spirits. On the appearance of such an object it awakes, as it were, from a dream: The blood flows with a new tide: The heart is elevated: And the whole man acquires a vigour, which he cannot command in his solitary and calm moments. Hence company is naturally so rejoicing, as presenting the liveliest of all objects.[42]

Man is crucially a social being. Nature asserts herself through such things as a game of backgammon and a good dinner-party: social pastimes. The world of common sense and consensus has much to do with convention: and convention is made in society. Of course, it is true that such a fundamental matter as our belief in causation and an external world, product of conditioning though it is, does not depend upon the influence of society, but rather upon a 'blind and powerful instinct of nature'.[43] But when it comes to morality, Hume's presumption is that our moral sentiments are sufficiently alike to provide a workable common standard—and this depends crucially on the influence of social custom:

> The intercourse of sentiments, therefore, in society and conversation, makes us form some general inalterable standard, by which we may approve or disapprove of characters and manners. And tho' the *heart* does not always take part with those general notions, or regulate its love and hatred by them, yet are they sufficient for discourse, and serve all our purposes in company, in the pulpit, on the theatre, and in the schools.[44]

That last sentence is remarkable. Our approval or disapproval of characters and manners by a general standard, is clearly distinguishable from the feelings of the heart. Humean morality is 'sufficient for discourse' and for all public purposes, but it depends upon

[41] See e.g. the essay 'Of Solitude'.
[42] *Treatise*, pp. 352 f. The emphasis on company can be understood as a reaction against the sense of personal and epistemological isolation expressed in the *Treatise*; see John Sitter, *Literary Loneliness in Mid-Eighteenth-Century England* (Ithaca, NY and London, 1982), pp. 19–49, e.g. p. 23: 'The chamber and the moment are the boundaries of Hume's experience as writer, and both are invoked frequently in ways which emphasize the privacy of all experience.'
[43] *Enquiries*, p. 151.
[44] *Treatise*, p. 603.

a species of social fiction, for our sentiments as participants in polite society are liable to differ from what they would otherwise be, or from what 'the *heart*' would recognize as its own:

In order to render conversation, and the intercourse of minds more easy and agreeable, good-manners have been invented, and have carried the matter somewhat farther. Wherever nature has given the mind a propensity to any vice, or to any passion disagreeable to others, refined breeding has taught men to throw the biass on the opposite side, and to preserve, in all their behaviour, the appearance of sentiments different from those to which they naturally incline.[45]

This is not to imply that the social world is the realm of downright deception and untruth. No-one who understands what participation in society involves, is positively deceived. Writing to his friend James Edmonstoune, Hume resisted the suggestion that a churchman who has doubts concerning the Christian faith should declare them, and resign from holy orders:

If the thing were worthy being treated gravely, I should tell him, that the Pythian oracle, with the approbation of Xenophon, advised every one to worship the gods—νομω πολεωσ [according to the law of the city]. I wish it were still in my power to be a hypocrite in this particular. The common duties of society usually require it; and the ecclesiastical profession only adds a little more to an innocent dissimulation, or rather simulation, without which it is impossible to pass through the world. Am I a liar, because I order my servant to say, I am not at home, when I do not desire to see company?[46]

This may sound like the most disreputable kind of worldly cynicism. Certainly it is a stance that could be used to license such cynicism. Yet Hume is no cynic; and his advice to Edmonstoune parallels his admiring description of Cicero as sceptic in 'The Natural History of Religion':

Whatever sceptical liberties that great man might use, in his writings or in philosophical conversation; he yet avoided, in the common conduct of life, the imputation of deism and profaneness. Even in his own family, and to his wife, *Terentia*, whom he highly trusted, he was willing to appear a devout religionist; and there remains a letter, addrest to her, in which he

[45] 'Of the Rise and Progress of the Arts and Sciences', in Hume, *Essays*, ed. Miller, p. 132.
[46] *The Letters of David Hume*, ed. J. Y. T. Greig, 2 vols. (Oxford, 1932), i.439 f. (no. 238; April 1764).

seriously desires her to offer sacrifice to *Apollo* and *Aesculapius*, in gratitude for the recovery of his health. . . . The same *Cicero*, who affected, in
his own family, to appear a devout religionist, makes no scruple, in a
public court of judicature, of treating the doctrine of a future state as a
most ridiculous fable.[47]

Cicero spoke differently about the gods in philosophical conversation, with his family, and in the law-court; this variousness, Hume
implies, is no hypocritical conformism but the true expression of
Cicero's scepticism. Such doubleness is not duplicity.[48] The charge
of *insincerity*, to which Cicero appears to lie so open, depends
upon the notion, perhaps essentially Romantic, of an authentic
inner self, that lies 'behind' social behaviour and gives the measure
of its truth and value. Yet Hume was capable of regarding the 'self'
as an illusion, being 'nothing but a heap or collection of different
perceptions', or 'a kind of theatre', where several perceptions
successively make their appearance';[49] this view must give corre-
spondingly greater reality to the way in which we perform
ourselves in public, to what is realized through our social role. In
an early letter written during his first stay in France, Hume
describes how 'Expressions of Politeness' should be managed:

These Ceremonies ought to be so contriv'd, as that, tho they do not
deceive, nor pass for sincere, yet still they please by their Appearance, &
lead the Mind by its own Consent & Knowledge, into an agreeable
Delusion. One may err by running into either of the two Extremes, that of
making them too like Truth or too remote from it; tho we may observe,
that the first is scarce possible, because whenever any Expression or Action
becomes customary it can deceive no body. . . . The French err in the
contrary Extreme, that of making their Civilities too remote from Truth;
which is a Fault, tho they are not design'd to be believ'd; just as it is a
Transgression of Rules in a Dramatic Poet to mix any Improbabilities with
his Fable; tho' tis certain that in the representation, the Scenes, Lights,
Company & a thousand other Circumstances, make it impossible he can
ever deceive.[50]

[47] David Hume, *The Natural History of Religion and Dialogues concerning
Natural Religion*, ed. A. Wayne Colver and John Valdimir Price (Oxford, 1976), pp.
73, 79.
[48] Similarly, in *A Letter from a Gentleman to his Friend in Edinburgh*
(Edinburgh, 1745; ed. Ernest C. Mossner and John V. Price, Edinburgh, 1967), in
which Hume protested the innocence of the doctrines in the *Treatise*, he cited Cicero
with Socrates as the 'most religious' of the classical philosophers, 'who both of them
carried their Philosophical Doubts to the highest Degree of Scepticism' (pp. 21).
[49] *Treatise*, pp. 207, 253.   [50] *Letters*, i.20 (no. 4; Sept. 1734).

This letter provides the perfect gloss on Hume's advice to Edmonstoune and his admiration for Cicero. Polite society at its finest provides the sceptic with a model of how to live by appearances, in a situation where there can be no direct access to truth. It becomes possible to see how the notion of an 'innocent . . . simulation, without which it is impossible to pass through the world', brings together the whole enterprise of Humean scepticism with the art of social living. Our belief in causation and an external world depends, according to Hume, on an act of simulation, a fiction of the imagination, but this is a fiction to which we are habituated at so deep a level, that only the most intense and abstruse effort of philosophical thought can, for a moment, expose it as such. But in the case of our moral beliefs, the element of fiction—the fiction by which we identify with our socially constructed selves, and accept consensus and convention as a real standard—lies much closer to the surface, right on the threshold of consciousness. Such beliefs can be entertained, with the mind's consent and knowledge, as an 'agreeable Delusion'; just as in the theatre (and perhaps in our experience of literature generally) we neither disbelieve nor are deceived. A manner which recognizes and expresses this state of affairs, fulfilling Hume's aim of 'preserving one's scepticism in the common affairs of life', readily allies itself with the manner required for intelligent participation in society, especially where the dominant culture is one of highly self-aware politeness, highly conscious sociability. Scepticism naturally tends to throw one back on established custom and convention, but Hume's concern with sociability goes deeper than that: not only does all his philosophy lead towards an emphasis on social cohesion and a cherishing of the social virtues, but the eighteenth-century game of polite society, whose participants must act and communicate through acknowledged conventions and surfaces without becoming conventional or superficial, offers ideal conditions for the sceptic to practise the common affairs of life without altogether abandoning the sceptical consciousness which brought him there. A great deal lies behind Hume's reference to 'that art, the most useful and agreeable of any, *l'Art de Vivre*, the art of society and conversation'.[51]

Hence the interest of the shape taken by Hume's literary career after the failure of the *Treatise* to win an audience. After that work

[51] 'Of Civil Liberty', in *Essays*, ed. Miller, p. 91.

fell '*dead-born from the press*'[52] in 1739–40, he first devoted himself to the more 'sociable' genre of the essay, with the model of the famous *Spectator* papers very much in view, and it was in an accessibly essayistic style that the core arguments of the *Treatise* were then recast as *An Enquiry concerning Human Understanding* (at first titled *Philosophical Essays concerning Human Understanding*), published in 1748, and *An Enquiry concerning the Principles of Morals*, published in 1751.[53] The felicity of the Addisonian essay lay in pitching itself, stylistically and intellectually, within the circle of the readily apprehensible and conventionally acceptable, while drawing on a reflective intelligence in a way that implied a certain critical detachment from that milieu: a felicity nicely figured in the transparent fiction of 'Mr Spectator', the nominal author, half participant in, half detached observer of the affairs of the social world. Addison wrote that he wished to bring philosophy into the coffee-houses and drawing-rooms of polite society, and as an essayist Hume similarly introduces himself to his public as an ambassador from the '*learned*' to the '*conversible*' world.[54] This idea is more fully developed at the start of the first *Enquiry*, where Hume proposes a distinction between two kinds of philosophizing: the analytic or 'abstruse', as typified by Aristotle or Locke, devoted to the investigation of its topic without being overly concerned to move or please its reader, and the rhetorically effective and 'easy', typified by Cicero or Addison, which appeals to the imagination and the affections in painting the most 'amiable' and eloquent picture of virtue, while never straying far from the natural sentiments of common life. The discussion of these two kinds is developed into an apology for the analytic or abstruse, warning the reader that some hard thinking lies ahead, but only while praising the easy kind so warmly, and conducting itself in such an Addisonian style of sweetly-reasonable consideration for where the reader is coming from, that the effect is of a double allegiance:

52 'My Own Life', in *Essays*, ed. Miller, p. xxxiv.
53 Two excellent accounts of this shift can be found in John Sitter, *Literary Loneliness in Mid-Eighteenth-Century England* (Ithaca, NY and London. 1982), ch. 1: 'Hume's Stylistic Emergence', and M. A. Box, *The Suasive Art of David Hume* (Princeton, 1990), whose analysis coincides with my own at several points, although always tending to identify Hume with the voice which plays down the disturbing potential of his scepticism.
54 'Of Essay-Writing', in *Essays*, ed. Miller, pp. 533–7.

Happy, if we can unite the boundaries of the different species of philosophy, by reconciling profound enquiry with clearness, and truth with novelty! And still more happy, if, reasoning in this easy manner, we can undermine the foundations of an abstruse philosophy, which seems to have hitherto served only as a shelter for superstition, and a cover to absurdity and error![55]

This goal of expressing the results of 'profound enquiry'—the fruits of the *Treatise*—in an Addisonian, 'easy manner' is fundamental to both *Enquiries*, as also to the *Dialogues concerning Natural Religion*, where the dialogue form is chosen because it 'carries us, in a manner, into Company; and unites the two greatest and purest Pleasures of human Life, Study and Society'.[56]

In the quotation just given, Hume speaks of 'reasoning in this easy manner'. That word 'easy' is worth dwelling on, as a term that holds together a social grace with an inner poise: it implies a state of freedom from all apparent effort or striving, in which all friction between consciousness and instinct has disappeared, and the self is perfectly assimilated to the available forms of expression, both linguistic and social. It stands for a widely held eighteenth-century ideal of social behaviour and literary style, of which Addison was the acknowledged model. To read Addison, and still more to read Pope, is to come into contact with an art that recognizes no dichotomy, although it may exploit a distance, between the conscious performance of a social gesture and the serious expression of personal conviction. But in the next generation, after the death of Pope, that ideal seems to have become increasingly impracticable: Johnson's *Rambler* essays were written in a style—strenuous, hard, complex, weighty—that was pointedly the opposite of 'easy'; in this style a dynamic sense of the likely inadequacy of the conventional currency of discourse is built into the medium. Such a non-easy manner places Johnson on one side of an opening divide, as asserting an individual integrity that cannot be altogether assimilated to the ethos of sociable living and polite culture. Even Hume's paradigm case of a wholly 'innocent simulation' ordained by social convention, telling one's servant to say one is not at home

---

[55] *Enquiries*, p. 16.
[56] *Religion*, p. 144. For an account of the *Enquiries*, in particular, which both overlaps with and differs from what follows, see John J. Richetti, *Philosophical Writing: Locke, Berkeley, Hume* (Cambridge, Mass., and London, 1983), pp. 254–63.

when one desires not to see company, is something that Johnson found dubious; Boswell records how Johnson 'would not allow his servant to say he was not at home when he really was. "A servant's strict regard for truth," (said he) "must be weakened by such a practice. A philosopher may know that it is merely a form of denial; but few servants are such nice distinguishers."' Boswell found such scrupulosity overdone, commenting that every servant 'understands saying his master is not at home, not at all as the affirmation of a fact, but as customary words, intimating that his master wishes not to be seen; so that there can be no bad effect from it.'[57] But it is precisely the use of 'customary words' to which Johnson is objecting. This is a tiny example, trivial in itself, of a fundamental stubbornness in Johnson that bears directly on his antagonism to Hume. This antagonism was, no doubt, fuelled largely by Hume's insinuations against Christianity, an area in which Johnson's own anxieties could render him too dogmatic to be intelligent; when Boswell reported that Hume was dying with every appearance of tranquillity, Johnson retorted that he must be either shamming or clinically insane. But Johnson could also criticize Humean scepticism in more interesting ways:

We can have no dependance upon that instinctive, that constitutional goodness which is not founded upon principle. I grant you that such a man may be a very amiable member of society. I can conceive him placed in such a situation that he is not much tempted to deviate from what is right . . . . But if such a man stood in need of money, I should not like to trust him; and I should certainly not trust him with young ladies, for *there* there is always temptation. Hume, and other sceptical innovators, are vain men, and will gratify themselves at any expence.[58]

Johnson finds a large objection in the thought that the end of Hume's ethics is to render man 'a very amiable member of society'. No one could place more emphasis than Johnson on the need to live in society rather than in solitude, but Johnsonian society is a congregation of individuals, a place of competition, exchange, and debate, in which a code of amiability, or an easy manner, cannot reach very far without becoming a kind of lie: 'We are formed for society, not for combination; we are equally unqualified to live in a close connection with our fellow beings, and in total separation from them: we are attracted towards each other by general sympathy, but kept back from contact by private interests.'[59]

Johnson's stance will be more fully discussed in a later chapter, but enough has been said to illustrate his suspicion of convention, and his reservations about sociability. The contrast with Hume supplies a kind of criterion for the success of Hume's writing. For the remainder of this chapter, I want to emphasize the 'sociable' as at the very heart of what Hume is doing in the two *Enquiries* and the *Dialogues*, to look at how his 'easy manner' in those works accommodates the radicalism of his sceptical thought, and to inquire how far that manner can resist the kind of critique that might be extrapolated from Swift or from Johnson.

*   *   *

These three works need to be treated separately, for each of them sets up a different relationship with its reader. The work which Hume regarded as 'incomparably the best'[60] was the *Enquiry concerning the Principles of Morals*, which is certainly the most *amiable* of all his longer writings. In rewriting Book Three of the *Treatise* as the *Principles*, Hume did more than just simplify the logic, shorten the sentences and supply concrete examples. He adopted an angle of presentation which is that of civilized and moderate common sense, writing in a manner that considerately offers to identify itself with the conventional good sense of the reader. This can be seen both in the changes he made to his material, and in the tone which he adopts. The *Principles* begins, 'Disputes with men, pertinaciously obstinate in their principles, are, of all others, the most irksome'[61] and we immediately know where we are: in the company of a man too well-bred to press an argument in a way that will be 'irksome' in company, and who knows (rather like Addison) the value of a proposition phrased in such a way that it seems no reasonable person could possibly disagree with it. The next paragraph dismisses those who, absurdly, have 'denied the reality of moral distinctions'—another impeccable gesture which assures us at once that our author is not a man to involve himself in such subversive paradoxes. And when

[59] *Johnson*, ii.359 f. (*Adventurer* 45).
[60] 'My Own Life', in *Essays*, ed. Miller, p. xxxvi; see also *Letters*, i.175 and i.227.   [61] *Enquiries*, p. 169.

Hume then opens the more substantial question of whether morals
are derived from reason or from sentiment, he appears to settle for
a tactful compromise:

These arguments on each side (and many more might be produced) are so
plausible, that I am apt to suspect, they may, the one as well as the other,
be solid and satisfactory, and that *reason* and *sentiment* concur in almost
all moral determinations and conclusions. The final sentence, it is probable, which pronounces characters and actions amiable or odious, praise-
worthy or blameable; that which stamps on them the mark of honour or
infamy, approbation or censure; that which renders morality an active
principle and constitutes virtue our happiness, and vice our misery: it is
probable, I say, that this final sentence depends on some internal sense or
feeling, which nature has made universal in the whole species. For what
else can have an influence of this nature? But in order to pave the way for
such a sentiment, and give a proper discernment of its object, it is often
necessary, we find, that much reasoning should precede, that nice distinctions be made, just conclusions drawn, distant comparisons formed.[62]

On the surface, this reads very unlike Book Three of the *Treatise*,
which begins with a section positively arguing that moral distinctions are not derived from reason, and that 'ought' can therefore
never be derived from 'is'—a principle which subverts 'all the
vulgar systems of morality'. In fact, Hume's position in the
Principles has not changed. We may need reason to establish the
facts of the case, but our moral response to those facts, once established, derives wholly from sentiment, not reason. However, the
primacy of sentiment is spelt out only in an appendix, and even
there Hume is careful to finish with the vague but pious-sounding
statement that the standard of our moral sentiments, 'arising from
the internal frame and constitution of animals, is ultimately derived
from that Supreme Will, which bestowed on each being its peculiar
nature, and arranged the several classes and orders of existence.'[63]
Meanwhile the corollary, that our moral judgements are not rationally justifiable, which Hume made so provocatively prominent in
the *Treatise*, is kept firmly out of sight.

   A similarly tactful omission is the emphasis on justice as an 'artificial' virtue, which dominated the central section of Book Three of
the *Treatise*. Hume understands justice as a pure convention
adopted for the benefit of society; the sense of justice is the prod-

[62] *Enquiries*, p. 172 f.   [63] Ibid. 294.

uct of enlightened self-interest and social conditioning. In the *Principles* Hume's analysis is the same, but from the socialized point of view from which it is now written, the inference that the sense of justice is artificial rather than natural can scarcely be registered. (It survives only in a footnote to one of the appendices, expressed in the most conciliatory and unemphatic terms.)[64] This permits Hume to put clear water between himself and such disreputable thinkers as Mandeville and Hobbes, who are stigmatized with the bugaboo term of 'sceptic':

From the apparent usefulness of the social virtues, it has readily been inferred by sceptics, both ancient and modern, that all moral distinctions arise from education . . . Nothing can be more superficial than this paradox of the sceptics; and it were well, if, in the abstruser studies of logic and metaphysics, we could as easily obviate the cavils of that sect, as in the practical and more intelligible sciences of politics and morals.[65]

Against the 'cavils' of the sceptics, Hume's tone assumes a solidarity with all right-thinking members of society. Even where their arguments seem to have force, those who entertain them are still 'that sect', a marginal group: 'we' are never sceptics. This wholesome impression is strengthened by the emphasis Hume places on rebutting those ugly theories which would reduce all morality to the principle of self-love. Spectacles of utility give us pleasure, Hume points out, even where there is no direct benefit to ourselves. In the *Treatise* this had been explained largely in terms of 'the force of *sympathy*'. 'As in strings equally wound up, the motion of one communicates itself to the rest; so all the affections readily pass from one person to another, and beget correspondent movements in every human creature.'[66] Hume's example there is the unease and anxiety we will feel in the presence of a patient being prepared for surgery (without anaesthetic, of course). But in the *Principles* this quasi-mechanical contagiousness of emotion is redescribed as 'the benevolent principle', a fundamental principle of 'humanity or a concern for others'.[67] Commentators differ over whether this

---

[64] 'Natural may be opposed, either to what is *unusual, miraculous*, or *artificial*. In the two former senses, justice and property are undoubtedly natural. But as they suppose reason, forethought, design, and a social union and confederacy among men, perhaps that epithet cannot strictly, in the last sense, be applied to them. . . . But all these disputes are merely verbal.' *Enquiries*, p. 307 n.

[65] Ibid. 214.   [66] *Treatise*, pp. 575 f.

[67] *Enquiries*, p. 231.

represents a shift in Hume's position, but what it certainly involves is a shift in tone: our capacity for benevolent pleasure in all that is useful or agreeable to mankind is the essence of morality, and, described in glowing terms, becomes a handsome compliment to human nature.

This sense of virtue as bound up in the codes of social approval, is nicely caught in the final section of the *Principles*, where Hume gives his portrait of the moral ideal. Cleanthes is not only the kind of man you would wish your daughter to marry, he is the kind of man your friends will congratulate you on your daughter marrying:

You are very happy, we shall suppose one to say, addressing himself to another, that you have given your daughter to Cleanthes. He is a man of honour and humanity. Every one, who has any intercourse with him, is sure of *fair* and *kind* treatment. I congratulate you too, says another, on the promising expectations of this son-in-law; whose assiduous application to the study of the laws, whose quick penetration and early knowledge both of men and business, prognosticate the greatest honours and advancement. You surprise me, replies a third, when you talk of Cleanthes as a man of business and application. I met him lately in a circle of the gayest company, and he was the very life and soul of our conversation: so much wit with good manners; so much gallantry without affectation; so much ingenious knowledge so genteelly delivered, I have never before observed in any one. You would admire him still more, says a fourth, if you knew him more familiarly. That cheerfulness, which you might remark in him, is not a sudden flash struck out by company: it runs through the whole tenor of his life, and preserves a perpetual serenity on his countenance, and tranquillity in his soul. He has met with severe trials, misfortunes as well as dangers; and by his greatness of mind, was still superior to all of them. The image, gentlemen, which you have here delineated of Cleanthes, cried I, is that of accomplished merit. Each of you has given a stroke of the pencil to his figure; and you have unawares exceeded all the pictures drawn by Gratian or Castiglione. A philosopher might select this character as a model of perfect virtue.[68]

It may be true that nothing can be added to this list. Cleanthes' four acquaintances together describe Hume's fourfold understanding of virtue: his qualities make him both useful and agreeable to himself and others. But it is hard to warm to a moral ideal whose merits can be so completely apprehended in the idiom of the eighteenth-century drawing-room; an impression of superficiality is hard to

[68] *Enquiries*, p. 269 f.

resist. This is where Johnson's ungenteel objection may shoulder its way in: 'We can have no dependence upon that instinctive, that constitutional goodness, which is not founded upon principle. I grant you that such a man may be a very amiable member of society . . . . But if such a man stood in need of money, I should not like to trust him.'[69] Hume actually anticipates this kind of objection at the end of the *Principles*:

That *honesty is the best policy*, may be a good general rule, but is liable to many exceptions; and he, it may perhaps be thought, conducts himself with most wisdom, who observes the general rule, and takes advantage of all the exceptions.

(If justice rests upon utility, and vice exists nowhere except in the disapproving consciousness of others, why not quietly pocket the wallet one sees dropped in the street?)

I must confess that, if a man think that this reasoning much requires an answer, it will be a little difficult to find any which will to him appear satisfactory and convincing. If his heart rebel not against such pernicious maxims, if he feel no reluctance to the thoughts of villainy or baseness, he has indeed lost a considerable motive to virtue; and we may expect that his practice will be answerable to his speculation.[70]

That is to say, such an act would not be the act of a gentleman. This is not, Johnson would think, a very strong reply. Swift might well hear in it the voice of a fool among knaves. Yet it is perfectly in keeping with the socially accommodating, amiable manner in which the whole of the *Principles* is cast: a manner which is not naive or effete, because informed by Hume's understanding of the folly of rejecting the claims of convention in the search for something more substantial. If the *Principles* seems bland, the value of such blandness can be glossed by this passage from the *History*, where Hume is discussing the actions of the parliamentarians during the Civil War:

Among the generality of men, educated in regular, civilised societies, the sentiments of shame, duty, honor, have considerable authority, and serve to counterballance and direct the motives, derived from private advantage: But, where fanaticism predominated to such a degree as among the parliamentary forces, all these salutary principles lost their credit, and were

69 Boswell, *Life*, i.443 f. (July 1763).
70 *Enquiries*, pp. 282 f.

regarded as mere human inventions, yea moral institutions, fitter for heathens than for christians . . . . And, beside the strange corruptions engendered by this spirit, it eluded and loosened all the ties of morality, and gave intire scope, and even sanction to the selfishness and ambition, which so commonly adhere to the human mind.[71]

What Hume achieves by his amiable manner is a powerful if largely tacit leverage against his real target: those false, because anti-social, moralities of repression, accusation, self-denial, and self-righteousness which include so much of traditional Christianity. Such 'strange corruptions' can have no *entrée* in polite society, which, at its best, understands, just as clearly as the philosophical sceptic, the necessary superficiality of the ties which hold society together.

One can thus understand why Hume thought the *Principles* his best work. His faithful translation of the radicalism of the *Treatise* into the idiom of innocent amiability is a remarkable feat. Yet one can also understand why few of Hume's readers have agreed with his high opinion. The translation is too smoothly done; Hume identifies himself so completely with the mores of polite society, he invokes the conventions so blandly from within, that we seem to lose all contact with any saving ironic consciousness of the true nature of the enterprise. Hume's innocence seems to be sealed in a compartment quite separate from his scepticism.

That is not entirely fair. A certain ironic consciousness attaches itself to the *Principles* merely from the fact that Hume wrote it. Given his notoriety as an infidel and an anti-religionist, the impeccable amiability of the *Principles* amounts almost to a provocation, like some of the local professions of innocence in the *Treatise*. Perfectly ingenuous in itself, we nonetheless understand it to be a gesture, a performance, a social act, an 'innocent simulation' which is also a conscious simulation of innocence. But this understanding depends upon our knowledge of Hume's other works, and remains finally hypothetical; it is not realized in the manner of the writing.

The same is not true of the *Enquiry concerning Human Understanding*. This offers a shorter and somewhat simplified version of Hume's sceptical epistemology, and here too, without falsifying the radicalism of his thought, Hume explicates his scepticism into generally wholesome and innocent outcomes. The final

---

[71] David Hume, *The History of Great Britain*, ed. Duncan Forbes (Harmondsworth, 1970), p. 627.

section, in particular, reprises the concluding section of Book One of the *Treatise* without any of that work's sense of immediate personal crisis: the giddying paradoxes and contradictions of Hume's radical scepticism are rehearsed, and their logical force acknowledged, by a Hume who stands outside them, on the further shore of common sense, and who treats them from the start as curiosities in the history of philosophical thought. This stance makes the 'turn' to common sense far less traumatic, distinctly 'easier', than it was in the *Treatise*:

The great subverter of *Pyrrhonism* or the excessive principles of scepticism is action, and employment, and the occupations of common life. These principles may flourish and triumph in the schools; where it is, indeed, difficult, if not impossible, to refute them. But as soon as they leave the shade, and by the presence of the real objects, which actuate our passions and sentiments, are put in opposition to the more powerful principles of our nature, they vanish like smoke, and leave the most determined sceptic in the same condition as other mortals. . . . When he awakes from his dream, he will be the first to join in the laugh against himself, and to confess, that all his objections are mere amusement, and can have no other tendency than to show the whimsical condition of mankind, who must act and reason and believe; though they are not able, by their most diligent enquiry, to satisfy themselves concerning the foundation of these operations, or to remove the objections, which may be raised against them.[72]

'He will be the first to join in the laugh against himself': the route to sanity lies, once more, through society. The real use of such *'excessive* scepticism', Hume continues, is in the *'mitigated* scepticism' to which it leads, once 'corrected by common sense and reflection'. Such corrected and mitigated scepticism teaches us two useful lessons in what might be described as intellectual good manners: not to be 'affirmative and dogmatical' in our opinions, and modestly to confine our speculations (except in pure mathematics) to the sphere of empirical fact.[73] All this seems sensible, moderate, and constructive—but not merely bland, for in this *Enquiry* the affirmations of innocence are accompanied by a play of irony that reminds us how Hume *might* be a dangerous subversive, even if that suggestion is, teasingly, made only to be withdrawn. The concluding paragraph is a striking example, as Hume returns to the destructive, rather than constructive, implications of his scepticism:

> When we run over libraries, persuaded of these principles, what havoc must we make? If we take in our hand any volume; of divinity or school metaphysics, for instance; let us ask, *Does it contain any abstract reasoning concerning quantity or number?* No. *Does it contain any experimental reasoning concerning matter of fact and existence?* No. Commit it then to the flames: for it can contain nothing but sophistry and illusion.[74]

The *Enquiry* closes with an image of Hume as his enemies saw him, maker of havoc and intellectual incendiary. This image is offered, however, with a smile, as a kind of joke; we feel this in the urbanity of tone and the consciously melodramatic swagger of the final sentence. Even while Hume insists, not unseriously, on the radicalism of his thought, we are aware of a play of irony which is not unsociable, akin to what Adam Smith described as Hume's special quality of delightful 'raillery' in company:

> His constant pleasantry was the genuine effusion of good-nature and good-humour, tempered with delicacy and modesty, and without even the slightest tincture of malignity, so frequently the disagreeable source of what is called wit in other men. It never was the meaning of his raillery to mortify; and therefore, far from offending, it seldom failed to please and delight, even those who were the objects of it.[75]

The pleasantry which connects the sceptical with the sociable, the play of irony in which depths are not altogether opposed to surfaces, enacts the reassurance that, despite or even because of the destructive potential of Hume's philosophy, its ultimate tendency is benign. The reader is encouraged to recall that the preceding page has listed many intellectual disciplines that do concern matters of fact and may therefore survive the flames; 'divinity or school metaphysics' may well be the *only* categories destined for the bonfire, and these, Hume's easy manner suggests, can readily be spared.

There is a further complication attached to this reading, however, and it lies with the word 'divinity' and the studied casualness with which Hume slips it into the pile marked for destruction. In a way that has no precedent in the *Treatise*, the *Enquiry* is structured so as to suggest that Hume's epistemological scepticism

---

74 *Enquiries*, p. 165.
75 'Letter . . . to William Strahan', in Hume, *Essays*, ed. Miller, p. xlviii.

leads to, and is advanced largely for the sake of, an attack upon religion. The work comprises twelve short sections. By the middle of the eighth section the exposition of the core arguments from the *Treatise* is effectively complete; Hume has just rehearsed his argument against the freedom of the will, based on his analysis of causation and necessary connection. He then pauses, as it were, to raise the question of where this argument tends:

There is no method of reasoning more common, and yet none more blameable, than, in philosophical disputes, to endeavour the refutation of any hypothesis, by a pretence of its dangerous consequences to religion and morality. When any opinion leads to absurdities, it is certainly false; but it is not certain that an opinion is false, because it is of dangerous consequence. Such topics, therefore, ought entirely to be forborne; as serving nothing to the discovery of truth, but only to make the person of an antagonist odious. This I observe in general, without pretending to draw any advantage from it. I frankly submit to an examination of this kind, and shall venture to affirm that the doctrines, both of necessity and liberty, as above explained, are not only consistent with morality, but are absolutely essential to its support.[76]

This declaration of wholesome intent, of the innocent consequences of his philosophizing, is supported, once more, by Hume's manner, by the offer of a 'frank' and easy relationship with the reader. To deny the freedom of the will sounds like a threat to conventional morality, but trust me, Hume tells us, and I will show you that it is nothing of the kind; in advancing these doctrines I have no hidden agenda. And he goes on to argue that the conventional notion of moral responsibility in fact depends upon determinism in his sense; the reality of 'moral ill', of the 'distinction between vice and virtue', is not in the least diminished. 'Nothing, therefore, can be more innocent, at least, than this doctrine.'[77] Yet a suspicious reader, jealous for the prerogatives of religion, might find something less than 'frank', something positively disingenuous, in the way Hume shifts, in the quotation given above, from 'religion and morality' to 'morality' alone. And indeed it transpires that the same argument which saves the notion of moral responsibility, jeopardizes religion; for the idea of a chain of causes running through the determinations of the will would seem, Hume rather pointedly confesses, to make God the ultimate 'author of sin and

[76] *Enquiries*, p. 96 f.   [77] Ibid. 97.

moral turpitude'.[78] Having raised this objection, Hume admits that
it cannot be resolved:

> These are mysteries, which mere natural and unassisted reason is very unfit
> to handle; and whatever system she embraces, she must find herself
> involved in inextricable difficulties, and even contradictions, at every step
> which she takes with regard to such subjects. . . . Happy, if she be thence
> sensible of her temerity, when she pries into these sublime mysteries; and
> leaving a scene so full of obscurities and perplexities, return, with suitable
> modesty, to her true and proper province, the examination of common life;
> where she will find difficulties enough to employ her enquiries, without
> launching into so boundless an ocean of doubt, uncertainty, and contra-
> diction![79]

Such sentiments are orthodox enough; Johnson makes a similar
point against Soame Jenyns. And the turn from the contradictions
uncovered by reason to the examination of common life is entirely
characteristic of Hume. No unprejudiced reader could feel sure that
'these sublime mysteries' amounts to a sneer. But the phrase does
sound, at the least, consciously diplomatic; the 'easy manner' no
longer seems quite trustworthy.

This trickle of suspicion turns into a flood when the reader
comes to sections 10 and 11. The notorious essay on miracles
argues that no testimony can ever amount to evidence strong
enough for the rational crediting of a miraculous event; most of the
examples are taken from pagan or Catholic (therefore 'supersti-
tious') claims, but it is clear that nothing excludes the miracles
recounted in Scripture from this critique. And having dealt with the
evidence of revelation, section 11 then deals with the evidence of
creation, denying that a providential deity or an afterlife can be
rationally inferred from such principles of organization as appear
in the world. Together, the two sections imply a comprehensive
attack on the foundations of religious belief. Placed where they are,
they seem to reveal the *Enquiry* as not disinterested, but a work
with a plot: the infidel has shown his hand.

Yet Hume still maintains his simulation of innocence. Both of
these notorious sections end with an explicit disclaimer: it is not
religious belief that is attacked, but the rationality of religious
belief. Once understood to be irrational, religious belief is, nomi-

nally, affirmed. In section 11, which is presented as a dialogue, Hume represents himself as making this reply to the friend 'who loves sceptical paradoxes'.[80] The friend has been defending the anti-religious position of Epicurus, and maintaining its innocuousness with regard to moral practice. Hume replies

> You conclude, that religious doctrines and reasonings *can* have no influence on life, because they *ought* to have no influence; never considering, that men reason not in the same manner you do, but draw many consequences from the belief of a divine Existence, and suppose that the Deity will inflict punishments on vice, and bestow rewards on virtue, beyond what appear in the ordinary course of nature. Whether this reasoning of theirs be just or not, is no matter. Its influence on their life and conduct must still be the same. And, those, who attempt to disabuse them of such prejudices, may, for aught I know, be good reasoners, but I cannot allow them to be good citizens and politicians.[81]

If we compare this with Gibbon's formulation in the *Decline and Fall*—'The various modes of worship, which prevailed in the Roman world, were all considered by the people, as equally true; by the philosopher, as equally false; and by the magistrate, as equally useful'[82]—we can feel how much more slippery is the irony of Hume. Gibbon's voice comprehends and expresses his irony; Hume's voice, so much more of the surface than Gibbon's ('may, for aught I know . . .'), is merely a factor in his. The 'easy' relation between Hume and his readership is jeopardized by the possibility that Hume is playing games with us, that he is wickedly offering one of the traditional arguments for the good effects of Christian belief in such a weak form as to invite its repudiation. At the end of the essay on miracles such a frank and easy relation between writer and reader is not so much jeopardized as exploded:

> I am the better pleased with the method of reasoning here delivered, as I think it may serve to confound those dangerous friends or disguised enemies to the *Christian Religion*, who have undertaken to defend it by the principles of human reason. Our most holy religion is founded on *Faith*, not on reason; and it is a sure method of exposing it to put it to such a trial as it is, by no means, fitted to endure . . . [Hume then specifies the irrationality of crediting the miracles recounted in the pentateuch] . . . Upon

[80] Ibid. 132.   [81] Ibid. 147.
[82] Edward Gibbon, *The History of the Decline and Fall of the Roman Empire*, ed. David Womersley, 3 vols. (Harmondsworth, 1994), i.56 (ch. 2).

the whole, we may conclude, that the *Christian Religion* not only was at first attended with miracles, but even at this day cannot be believed by any reasonable person without one. Mere reason is insufficient to convince us of its veracity: And whoever is moved by *Faith* to assent to it, is conscious of a continued miracle in his own person, which subverts all the principles of his understanding, and gives him a determination to believe what is most contrary to custom and experience.[83]

Theologically this is tenable; and of course for Hume *no* belief is 'reasonable', strictly speaking; and *something* must indeed be causing belief in those who sincerely profess Christianity; yet it is almost impossible not to hear the play of irony here as a destructive sarcasm, a simulation of conventional piety which is not innocent but thoroughly disingenuous. The characteristic movement of reassurance is here not truly sociable, but divisive in its effect. Just as the world is split between those with and those without this miraculous experience of faith, so Hume's manner here implicitly divides his readers between the enlightened and the credulous: for only the credulous could read those final sentences innocently, at their face value. To hear in them a satirical irony is to have lost one's innocence; and all Hume's readers were duly incriminated. The essay works beautifully as a polemic: but, for that reason, it runs counter to, and destabilizes, the tendency of the *Enquiry* as a whole.[84] What, in retrospect, should we now make of earlier passages where Hume professes the innocence of his doctrine, as for example on the non-freedom of the will? Our sense of an underlying, undeclared authorial purpose destroys the effect of the easy manner.

It seems from this that the double tendency of Hume's thought—to be subversive of theory but conservative of practice—operates everywhere except with regard to religion, where alone the irony has an unequivocal cutting edge. Hume could invite his readers to go on believing in causation, making moral judgements and professing allegiance to George II while knowing that there was no rational basis for doing so, but he could not—at least in the *Enquiry*—invite them to have faith in God in the same spirit. This

---

[83] *Enquiries*, pp. 129–31.

[84] Hume's later change of title, from *Philosophical Essays* to *An Enquiry*, suggests a degree of uncertainty as to the unity of the whole work; a version of 'Of Miracles' was in fact written much earlier, and originally intended for the *Treatise*, from which it was omitted on prudential grounds.

is an observation about Hume's readership as well as about his writing. Where his philosophical writing presses so strongly the question of how it will be read, its meaning becomes inextricably bound up with the kind of reader that can be imagined for it. This is partly a stylistic matter (in so far as great literature can extend its reader's powers, can call into being a fit audience for itself), but partly also a matter of historical context. The animus in Hume's writing on religion exists in relation to the climate in which he is writing, a climate in which the rational defensibility of the Christian faith was, by many, gripped anxiously tight. In a period when, as Bishop Butler wrote in 1736, it was come 'to be taken for granted, by many Persons, that Christianity is . . . now at length, discovered to be fictitious',[85] to profess Christian faith was, increasingly, to make a conscious and deliberate assertion of belief in a way that could have no truck with the Humean insinuation that all beliefs, whether supernatural or quotidian, are fictions of the imagination. Boswell has recorded Johnson's revealing explanation of how the classical writers were able to argue about the gods with such tolerance and good humour:

Sir, they disputed with good humour, because they were not in earnest as to religion. Had the ancients been serious in their belief, we should not have had their Gods exhibited in the manner we find them represented in the Poets . . . They disputed with good humour upon their fanciful theories, because they were not interested in the truth of them: when a man has nothing to lose he may be in good humour with his opponent . . . . Every man who attacks my belief diminishes, in some degree, my confidence in it, and therefore makes me uneasy; and I am angry with him who makes me uneasy.[86]

In this theological climate, the sociable good humour that Hume seeks to achieve, is inevitably compromised by the 'uneasiness' of his Johnsonian readers, whose mere existence among the audience threatens to reduce Hume's sceptical irony—the good-humoured raillery of his opponent which, according to Adam Smith, gave pleasure to all parties—into an offensive act.

If this problem stands behind the sections on religion in the *Enquiry concerning Human Understanding*, and somewhat spoils

---

[85] Joseph Butler, *The Analogy of Religion Natural and Revealed to the Constitution and Course of Nature* (London, 1736), 'Advertisement'.
[86] Boswell, *Life*, iii.10 f. (April 1776).

the coherence of the work as a whole, it itself becomes part of the subject-matter of the posthumous *Dialogues concerning Natural Religion*, which is in many ways Hume's finest work of literature. The dialogue is narrated by the youthful Pamphilus, who recounts a discussion triggered by the question of his religious education. There are three speakers: Philo the sceptic, who seems to stand for Hume himself; Demea, the orthodox religionist; and Cleanthes, fatherly tutor to Pamphilus, and the exponent of a reasoned deism based on the evidence of design in the creation. Demea dislikes this new-fangled way of thinking about God, which rests on the potentially impious assumption that God is sufficiently like man for arguments from analogy to be reliable, and depends upon a dangerous confidence in the power of human reason to penetrate into matters of religion. He is therefore delighted when Philo appears to side with him against Cleanthes:

> Let *Demea*'s Principles be improv'd and cultivated: Let us become thoroughly sensible of the Weakness, Blindness, and narrow Limits of human Reason: Let us duely consider its Uncertainty and endless Contrarieties, even in Subjects of common Life and Practice . . . . When these Topics are display'd in their full Light, as they are by some Philosophers and almost all Divines; who can retain such Confidence in this frail Faculty of Reason as to pay any Regard to its Determinations in Points so sublime, so abstruse, so remote from common Life and Experience? . . .
>
>   While *Philo* pronounc'd these Words, I cou'd observe a Smile in the Countenances both of *Demea* and *Cleanthes*. That of *Demea* seem'd to imply an unreserv'd Satisfaction in the Doctrines deliver'd: But in *Cleanthes*'s Features, I cou'd distinguish an Air of Finesse, as if he perceiv'd some Raillery or artificial Malice in the Reasonings of *Philo*.[87]

What Cleanthes understands, of course, is that the scepticism which Demea welcomes as an ally will end by undermining Demea's own position, as well as that of his opponent. But that 'Raillery or artificial Malice' does not declare itself for some time. The body of the *Dialogues* is taken up with a rigorous philosophical examination of the argument from design, resourcefully defended by Cleanthes, who is by no means a straw man, but even more powerfully attacked by the sceptical Philo, who wins point after point. As their debate nears its end, Demea is glad to feel that the weakness of deistical reasoning has been exposed by his scepti-

---

[87] *Religion*, p. 147 f. (Part 2).

cal companion, and is happy to endorse the declared tendency of Philo's scepticism, 'that Men ever did, and ever will, derive their Religion from other Sources than from this Species of Reasoning'.[88] For Demea, man's deepest motive to belief in God is not a matter of reasoning, but rather the manifest 'Miseries of Life, the Unhappiness of Man, the general Corruptions of our Nature',[89] and he is gratified to find that Philo supports him even more warmly in this. But Philo then takes that idea to the limit: he expounds the pain, misery, and imperfection of human life to the point where the idea of a benevolent Almighty becomes absurd, and Demea at last begins to take alarm:

Hold! Hold! cry'd *Demea*: Whither does your Imagination hurry you? I join'd in Alliance with you, in order to prove the incomprehensible Nature of the divine Being, and refute the Principles of *Cleanthes*, who wou'd measure every thing by a human Rule and Standard. But I now find you running into all the Topics of the greatest Libertines and Infidels; and betraying that holy Cause, which you seemingly espous'd. Are you secretly, then, a more dangerous Enemy than *Cleanthes* himself?

And you are so late in perceiving it? reply'd *Cleanthes*. Believe me, *Demea*; your Friend, *Philo*, from the beginning, has been amusing himself at both our Expence; and it must be confessed, that the injudicious Reasoning of our vulgar Theology has given him but too just a handle of ridicule.[90]

This, Pamphilus records, proves too much for Demea: 'Thus *Philo* continu'd to the last his Spirit of Opposition, and his Censure of establish'd Opinions. But I cou'd observe, that *Demea* did not at all relish the latter Part of the Discourse; and he took Occasion soon after, on some Pretence or other, to leave the Company.'[91] Demea is angry to find that he has been teased and trifled with on such a serious question: he makes some excuse and leaves the party, rather as Johnson immediately left the room on the one occasion when he found himself in company with Hume. To him, clearly, Philo's defence of 'the adorable Mysteriousness of the divine Nature'[92] is revealed as a malicious sarcasm; his air of innocence, a dissimulation.

However, what Hume gives us in the twelfth and final section of

---

[88] Ibid. 219 (Part 9).   [89] Ibid. 220 (Part 10).
[90] Ibid. 242 f. (Part 11).   [91] Ibid. 244 (Part 11).
[92] Ibid. 166 (Part 2).

the *Dialogues*, after Demea has left, suggests that such a judge-ment, although understandable, may have been premature, and that Philo's play of irony—he speaks 'somewhat between Jest and Earnest', Pamphilus says[93]—is finer than Demea even now under-stands. For with Demea gone, and the Johnsonian presence (so to speak) departed from his audience, Philo is able to strike a new note in his conversation with Cleanthes:

> I must confess, reply'd *Philo*, that I am less cautious on the Subject of natural Religion than on any other; both because I know that I can never, on that head, corrupt the Principles of any Man of common Sense, and because no-one, I am confident, in whose Eyes I appear a Man of common Sense, will ever mistake my Intentions. You in particular, *Cleanthes*, with whom I live in unreserv'd Intimacy; you are sensible, that, notwithstand-ing the Freedom of my Conversation, and my Love of singular Arguments, no-one has a deeper Sense of Religion impressed on his Mind, or pays more profound Adoration to the divine Being, as he discovers himself to Reason, in the inexplicable Contrivance and Artifice of Nature. A Purpose, an Intention, a Design strikes every where the most careless, the most stupid Thinker; and no man can be so harden'd in absurd Systems, as at all times to reject it.[94]

In this more genuinely sociable environment, Philo is able to make the characteristic Humean turn from the realm of sceptical reason-ing to the realm of natural feeling and 'common sense'. From this perspective, his stream of brilliant rebuttals of the argument from design can seem to have been mere intellectual ingenuity, 'singular arguments' that smack of 'absurd systems'.[95] Not—it is important to be clear—that anything is being recanted or withdrawn: this is a paradigm shift, not a volte-face. Philo had already been 'a little embarrass'd and confounded' earlier in the *Dialogues*, when Cleanthes appealed to how 'the plain Instincts of Nature' respond to the manifest wonders of bodily organization: 'Consider, anato-mize the Eye: Survey its Structure and Contrivance; and tell me, from your own Feeling, if the Idea of a Contriver does not imme-diately flow in upon you with a Force like that of Sensation.'[96] Philo had no answer to this at the time, and he now confesses the

---

[93] *Religion*, p. 170 (Part 2).   [94] Ibid. 244 f. (Part 12).
[95] Though a distinction should be drawn between the inference to intelligent design and that to moral or providential design. Philo feels on much stronger ground when attacking the latter. See *Religion*, pp. 230 f. (Part 10).
[96] Ibid. 176–8 (Part 3).

force of such an appeal, although in terms which distinguish such a *feeling* of belief ('a Force like that of Sensation') from rational knowledge. To confess that he has a profound '*sense* of religion' (my emphasis) impressed on his mind is simply to record a matter of fact, an instinctive, natural response to the appearances of design in the world. This is not, however, knowledge; no rational inference about God can be drawn from this 'sense' or feeling. Hume has by no means left his scepticism behind, and in case we should suppose that Philo is subsiding into a simple piety of sentiment, he moves straight into his final and most dazzling paradox: that the difference between theism and atheism is merely verbal, merely one of emphasis. While on the one hand the atheist cannot deny that the world offers principles of order that suggest 'some remote inconceivable analogy' with works of human intelligence, the pious theist must equally agree that the difference between human and divine intelligence is inconceivably great.

Where then, cry I to both these Antagonists, is the Subject of your dispute? The Theist allows, that the original Intelligence is very different from human reason: The Atheist allows, that the original Principle of Order bears some remote Analogy to it. Will you quarrel, Gentlemen, about the degrees, and enter into a controversy, which admits not of any precise meaning, nor consequently of any determination? If you shou'd be so obstinate, I shou'd not be surpriz'd to find you insensibly change sides.[97]

Hume elsewhere described a radically sceptical argument as one which admits of no answer, while producing no conviction.[98] That description may seem to fit Philo's audacious paradox, that nothing much really divides the theist from the atheist. But this is, when taken in its dramatic context, not one of those 'singular arguments' which have no connection with common life. Philo is clearly advancing it as much for the outcome it makes possible, as for its inherent truth: his hypothetical address to theist and atheist offers to bring them out of their state of incipient quarrel into a more sociable frame of mind. This *rapprochement* is made possible partly by the force of Philo's paradox, but also by the mix of jest and earnest in his tone, the play of irony which—like the dialogue form as Hume employs it—identifies a certain comedy in the limitations of philosophical argument.

This imagined reconciliation broadly mirrors Philo's own relationship with Cleanthes at this point. Their philosophical differences over the argument from design seem much less significant after Philo has presented this paradox, which Cleanthes appears to accept. Those differences have in any case always been compatible with a warm mutual understanding: Cleanthes has appreciated Philo's subtlety from the beginning, as we have seen, and Philo speaks of living with Cleanthes 'in unreserved intimacy'. It is crucial to the success of the *Dialogues* that such intimacy should be conceivable, that, for all Philo's scepticism, the gesture of sociability need not involve dissimulation:

These, *Cleanthes*, are my unfeign'd Sentiments on this Subject; and these Sentiments, you know, I have ever cherish'd and maintained. But in proportion to my Veneration for true Religion, is my Abhorrence of vulgar Superstitions; and I indulge a peculiar Pleasure, I confess, in pushing such Principles, sometimes into Absurdity, sometimes into Impiety.[99]

Philo is certainly unequivocating as he goes on to expound this abhorrence of 'vulgar Superstitions'. Popular religion naturally tends to foster faction and persecution; in its influence on morality it is either inert or undesirable; it promotes, and is promoted by, fear and melancholy; it commonly degrades the Deity by its representation of him. Such is 'Religion, as it has commonly been found in the World'.[100] What remains is the distinct category of 'true' or 'philosophical' religion, which has 'no such pernicious Consequences', but the philosophical content of such religion is minimal: it involves assent only to 'one simple, tho' somewhat ambiguous, at least undefin'd Proposition, *that the Cause or Causes of Order in the Universe probably bear some remote Analogy to human Intelligence*'.[101]

However, having concluded this analysis, Philo then ends by inquiring what feelings it is likely to provoke, and the *Dialogues* takes yet another surprising turn:

99 *Religion*, p. 251 (Part 12).   100 Ibid. 256 (Part 12).
101 Ibid. 256, 260 (Part 12).

Some Astonishment indeed will naturally arise from the Greatness of the Object: Some Melancholy from its Obscurity: Some Contempt of human Reason, that it can give no Solution more satisfactory with regard to so extraordinary and magnificent a Question. But believe me, *Cleanthes*, the most natural Sentiment, which a well dispos'd Mind will feel on this Occasion, is a longing Desire and Expectation, that Heaven wou'd be pleas'd to dissipate, at least alleviate this profound Ignorance, by affording some more particular Revelation to Mankind, and making Discoveries of the Nature, Attributes, and Operations of the divine Object of our Faith. A Person, season'd with a just Sense of the Imperfections of natural Reason, will fly to reveal'd Truth with the greatest Avidity: While the haughty Dogmatist, perswaded, that he can erect a compleat System of Theology by the mere Help of Philosophy, disdains any farther Aid, and rejects this adventitious Instructor. To be a philosophical Sceptic is, in a man of Letters, the first and most essential Step towards being a sound, believing Christian; a Proposition, which I would willingly recommend to the Attention of *Pamphilus*: And I hope *Cleanthes* will forgive me for interposing so far in the Education and Instruction of his Pupil.[102]

There has been much controversy over how to interpret the end of the *Dialogues*,[103] together with some feeling that Hume has here been too clever by half, but the sense of a problem stems, I think, from an inappropriate desire in some commentators to establish where Philo (or Hume) really stands, a desire which is inappropriate because *ill-mannered*. The conclusion is best understood as the kind of innocent simulation which scepticism makes possible, a social and sociable gesture, where Philo's sociability is an extension of Hume's. It will not do to explain the passage away as Hume

---

[102] Ibid. 260 f. (Part 12).

[103] For a clear-headed summary of the main points of difficulty, see Jonathan Dancy, ' "For Here the Author is Annihilated": Reflections on Philosophical Aspects of the Use of the Dialogue Form in Hume's *Dialogues concerning Natural Religion*', in *Philosophical Dialogues: Plato, Hume, Wittgenstein*, ed. Timothy Smiley, Proceedings of the British Academy, 85 (Oxford, 1995), pp. 29–60. Dancy's own conclusion, in part following Simpson ('Hume's Intimate Voices', pp. 88 f.), finds that the author has disappeared altogether from the *Dialogues*; just as there is no way back from the creation to its Author, so there is no way back from Hume's text to its author. But for Dancy to perceive that 'this situation is intentional. The text is designed to be effectively uninterpretable' (p. 46), is surely to overthrow his own case. Readings of the end of the *Dialogues* more compatible with my own include Nelson Pike's commentary in his edition (Indianapolis, 1970), Robert J. Fogelin, 'The Tendency of Hume's Skepticism', in *The Skeptical Tradition*, ed. Miles Burnyeat (Berkeley and Los Angeles, 1983), pp. 397–412, esp. pp. 404–8, and W. B. Carnochan, 'The Comic Plot of Hume's *Dialogues*', in *Modern Philology* 85 (1988), 514–22.

covering himself against criticism for his infidelity. In the first place, the immediately preceding attack on popular religion manifestly has historical Christianity in its sights; in the second, Hume's infamy among the faithful was already irreversible; in the third, the *Dialogues* was published posthumously, and was intended by Hume to be so published, partly to exclude such considerations of personal self-defence. At the same time, it would also be wrong to hear either hypocrisy or sarcasm, in Philo or in Hume. The conscious innocence of this conclusion is not at all the same as the mock-innocence with which Hume concludes 'Of Miracles'. Philo can mean just what he says, without self-contradiction or the kind of inconsistency that demands to be interpreted as a positive irony. For he says nothing about the truth of Christianity, nor claims to be a Christian himself, but speaks only about the psychology ('natural sentiment', 'desire', 'avidity') which might prompt a move from philosophical scepticism to Christian belief. To speak of a first step 'towards' Christian belief is not to say that a second must follow; everything that Philo says could be endorsed by Hume as infidel. One can even glimpse the outlines of a psychological explanation for the rise and success of Christianity, of the kind which Gibbon was to elaborate in the *Decline and Fall*. Yet it is also true, of course, that Philo's phrasing conveys a positively friendly attitude towards being 'a sound, believing Christian', and that this is a surprising turn of events. What we have—what Philo asks us to recognize—is a simulation of innocence in which there is no dissimulation. As Philo turns from the conclusion permitted by philosophical scepticism to the conclusion desiderated by natural sentiment (here indistinguishable from social convention, as so often in Hume), so he allows the exposition of his own views to become sensitive to the immediate social realities: the education of young Pamphilus in a conventionally Christian society. Without any essential compromise of his scepticism, he tactfully finds room for the notion of a 'sound' Christianity which might, after all, be free from the weaknesses and vices normally associated with religious belief. The play of irony succeeds in accommodating both Philo's sceptical intelligence and the necessity, after all, of returning to the realm of natural feeling and common sense, even in this most sensitive area.

The same kind of irony invests the paragraph which follows, in which Pamphilus concludes the whole work, and Hume shows that he remembers the society in which that work will be read, and to which it must be submitted:

> *Cleanthes* and *Philo* pursu'd not this Conversation much farther; and as nothing ever made greater Impression on me, than all the Reasonings of that day; so, I confess, that, upon a serious Review of the Whole, I cannot but think, that *Philo*'s Principles are more probable than *Demea*'s; but that those of *Cleanthes* approach still nearer to the Truth.[104]

For Hume to have Pamphilus vote loyally in favour of Cleanthes, the temperate, rational, constructive natural religionist, over the slippery scepticism of Philo—who has won almost every point in the debate, and with whom every reader naturally associated Hume himself—is just the same kind of gesture as Philo makes in recommending scepticism as the first step to Christianity. It is to be felt as a piece of good manners on the part of the author, a manifestation of that good breeding which, Hume wrote in the *Essays*, teaches those who might otherwise give offence to their company, to preserve 'the appearance of sentiments different from those to which they naturally incline'.[105] This appearance is not intended to deceive, or it would give no pleasure, but to be recognized as a simulation, a stroke of artifice: the consciousness of artifice is heightened by the way Pamphilus' conclusion echoes the end of Cicero's *On the Nature of the Gods*, the classical model for the *Dialogues*; the consciously socialized gesture is also a consciously literary one.[106] Yet it is also a gesture which tells a truth: for Philo to gain only second prize from Pamphilus at the conclusion, is for Hume to acknowledge the ultimate unpersuasiveness of scepticism, which can scarcely hope to travel far outside the study or the text. (The end of the *Dialogues* is in that respect just a little like the epilogue to *The Tempest*.) Hume's concluding gesture hopes to be recognized as at once generous, ironic, and resigned, and expresses, perhaps more perfectly than anywhere else in his writing, what is

---

[104] *Religion*, p. 261 (Part 12).
[105] *Essays*, ed. Miller, p. 132.
[106] 'This then was the end of our discussion and we went our ways, Velleius thinking that Cotta had the best of the argument while to me it seemed that the reasoning of Balbus brought us nearer to an image of the truth' (Cicero's conclusion to *The Nature of the Gods*, trans. Horace C. P. McGregor (1972), p. 235). Cotta is a sceptic, who would seem to have had the best of the argument and to be closest to Cicero's historical views; Balbus represents the Stoic position; Cicero represents himself as the narrator.

involved in the necessary turn from the realm of scepticism to that of common sense and social convention.

The final section of the *Dialogues* is a wonderful achievement. Yet we may note that Demea had to leave for that achievement to be possible. The circle of congenial company which can appreciate Philo, and on which his achievement finally depends, is small, select, and tightly drawn. Pamphilus' vote for Cleanthes at the end suggests, along with all its other implications, Hume's tribute to Cleanthes for being such an intelligent friend to Philo. Such an enabling audience had only the most fragile reflection in social reality. Hume never felt able to publish the *Dialogues*, which he had by him, in one version or another, for some twenty-five years. He showed it only to a few friends, and came to feel that he was writing a necessarily posthumous work; indeed, he had to go to considerable lengths to ensure that it would be published even after his death. This sense of the *Dialogues* as unpublishable focuses a larger observation about Hume: that the fineness of his irony depends upon the quality of his audience, just as his ethics depends upon the quality of social convention and consensus, those general notions that, although they may differ from the feelings of the heart, still 'serve all our purposes in company, in the pulpit, on the theatre, and in the schools'. (Everything, for Hume, depends upon society being *sociable*: a Humean moralist who found himself in a predominantly brutal or inhumane society, where, say, the persecution of a minority was widely regarded as 'useful and agreeable', would be helpless to resist or protest.) The unpublished *Dialogues*, which creates and contains its own audience, is something of a special case; elsewhere, Hume's rhetorical self-consciousness and his commitment to sociability meant that he could not but write in terms that were highly attentive and responsive to his society. This does not make him a fool among knaves, but it does produce the problems of rhetorical register which I have tried to identify in the *Enquiries*, and it may also be relevant to the literary silence of his final years, when he declined to continue with his *History of England*, whose politics had been found tendentious and controversial. Several letters from this period express his sharp disenchantment with the quality of his readership:

Considering the Treatment I have met with, it woud have been very silly for me at my Years to continue writing any more; and still more blameable to warp my Principles and Sentiments in conformity to the Prejudices of a stupid, factious Nation, with whom I am heartily disgusted. . . . That Nation [England] is so sunk in Stupidity and Barbarism and Faction that you may as well think of Lapland for an Author.[107]

From the so good-tempered Hume, this flash of 'hearty disgust' suggests both how fine and how fragile is the implied rapport with his reader that he established in his best passages; it also implies that the commitment to sociability was not without its cost.

*   *   *

The letter just quoted continues like this:

The best Book, that has been writ by any Englishman these thirty Years [i.e. since the death of Pope] . . . is Tristram Shandy, bad as it is. A Remark which may astonish you; but which you will find true on Reflection.[108]

Tristram Shandy is certainly not a work that is concerned to conform, even in appearance, to its readers' sense of proprieties. If Hume's scepticism is bound up, for better and worse, with his sociability, the no less radical scepticism which informs *Tristram Shandy* offers a significant contrast, for it laughs at social convention and revels in the idiosyncrasy of individual experience.

This will be the subject of the next chapter.

---

[107] *Letters*, ii.269 (no. 482; 30 Jan. 1773).   [108] Ibid.

5

Tristram Shandy: Singularity and the Single Life

The first, irresistible impression made by *Tristram Shandy*—a work which encourages us to go with our first impressions—is of freedom and spontaneity. 'Of all the several ways of beginning a book which are now in practice throughout the known world,' declares Tristram, 'I am confident my own way of doing it is the best—— I'm sure it is the most religious——for I begin with writing the first sentence——and trusting to Almighty God for the second.'[1] This freedom is not, indeed, the freedom of agency, the freedom to make or to pursue significant choices, but rather its opposite: the freedom that comes with submission, with the acceptance of whatever God sends, or Tristram's destiny decrees, or the chance quirks and associations of the writer's mind happen to throw up, from moment to moment, as he sets down, in such helpless and loving detail, the circumstances of his conception, his birth, and his early family life. Such freedom is like a religious faith in Almighty God, or it may even be, as Tristram suggests, an expression of such faith. Certainly, the narrative attitude of openness and relaxation is felt as benign, almost as blest. The reader is more pleasured than perplexed by the narrative chaos that results from Tristram's digressive swerves and meanders, and the eccentricity of the book, like the eccentricity of its characters, seems less an aberration from any retrievable norm than a beautifully appropriate adaptation to a world of pure contingencies. In this world any attempt to rationalize the phenomena is felt as ludicrously misguided or problematic. Scepticism's natural relation to comedy emerges here; the comedy of *Tristram* celebrates scepticism's vision of human

---

[1] *Tristram Shandy*, viii. ch. 2: p. 656.

contrivance and deliberation as foolish and futile. 'A mightier Pow'r the strong direction sends', Pope had written in the *Essay on Man*;[2] the life-forces and spontaneities that shape and unshape Tristram's narrative may lack any 'strong direction', but they are nonetheless aligned with that ultimately comic power. Reason, in Pope, must understand its subordination to the forces of Passion and of Instinct; Hume is rescued from the vortex of scepticism by submission to 'the current of nature';[3] and in a similar way, though taken to a comic extreme, 'Shandeism' saves us from the fruitlessness of mere thinking:

And now that you have just got to the end of these four volumes——the thing I have to *ask* is, how you feel your heads? my own akes dismally— as for your healths, I know, they are much better——True *Shandeism*, think what you will against it, opens the heart and lungs, and like all those affections which partake of its nature, it forces the blood and other vital fluids of the body to run freely thro' its channels, and makes the wheel of life run long and chearfully round.[4]

It is appropriate that the chief antagonist or foil to this spirit of sceptical comedy should be an intellectual. Tristram's father, Walter, is 'an excellent natural philosopher, and much given to close reasoning upon the smallest matters', 'a philosopher in grain,—speculative,—systematical'.[5] Tristram's belief in writing spontaneously is the very opposite of Walter's theory (which he has, of course, from a learned authority) that a writer's 'first thoughts were always the temptations of the evil one', and that the first duty of a Christian author was therefore that of 'RESIS-TANCE'.[6] This attitude, that stands on guard against spontaneity, makes the writing of Walter's own book on the education of his child an infinitely protracted business, an absurdly belated piece of theorizing; it informs his comically misguided endeavours to rationalize and to control the flow of events; and it is expressed also in his dislike of the instinctual spontaneity of the body and in particular the 'unruly appetite' of sexual desire.[7] Walter—'one of the most regular men in every thing he did . . . that ever lived'—has sex with his wife on the first Sunday night of every month, immediately after winding up the clock that stands on the landing, so as to be

[2] *Essay on Man*, ii.165; Pope, p. 255.   [3] *Treatise*, p. 269.
[4] *Tristram Shandy*, iv. ch. 32: p. 401.   [5] Ibid. i. ch. 3: p. 4; i. ch. 21: p. 76.
[6] Ibid. v. ch. 16: p. 447.   [7] Ibid. ix. ch. 32: p. 805.

no more 'plagued and pester'd' with either matter for the rest of the month.[8] Such a determination to regulate life is a natural target for comedy, and Walter's 'interruption' on the occasion of Tristram's conception by his wife's unfortunate association of ideas—'*Pray, my dear,* quoth my mother, *have you not forgot to wind up the clock?*'[9]—is only the first of a series of comic mortifications, as his rationalism is repeatedly frustrated and undone by the irrepressible contingencies of life.

So far, this seems like the classic formula for one familiar kind of comedy: a joyous spontaneity triumphantly opposed to a narrow and overweening rationality. But comedy likes to end with closure and a marriage, while *Tristram Shandy* pointedly ends with the frustration of both those desires. In fact, what Sterne offers us, all through, is not quite comedy of that familiar kind. Neither the rationality, nor the vitality which overthrows it, are quite what such comedy would have them be. In the first place, rationality cannot be put in its place in *Tristram Shandy* because it is never really granted admission. Walter, although nominally a philosopher and the antagonist of the spirit that animates the book, is rescued for the Shandean circle in that his concern for 'philosophy' is itself so clearly a non-rational instinct, a 'ruling passion' (in Pope's terminology) or a 'hobby-horse' (in Tristram's). His most cherished opinions are not the product of thought, but 'picked up' as though they were physical objects:

What a shuttlecock of a fellow would the greatest philosopher that ever existed, be whisk'd into at once, did he read such books, and observe such facts, and think such thoughts, as would eternally be making him change sides!

Now, my father, as I told you last year, detested all this.—He pick'd up an opinion, Sir, as a man in a state of nature picks up an apple.—It becomes his own,—and if he is a man of spirit, he would lose his life rather than give it up.[10]

Hence Tristram can speak of Walter's favourite notions as 'sceptical', even though he clearly holds them with the most dogmatic certainty:

He had a thousand little sceptical notions of the comick kind to defend,——

[8] *Tristram Shandy*, i. ch. 4: p. 6.   [9] Ibid. i. ch. 1, p. 2.
[10] Ibid. iii. ch. 34: pp. 262 f.

most of which notions, I verily believe, at first enter'd upon the footing of mere whims, and of a *vive la Bagatelle* ... [11]

In truth, there was not a stage in the life of man ... but he had some favourite notion to himself, springing out of it, as sceptical, and as far out of the high-way of thinking, as these two which have been explained.

——Mr. *Shandy*, my father, Sir, would see nothing in the light in which others placed it;—he placed things in his own light. [12]

Such notions are 'sceptical', not because they are undogmatically held, but because they are so unembarrassed by their eccentricity. The implicit suggestion is that, in a world in which people's opinions have so little to do with reason, Walter's may be as good as any other. Opinions, in the mid-eighteenth century, were increasingly described as 'sentiments', and sentiments, as Hume understood, are not the product of reasoning, however much they may be rationalized after their arrival. This is obviously true of Walter's beliefs about the formative importance of names and noses. But even where his philosophical sentiments are not in themselves eccentric, as over the death of his son Bobby, Sterne shows us this discourse too as a mere ride upon the hobby-horse of philosophy and rhetoric. As Walter enthusiastically strings together his favourite classical topics of philosophical consolation in a great declamatory anthology, carried away by the energy of his own performance, he loses touch altogether with the reality of death, his nominal subject. He also loses touch with his audience: for uncle Toby is bemused by Walter's apparent reference to his experiences in the first century BC.

My uncle *Toby* had but two things for it; either to suppose his brother to be the wandering *Jew*, or that his misfortunes had disordered his brain.— 'May the Lord God of heaven and earth protect and restore him,' said my uncle *Toby*, praying silently for my father, and with tears in his eyes.

—My father placed the tears to a proper account, and went on with his harangue with great spirit. ... [13]

Walter's flow of discourse has sealed him within the bubble of his own language, triggering a splendidly comic sequence of communication breakdowns between himself and those around him. His philosophical reflections are, as he delivers them, empty of serious

---

[11] Ibid. i. ch. 19: p. 60.   [12] Ibid. ii. ch. 19: p. 170.
[13] Ibid. v. ch. 3: p. 423.

reflection; mortality is much spoken about, but nothing of mortality is really present to Walter's experience. One might say the same of the stoic philosopher in *Rasselas*, who

enumerated many examples of heroes immovable by pain or pleasure, who looked with indifference on those modes or accidents to which the vulgar give the names of good and evil. He exhorted his hearers to lay aside their prejudices, and arm themselves against the shafts of malice or misfortune, by invulnerable patience; concluding, that this state only was happiness, and that this happiness was in every one's power.[14]

Rasselas is initially impressed; but when the philosopher's daughter dies of a fever, the father is desolated; confronted with the reality of experience, these fine theoretical reflections count for nothing. Sterne's scepticism works here quite differently from Johnson's, for Walter *is* consoled by his philosophizing—consoled not, indeed, by any rational strength that there may be in his reflections, but by the energy with which he rehearses and performs them. It is his pleasure in philosophizing that enables him, as Tristram tells us, to get rid of his affliction: and if we as readers find nothing problematic in this, it is because the life and death of Bobby have so little part in Tristram's immediate consciousness, and hence—since everything is mediated through Tristram's consciousness—in our own minds. Bobby's death enters the story only as an occasion for pleasure, for Walter's pleasure in his philosophical eloquence, at one level, and for Tristram's comic representation of philosophical eloquence, at another. These two levels chime with one another so successfully as diverting, and diversionary, activities that we are hardly aware of what we are being diverted from. The difference between them is that Tristram is self-aware in his Shandeism as Walter is not; but at bottom, what might be called the *mentalism* of Walter's approach to life harmonizes with Shandeism well enough. Unlike Johnson, Sterne is happy to make the most of the situation in which the great realities of death and bereavement can hardly find lodgement in our minds, can hardly penetrate the energetic fizz of mental static which accompanies the reception of all signals from outside our individual subjectivities.

The episode which immediately follows may seem to contradict

---

[14] *Johnson*, xvi.72f (ch. 18).

that general proposition, but, in the end, supports it. Walter's self-enclosing discourse in response to his son's death is contrasted with the reception of the same news below stairs, and the immeasurably more effective method of Trim's eloquence:

He was alive last *Whitsontide*, said the coachman.—*Whitsontide!* alas! cried *Trim*, extending his right arm, and falling instantly into the same attitude in which he read the sermon,—what is *Whitsontide, Jonathan* (for that was the coachman's name), or *Shrovetide*, or any tide or time past, to this? Are we not here now, continued the corporal, (striking the end of his stick perpendicularly upon the floor, so as to give an idea of health and stability)—and are we not—(dropping his hat upon the ground) gone! in a moment!—'Twas infinitely striking! *Susannah* burst into a flood of tears.—We are not stocks and stones.—*Jonathan, Obadiah*, the cook-maid, all melted.—The foolish fat scullion herself, who was scouring a fish-kettle upon her knees, was rous'd with it.—The whole kitchen crouded about the corporal.[15]

Until the moment of Trim's great funeral elegy, his audience had been in the normal Sternean condition, pursuing their private trains of association: Susannah thinking about mourning wear, Obadiah about the project of land enclosure which will now go forward, the scullion congratulating herself on her survival of a dropsy. From this condition of more or less enclosed subjectivity, Trim's gesture has the power to deliver them, as all Walter's resounding quotations from Servius Sulpicius could not. For a moment, what Tristram goes on to call 'the sentiment of mortality'—a sentiment, something more akin to a sensation than a thought—touches them all and brings them together. Trim's gesture seems to amount to a true communication, a precious release from the enclosure of the mind: and this is largely because it by-passes the idiosyncrasies and truisms of language, and works upon the soul directly through the senses.

This notion of a non-verbal communication more potent and direct than language can provide recurs frequently. We have the black page marking the death of Yorick,[16] or the actual drawing out of the shape cut through the air by the flourish of Trim's stick in praise of freedom: 'A thousand of my father's most subtle syllogisms could not have said more for celibacy'.[17] We have Toby's

[15] *Tristram Shandy*, v. ch. 7: p. 431.   [16] Ibid. i. ch. 12: p. 38.
[17] Ibid. ix. ch. 4: p. 744.

happy progression from unsatisfactory verbal descriptions of the
siege of Namur to physical models of the fortifications constructed
on the bowling-green.[18] In *A Sentimental Journey*, we have
Yorick's skill at what he calls 'translation', the reading of body-
language, so that he claims the ability to render

the several turns of looks and limbs, with all their inflections and delin-
eations, into plain words. For my own part, by long habitude, I do it so
mechanically, that when I walk the streets of London, I go translating all
the way; and have more than once stood behind in the circle, where not
three words have been said, and have brought off twenty different
dialogues with me, which I could have fairly wrote down and sworn to.[19]

In Swift's Academy of Lagado, the philosophers who communicate
with physical objects rather than words are ludicrous figures, material for satire: there is no escape from the imperfections of
language. But in Sterne, these passages are not satirical; they
suggest the possibility of a spontaneous, 'sentimental' communication that by-passes the inauthenticities of language and rational
reflection, uncovering a continuum between mind and body, root-
ing the mental in the physical. There is something tonic in the
image of Walter picking up an opinion like an apple. What Swift
derided as 'the mechanical operation of the spirit'—a degrading (if
perversely fascinating) model of human behaviour—becomes in
Sterne a much more appealing, even therapeutic, idea. It is precisely
the virtue of Shandeism that it has physiological effects and
promotes the bodily health of the reader, 'opens the heart and
lungs, and . . . forces the blood and other vital fluids of the body to
run freely thro' its channels'.[20]

However, Sterne never allows us to rest in such a vision of
immediate rapport between the mental and the physical. Trim's
gesture with his hat touches his audience as Walter's discourse
could not, but for Tristram to elaborate on the episode of Trim's
hat as he immediately proceeds to do, altogether changes the quality of the moment. The quotation continues from that given above
without a break:

[18] *Tristram Shandy*, ii. ch. 1–5: pp. 93–114.
[19] *The Florida Edition of the Works of Laurence Sterne. Volume VI: A
Sentimental Journey through France and Italy AND Continuation of the Bramine's
Journal*, ed. Melvyn New and W. G. Day (Gainesville, Fla., 2002), p. 77.
[20] *Tristram Shandy*, v. ch. 32: p. 401.

Now as I perceive plainly, that the preservation of our constitution in church and state,—and possibly the preservation of the whole world—or what is the same thing, the distribution and balance of its property and power, may in time to come depend greatly upon the right understanding of this stroke of the corporal's eloquence—I do demand your attention,—your worships and reverences, for any ten pages together, take them where you will in any other part of the work, shall sleep for it at your ease.

I said, 'we were not stocks and stones'—'tis very well. I should have added, nor are we angels, I wish we were,—but men cloathed with bodies, and governed by our imaginations;—and what a junketting piece of work of it there is, betwixt these and our seven senses, especially some of them, for my own part, I own it, I am ashamed to confess. Let it suffice to affirm, that of all the senses, the eye, (for I absolutely deny the touch, though most of your *Barbati*, I know, are for it) has the quickest commerce with the soul,—gives a smarter stroke, and leaves something more inexpressible upon the fancy, than words can either convey—or sometimes get rid of.

—I've gone a little about—no matter, 'tis for health—let us only carry it back in our mind to the mortality of *Trim*'s hat.—'Are we not here now,—and gone in a moment?'—There was nothing in the sentence—'twas one of your self-evident truths we have the advantage of hearing every day; and if *Trim* had not trusted more to his hat than his head—he had made nothing at all of it.

————'Are we not here now;'—continued the corporal, 'and are we not'—(dropping his hat plumb upon the ground—and pausing, before he pronounced the word)——'gone! in a moment?' The descent of the hat was as if a heavy lump of clay had been kneaded into the crown of it.——Nothing could have expressed the sentiment of mortality, of which it was the type and fore-runner, like it,—his hand seemed to vanish from under it,—it fell dead,—the corporal's eye fix'd upon it, as upon a corps,—and *Susannah* burst into a flood of tears. . . .

Ye who govern this mighty world and its mighty concerns with the *engines* of eloquence,—who heat it, and cool it, and melt it, and mollify it,——and then harden it again to *your purpose*——

Ye who wind and turn the passions with this great windlass,—and, having done it, lead the owners of them, whither ye think meet—

Ye, lastly, who drive——and why not, Ye also who are driven, like turkeys to market, with a stick and a red clout—meditate—meditate, I beseech you, upon *Trim*'s hat.[21]

'Meditate' is a joke because it is such a giddyingly undefined imperative. To insist that we *meditate* upon Trim's hat is precisely to

[21] Ibid. v. ch. 7: pp. 431–3.

alienate us from the life of instinctive, spontaneous, immediate apprehension for which, at the beginning of the passage, it appeared to stand. Tristram's elaborate commentary obtrusively turns the spontaneity of event into an object of separate and distanced consciousness. The reprise, in particular, encourages us to see the effect with the hat as a (repeating) mechanism: which then leads naturally enough into the images of manipulative rhetorical machinery whose unlovely political employers are apostrophized in the final paragraphs. If 'the *engines* of eloquence' seem at first to be contrasted to Trim's laconic but telling gesture, so that those who practise the calculating arts of political rhetoric are being urged to mend their ways by meditating upon the truer language of the heart, by the end Trim's eloquent hat can be seen, in hindsight, as itself (like sticks and red clouts) just such an engine of manipulation; by this reading the politicians are being urged to attend to Trim as a master in their own art. This ambiguity means that, even while we recognize the superiority of Trim's instinctual to Walter's intellectual eloquence, the effect of Tristram's narrative on us its alert readers cannot be automatic or compelling. Those who meditate on Trim's hat will no longer be driven like turkeys to market. Despite the attractions of immediacy, the mind ends by keeping its distance.

The concerns shaping the movement I am tracing here are explicitly set down in a passage in one of the sermons, 'Philanthropy Recommended', in which Sterne discusses the compassion of the Samaritan. His emphasis falls on the idea of compassion as a natural instinct, uncontaminated by even the most refined or indirect calculations of self-love:

In such calamities as a man has fallen into through mere misfortune, to be charged upon no fault or indiscretion of himself, there is something then so truly interesting, that at the first sight we generally make them our own, not altogether from a reflection that they might have been or may be so, but oftener from a certain generosity and tenderness of nature which disposes us for compassion, abstracted from all considerations of self. So that without any observable act of the will, we suffer with the unfortunate . . . . In benevolent natures the impulse to pity is so sudden, that like instruments of music which obey the touch—the objects which are fitted to excite such impressions work so instantaneous an effect, that you would think the will was scarce concerned, and that the mind was altogether passive in the sympathy which her own goodness has excited. The truth is,—the soul is generally in such cases so busily taken up and wholly engrossed by the object of pity, that she does not attend to her own operations, or take leisure to examine the principles upon which she acts. So that the Samaritan, though the moment he saw him he had compassion on him, yet sudden as the emotion is represented, you are not to imagine that it was mechanical, but that there was a settled principle of humanity and goodness which operated within him.[22]

Like many another eighteenth-century promoter of sensibility against the theorists of self-love, Sterne warms to the account of compassion as a spontaneous instinct, operating quite independently of any activity of cognition or volition. But there is at the same time an anxiety attached to the idea of such spontaneity: 'you are not to imagine that it was mechanical'. Accordingly, 'without any observable act of the will' is revised into the more wary 'you would think the will was scarce concerned', and Sterne feels obliged to supply an extended account of the 'train of reflections' that would have risen in the Samaritan's mind:

'Good God! what a spectacle of misery do I behold—a man stripped of his raiment—wounded—lying languishing before me upon the ground just ready to expire,—without the comfort of a friend to support him in his last agonies, or the prospect of a hand to close his eyes when his pains are over. But perhaps my concern should lessen when I reflect on the relations in which we stand to each other—that he is a Jew and I a Samaritan.—But are we not still both men? partakers of the same nature—and subject to the same evils?—let me change conditions with him for a moment and consider, had his lot befallen me as I journeyed in the way, what measure I should have expected at his hands.—Should I wish when he beheld me wounded and half-dead, that he should shut up his bowels of compassion from me, and double the weight of my miseries by passing by and leaving them unpitied?—But I am a stranger to the man—be it so,—but I am no stranger to his condition—misfortunes are of no particular tribe or nation, but belong to us all, and have a general claim upon us, without distinction of climate, country, or religion. Besides, though I am a stranger—'tis no fault of his that I do not know him, and therefore unequitable he should suffer by it:—Had I known him, possibly I should have had cause to love and pity him the more—for aught I know, he is some one of uncommon merit, whose life is rendered still more precious, as the lives and happiness of others may be involved in it: perhaps at this instant that he lies here

[22] *The Florida Edition of the Works of Laurence Sterne. Volume IV: The Sermons*, ed. Melvyn New (Gainesville, Fla., 1996), pp. 23, 26 f.

forsaken, in all this misery, a whole virtuous family is joyfully looking for his return, and affectionately counting the hours of his delay. Oh ! did they know what evil hath befallen him—how would they fly to succour him.— Let me then hasten to supply those tender offices of binding up his wounds, and carrying him to a place of safety—or if that assistance comes too late, I shall comfort him at least in his last hour—and, if I can do nothing else,—I shall soften his misfortunes by dropping a tear of pity over them.'

'Tis almost necessary to imagine the good Samaritan was influenced by some such thoughts as these, from the uncommon generosity of his behaviour.[23]

Sterne's approving exposition of the processes of instinct is now thoroughly counter-instinctive. The passage of internal reflection is so long, so elaborately conscious, and so fully rationalized as to neutralize or reverse the earlier emphasis on compassion as instantaneous and unreflecting. The Samaritan's warmly sentimental consciousness, which if offered as a transparent representation of his true state of self would be felt as highly implausible, is confessedly mediated to us as Sterne's self-consciously projected fiction, rather as the Samaritan elaborates his own imaginative scenario of the Jew's virtuous family and his own tear of pity at the deathbed. The act of compassion which instantaneously united Samaritan and Jew ('we suffer with the unfortunate') has been resolved into an activity of internal consciousness that emphasizes the distance separating Samaritan from Jew, as reader from Samaritan.

A similar movement can be traced in other passages: for example, the passage on the Bastille in *A Sentimental Journey*. Yorick finds himself in Paris without a passport, and contemplates the possibility of arrest and imprisonment. But he is not alarmed; he responds with a kind of philosophical nonchalance, and rehearses reasons for thinking that much of the evil of imprisonment in the Bastille lies merely in the terror which the mind projects onto the idea: in a more sanguine view it appears as nothing worse than a confinement through illness, and can be relatively easily borne. This may recall Hamlet on 'imprisonment' in Denmark—'there is nothing either good or bad but thinking makes it so'—although Yorick embraces not only the mind's priority but also its freedom of agency, its power to refashion its experience. In this sense, it is

[23] Sterne, *Sermons*, pp. 27 f.

a kind of Walter-ism. 'I could not bring down my mind', Yorick tells us, to think of the Bastille with real concern; 'I walk'd down stairs in no small triumph with the conceit of my reasoning.'²⁴ But he is then 'interrupted in the hey-day of this soliloquy' by a voice, which proves to be that of a starling in a cage, repeating over and over, 'I can't get out', and this immediately, if irrationally, punctures his former attitude. The sentiments of nature sweep aside the posturings of reason:

I vow, I never had my affections more tenderly awakened; or do I remember an incident in my life, where the dissipated spirits, to which my reason had been a bubble, were so suddenly call'd home. Mechanical as the notes were, yet so true in tune to nature were they chanted, that in one moment they overthrew all my systematic reasonings upon the Bastile; and I heavily walk'd up stairs, unsaying every word I had said in going down them.

Disguise thyself as thou wilt, still slavery! said I—still thou art a bitter draught.²⁵

Like Trim's hat, the starling in the cage seems to effect an epiphany, penetrating an enclosed attitude of mind—'the hey-day of this soliloquy'—with a more substantial reality. Yet, as with Trim's hat, there is more to be said. As Yorick elaborates his new sentiments in an address to the fair goddess Liberty, we register an element of rhetorical excess, a note of conscious over-performance, which distinguishes Sterne's very particular brand of sentimentalism:

With thee to smile upon him as he eats his crust, the swain is happier than his monarch, from whose court thou art exiled—Gracious heaven! cried I, kneeling down upon the last step but one in my ascent—grant me but health, thou great Bestower of it, and give me but this fair goddess as my companion—and shower down thy mitres, if it seems good unto thy divine providence, upon those heads which are aching for them.²⁶

The passion of the dramatic speaker is shot through with a more detached narratorial consciousness, in a way that allows Sterne to be both sentimentalist and ironist at once. The phrase 'kneeling down upon the last step but one in my ascent', as though the actor were to include a stage direction within his speech of passion, strikes a distancing, faintly ludicrous note. Yorick, we are

²⁴ Sterne, *Sentimental Journey*, p. 94.   ²⁵ Ibid. 95 f.
²⁶ Ibid. 96.

reminded, expresses one set of sentiments when he goes down the stairs, and an opposite set when he goes up. This momentary linking of his sentiments with his physical actions presents the spontaneous reversal in those sentiments in a comic light, as a kind of mechanism, triggered by the 'mechanical' notes of the starling, sounds whose meaning for the listener is supplied entirely by the listener (as is the case of so much utterance in Sterne). This no longer seems like the necessary response to an overwhelming moral reality. Yorick then goes up to his room and sets himself to imagine some particular prisoner and the miseries of his situation, until he bursts into tears: 'I could not sustain the picture of confinement which my fancy had drawn'.[27] If at one level we feel that Yorick is now closer to the reality of the Bastille, at another we also feel his new sentiments are just as subjective, as composed of 'fancy', as his old. The starling's cry, 'I can't get out' is a resonant phrase because of the way in which Sterne's play of irony continually returns us to the enclosure of the mind.

Such self-enclosing consciousness both values unreflecting impulse and observes its own distance from it; it is from that distance that such impulse appears as mechanical. This ambiguous benignity of mechanism is regularly expressed in *Tristram Shandy* through Corporal Trim. In the fifth book, Walter is discussing the nature of the respect owed by the child to its father and mother with his usual hyper-ingenious philosophical subtlety. Yorick replies that this is a much simpler matter than Walter implies, and is perfectly well dealt with in the catechism, of which Trim, Toby then declares, can repeat every word by heart. But when Yorick asks Trim for the fifth Commandment, Trim cannot well reply.

I must begin with the first, an' please your honour, said the corporal.——
——*Yorick* could not forbear smiling.—Your reverence does not consider, said the corporal, shouldering his stick like a musket, and marching into the middle of the room, to illustrate his position,—that 'tis exactly the same thing, as doing one's exercise in the field.—
'*Join your right-hand to your firelock,*' cried the corporal, giving the word of command, and performing the motion.—
'*Poise your firelock,*' cried the corporal, doing the duty still of both adjutant and private man.—

[27] Sterne, *Sentimental Journey*, p. 98.

'*Rest your firelock*,'—one motion, an' please your reverence, you see leads into another.—If his honour will begin but with the *first*—
THE FIRST—cried my uncle *Toby*, setting his hand upon his side—* *
* * * * * * * * * * * * * * * .

THE SECOND—cried my uncle *Toby*, waving his tobacco-pipe, as he would have done his sword at the head of a regiment.—The corporal went through his *manual* with exactness; and having *honoured his father and mother*, made a low bow, and fell back to the side of the room.[28]

The mechanical, non-rational quality of Trim's rote-learning is brought out by its close correlation, almost identification, with physical movement: it is by gesture, of course, that he illustrates his 'position'; he both gives the word of command, and performs the motion; he honoured his father and mother, and made a low bow. The effect of this is absurd, but also oddly cheering: Toby's enthusiasm ('waving his tobacco-pipe') is infectious, the pretence that the physical and the mental act are one makes for a certain real release of energy and exuberance. But Walter, speaking in the name of true intellectual enlightenment, can see in this notably corporal Corporal only material for satire:

—SCIENCES MAY BE LEARNED BY ROTE, BUT WISDOM NOT.
Yorick thought my father inspired.—I will enter into obligations this moment, said my father, to lay out all my aunt *Dinah*'s legacy, in charitable uses (of which, by the bye, my father had no high opinion) if the corporal has any one determinate idea annexed to any one word he has repeated.—Prythee, *Trim*, quoth my father, turning round to him,—What do'st thou mean, by '*honouring thy father and mother?*'
Allowing them, an' please your honour, three halfpence a day out of my pay, when they grew old.—And didst thou do that, *Trim?* said *Yorick*.—He did indeed, replied my uncle *Toby*.—Then, *Trim*, said *Yorick*, springing out of his chair, and taking the corporal by the hand, thou art the best commentator upon that part of the *Decalogue*; and I honour thee more for it, corporal *Trim*, than if thou hadst had a hand in the *Talmud* itself.[29]

Clearly, the intellectualism of Walter, who had no high opinion of charitable uses for one's money, is the foil to Trim's unreflecting charity; and yet Walter's criticism of Trim's rote-learning is not obviously foolish, and indeed earns Yorick's endorsement (he 'thought my father inspired'). There is an unresolved ambivalence here, reflected in the way Yorick applauds both Walter and Trim,

---

[28] *Tristram Shandy*, v. ch. 32: p. 469.   [29] Ibid. 470 f.

and a real gap between reflection and action. While Walter has no
high opinion of laying out money in charitable uses, which would
be to translate precept into action, Trim cannot apprehend precept
except through action, in a way that gives point to Walter's criticism, for Trim's filial piety may well seem, in its regularity ('three
half-pence a day'), as automatic as his recitation. Like the compassion of the Samaritan in Sterne's sermon, it rehearses itself 'without
any observable act of the will': a quality which guarantees its
blessed immunity from the dissipating effect of reflection, but also
evokes the idea of mechanism.

Mechanical models of human psychology were widely discussed
in the eighteenth century, largely because of Lockean epistemology,
which derived all knowledge from sensation, and had floated the
startling suggestion that the thinking soul might (for all we know)
be material. When Tristram describes Locke's *Essay* as 'a history
. . . a history-book . . . of what passes in a man's own mind' he
recalls Voltaire's description in the *Lettres philosophiques*: 'So
many thinkers having written the novel of the soul, a wise man has
appeared who has modestly written its history. Locke has
expounded human understanding to mankind as an excellent
anatomist explains the mechanism of the human body.'[30] As
Voltaire's simile suggests, Locke's analysis offered hospitality to
associationist models of psychology and to hypotheses about the
physiology of perception and, ultimately, of consciousness itself.[31]
The implications were much debated: did physiological processes
accompany perception, or did they constitute perception? How far
could an understanding of the body as mechanism be extended to
the workings of the mind? Could accounts which emphasized how,
as Trim explained it, 'one motion . . . leads into another' leave
room for conscious volition and free agency? After La Mettrie had
openly asserted the most extreme position in *L'Homme machine*
(1748), Johnson refused even to enter into the ensuing debate:
'With all the evil that there is, there is no man but would rather be
a free agent, than a mere machine without the evil . . . . If a man
would rather be the machine, I cannot argue with him. He is a

[30] *Tristram Shandy*, ii. ch. 2: p. 98; Voltaire, *Letters on England*, trans. Leonard
Tancock (Harmondsworth, 1980), p. 63.
[31] See John W. Yolton, *Thinking Matter: Materialism in Eighteenth-Century
Britain* (Oxford, 1984).

different being from me.'³² Just as one cannot wish to be a machine, so no-one could wish to be Trim, admirable though his behaviour may be. This gap between reflection and action is the source of Sterne's comedy, and the gesture at overcoming that gap here through Yorick's approval of Trim is revealingly unsuccessful: a notably witty and clever consciousness ('than if thou hadst a hand in the *Talmud* itself') exclaims in praise of simple-mindedness, or at least of a quality intimately associated with simple-mindedness, and the effect is uncomfortably close to condescension. The consciousness that appreciates the automatic quality of Trim's piety, and does so with a curious mixture of envy and amusement, confesses its own distance from such a mode of being.

In all these examples, the relation between body and mind is never far away. Tristram pauses in his discussion of Trim's hat to reflect on the 'junketting piece of work' that there is between the senses and the imagination, and to inquire which of the senses 'has the quickest commerce with the soul'; Sterne compares the Samaritan's impulse to pity with the sounding of a musical instrument which instantaneously responds to the touch; Yorick, moved by the sound of the starling, speaks of how his 'dissipated spirits' were 'suddenly called home'. This last is not the vague metaphor which it seems to the modern reader, but invokes the established physiological theory of 'animal spirits'; Locke used this theory in discussing the habitual association of ideas, in a paragraph echoed in the very first paragraph of *Tristram Shandy*. This is Locke:

Custom settles habits of Thinking in the Understanding, as well as of Determining in the Will, and of Motions in the Body; all which seems to be but Trains of Motion in the Animal Spirits, which once set a going continue on in the same steps they have been used to, which by often treading are worn into a smooth path, and the Motion in it becomes easy and as it were Natural. As far as we can comprehend Thinking, thus *Ideas* seem to be produced in our Minds; or if they are not, this may serve to explain their following one another in an habitual train, when once they are put into that tract, as well as it does to explain such Motions of the Body.³³

³² Boswell, *Life*, v.117 (Aug. 1773).
³³ Locke, *Essay*, ii.xxxiii.6: p. 396.

Thus Trim can reach the fifth commandment only by passing through the first four; and thus Mrs Shandy habitually associates activities that take place on the first Sunday night of every month:

> You have all, I dare say, heard of the animal spirits, as how they are trans-fused from father to son, &c. &c.—and a great deal to that purpose:—Well, you may take my word, that nine parts in ten of a man's sense or his nonsense, his successes and miscarriages in this world depend upon their motions and activity, and the different tracks and trains you put them into; so that when they are once set a-going, whether right or wrong, 'tis not a halfpenny matter,—away they go cluttering like hey-go-mad; and by tread-ing the same steps over and over again, they presently make a road of it, as plain and smooth as a garden-walk, which, when they are once used to, the Devil himself sometimes shall not be able to drive them off it.
>
> *Pray, my dear*, quoth my mother, *have you not forgot to wind up the clock?*[34]

The passage in Locke proposes a close connection, falling only just short of identification, between mind and body: mental disposi-tions are very like physical dispositions, and both come into being through the physical motion of the animal spirits. In borrowing the passage, Sterne preserves this closeness of connection, for he uses it not only to illustrate Mrs Shandy's mechanical association of ideas—which further suggest the idea of sex as mechanical, like clockwork—but also to set up the notion that Tristram's tempera-ment and course of life have been all but determined by the physi-cal circumstances of his conception. This is whimsical, of course, but, notwithstanding, Sterne's representation of the life of the mind as intimately bound up with physical contingencies has a curious attractiveness. Locke had seen the chance association of ideas as something to be deplored; although almost universal, it was, prop-erly speaking, 'Madness', a 'Weakness' and 'Taint' that called for 'Prevention and Cure'.[35] In the passage which opens *Tristram Shandy*, by contrast, it is entirely characteristic that the habitual,

---

[34] *Tristram Shandy* i. ch. 1, pp. 1 f.

[35] Locke, *Essay*, II.xxxiii.4: p. 395. Locke's pejorative emphasis would chime with Bergson's theory in *Laughter*: people behaving in a mechanical way are comic because they bring home to us that we are not machines. But such a theory of comedy will not fit *Tristram Shandy*, where mechanism is attractive as well as comic, and 'Sterne's adaptations of associationism imply a . . . transvaluation of Lockean understanding'. See the excellent general discussion of Sterne's relation to Locke by Peter M. Briggs, 'Locke's *Essay* and the Tentativeness of *Tristram Shandy*', *Studies in Philology* 82 (1985), pp. 493–520: p. 506.

conditioning association of ideas should be thought of as a force for good as well as ill, indeed as offering protection against 'the Devil himself'; psycho-physiological determinism guarantees a kind of innocence.

These matters are everywhere in play in *Tristram*, but nowhere more intelligently explored than at the end and climax of the book, when Tristram comes—at last—to the story of Uncle Toby's amours. Here the relation of body and mind takes its most interesting form: the place of the body in the passion of love. The sequence begins with the final chapers of book eight, where corporal Trim once more offers the ideal of fine feeling as indistinguishable from the motions of the body. He describes the period when a young beguine nursed his wounded knee.

My fever ran very high that night—her figure made sad disturbance within me—I was every moment cutting the world in two—to give her half of it—and every moment was I crying, That I had nothing but a knapsack and eighteen florins to share with her——The whole night long was the fair Beguine, like an angel, close by my bedside, holding back my curtain and offering me cordials—and I was only awakened from my dream by her coming there at the hour promised, and giving them in reality. In truth, she was scarce ever from me, and so accustomed was I to receive life from her hands, that my heart sickened, and I lost colour when she left the room: and yet, continued the corporal, (making one of the strangest reflections upon it in the world)——

——'It *was not* love'——for during the three weeks she was almost constantly with me, fomenting my knee with her hand, night and day—I can honestly say, an' please your honour—that * * * * * * * * * * * * * * * * * * * once.

That was very odd, Trim, quoth my uncle Toby——
I think so too—said Mrs. Wadman.
It never did, said the corporal.[36]

Nevertheless, Trim did fall in love with the fair beguine, as he was 'predestined' to: there is, he explains, 'no resisting our fate'.[37] It happened on a Sunday afternoon, while she was rubbing the itching flesh around the wound with particular care:

The fair Beguine, said the corporal, continued rubbing with her whole hand under my knee—till I fear'd her zeal would weary her——'I would

[36] *Tristram Shandy*, viii. ch. 20: pp. 699 f.
[37] Ibid. ch. 22: p. 701.

do a thousand times more,' said she, 'for the love of Christ'——In saying
which she pass'd her hand across the flannel, to the part above my knee,
which I had equally complained of, and rubb'd it also.

I perceived, then, I was beginning to be in love——

As she continued rub-rub-rubbing—I felt it spread from under her
hand, an' please your honour, to every part of my frame——

The more she rubb'd, and the longer strokes she took——the more the
fire kindled in my veins——till at length, by two or three strokes longer
than the rest——my passion rose to the highest pitch——I seiz'd her
hand——

——And then, thou clapped'st it to thy lips, Trim, said my uncle
Toby——and madest a speech.

Whether the corporal's amour terminated precisely in the way my uncle
Toby described it, is not material; it is enough that it contain'd in it the
essence of all the love-romances which ever have been wrote since the
beginning of the world.[38]

Sterne (or Tristram) makes the reader supply the idea that to be in
love is, in its 'essence', to be physically aroused and to approach
orgasm. Montaigne says almost the same, in an essay referred to at
the beginnng and end of *Tristram Shandy*: 'laying Books aside, and
more simply and materially speaking, I find after all, that *Love is
nothing else but the thirst of enjoying the object desir'd*; neither is
Venus any other thing than the pleasure of discharging the
Vessels'.[39] But where Sterne differs from Montaigne is in using
innuendo: the text suggests the grossly physical reading, but does
not accept responsibility for it. Instead, it is we who must supply it,
as an imagined inference rather than a flesh-and-blood presence in
the text, after the exquisite anti-climax of Toby's modest interruption (in this text full of interruptions) turns the reality of the
moment into witty ambiguity and literary self-consciousness. In
this distanced perspective Trim's manner of falling in love can
appear as genuinely attractive, and the opposition between the
flesh and the spirit can become 'not material', an illusion thrown
up by interpretation. The final sentence draws the thinnest veil over

[38] *Tristram Shandy*, 703 f.
[39] Montaigne, iii.150 (ch. 5). This essay, 'On Some Verses of Virgil', is
Montaigne's fullest treatment of sexuality; it is referred to near the start of *Tristram
Shandy* (i. ch. 4: p. 5) and provides Walter with his speech at the end (ix. ch. 33: p.
806). In the latter case Sterne's immediate source is Charron, whose more censori-
ous phrasing better suits Walter's way of thinking, but Sterne remembers Montaigne
well enough to reunite the passages which Charron had separated.

a bawdy thought, yet defies us to see the identification of the sentimental and the physical as reductive.

This tenuously idyllic note in Trim's love for the fair beguine is
reinforced by the contrast which Sterne then introduces. Once
more, Trim's antagonist is Walter. The body, for Walter, is an ass,
'a beast concupiscent' who must be made to leave off kicking, and
he is in the matter of love a convinced dualist, urging upon Toby
by the authority of Plato the doctrine of 'two different and distinct
kinds of *love*', the one '*rational*', in which 'Venus had nothing to
do', involving 'the desire of philosophy and truth', and the other
'*natural*', which 'excites to *desire*, simply'.[40] This exasperated
opposition of mind to body is clearly bound up with Walter's
misogyny, his pedantry, and his comically absurd mentalism. It gets
firm rebuttal: 'What signifies it, brother Shandy, replied my uncle
Toby, which of the two it is, provided it will but make a man
marry, and love his wife, and get a few children.'[41] The comedy
here seems rooted in the inseparability of mind and body, and plays
its humour against any attempt to set up the realm of the mind as
a thing apart.

Yet what Sterne leaves us with is nothing so simple as the
triumph of a comedy which celebrates the body over a Walterism
which degrades it. The protagonist of these final scenes is Toby:
Toby in love with the widow Wadman. The effect of listening to
Trim's story about the beguine leaves him vulnerable to the
amorous widow's advances; he looks into her eye, as an immediate
consequence falls in love, and, like Trim, acquiesces in his fate. But
Tristram Shandy does not end with a marriage. The widow is
concerned to discover the exact nature of the wound to his groin
which Toby sustained at the siege of Namur, and when the innocent Toby, who had taken this concern as an instance of her
compassionate nature, learns from Trim that her interest is of a
thoroughly practical, reflective, deliberate kind, he is profoundly
shocked, even traumatized. The courtship collapses. Walter's
response to this will be a diatribe against women and against lust,
which plainly tells us more about Walter than about women. Yet,
within the circle of the novel, the widow Wadman does indeed
function as the threatening force of Walter's paranoia: that is to

[40] *Tristram Shandy*, viii. ch. 31: p. 716; viii. ch. 33: pp. 718–21.
[41] Ibid. ch. 33: p. 718.

say, the gentle, amiable, trusting Uncle Toby really does get hurt. The widow's behaviour, we are told, induces in Toby a lifelong modesty. It is entirely reasonable to ask why. For although the most innocent of sentimentalists, Toby is neither prudish nor sexless. He is not, in fact, disabled from the marriage state, as Tristram unequivocally tells us; he is capable of speaking to the widow of the pleasures of the marriage-bed, and gives his reasons for wanting to marry as those 'written . . . in the Common-Prayer Book'.[42] Or, to put the question in a less character-based form: how is it that such a sexually knowing work as *Tristram Shandy*, with bawdy insinuation on so many of its pages, should take as its shocking climax the revelation of a woman's interest in whether or not the man she has it in mind to marry is sexually disabled? It is this discovery which brings the whole apparently never-ending narrative to a sudden halt, and blocks comedy's conventional progress towards resolution in marriage: but why should this be?

The answer is, I think, that widow Wadman is the nearest thing in *Tristram Shandy* to a moral agent. That is to say, she has intentions, and acts accordingly. Her behaviour connects reflection with action, mind with body, and does so without any Trim-like quality of automatism. In particular, her designs on Toby threaten to raise sex above the level of either innuendo or mechanism into the realm of the conscious will. This is such a shock that the screen goes blank, so to speak, and we become aware of a sense in which Toby's modesty is shared by the book as a whole. Her wish for intercourse is felt as such a threat—a kind of violation—because of our strong sense of Toby's *singularity*, a singularity which he shares with the book in which he appears.

That last point is worth dwelling on. Toby's singularity is most evident in his 'hobby-horse', his obsession with military fortification: but this makes him only the most extreme figure in Sterne's gallery of eccentrics. Their singularity is what they have in common. This singularity extends to Tristram himself, who fulfils his father's opinion that he 'should neither think, nor act like any other man's child',[43] and of course to the book which records his life and opinions. 'Nothing odd will do long. "Tristram Shandy"

[42] Viz. for the procreation of children; to avoid fornication; and for the mutual society, help, and comfort of man and wife. *Tristram Shandy*, ix. 'The Eighteenth Chapter': p. 787.
[43] Ibid. ch. 1: p. 737.

did not last',[44] growled Johnson, asserting the claims of 'general nature' in literature as in life, and putting his finger on something fundamental in his opposition to Sterne. For to be as 'odd' as *Tristram Shandy*, or as singular as Tristram or Toby, is to be well adapted to the atmosphere of Shandean contingency, in which normative judgement cannot operate, and the particulars of the case resist generalization: what is particular or private acquires a kind of sanctity, or at least a new authenticity, of a kind that would not have been recognized in the previous century. This can be linked to the steady tendency in contemporary philosophy to erode the reality of the general in favour of the particular. For Locke, 'general natures' had no existence out in the world, but existed only in our ideas. Berkeley took this further with the argument that even our ideas are always, in fact, of particulars, and that generality exists only in language: a discovery which Hume thought the most significant to have been made in recent philosophy.[45] But more importantly, this emphasis in recent philosophy went with cultural changes that placed a new value on individuality. To be odd or eccentric, or in an earlier idiom to 'have a humour', was no longer to invite a normative, corrective ridicule; 'humour' came increasingly to be contradistinguished from 'wit' or 'ridicule' and to suggest something amiable or even admirable.[46] Steele wrote in the *Guardian*:

There is scarce an *Englishman* of any Life and Spirit, that has not some odd Cast of Thought, some Original Humour, that distinguishes him from his Neighbour. Hence it is, that our Comedies are enriched with such a Diversity of Characters, as is not to be seen upon any other Theatre in *Europe*. . . . This makes it as impracticable to Foreigners to enter into a thorough Knowledge of the English, as it would be to learn the *Chinese* Language, in which there is a different Character for every individual Word. . . .

Though this Singularity of Temper, which runs through the Generality of us, may make us seem whimsical to Strangers; yet it furnishes out a perpetual Change of Entertainment to our selves, and diversifies all our

---

[44] Boswell, *Life*, ii.449 (March 1776).
[45] Locke, *Essay*, III.iii.9–11: pp. 412–14; Berkeley, 'Introduction' to *A Treatise concerning the Principles of Human Knowledge*: *Works*, ed. Luce and Jessop, II.25–40; Hume, *Treatise*, p. 17.
[46] This is helpfully documented in Stuart Tave, *The Amiable Humorist* (Chicago, 1960).

Conversations with such a variety of Mirth, as is not to be met with in any other Country. . . .

Ours is the only Country, perhaps, in the whole World, where every Man, rich and poor, dares to have a Humour of his own, and to avow it upon all Occasions. I make no doubt, but that it is to this great Freedom of Temper, and this unconstrained manner of Living, that we owe, in a great Measure, the Number of shining *Genius's*, which rise up amongst us from time to time.[47]

Singularity makes for humour; it also goes together with 'life and spirit', promotes genius, and guarantees authenticity. This newly positive evaluation implies a mistrust of the conventions of society, a mistrust that was putting down deep roots in the middle of the eighteenth century. The extreme statement is by Rousseau, described by Hume as 'a great Humourist' with 'great singularities',[48] who was writing his *Confessions* at about the same time that Sterne was completing *Tristram Shandy*:

I have resolved on an enterprise which has no precedent, and which, once complete, will have no imitator. My purpose is to display to my kind a portrait in every way true to nature, and the man I shall portray will be myself.

Simply myself. I know my own heart and understand my fellow man. But I am made unlike any one I have ever met; I will even venture to say that I am like no one in the whole world. I may be no better, but at least I am different.[49]

Such absolute difference becomes a virtue in a world where the channels of social communication seem blocked or unhealthy or intolerably shallow. Sterne's characters are sentimentally reassuring partly because each is so inalienably himself, so free from deformation by the pressures of society. (How innocently Toby and Trim have passed through army life!) Toby is sublimely immune to such pressures, and if this makes him, from one point of view,

[47] Steele, *The Guardian*, ed. John Calhoun Stephens (Lexington, Ky., 1982), pp. 474 f.: no. 144. Tristram refers to this as a familiar position when introducing the reader to Uncle Toby: *Tristram Shandy*, i. ch. 21: p. 71.

[48] *The Letters of David Hume*, ed. J. Y. T. Greig, 2 vols. (Oxford, 1932), ii.13 (no. 303; 11 Feb. 1766); ii.15 (no. 304; 16 Feb. 1766). Hume was to discover at first hand how acutely problematic was Rousseau's ability to understand or be understood by others; see Ernst Campbell Mossner, *The Life of David Hume* (Edinburgh, 1954), pp. 521 ff.

[49] *The Confessions of Jean-Jacques Rousseau*, trans. J. M. Cohen (Harmondsworth, 1953), p. 17.

mildly insane, it also makes him the great model of Tristram's sentimental morality:

> ... my uncle *Toby* had scarce a heart to retalliate upon a fly.
>
> —Go,—says he, one day at dinner, to an over-grown one which had buzz'd about his nose, and tormented him cruelly all dinner-time,—and which, after infinite attempts, he had caught at last, as it flew by him;—I'll not hurt thee, says my uncle *Toby*, rising from his chair, and going a-cross the room, with the fly in his hand,—I'll not hurt a hair of thy head:—Go, says he, lifting up the sash, and opening his hand as he spoke, to let it escape;—go poor Devil, get thee gone, why should I hurt thee?——This world surely is wide enough to hold both thee and me.[50]

Wide enough to hold both thee and me, in the utterness of our difference one from another. Sternean sentiment implies such difference, is in a sense a compensation for it. Toby cannot communicate with the fly (as Sterne makes us feel by having him talk to the creature), they have nothing (except their vulnerability) in common, only an infinitely wide and undefined world could hold them both, and it is precisely this which makes Toby's compassion so moving, so absurd, and itself so pitiable. Tristram tells us that his witnessing of this action of Toby's has constituted the best part of his moral education: and indeed Toby's forbearance toward the fly is writ large in the tolerance Tristram extends toward the idiosyncrasies of all mankind:

> Have not the wisest of men in all ages, not excepting *Solomon* himself,— have they not had their HOBBY-HORSES;—their running horses,—their coins and their cockle-shells, their drums and their trumpets, their fiddles, their pallets,——their maggots and their butterflies?—and so long as a man rides his HOBBY-HORSE peaceably and quietly along the King's highway, and neither compels you or me to get up behind him,——pray, Sir, what have either you or I to do with it?[51]

'*De gustibus non est disputandum*;—that is, there is no disputing against HOBBY-HORSES' is how Tristram begins the chapter immediately following. A hobby-horse is a personal, incommensurable thing; its fascination is not communicable. Singularity is jeopardized by communication, and the difficulties which Sterne's characters have in communicating with each other, and which

---

[50] *Tristram Shandy*, ii. ch. 12: pp. 131 f.
[51] Ibid. i. ch. 7: p. 12.

Tristram feigns or fabricates in communicating with the reader, both express that singularity and protect it.[52] Locke had written that words properly *'stand for nothing, but the* Ideas *in the Mind of him that uses them'*, yet men secretly refer them to ideas in the minds of others, and to the reality of things, because '*Men* would not be thought to talk *barely* of their own Imaginations, but of Things as really they are'.[53] It is, in other words, the pressure of social convention and expectation ('Men would not be thought . . .') that fends off a kind of solipsism, where each individual's experience would become a country with its own language. In *Tristram Shandy* such social pressures are weak or negligible or positively flouted; words become markedly idiosyncratic and subjective in their reference; and hobby-horses thrive.

Locke was writing specifically about words, and the spectacular failures of communication in *Tristram Shandy* are linguistic. As already noted with Trim's hat, much play is made with gesture and other forms of non-verbal representation as having the potential to avoid the problems of language. The paradigm case is Toby's progress after his wound. His wish to describe or narrate the siege of Namur with a proper attention to particularities, involves him in perplexity, due to 'the almost insurmountable difficulties he found in telling his story intelligibly, and giving such clear ideas of the differences and distinctions between the scarp and counterscarp,— —the glacis and covered way,——the half-moon and ravelin,—— as to make his company fully comprehend where and what he was about'.[54] Toby's struggles in this quintessentially Lockean area of difficulty—'the unsteady uses of words which have perplexed the

---

[52] For a fine discussion that bears intelligently on this matter, see John Mullan, 'Laurence Sterne and the "Sociality" of the Novel', in *Sentiment and Sociability: The Language of Feeling in the Eighteenth Century* (Oxford, 1988), pp. 147–200. Mullan's account differs from mine in so far as he draws a sharp distinction between the instances of non-communication within the novel and the 'sociality' established between novel and reader: 'the sympathy that can bridge the gulf between perceptions' allows us to feel that 'the misunderstandings and non-communications . . . are only apparent' (pp. 160 f.). Later in his discussion, however, he also speaks of 'the impossibility of generalizing sympathy and sociability': 'the relationship between reader and text (that "sociality") works because it can purport to be unique, and unrealizable outside the confines of the closet in which the book is read' (p. 192). His immediate reference there is to *A Sentimental Journey*; I find that sense of singularity equally in *Tristram*.

[53] Locke, *Essay concerning Human Understanding*, III.ii.2, 4 f.: pp. 405–7.

[54] *Tristram Shandy*, ii. ch. 1: p. 94.

clearest and most exalted understandings'⁵⁵—are such as to aggra-
vate his wound and threaten his very existence. 'By heaven! his life
was put in jeopardy by words.'⁵⁶ But recovery comes as he moves
first from words to maps, and then from maps to models on the
bowling-green, and so frees himself 'from a world of sad explanations'⁵⁷ (wonderful phrase!) to the condition of Shandean bliss in
which signs are as concrete as the things for which they were once
supposed to stand, and particulars require no explanation. This is
a healing progression—'the happy means ... of procuring my
uncle *Toby* his HOBBY-HORSE'⁵⁸—but it implies the abandonment
of communication. Where individuals differ, *only* terms whose
meaning is governed by convention—words, not things—can function as a medium of exchange. Gesture, as Sterne deploys it, only
plays at communication: what the black page marking the death of
Yorick actually communicates is not grief or commemoration, but
an idea about the inadequacy of language to express grief or
commemoration: it describes the enclosing circle of its own self-
consciousness. What it really expresses is isolation. This is largely
whimsical; but there can be real emotional power in Sterne's
silences or in gestures which imply the inexpressible, like Toby's
whistling of Lillibulero at moments of stress, or above all in the
gesture by which, at the book's great climax, he signifies his understanding of the widow Wadman's low designs:

My uncle Toby gave a long whistle——but in a note which could scarce
be heard across the table.
  The Corporal had advanced too far to retire——in three words he told
the rest——
  My uncle Toby laid down his pipe as gently upon the fender, as if it had
been spun from the unravellings of a spider's web——
  ——Let us go to my brother Shandy's, said he.⁵⁹

If what threatens Toby here is sex raised into full consciousness, it
is also full communication: intercourse in both senses. Trim
enlightens Toby about the widow 'in three words': perhaps the
only instance of straightforward communication to be achieved in
the entire nine volumes. And the immediate consequence is hurt: as
though Sterne feared that the only likely outcome of real human

⁵⁵ Ibid. ch. 2: p. 100. ⁵⁶ Ibid. 101.
⁵⁷ Ibid. ch. 1: p. 96. ⁵⁸ Ibid.
⁵⁹ Ibid. ix. ch. 31: p. 803.

interaction will be hurt. That is why goodness, above all else, is a matter of forbearance, tolerance, respect for the singularity of the individual, allowing each man to ride his hobby horse peaceably down the King's Highway. Tristram's own forbearance with regard to Toby at this moment is a fine example. What he gives us first is an image of enormous implicit vulnerability: Toby lays down his pipe, one of his chief comforters throughout the book, as suddenly become hugely fragile: the spider's web, traditional image of self-sufficient subjectivity,[60] unravels here. Then, most poignantly, we have the double dash, to end one paragraph and begin another, as though Tristram, at least, will respect Toby's privacy. His thoughts and feelings are not to be communicated; we shall not intrude. And then, finally, in recoil from this moment of real risk and real encounter, 'Let us go to my brother Shandy's': to the bosom of one's family, who can be relied upon for talk that does not threaten communication or understanding, to the body-hating Walter, and, beyond that, to the refuge of perpetual bachelordom and lifelong 'modesty'. It is a recoil abetted, with perfect tact, by Tristram as narrator, who eschews all 'sad explanations' by returning us to the familiar pleasures of the Shandy hearth in a comic finale of Shandean insouciance. Walter, indignant 'at the trespass done his brother', is moved to an oration on sexual desire as the root of all evil and disorder,

Yorick was rising up to batter the whole hypothesis to pieces——
——When Obadiah broke into the middle of the room with a complaint, which cried out for an immediate hearing . . .

And the novel ends, both pointedly and inconsequentially, with the story of the alleged impotence of the town bull. Toby's distress, thus diverted into jest, evaporates; and these momentarily serious, painful matters turn into mere talk and text on the one hand, and amusement on the other.

L- -d ! said my mother, what is all this story about?——
A COCK and a BULL, said Yorick——And one of the best of its kind, I ever heard.[61]

Nowhere does Sterne show us more clearly what Shandeism is for.

---

[60] e.g. 'My father spun his [knowledge], every thread of it, out of his own brain.' *Tristram Shandy*, v. ch. 16: p. 445.
[61] *Tristram Shandy*, ix. ch. 32–3: pp. 804–9.

* * *

It is harder to decide what Shandeism is worth. Its function, I have tried to show, lies in realising a play of consciousness in which—for all the seeming determinism of event—nothing is consequential, and which seems capable of subduing all experience to its own quality. This play of consciousness is both delightful in itself, in the way it *flirts* with experience, and protective, in the way it deflects any substantial encounter with realities outside its own enchanted circle. Sterne referred to his writing as his hobby-horse,[62] and within the text we feel how the writing of *Tristram Shandy* is Tristram's own hobby-horse, an absorbing activity which, like Toby's fortifications on the bowling-green, interposes a huge distance between itself and the realities in which it originates. By writing his life and opinions in the way that he does, Tristram sets out towards the region of sad explanations in the happy knowledge that he will never reach it. Shandeism can thus be described as a form of *diversion*. But if it diverts the mind from what threatens hurt, it does so with a self-awareness that rebuffs any charge of simple escapism. Such a charge would be misplaced, partly because the comedy of *Tristram* queries whether anything can be more real to experience than the play of consciousness, and partly because what animates the book is, in truly sceptical spirit, less the mind's unwillingness than its *incapacity* for holding to realities.

This is true in particular of those realities which insist on the mind's finally inevitable relation to the body, and so jeopardize that free play of consciousness in which Tristram delights. Sex is pre-eminently one such reality; death is another. Samuel Johnson believed that mortality is what makes life serious, although he found the idea of death so dreadful that he could say that 'the whole of life is but keeping away the thoughts of it'.[63] In *Tristram Shandy* that sentiment is transposed into a much lighter key: the 'keeping away' is so successfully and energetically performed, that death itself—whether Bobby's, Yorick's, or Tristram's—seems to have no compelling power: it appears only at the margins of consciousness, and is quite unable to gain a hold on Tristram's 'good spirits':

[62] *Letters of Laurence Sterne*, ed. Lewis Perry Curtis (Oxford, 1935), p. 143: to Lady Dacre, Sept. 1761.
[63] Boswell, *Life*, ii.93 (Oct. 1769).

In dangers ye gilded my horizon with hope, and when DEATH himself
knocked at my door—ye bad him come again; and in so gay a tone of careless indifference, did ye do it, that he doubted of his commission——
    '—There must certainly be some mistake in this matter,' quoth he.[64]

It is easy to see why Johnson would not greatly care for this. There
is a limit to how impressed we can be by Tristram's gaiety in the
face of death, because the Shandean text does not seriously grant
death admission in the first place. (Imagine recommending
Tristram to someone diagnosed with a terminal illness.) *Tristram
Shandy* has always been a troublesome work for those who want
literature to help us grasp realities—thereby better to enjoy life, or
better to endure it, in Johnson's words—rather than help us evade
them. But dissatisfaction of the Johnsonian kind finally tells us
little; it hardly engages with what Sterne is offering, but merely
pushes against an open door. For *Tristram Shandy* confesses at
every point its unseriousness, its irresponsibility towards realities as
they may exist outside Tristram's play of consciousness.[65] Any
attempt to evaluate Shandeism by the yardstick of the reality principle which it rejects, or (rather) simply sets aside, is always liable
to miss the book altogether. Richard Lanham is one of the writers
on Sterne who have seen this most clearly; he insists that the playfulness of *Tristram* defines our experience of it, that the pleasure it
generates is its own sufficient *raison d'être*: 'We may, I suppose,
talk about [Walter and Toby] not accepting "the full consequences
of the human state." But those consequences, whatever they are,
are nowhere suggested in *Tristram Shandy*. Its sphere *is* the game
sphere. This is its reality.'[66] Critics of Sterne regularly wish to pull
the buoyancy of *Tristram* down to earth, to see the playfulness as
instrumental in some more serious end or as holding some large
general significance about narrative or discourse or how we understand the world: but these 'sermonizing' impulses, Lanham insists,
go against the grain of the novel, which celebrates without embar-
rassment 'those endless resources of self-deception that protect our

    [64] *Tristram Shandy*, vii. ch. 1: pp. 575 f.
    [65] 'Sterne was perhaps the first eighteenth-century writer of consequence to shake
himself free of the fear of subjectivity.' Michael V. Deporte, *Nightmares and
Hobbyhorses: Swift, Sterne, and Augustan Ideas of Madness* (San Marino, Calif.,
1974), p. 133.
    [66] Richard A. Lanham, *Tristram Shandy: The Games of Pleasure* (Berkeley and
Los Angeles,1973), p. 80.

pleasures. Sermonizing ignores the resources of game, of self-infatuation.'[67]

This makes the task of judgement peculiarly delicate. In an attempt to get some critical purchase on *Tristram* without ignoring 'the resources of game', let me develop the comparison with Montaigne: a comparison that will not introduce alien, 'sermonizing' premises about what Sterne ought to have been doing. Sterne knew and admired Montaigne's *Essais*; he draws on them at several points in *Tristram*; and when one of his readers suggested that he must know his Montaigne as well as his prayer-book he was happy to agree.[68] Clearly, Tristram shares a great deal with Montaigne, beyond the absorbing project of writing the self. There is the spontaneity of utterance:

> I fall to without premeditation, or design; the first word begets the second, and so to the end of the Chapter[69]

the pleasure in digression:

> Good God, how beautiful then are [Plutarch's] variations and digressions, and then most of all when they seem to be fortuitous, and introduc'd for want of heed. 'Tis the indiligent Reader that loses my subject, and not I; there will always be found some words or other in a corner that are to the purpose, though it lie very close. I ramble indiscreetly and tumultuously . . .[70]

and the extraordinary tolerance of heteronomy and the self-sufficiency of performance:

> I pretend to no other fruit by acting than to act, and add to it no long pursuit nor proposals; every action plays its own Game, win if it can.[71]

[67] Ibid. 136. See also Iain McGilchrist, *Against Criticism* (London, 1982), pp. 131–75, for a fine essay on Sterne that consciously resists the sermonizing impulse of much criticism.

[68] *Letters*, p. 122: to Rev. Robert Brown, 9 Sept. 1760. See Jonathan Lamb, 'Sterne's Use of Montaigne', *Comparative Literature* 32 (1980), 1–41, for an interesting if dizzying discussion of aspects of this relationship; some of the ideas are developed further in Jonathan Lamb, *Sterne's Fiction and the Double Principle* (Cambridge, 1989). Lamb's discussion is much better than that by Donald R. Wehrs, 'Sterne, Cervantes, Montaigne: Fideistic Skepticism and the Rhetoric of Desire', in *Comparative Literature Studies* 25 (1988), 127–51. Painting with a very broad brush, Wehrs notes how these writers (along with Erasmus) prompt multiple interpretations, briskly interprets this phenomenon in terms of the *epoche* of classical scepticism, and then interprets that suspense of judgement as Christian fideism.

[69] Montaigne, i.400 (ch. 39).

[70] Ibid. iii.348 f. (ch. 9).

[71] Ibid. 5 (ch. 1).

Moreover, Montaigne has his own version of Shandean diversion. In the essay entitled 'Of Diversion', Montaigne writes of how no-one (except only Socrates) has ever really confronted death in their thoughts; even those on the scaffold, or those falling in a battle or fighting in a duel, are always thinking of something else. This fluid mobility of the mind is what Montaigne can actively make use of in ridding himself of any undesirable passion or obsessive idea:

> If I am not able to contend with it, I escape from it; and in avoiding it, slip out of the way, and make my doubles: Shifting of Place, Business, and Company, I secure my self in the crowd of other Thoughts and Fancies, where it loses my trace, and I escape.[72]

The subjectivity of those 'other thoughts and fancies' is allowed its own share of reality; the free play of consciousness can reconstitute experience:

> A frivolous Cause you will say, How a Cause? There needs none to agitate the Mind; a mere whimsy without body, and without subject will rule and sway it. Let me think of building Castles in *Spain*, my Imagination suggests to me Conveniences and Pleasures, with which my Soul is really delighted and pleased.[73]

The dual implication there—of the utter foolishness of the mind, and of a precious resource that lies precisely in that foolishness—is not unShandean. Montaigne's castles in Spain are more ephemeral constructions of the mind than Sterne's hobby-horses, but they work in a similar way.

Yet there is also a difference between them. In the last sentence quoted above, the consciousness that recalls its real pleasure in the fancies of the mind is *identical* with the consciousness that recognizes such fancies as private illusions. One might express this by saying that in Montaigne the play of subjectivity is in full communication with realities outside the mind, including, most obviously and prominently, the reality of the body. Take, for example, a passage from the great final essay, 'Of Experience', where Montaigne displays the *eschapatoires*, or stratagems for escape, by which his mind diverts itself from the reality of his sick and aging body. He rehearses the series of consoling reflections which his mind supplies his imagination about the relative merits and advantages of suffering the agonies of kidney-stones, and as he does so—

[72] Montaigne, iii.79 (ch. 4).   [73] Ibid. 85 (ch. 4).

over several pages—he himself appears to enter into those arguments, to give himself up to his own performance, so that what began as the exemplification of a mental strategy, externally regarded, becomes an immediate reality of consciousness, a philosophical attitude animated from within. This is a little like Walter's philosophical self-consolation at the news of Bobby's death, but the crucial difference between them can be felt in the way that Montaigne ends this sequence of consolations and, in a wonderful passage, reflects on their efficacy:

> By such like arguments, weak and strong, as *Cicero* did the disease of his Old Age, I try to rock asleep and amuse my imagination, and to dress its Wounds. If I find them worse to morrow, I will provide new remedies and applications. That this is true, I am come to that pass of late, that the least motion forces pure blood out of my Reins: And what of that, I stir nevertheless as before, and ride after my Hounds with a Juvenile ardour; And find that I have very good satisfaction for an accident of that importance, when it costs me no more but a little heaviness and uneasiness in that part. 'Tis some great Stone that wastes and consumes the substance of our Kidneys, and of my Life, which I by little and little evacuate, not without some natural pleasure, as an excrement henceforward superfluous and troublesome.[74]

Diversion here does not distance itself from the realities of the body, which can be very fully acknowledged without putting an end to the play of consciousness. Montaigne knows, as an intelligent sceptic must, that all his moralist's arguments, his 'remedies and applications' are *eschapatoires*, kinds of diversion or escape offered by the intellect to the imagination, the question of whose truth Montaigne contemplates with a certain generous irony. There is enough truth in them to serve his turn, at least for a while: enough *vraisemblance* for performance. Which is to say that this irony is not exactly detachment. 'If I find them worse to morrow, I will provide new remedies.' And the magnificent assertions that follow (and that were indeed provided 'tomorrow', i.e. added to the later edition) dissolve any remaining dichotomy between escapist play of mind and the embracing of reality: for even while they offer themselves as just such a further *eschapatoire* for the mind, they equally lay claim to the immediacy of vivid physical sensation. What Montaigne little by little evacuates, according to

[74] Ibid. 520 (ch. 13).

the French as the English syntax, is both his kidney-stone and his life: a phrase both metaphorical and literal, in which mind and body play into one another; just so, the physicality of Montaigne's 'juvenile ardour' in riding with his hounds is splendid precisely because of the juvenile ardour with which the old man's imagination relishes and recites it. The end of all this exploration of the freedom and resourcefulness of subjectivity is that Montaigne can finish, remarkably, by affirming the continual, necessary, natural interconnectedness of mind and body:

I, who but crawl upon the Earth, hate this inhuman Wisdom, that will have us despise and hate all culture of the Body. I look upon it as an equal Injustice to loath natural Pleasures, as to be too much in love with them. . . . A Man should neither pursue nor Flie, but receive them. I receive them I confess a little too affectionately and kindly, and easily suffer my self to follow my natural Propension. We have nothing to do to exaggerate their inanity, they themselves will make us sufficiently sensible of it. Thanks be to our sick Minds that abate our Joys, and put them out of taste with them, as with themselves. They entertain both themselves and all they receive, one while better, and another worse, according to their insatiable, vagabond, and versatile Essence . . . . The pure Pleasures, as well as the pure Displeasures of the Imagination, say some, are the greatest . . . . 'Tis no wonder; It makes them to its own liking, and cuts them out of the whole Cloth: Of which I every day see notable Examples, and peradventure to be desir'd. But I, who am of a mixed and heavy Condition, cannot snap so soon at this one simple Object but that I negligently suffer my self to be carried away with the present Pleasures of the general human *Law*. Intellectually sensible, and sensibly intellectual.[75]

Although Montaigne cannot sustain the pure pleasures of the imagination, his 'mixed and heavy condition' makes possible pleasures of a different kind. These are pleasures of 'the general human law': through grasping the interrelation of mind and body Montaigne moves beyond strictly individual experience. This movement beyond what is individual is a moment of breakthrough. The sceptical starting-point of the essay had been an assertion of the singularity of things, a singularity which renders desperate all attempts at generalization:

Reason has so many forms, that we know not which to take; *Experience* has no fewer. The Consequence we will draw from the conference of

Events is unsure, by reason they are always unlike. There is no quality so universal in this Image of things, as diversity and variety. Both the Greeks, the Latins, and we, for the most express Example of similitude, have pitch'd upon that of Eggs. And yet there have been Men, particularly one at *Delphos*, who could distinguish Marks of difference amongst Eggs so well, that he never mistook one for another: And, having many *Hens*, could tell which had laid it.[76]

The anecdote of the eagle-eyed poultry-farmer from Delphi is one of those scarcely credible, mildly absurd, pointedly *localized* exempla which Montaigne loves to use: its weakness as significant evidence, as support for a generalization concerning the weakness of generalizations, is all to the point. The uniqueness of particular experience can never support general knowledge; cases never establish laws, and laws never quite fit cases. Montaigne goes on to tell how he has, accordingly, abandoned the precepts and prescriptions of medicine, and fallen back, by way of self-therapy, on merely his own highly particular habits and inclinations. We hear, at length and in detail, about his preferences in sleeping, eating, drinking (out of glass only), heating (German stoves, not French hearths), washing, noise, defaecation, sex, clothing, dental care, and so on: his singularities and idiosyncrasies, certainly, if not quite his hobby-horses. Yet, as he wrote elsewhere, 'Every Man carries the entire form of human Condition',[77] and so it proves: by the end of the essay his embrace of subjectivity has carried beyond itself, to 'the general human *Law*. Intellectually sensible, and sensibly intellectual'.

That note is beyond anything in *Tristram Shandy*, and the difference is reflected in one particular passage in which Montaigne is cited by name. What this passage suggests is that Tristram sees in Montaigne only an achievement like his own, which is all to do with the freedom and detachment of the mind:

A man's body and his mind, with the utmost reverence to both I speak it, are exactly like a jerkin, and a jerkin's lining;—rumple the one—you rumple the other. There is one certain exception however in this case, and that is, when you are so fortunate a fellow, as to have had your jerkin made of a gum-taffeta, and the body-lining to it, of a sarcenet or thin persian.

---

[76] Ibid. 466 (ch. 13).   [77] Ibid. 27 (ch. 2).

Zeno, Cleanthes, Diogenes Babylonius, Dyonisius Heracleotes, Antipater, Panaetius and *Possidonius* amongst the *Greeks;—Cato* and *Varro* and *Seneca* amongst the *Romans;—Pantenus* and *Clemens Alexandrinus* and *Montaigne* amongst the Christians; and a score and a half of good honest, unthinking, *Shandean* people as ever lived, whose names I can't recollect,—all pretended that their jerkins were made after this fashion,——you might have rumpled and crumpled, and doubled and creased, and fretted and fridged the outsides of them all to pieces;—in short, you might have played the very devil with them, and at the same time, not one of the insides of 'em would have been one button the worse, for all you had done to them.

I believe in my conscience that mine is made up somewhat after this sort . . . [78]

We can recognize here the same movement that is now familiar from other passages. The opening assertion of the unity of mind and body—'rumple the one—you rumple the other'—is given with a comical banality, an apprehension of such unity as merely automatic or mechanical, that positively encourages the counter-assertion of the autonomy of the mind. Hence the metaphor begins as a simile, but ends as a conceit: it offers to bring mind and body together, embodying a concept (the unity of body and mind) in a physical image (jerkin and lining) which it is said to be 'exactly like', but it then runs into a comical, quasi-Swiftian literalism in which the metaphorical significance is absorbed and dissipated by concentration upon the physical vehicle (the 'body-lining' being, with happy irresponsibility, a metaphor for the *mind*). The metaphor is so self-consciously elaborated as to convey a certain whimsical detachment, as though the notion that the life of the mind could ever be expressed and realized in an image drawn from the world of physical reality were itself a kind of joke: an attitude perfectly congenial to what Tristram remarks as the common ground between Shandeism and Stoicism, the claim for the mind's independence of body and circumstance. Here again there is a swift shift of viewpoint, a kind of feint at the physical, which turns on the word 'pretended'. 'All pretended that their jerkins were made after this fashion.' In 1760 'pretended' could still, just about, be a neutral term, simply meaning 'claimed', but it was already liable to carry its modern implication of making a claim which is untrue.

[78] *Tristram Shandy*, iii. ch. 4: pp. 189 f.

According to Johnson's *Dictionary*, 'it is seldom used without
shade of censure'. The all-too-scholarly list of Great Stoics (lifted,
with two significant exceptions, from Chambers' *Cyclopaedia*)
sounds likely to be a catalogue of comic presumption, and sets up
an expectation that this 'pretending' to the autonomy of the mind
will be exposed as a delusion, will inevitably trip up on the world
of physical realities. This expectation would be strengthened for
any reader who recognized the first name Sterne added to
Chambers' list, Dionysius Heracleotes, a pupil of Zeno who gave
up stoicism because of a painful eye disease.[79] But the pejorative
implication of 'pretended' that we anticipate, never in fact materi-
alizes, and the clauses which follow ('you might have rumpled . . .')
effectively confirm what is pretended as truth—or rather, they
adopt the viewpoint of 'pretence' so completely that no way of
checking pretence against reality is available. Tristram voicing
what the stoics thought about themselves, in what would be a case
of free indirect style, becomes indistinguishable from Tristram
reporting on how they lived. What the mind pretends is sovereign
within its own sphere; it encounters, or registers, no resistance.
And this, as Tristram says, is his own case. If he pretends to
respond to his hostile critics with quasi-stoical good humour
(which is where the passage is heading), then, within the sphere of
his own self-consciousness, which is also the sphere of the text (and
we cannot go outside it), he does so. The whole book, after all, is
nothing more nor less than Tristram's play of consciousness, the
activity of Tristram *pretending*.

Montaigne is the other name Sterne added to the list of stoics
lifted from the *Cyclopaedia*. This is not Montaigne as I have been
describing him, but it is perfectly possible to see why Sterne should
think to place Montaigne in this company. Some of the earlier
essays in particular have passages that readily could be described as
stoical, where the sceptical emphasis on the subjectivity of judgement is explored as promoting an inner freedom and self-posses-
sion. The epigraph of *Tristram Shandy*, which is taken from the
stoic Epictetus, forms the basis of one of the most substantial
essays in Montaigne's first book:

[79] See Melvyn New, ed., *The Life and Opinions of Tristram Shandy, Gentleman*,
3 vols. (Gainesville, Fla., 1984): *Volume III: The Notes*, p. 208.

Men (says an ancient *Greek* Sentence) are tormented with the Opinions they have of things, and not by the things themselves. It were a great Victory obtain'd for the relief of our miserable Human condition, could this proposition be establish'd for certain, and true throughout. For if evils have no admission into us, but by the judgment we our selves make of them, it should seem that it is then in our own power to despise them, or to turn them to good. If things surrender themselves to our mercy, why do we not convert, and accommodate them to our advantage? If what we call Evil, and Torment, is neither Evil, nor Torment of it self, but only that our Fancy gives it that Quality, and makes it so, it is in us to change, and alter it, and it being in our own choice, if there be no constraint upon us, we must certainly be very strange Fools to take Arms for that side, which is most offensive to us, and to give Sickness, Want, and contempt, a nauseous taste, if it be in our power to give them a more graceful Relish, and if Fortune simply providing the matter, 'tis for us to give it the form.[80]

'Fortune simply providing the matter, 'tis for us to give it the form', could be the perfect motto for the extreme rhetorical self-consciousness with which Tristram narrates his life. And as Montaigne tries out Epictetus' thesis, he sketches an account of the mind's supremacy that must have appealed to Tristram:

That which makes us suffer Pain with so much Impatience is the not being accustomed to repose our chiefest Contentment in the Soul, that we do not enough rely upon her who is the sole and soveraign Mistress of our Condition. The Body, saving in greater or less proportion, has but one and the same Bent and Biass; whereas the Soul is variable into all sorts of forms; and subjects to her self, and to her own Empire, all things whatsoever: both the Senses of the Body, and all other Accidents: and therefore it is that we ought to study her, to enquire into her, and to rouse up all her powerful Faculties.[81]

But this elevation of the mind is not, as we have seen, where Montaigne's scepticism is heading in the later essays, where the play of mind is part of a larger process that leads back to the inter-dependence of mind and body. In 'Of Experience' Montaigne can partly escape the agonies of the stone through the reflections of his mind; in 'On Some Verses of Vergil' he can oppose the vivacity of his erotic imagination to the sluggishness of his aging body. But in both essays the point of maximum reality, the point where human-ity can discover itself, lies finally in the interaction between mind

---

[80] Montaigne, i.401 f. (ch. 40).   [81] Ibid. 415 (ch. 40).

and body, not in the release or triumph of the mind. It would therefore seem that Tristram must be thinking only of the earlier, and in
some ways inferior, Montaigne. And even in the early essay which
draws on Epictetus, Montaigne is not quite Tristram's Shandean
stoic. Epictetus' proposition is enthusiastically explored, but it is
also treated conditionally. The sentences that sketch the 'great
victory' for the human condition that this *would* imply, are nicely
poised between exhortation—let's go ahead and do it—and the
observation that our opinions of things seem not, in fact, to be in
our own power. As we have seen, all Montaigne's play of mind
does not preclude—indeed, in the later essays, it leads naturally
into—the understanding of mind and body as profoundly interde-
pendent. Sexuality, illness, mortality are realities in the *Essais*, as
they are not for Tristram—at least in the pages of his book, where
consciousness is all.

To recognize the *Essais* as a more substantial work than
Tristram Shandy is to find some basis for disagreement with those
critics who would have us see Sterne as a profound moralist, as
though Tristram were Everyman, and his book comprehended
some fundamental aspect of the human condition.[82] It is not,
however, to register any lack of intelligence in *Tristram* itself.
Although the text cannot reach beyond the singularity of
Tristram's consciousness, Sterne knows that well enough, and
delimits that consciousness with a tact that acknowledges the existence of the inaccessible world beyond its reach. Why else would
Sterne choose for inclusion an (albeit much interrupted) sermon
which preaches such a profoundly un-Shandean, anti-subjectivist,
and anti-sentimental moral: that the testimony of conscience
counts for little or nothing by comparison with the fruits of action?

---

[82] Still one of the most impressive of these critics is John Traugott, in his seminal
Tristram Shandy's World: Sterne's Philosophical Rhetoric (Berkeley and Los
Angeles, 1954). Traugott is stimulating on Sterne's relation to scepticism, but he
finds the same kind of weight and centrality in *Tristram Shandy* that I find rather in
Montaigne; there is, moreover, some unresolved tension between his emphasis on
Sterne's moral vision and his perception that this is all the effect of 'rhetoric'. 'As a
rhetorician Sterne had to subvert the reason so that he could persuade his reader of
the moral substance of that ultimate sympathy which reconciles the eccentric egos
of the Shandy world. Another effort of rhetoric demonstrates that those egos indeed
are not eccentric at all, or are at least very similar to that of His Worship the Reader.
The undermining skeptical arguments of Hume (which recommend his doctrine of
sympathy) find almost a descriptive statement in *Tristram*' (p. 19).

'*By their fruits ye shall know them.*'[83] The reality of death (as in Tristram's haemorrhage of blood, which was also the consumptive Sterne's),[84] or the reality of a possible fruitful relationship with widow Wadman, or the reality of the mutuality of mind and body that we are told Yorick would have asserted at the end, had he not been (of course!) interrupted by Obadiah and the last of many diversions—these things are known about, yet can have no more than a ghostly presence inside the circle of the text, rather like Tristram's relationship with 'dear *Jenny*'.[85] The fleeting, teasing, unelaborated references to that relationship function in the book as boundary markers: icons on a computer screen of files that will not open. It is within the circle of textual self-consciousness that Shandeism thrives, and from the clarity with which Sterne draws that circle around it that it gains its energy, intelligence, and wit.

To see what Shandeism looks like without that circle, one can turn to a revealingly lesser work: Sterne's *Bramine's Journal* or *Journal to Eliza*. This was ostensibly written for, and addressed to, a real woman, Eliza Draper; the part which has come down to us was written during the period of her voyage from England back to her husband in India. Sterne seems to have enjoyed a flirtation with her in the weeks before her departure, and in the journal he figures

---

[83] *Tristram Shandy*, ii. ch. 17: p. 163. Sterne's Florida editor, Melvyn New, has drawn attention to the explicitly Christian, often orthodox Anglican, sources and contexts from which many passages in *Tristram Shandy* derive, and argues that these sources and contexts should be regarded as elements in the meaning of the work; he is also inclined to gloss scepticism in Sterne in terms of a traditional strain of 'skeptical Christianity' or 'unknowingness' that descends from Renaissance thought to the Latitudinarians. Certainly, there is nothing in *Tristram Shandy* that need call into doubt the sincerity of Sterne's Anglicanism. But that is not to say that the scepticism of *Tristram Shandy* expresses a positively Christian vision, in the tradition of (e.g.) Erasmus' *Praise of Folly*. Christianity and scepticism may be compatible, but they *fuse* only at extraordinarily high imaginative temperatures. A counter-argument hostile to New might observe that it is only when these passages are stripped away from their defining religious contexts that they acquire, in Sterne's reworking, such vitality. But it would be more just simply to say that the reality of Christianity, like other realities, is left largely outside the circle of the text—unchallenged, occasionally referred to, but not an informing presence. For New's argument here, see e.g. *Tristram Shandy: A Book for Free Spirits* (New York, 1994), pp. 28–45; 'The Odd Couple: Laurence Sterne and John Norris of Bemerton', in *Philological Quarterly* 75 (1996), pp. 361–85; *The Life and Opinions of Tristram Shandy, Gentleman*, ed. Melvyn and Joan New (Harmondsworth, 1997), pp. xxxviii f.

[84] *Tristram Shandy*, viii. ch. 6: p. 663.

[85] See *Tristram Shandy*, i. ch. 18: pp. 51, 56; vii. ch. 29: p. 624; ix. ch. 8: p. 754.

himself as her ardent sentimental lover, and supposes that those feelings are to some degree returned. He addresses her directly, although this portion of the journal was never to be sent; and speaks of himself as living for her return (even preparing a room for her in his house), although the circumstances under which she might return to England to live with him were wildly hypothetical and remote. The *Journal* is thus a piece of Shandean 'pretending', as well as a Shandean diversion from Sterne's immediate difficulties: he was seriously ill at the time of writing, and awaiting a troublesome visit from his estranged wife who was demanding a financial settlement. Such unpleasant actualities merely intensify his need to spend time, in imagination, with Eliza, as he explains to her: 'I have you more in my mind than ever—and in proportion as I am thus torn from your embraces—*I cling the closer to the Idea of you*'.[86] But those 'embraces' are, of course, themselves fanciful and figurative. His feelings toward her are ideal only, enclosed within the mind; the moment of her departure was for him 'the Separation of Soul & Body'[87] in a rather literal, as well as an extravagantly metaphorical sense. It is Eliza's absence as she sails back to India, her physical as well as moral inaccessibility, that liberates Sterne's sentimental 'pretending': he can write that he finds in her 'as many virtues as my Uncle Toby's widow' while knowing it impossible (as her ship sets sail) 'for any *Trim*' to bring him to disillusionment; he can also write of intending to marry her while knowing that this intention, like Toby's, must come to nothing.[88] This situation of passion in separation, barred from or renouncing fruition, is in many ways the archetypal situation of sentimental fiction—it is at the centre of Rousseau's *Julie, or the New Eloisa*, the supreme sentimental novel of the eighteenth century—but in Sterne's *Journal* the element of 'pretending' lies on the surface of consciousness, so that the effect is awkwardly thin and unconvincing:

... I continue writing ... to thee Eliza who art the *Woman of my heart*, & for whom I am ordering & planning this, & every thing else—be

---

[86] *The Florida Edition of the Works of Laurence Sterne. Volume VI: A Sentimental Journey through France and Italy AND Continuation of the Bramine's Journal*, ed. Melvyn New and W. G. Day (Gainesville, Fla., 2002), p. 216: 7 July 1767.

[87] Sterne, *Bramine's Journal*, p. 215: 6 July 1767.

[88] *Letters*, pp. 318 f.: to Mrs Daniel Draper, March 1767.

assured my Bramine that ere every thing is ripe for our Drama,—I shall
work hard to fit out & decorate a little Theatre for us to act on—but not
before a crouded house—no Eliza—it shall be as secluded as the elysian
fields—retirement is the nurse of Love and kindness—& I will Woo &
caress thee in it in such sort, that every thicket & grotto we pass by, *shall*
sollicit the remembrance of the mutual pledges We have exchanged of
Affection with one another—Oh! these expectations—make me sigh, as I
recite them—& many a heart-felt Interjection! do they cost me, as I saunter
alone in the tracks we are to tread together hereafter—still I think thy
heart is with me—& whilst I think so, I prefer it to all the Society this
world can offer.[89]

It is that hardly veiled consciousness of 'pretending' that weakens
the rhetoric of intense feeling (Sterne 'saunters' as he 'sighs'), even
while it betrays a more intelligent understanding of the nature of
sentimental fiction than a published novel could well admit. That
consciousness cannot properly declare itself, however, for the
Journal confessedly documents a real situation, and lacks the
conscious textual fictionality which, in *Tristram Shandy* and *A
Sentimental Journey*, clearly bounds the play of mind. 'Eliza' does
feature in *A Sentimental Journey*, but only as 'Jenny' features in
Tristram, as a reference to an off-stage reality which cannot be
brought into consciousness. Any attempt to do so—whether by the
expression of sentiment, or by the appeal to the body—triggers a
countermovement of irony which reinstates the text as the immediate reality.

The general principle is most perfectly illustrated by the brilliant
ending of *A Sentimental Journey*. Here Yorick finds himself obliged
to share a bedchamber at an inn with a female traveller and her
chambermaid. The beds are scrupulously separated, but the situation is one of strong sexual possibility, and Yorick lies restlessly
awake until, 'Nature and patience both wearing out—O my God!
said I'. The lady complains that Yorick has broken his promise to
remain silent, but he insists that 'it was no more than an ejacula-
tion', and protests the innocence of his intentions:

Upon my word and honour, Madame, said I—stretching my arm out of
bed, by way of asseveration—
   —(I was going to have added, that I would not have trespass'd against
the remotest idea of decorum for the world)—

[89] Sterne, *Bramine's Journal*, p. 214: 5 July 1767.

—But the Fille de Chambre hearing there were words between us, and fearing that hostilities would ensue in course, had crept silently out of her closet, and it being totally dark, had stolen so close to our beds, that she had got herself into the narrow passage which separated them, and had advanc'd so far up as to be in a line betwixt her mistress and me—

So that when I stretch'd out my hand, I caught hold of the Fille de Chambre's[90]

And so the book ends, as *Tristram Shandy* begins, with an interruption. The sexual tease resolves itself into a textual joke: we stare both into and at the final space, which may equally stand for something and for nothing. If a full stop were added, the sentence would be grammatically complete, for 'hand' would then be understood as the object: touching hands have figured more than once in the narrative as an erotically charged yet crucially non-consequential mode of sentimental contact. But by breaking off, the text suggests that some more improper reality may lie behind the space, while reminding us that nothing lies behind it, that the narrative is a fiction, and that fiction's illusion of referentiality is just a piece of pretending. It is, in itself, a slight enough joke: yet it carries the great conceit on which Sterne's art rests, that the 'pretending' of the fictional text maps perfectly onto the 'pretending' of an enclosed and singular subjectivity. To pretend is, etymologically, to stretch forward or extend, and when Yorick stretches out his hand it creates the possibility of some really consequential contact and communication with another human being. It is both a small joke and a resonant one that Sterne's modesty will not allow him to proceed.

[90] Sterne, *Sentimental Journey*, pp. 164 f. Some later editions knowingly add a final dash.

6

Johnson's Conclusiveness

What then is to be done? said Rasselas; the more we enquire, the less we can resolve.

Sceptical thinking, as I have been describing it, involves an essential tension or doubleness: a power of affirmation that emerges from, without denying or transcending, the inadequacy of intellect to master the fluidity and variousness of things. It may seem surprising, therefore, to include Johnson in this company, who is so readily associated with the exercise of intellectual mastery, and was overtly hostile to scepticism in many of its forms. With regard to the sceptical thinking of Pope, Hume, and Sterne, Johnson has repeatedly appeared in this study as a contrasting and antagonistic voice. He queries the logic of the *Essay on Man*, raising an eyebrow at Pope's combination of 'argument' with 'poetry'; he attacks Hume for his treatment of religion, for the vanity involved in his manufacture of paradoxes, and for displacing fixed principles by mere social conventions; and he disparages *Tristram Shandy* for its oddity. Although he seems to praise Montaigne's 'vivacity' of thought, which he relates to the 'lightness and agility' of classical lyric, he then largely cancels that praise by insisting that such immethodical play of mind is not a desirable model for imitation. 'To proceed from one truth to another, and connect distant propositions by regular consequences, is the great prerogative of man':[1] there could hardly be a more unsceptical assertion. In the same vein, and also in the *Rambler*, he holds up the portrait of Pertinax the sceptic as a warning against such misuse of the intellect. Pertinax was a logician and intellectual who could argue brilliantly on both sides of any issue, and assemble objections to any position.

---

[1] *Johnson*, v.77 f. (*Rambler* 158).

But this habit of mind led not to the tranquillity envisaged by the classical theory, nor to any version of Hume's 'mitigated scepticism', but, by Pertinax's own account, to a much more alarming and painful condition of being:

I had deadened the sense of conviction, and abandoned my heart to the fluctuations of uncertainty, without anchor and without compass, without satisfaction of curiosity or peace of conscience; without principles of reason or motives of action. . . . I was weary of continual irresolution, and a perpetual equipoise of the mind.[2]

The strength of phrasing there suggests that Johnson knows this condition from the inside, that in treating this 'intellectual malady'[3] he writes, in Eliot's terms, as a 'wounded surgeon'.[4] The essay certainly acknowledges that such intellectual self-paralysis is possible, that reason can be engaged 'against its own determination'. But the same strength of phrasing ('I shuddered at my own corruption') will not stay to explore the implications of that state, but energetically repudiates it.[5]

This energy of assertion characterizes Johnson's thinking more generally, even when scepticism is not itself under discussion. 'Sir, there is nothing *conclusive* in his talk', he complained of some acquaintance who failed to give him what he expected from good conversation.[6] It seems unlikely that such a complaint was often made of Johnson himself. The 'Doctor Johnson' who lives so vividly in the pages of Boswell as an almost mythic presence, an icon of intellectual authority, delivers strikingly positive judgements in the most emphatic manner. It is true that this figure meets Boswell's personal needs and artistic purposes in ways that say as much about him as about Johnson. Yet the famous assertiveness, although amplified and no doubt distorted in transmission, is not Boswell's creation; it can also be heard clearly enough in Johnson's own prose, in the vigour of his judgements, the scope of his generalizations, and the special weightiness of his style. Entirely characteristic is the assertion in the preface to his edition of Shakespeare, 'The mind can only repose on the stability of truth.'[7] This is not, it

---

[2] *Johnson*, iv.147 (*Rambler* 95).   [3] Ibid. 143 (*Rambler* 95).
[4] In *East Coker*: 'The wounded surgeon plies the steel | That questions the distempered part.'
[5] *Johnson*, iv.147 (*Rambler* 95).   [6] Boswell, *Life*, iii.57 (May 1776).
[7] *Johnson*, vii.62.

is true, dogmatic in the way that it sounds. What Johnson means by 'the stability of truth' here is not a matter of propositional truth. On the contrary, the truth of Shakespeare's vision manifests itself to Johnson as a comprehensive resistance to categorization and to anything so one-sided as the abstraction of meaning:

Shakespeare's plays are not in the rigorous and critical sense either tragedies or comedies, but compositions of a distinct kind; exhibiting the real state of sublunary nature, which partakes of good and evil, joy and sorrow, mingled with endless variety of proportion and innumerable modes of combination; and expressing the course of the world, in which the loss of one is the gain of another; in which, at the same time, the reveller is hasting to his wine, and the mourner burying his friend; in which the malignity of one is sometimes defeated by the frolick of another; and many mischiefs and many benefits are done and hindered without design.[8]

In that affirmation of the endless interrelations and counterbalances of things, one can see how the Shakespearean truth to nature speaks to a profoundly sceptical intelligence. But Johnson does not speak of it in a sceptical voice. Diversity and flux become, in Johnson's prose, 'stability', a stabilizing which is in the first place an effect of style. The 'stability of truth' ends a clause which, coming at the end of a longer and more complex sentence, closes down the alternatives previously canvassed, and does so with a rhythmic and syntactical inevitability that claims to settle the matter:

The irregular combinations of fanciful invention may delight a-while, by that novelty of which the common satiety of life sends us all in quest; but the pleasures of sudden wonder are soon exhausted, and the mind can only repose on the stability of truth.[9]

Nothing odd will do long, as Johnson said of *Tristram Shandy*. The weighty final clause insists that all experiences are not of equal weight. Those which are *merely* of the mind—the combinations of fanciful invention—have a limited scope and duration; they necessarily yield to those grounded in truth, which stands outside the realm of individual subjectivity. Hence the strength of assertion is expressed through an appeal to the general experience of mankind; in Johnson it always, I think, implies the possibility of such an appeal.

---

[8] *Johnson*, vii.66.   [9] Ibid. 61 f.

This confidence in positive generalization immediately suggests how Johnson's scepticism differs from Sterne's. Sterne's scepticism expresses itself in the affirmation of singularity, the incommensurability of the subjective: but Johnson elevates Shakespeare's truth to general nature over lesser writers' representation of 'particular manners',[10] and regularly interprets singularity as affectation or self-deception. This is the theme of two papers in the *Adventurer*, no. 84 and no. 131, where he declares 'singularity . . . universally and invariably displeasing. . . . All violation of established practice, implies in its own nature a rejection of the common opinion, a defiance of common censure, and an appeal from general laws to private judgment.'[11] Johnson's emphasis on the common and the general could lead him to discount altogether subjective experience which seemed to him anomalous. If Hume reported that he felt no fear of death, this must be affectation, or even derangement, rather than a true account of Hume's particular sensibility.[12] An even more extreme, but still characteristic example is given by Mrs Thrale:

Mr Johnson did not like any one who said they were happy, or who said any one else was so. 'It is all *cant* (he would cry), the dog knows he is miserable all the time.' A friend whom he loved exceedingly, told him on some occasion notwithstanding, that his wife's sister was *really* happy, and called upon the lady to confirm his assertion, which she did somewhat roundly as we say, and with an accent and manner capable of offending Mr Johnson, if her position had not been sufficient, without any thing more, to put him in very ill humour. 'If your sister-in-law is really the contented being she professes herself Sir (said he), her life gives the lie to every research of humanity; for she is happy without health, without beauty, without money, and without understanding.'[13]

It is only an anecdote: but it captures, almost to the point of caricature, the Johnsonian assertiveness: authoritative, aggressive, overbearing, unanswerable, conclusive. Nothing could be more opposed to the spirit of Shandeism. Even in the matter of happiness, individual subjectivity cannot stand as its own witness, or create its own reality. 'We are never so happy or so unhappy as we

[10] Ibid. 61.   [11] Ibid. ii.485.
[12] Boswell, *Life*, ii.106 (Oct. 1769); iii.153 (Sept. 1777).
[13] Hester Lynch Piozzi, *Anecdotes of the Late Samuel Johnson*: in *Johnsonian Miscellanies*, ed. G. B. Hill, 2 vols. (Oxford, 1897), i.335.

imagine ourselves', wrote La Rochefoucauld,[14] and onto the poor sister-in-law's claim to know what she really feels, Johnson lowers the massive weight of the general human condition. 'Her life gives the lie to every research of humanity'. Such weighty assertion is very unlike the kind of oblique, teasing, subtle play of irony to be heard in Pope, or Hume, or Sterne: it might seem the very antithesis of a sceptical voice.

Yet absolutely fundamental to Johnson's thinking are some powerful sceptical principles that severely restrict the force and scope of generalization. The implications of these are most fully worked out in *Rasselas*, but they are also explored in certain of the periodical essays. In *Adventurer* no. 107, in particular, Johnson explains why the exercise of intelligence is bound to lead to 'difference of opinion', so that definitive conclusions can never be intelligently drawn:

> As a question becomes more complicated and involved, and extends to a greater number of relations, disagreement of opinion will always be multiplied, not because we are irrational, but because we are finite beings, furnished with different kinds of knowledge, exerting different degrees of attention, one discovering consequences which escape another, none taking in the whole concatenation of causes and effects, and most comprehending but a very small part; each comparing what he observes with a different criterion, and each referring it to a different purpose.[15]

As the syntax of that sentence unfolds, and itself 'extends to a greater number of relations', it mimics the complicated multiplicity which it describes. Strong general propositions which might have been emphatically conclusive ('not ... irrational, but ... finite beings') generate ever further ramifications ('one discovering ... none taking in ... and most comprehending ... each comparing ... and each referring ...'). The possibility of conclusiveness is dissipated, displaced by a more open-ended sense of relations and differences (such as the difference between comparing something with a criterion and referring it to a purpose). The prose communicates a certain pleasure in this diversity, invigorated by the stretch to apprehend that which by its very nature resists comprehensive summary. The main impression is of the vitality of a field

---

[14] 'On n'est jamais si heureux ni si malheureux qu'on s'imagine.' La Rochefoucauld, *Maximes*, ed. Jacques Truchet (Paris, 1967), p. 17: no. 49.
[15] *Johnson*, ii.441.

of attention which will not support any single master-interpretation; one begins to see how scepticism might break the mind open to that rich sense of multiplicity which Johnson found in Shakespeare. Yet there is also a darker side to this. When Johnson draws a natural corollary, and remarks how this plurality is something which any self-aware individual can find within himself, the potential discomfort of scepticism begins to make itself felt:

We have less reason to be surprised or offended when we find others differ from us in opinion, because we very often differ from ourselves: how often we alter our minds, we do not always remark; because the change is sometimes made imperceptibly and gradually, and the last conviction effaces all memory of the former; yet every man, accustomed from time to time to take a survey of his own notions, will by a slight retrospection be able to discover, that his mind has suffered many revolutions, that the same things have in the several parts of his life been condemned and approved, persued and shunned: and that on many occasions, even when his practice has been steady, his mind has been wavering, and he has persisted in a scheme of action, rather because he feared the censure of inconstancy, than because he was always pleased with his own choice.[16]

Johnson here is very close to Pope in the *Epistle to Bolingbroke*; and like Pope, Johnson does not find that this 'wavering' of the mind can be settled or resolved. He illustrates this, a little schematically, by quoting one Greek epigram expounding the misery of all conditions of life, and setting against it another, equally cogent, to the effect that every state of life has its felicity. Each generalization is true in different respects, so that 'no absolute determination ever can be formed', and their partial and opposite truths can never be brought to bear on a specific question—such as whether children will bring more pain or pleasure to their parents—in such a way as to resolve it. The consequence is that we are bound to make our life-decisions according to more or less arbitrary impulses, 'the hope or fear that shall happen to predominate', 'the caprices of imagination' that fill the vacuum left by the absence of clinching rational considerations:

We may examine, indeed, but we never can decide, because our faculties are unequal to the subject: we see a little, and form an opinion; we see more, and change it.[17]

[16] Ibid. 442.   [17] Ibid. 444.

This kind of scepticism—in which thinking is a process without conclusion, an unresolved dialectic—envisages a mind perpetually in movement, a mind that never reposes on the stability of truth. It supplies a kind of methodology for a good deal of Johnson's intellectual practice: his willingness to speak on either side of a question, and his preference for replying to another's argument rather than beginning with his own. It underwrites his hostility to high theory and grand intellectual system. It fits with the reactive, occasional nature of so many of his arguments, which may be presented as large generalizations, but whose force and point often depend on the proposition, stated or understood, to which they respond. And it is well expressed in the periodical essay as a form which interrogates an opening proposition, 'sees more', and modifies or complicates it, without pretence to finality or system, since implicit in the genre is the awareness that another day will bring another essay with a different starting-point.

Yet if Johnson is a sceptic, he is also a moralist. (One might also put this in another form: he is so much a sceptic that he will not repose even on the unrepose of scepticism.) 'We may examine, indeed, but we never can decide' is a troubling principle by which to live, as Rasselas will complain. For all Johnson's scepticism, he also recognizes, as we have seen, a powerful need for conclusions, a desire for a place for the mind to repose. In *Adventurer* no. 107 this is expressed, as one would expect, at the conclusion of the essay:

Life is not the object of science: we see a little, very little; and what is beyond we only can conjecture. If we enquire of those who have gone before us, we receive small satisfaction; some have travelled life without observation, and some willingly mislead us. The only thought, therefore, on which we can repose with comfort, is that which presents to us the care of Providence, whose eye takes in the whole of things, and under whose direction all involuntary errors will terminate in happiness.[18]

Johnson certainly believed that what lies beyond scepticism is God, 'whose eye takes in the whole of things', and whose conclusions are therefore not provisional. But although Johnson's final sentence terminates in happiness, it reads as a fragile, almost perfunctory gesture, too close to a conventionally pious signing-off to function

---

[18] *Johnson*, ii.445.

as the true conclusion of such a substantial essay. The 'care of Providence' comes in as something to fall back on only after inquiry fails, gingerly hypothetical, rather than a reality known to experience or to faith. It is distanced, with a kind of Lockean fastidiousness, as first and foremost an idea in the mind, something which a 'thought' may 'present to us', and it is syntactically preceded by the desire for comfort, in which it may well seem to have its origin. The essay must have a conclusion, a formal point of repose, and as a termination this will do well enough: but the scepticism expressed in the essay does not lead towards conclusion.

If the thought of how things conclude is not very fully realized in that essay, this may be because it was, in truth, a thought less productive of comfort than of dread. In *Idler* no. 103, the essay which concluded the series, Johnson inquired why the idea of something happening for the last time should affect us as it does:

There are few things not purely evil, of which we can say, without some emotion of uneasiness, 'this is the last.' Those who never could agree together, shed tears when mutual discontent has determined them to final separation; of a place which has been frequently visited, tho' without pleasure, the last look is taken with heaviness of heart; and the Idler, with all his chillness of tranquillity, is not wholly unaffected by the thought that his last essay is now before him.

This secret horrour of the last is inseparable from a thinking being whose life is limited, and to whom death is dreadful. We always make a secret comparison between a part and the whole; the termination of any period of life reminds us that life itself has likewise its termination. . . . I hope that [when my readers] see this series of trifles brought to a conclusion, they will consider that by outliving the *Idler*, they have passed weeks, months, and years which are now no longer in their power; that an end must in time be put to every thing great as to every thing little; that to life must come its last hour, and to this system of being its last day, the hour at which probation ceases, and repentance will be vain; the day in which every work of the hand, and imagination of the heart shall be brought to judgment, and an everlasting futurity shall be determined by the past.[19]

In that overwhelming final sentence, with terrible absoluteness, Johnson's voice identifies with the great doom itself: the Christian moralist, admonishing his readers in Easter Week to lead better lives, merges with a voice from beyond the grave, cursing his readers for outliving him, and bequeathing them a consciousness which is very like despair.

The horror at finality expressed in *Idler* no. 103 runs deep in Johnson. Clearly, this is intimately involved with, and often expressed as, a specifically religious fear of divine judgement. He could never get to the end of the *Dies Irae*, Mrs Thrale tells us, but would break down in a flood of tears.[20] On his watch was engraved a verse from John's gospel, 'the night cometh, when no man can work'. After his sixty-fourth birthday, he wrote in his journal, 'I have great reason to fear lest Death should lay hold upon me, while I am yet only designing to live'. He then added, 'But, I have yet hope.'[21] This hope meant that he would, at least, continue *designing* to live. The *Prayers and Meditations* record, over a period of many years, Johnson's regular renewals of resolutions regularly broken: a process redeemed from absurdity by the sense of a quasi-liturgical annual cycle in these moments of self-review (often undertaken at Easter or on the anniversary of his wife's death), and also by the sheer importance of keeping going.

When I look back upon resolutions of improvement and amendments, which have year after year been made and broken, either by negligence, forgetfulness, vicious idleness, casual interruption, or morbid infirmity, when I find that so much of my life has stolen unprofitably away, and that I can descry by retrospection scarcely a few single days properly and vigorously employed, why do I yet try to resolve again? I try because Reformation is necessary and despair is criminal.[22]

Failure, no matter how often repeated, cannot be accepted as conclusive; such conclusion would be dreadful.

This is, however, not only, perhaps not even fundamentally, a specifically Christian dread, nor even concerned only with mortality. It has to do with Johnson's more general sense of how conclusions—of which death is the great type and example—always tend to uncover the vanity of human striving and pretension. The key text here is *The Vanity of Human Wishes*, Johnson's imitation of Juvenal's tenth satire, a poem which supplies *Idler* no. 103 with its epigraph. The verse is *respicere ad longae jussit spatia ultima vitae,*

²⁰ *Johnsonian Miscellanies*, i.284.
²¹ *Johnson*, i.160 (24 Sept. 1773).
²² Ibid. 225 (Good Friday, 14 April 1775).

rendered by Johnson as 'caution'd to regard his end',[23] and a key line in the poem, which insists that all human wishes be seen in relation to, and judged in terms of, their final outcome. People wish for power, or wealth, or knowledge, or beauty, or long life, but these apparent goods are never, in the end, means to happiness; their achievement leads to nothing on which the mind can finally repose, but only, in one way or another, to downfall, disappointment, and undoing. People wish, in fact, for their own wretchedness: this is the general truth about the folly of human aspiration, the supreme generalization which includes all experience within it:

> Let observation with extensive view,
> Survey mankind from *China* to *Peru*;
> Remark each anxious toil, each eager strife . . .[24]

This sense of an overarching viewpoint, a massive comprehensiveness, permits Johnson's poem to be massively definitive in its conclusions. The diction is markedly more generalized than in Juvenal's original (or Dryden's translation), and the poem invests Juvenal's propositions with a double generality through the working of the imitation—the case of the classical Sejanus being duplicated by that of the modern Wolsey, Hannibal by Charles XII of Sweden, and so on. Elsewhere Johnson's generalizations are often shadowed by ironies, but in the *Vanity* the generality of the diction marches resolutely in step with the law of life which it observes. Just as nemesis inexorably visits the characters' desires for distinction and happiness, so the individual cases lead inexorably to the one great general truth which they exemplify. The poem is in consequence a work of quasi-tragic force, partly because the supreme generalization that admits of no exceptions is that everything comes to an end, but also because the poem's own impulse to intellectual domination, to a power of total comprehension which offers itself as comprehensive power, confesses itself as inextricably implicated in its own satire. The passage on the ultimate nullity of intellectual ambition (Johnson broke down when reading it out) has only a slim source in the original Latin, and the self-reflexive conclusion to the portrait of Charles XII associates the nullity of military conquest with the nullity of a moral tale which records that judgement:

---

[23] *Johnson*, vi.106 (l. 314).   [24] Ibid. 91 f. (ll. 1-3).

> His fall was destin'd to a barren strand,
> A petty fortress, and a dubious hand:
> He left the name, at which the world grew pale,
> To point a moral, or adorn a tale.[25]

This quality of self-implication gives the poem a powerful integrity, and a dark complexity of feeling. Johnson's own aspiration as poet, to sum up all human life in a single 'extensive view', is a Faustian wish, fulfilled only at the cost of turning all human aspiration to dust and ashes. As in *Idler* 103, or as with his friend's sister-in-law, *total* knowledge functions as a kind of blight or curse.

This is much darker than Juvenal, who derides human folly with a relieving, comic ferocity that clearly comes from outside the circle of folly, vice, and misery, and makes possible a vigorously positive ending to his poem:

> Still, if you *must* pray for *something*, if at every shrine you offer
> the entrails and holy chitterlings of a white piglet,
> then ask for a healthy mind in a healthy body,
> demand a valiant heart for which death holds no terrors,
> that reckons length of life as the least among the gifts
> of Nature, that's strong to endure every kind of sorrow
>
> .   .   .   .
>
> What I've shown you, you can bestow on yourself: there's one
> path, and one only, to a tranquil life—through virtue.
> Fortune has no divinity, could we but see it: it's we,
> we ourselves, who make her a goddess, and set her in the heavens.[26]

Juvenal finishes with a dynamic assertion, a rallying-cry. Johnson's ending, with Christianity to help or to hinder him, is by comparison muffled and uncertain in its articulation of any positive object for the will:

> Enquirer, cease, petitions yet remain,
> Which heav'n may hear, nor deem religion vain.
> Still raise for good the supplicating voice,
> But leave to heav'n the measure and the choice
>
> .   .   .   .
>
> Yet when the sense of sacred presence fires,
> And strong devotion to the skies aspires,

---

[25] *Johnson*, vi.102 (ll. 219–22).
[26] Juvenal, *The Sixteen Satires*, trans. Peter Green, 3rd ed. (Harmondsworth, 1998), p. 86.

> Pour forth thy fervours for a healthful mind,
> Obedient passions, and a will resign'd;
> For love, which scarce collective man can fill;
> For patience sov'reign o'er transmuted ill;
> For faith, that panting for a happier seat,
> Counts death kind Nature's signal of retreat.[27]

Even without recalling how little these sentiments correspond to Johnson's own religious attitude, with his emphasis on practice and his fear of death, one feels an awkward tension between the advocacy of spiritual humility—Be it unto me according to Thy will—and those assertive, demanding imperatives. Love, patience, and faith, as here described, seem thin abstractions by comparison with the desires canvassed earlier in the poem, which they are now called upon to supersede. Johnson does manage a resolution of sorts at the end, keeping some sense of human agency in play even while he offers to celebrate religious resignation:

> These goods for man the laws of heav'n ordain,
> These goods he grants, who grants the pow'r to gain;
> With these celestial wisdom calms the mind,
> And makes the happiness she does not find.[28]

'Celestial wisdom' stands in the penultimate line as a paraphrase for God, but as we read on it slips retrospectively towards suggesting a human faculty or virtue, so that some of God's 'making' in the final line gets associated with our own 'pow'r to gain'. But this depends upon a grammatical sleight of hand and a blurring of focus unusual for Johnson; the ending as a whole will not bear any great weight, but reads—rather like the hypothesis of Providence at the end of *Adventurer* no. 107—as an ending but not a conclusion, a cessation ('Enquirer, cease') rather than a resolution of enquiry.

Specifically, the ending does not adequately address the urgent questions which precede it, and which provide the true climax, and crisis, of the poem:

> Where then shall Hope and Fear their objects find?
> Must dull Suspence corrupt the stagnant mind?
> Must helpless man, in ignorance sedate,
> Roll darkling down the torrent of his fate?[29]

[27] *Johnson*, vi.108 (ll. 349–64). [28] Ibid. 109 (ll. 365–8).
[29] Ibid. 107 f. (ll. 343–6).

Although Johnson has reached it by a different route, this is recog-
nizably the same 'dangerous dilemma' which Hume set out at the
end of Book One of the *Treatise*. Rational inquiry uncovers the
groundlessness of our attachments to life, and leads to a fully sceptical *aporia*, or helplessness. The only alternative to the paralysis of
'dull Suspense' is to give oneself blindly up to forces beyond justification or control: and in fact these are not even alternatives, for
it is 'dull Suspense' in the mind that leaves one abandoned to the
torrent. For Hume, as I have tried to show, the sceptical crisis
makes possible a relaxation of the will and the entry into a fuller
mode of being. Through yielding to 'nature'—playing backgammon and conversing with his friends over dinner—Hume finds that
he can disperse his 'philosophical melancholy'. For Johnson this is
much more problematic. 'In ignorance sedate | Roll darkling down
the torrent of his fate' envisages the same outcome as Hume—'I
may, nay I must yield to the current of nature . . . and in this blind
submission I shew most perfectly my sceptical disposition and principles'[30]—but in a very different tone. The phrase 'in ignorance
sedate'—which might describe Hume—is terrifyingly dissonant
with the sense of threat and violence expressed in the line that
follows. Johnson invests what is fundamentally the same image
with a sense of huge anxiety; in terms of the metaphor, he cannot
help but think about where the current is heading. This is echoed
by his use of the same image in the essays, particularly in the
Rambler essays (1750–2), written closest in time to the *Vanity*
(1749). *Rambler* no. 102, for example, offers the fully expanded
allegory of life as a voyage, reflecting upon 'the thoughtlessness
with which [man] floats along the stream of time', propelled by 'the
current of life' towards rocks and whirlpools. 'So numerous,
indeed, were the dangers, and so thick the darkness, that no
caution could confer security.'[31] If so, it is not clear what can be
gained when the essayist is awoken at the conclusion by 'an admo-
nition from some unknown Power, "Gaze not idly upon others
when thou thyself art sinking." '[32] Shipwreck, we are told, sooner
or later, is inevitable. Or *Rambler* no. 127 tells how the man who
gives up on some laudable pursuit, disillusioned to discover that it
does not bring the rewards it promised, 'often abandons himself to

---

[30] *Treatise*, p. 269.   [31] *Johnson*, iv.179, 182, 180.
[32] Ibid. 184.

chance and to the wind, and glides careless and idle down the current of life, without resolution to make another effort, till he is swallowed up by the gulph of mortality'.[33] Both essays express the demand for some kind of effective agency ('Gaze not idly', 'without resolution to make another effort')—thereby heightening the sense of anxiety and guilt—but do little or nothing to fill out that demand with content.

In both those examples from the *Rambler*, the figure carried along by the current of life is described as 'idle'. A few years later, Johnson was to write as 'The Idler' in a series of essays contributed to the *Universal Chronicle* (1758–60) around the time that he composed *Rasselas* (1759). These essays range widely, but those that concern themselves explicitly with 'idleness' (mostly near the beginning of the series, just preceding *Rasselas*) interestingly modify Johnson's earlier representation. In both the *Rambler* passages just discussed, the implication is firstly, that such idleness is highly dangerous (another *Rambler* concludes firmly that 'to be idle is to be vicious'),[34] and secondly, that it could be dispelled by a sufficient taking of thought. When idleness appears in the *Idler* essays it is as a highly *conscious* attitude, as one would expect from the essayist's self-designation; the persona, in those essays where Johnson adopts it, is clearly that, yet also easily blends with an authorial intelligence. 'The Idler, who habituates himself to be satisfied with what he can most easily obtain, not only escapes labours which are often fruitless, but sometimes succeeds better than those who despise all that is within their reach.'[35] There speaks one who is indeed convinced of the vanity of human wishes; personal idleness seems the natural response to the idleness of striving and the idleness of existence as revealed by sceptical thought. A satirical, pejorative implication is still present, of course. The idler is pathetically grateful for any relief from vacancy and *ennui*;[36] and with his careful instructions in the art of 'wasting life' and extinguishing 'reflection on the past, and solicitude for the future',[37] he is clearly 'not productive of good' (definition 5 of IDLE in the *Dictionary*). But his own conscious lack of enterprise expresses an awareness of how much of human activity is 'vain' or 'trifling'

---

[33] Ibid. 314.
[35] Ibid. ii.3 (*Idler* 1).
[37] Ibid. 31 (*Idler* 9).

[34] Ibid. 87 (*Rambler* 85).
[36] Ibid. 11 (*Idler* 3).

(definitions 4 and 6), in a way that chimes with the new slightness of theme and lightness of manner that distinguish many of the *Idler* essays. In *Idler* no. 9, for example, idleness is described as a high art with its own precepts and degrees, where the elite may in time descend into the 'regions of undelighted quiet', and where the consciousness of existence persists only as 'an obtuse languor, and drowsy discontent'.[38] This is the same 'dull Suspence' which, in the *Vanity*, corrupts the stagnant mind, but is here more often treated as comic than threatening; the mock-heroic idiom relishes the paradox of idleness as an aim and a discipline, of unconsciousness made self-conscious. The note of comic detachment allows the reader imaginatively to entertain, without danger of identifying with, the idler's 'chillness of tranquillity', the *ataraxia* classically alleged to flow from the sceptical suspension of belief and engagement. [39]

These essays express a comic vision, but in the best of them the thread of comedy is drawn very fine. *Idler* no. 32 reflects first on sleep and then on day-dreaming as forms of unconsciousness that gratify 'our desire of abstraction from ourselves'.[40] The concept of day-dreaming is developed until it seems to include most of mental life.

Many have no happier moments than those that they pass in solitude, abandoned to their own imagination . . . . It is easy in these semi-slumbers to collect all the possibilities of happiness, to alter the course of the sun, to bring back the past, and anticipate the future, to unite all the beauties of all seasons, and all the blessings of all climates, to receive and bestow felicity, and forget that misery is the lot of man. All this is a voluntary dream, a temporary recession from the realities of life to airy fictions; an habitual subjection of reason to fancy.

Others are afraid to be alone, and amuse themselves by a perpetual succession of companions, but the difference is not great, in solitude we have our dreams to ourselves, and in company we agree to dream in concert. The end sought in both is forgetfulness of ourselves.[41]

And there the essay ends. In the *Rambler* day-dreaming had been

<hr />

[38] *Johnson*, ii.31 *(Idler* 9). Johnson draws on the mock-heroic vision of a sublime, majestic idleness in Boileau's *Lutrin*, Dryden's *MacFlecknoe* and Pope's *Dunciad*.

[39] *Johnson*, ii.314 f. (*Idler* 103). Explicit references in the *Idler* to the suspension of judgement induced by scepticism (nos. 24, 83) are strikingly more comic and relaxed in tone than the corresponding portrait of Pertinax in the *Rambler* (no. 95).

[40] *Johnson*, ii.100.   [41] Ibid. 101.

vigorously condemned,[42] but here, although Johnson duly notes how we lose hold of reality and reason, there is no condemnation, but rather a striking tenderness and poignancy in the description. The need for a counter-assertion of realities is met simply through the acknowledgement that that is how things are for mankind. A similar note can be heard in the immediately preceding, perhaps even finer essay. This offers a portrait of Johnson's 'old friend Sober'—an acknowledged self-portrait[43]—as a master in the art of idleness:

The art is, to fill the day with petty business, to have always something in hand which may raise curiosity, but not solicitude, and keep the mind in a state of action, but not of labour.

This art has for many years been practised by my old friend Sober, with wonderful success. Sober is a man of strong desires and quick imagination, so exactly ballanced by the love of ease, that they can seldom stimulate him to any difficult undertaking; they have, however, so much power, that they will not suffer him to lie quite at rest, and though they do not make him sufficiently useful to others, they make him at least weary of himself.

Mr Sober's chief pleasure is conversation; there is no end of his talk or his attention; to speak or to hear is equally pleasing; for he still fancies that he is teaching or learning something, and is free for the time from his own reproaches.

But there is one time at night when he must go home, that his friends may sleep; and another time in the morning, when all the world agrees to shut out interruption. These are the moments of which poor Sober trembles at the thought. But the misery of these tiresome intervals, he has many means of alleviating. . . . His daily amusement is chemistry. He has a small furnace, which he employs in distillation, and which has long been the solace of his life. He draws oils and waters, and essences and spirits, which he knows to be of no use; sits and counts the drops as they come from his retort, and forgets that, while a drop is falling, a moment flies away.

Poor Sober! I have often teaz'd him with reproof, and he has often promised reformation; for no man is so much open to conviction as the idler, but there is none on whom it operates so little. What will be the effect of this paper I know not; perhaps he will read it and laugh, and light the fire in his furnace; but my hope is that he will quit his trifles, and betake himself to rational and useful diligence.[44]

---

[42] In *Rambler* 89: *Johnson*, iv.105-7.   [43] *Johnsonian Miscellanies*, i.178.
[44] *Johnson*, ii.97 f. (*Idler* 31).

Samuel Beckett said that the writer who meant most to him, who
was always with him, was Johnson,[45] and in this passage one
glimpses what Beckett may have meant. To Johnson's 'old friend
Sober' nothing seems enough worth doing, yet to do nothing leads
to 'moments of which poor Sober trembles at the thought'. This is
a condition 'exactly ballanced', recalling the *isostheneia* of classical
scepticism: the idler is entirely 'open to conviction', entirely incapable of it. The best remedy for Sober's depression is conversation,
precisely because in conversation 'there is no end', no teleological
demand or necessity of conclusion. Where this fails, Sober has
other resources: his experiments in chemistry, which he knows to
be useless in themselves, are 'the solace of his life'. From the
perspective of Hume or Sterne, and like Pope's 'starving chemist in
his golden views', Sober is doing pretty well. And indeed when
Johnson speaks of Sober's 'wonderful success' in the art of filling
the day, the phrase is barely ironic, the irony barely satirical. There
is here a distinct shift from the note struck in the earlier *Vanity* and
Rambler essays. The stressful moral urgency, expressing the need
for some strong point of resolution that cannot be found—an
alarm bell ringing, but with nowhere to run—has disappeared,
replaced by a comedy that is both unsentimentally clear-eyed and
unexpectedly elegiac: 'poor Sober!' Something that was being
resisted has now been accepted. Yet Johnson's attitude to Sober's
chemistry can still be distinguished from Hume's attitude to playing backgammon. When Johnson describes Sober's art of getting
through life, he does so without abandoning the possibility that
there may be some more substantial, more rationally justifiable
way of acting in and on the world. Sober's concern is with keeping
going, but Johnson's prose looks toward conclusions—the reflections which haunt Sober's solitude, the moments that fly irrecover-
ably away, the quasi-judicial summing up with its threat of a final
judgement, and the conclusion of the essay itself, ending as it does
with the notion of 'rational and useful diligence'. Johnson keeps

---

[45] 'They can put me wherever they want, but it's Johnson, always Johnson, who
is with me. And if I follow any tradition, it is his.' The remark, from 1972, is quoted
in Deirdre Bair, *Samuel Beckett* (1978), p. 257. Beckett's first attempt at drama,
Human Wishes, took Johnson as protagonist; the project is discussed in Ruby Cohn,
Just Play: Beckett's Theater (Princeton, 1980), pp. 143–62, and the surviving fragment is reprinted in Cohn's book and in *Disjecta: Miscellaneous Writings and a
Dramatic Fragment* (London, 1983).

this undefined, and clearly feels little confidence that Sober can or will reform his life; the writing of this *Idler* may well be itself an idle act, as finally useless as one of Sober's chemical experiments. In the last of the *Idler* essays, when Johnson looks back from a point of conclusion, he will refer to the whole sequence as 'this series of trifles'.[46] But by sustaining the mere idea of rational action and significant labour—even as a felt absence, like Beckett's Godot—Johnson sharpens our sense of the emptiness of Sober's way of getting through life, and modifies the way in which we acquiesce in these processes of diversion and distraction, profoundly human though they are. It is equally human to require that they be not allowed the last word: which makes Sober's situation both more serious and more comic. Sober will go on promising reformation, just as Johnson at sixty-four, and as yet 'only designing to live', will go on renewing his resolutions to begin living indeed: even if the notion of truly living is realized largely through the sense of alienation from it.

The key issue here is the attitude to agency and resolution, or what I have been calling the sceptical relaxation of the will. Scepticism tends to undermine resolution, and promote 'idleness', in at least three ways. It counterbalances one consideration with another, so that the knowledge which would support resolution is never established; it empties prospective action of its significance or its promise of good, weakening motivation; and it observes the ineffectiveness of resolution, the gap between intention, however well-informed, and action. *Idler* no. 27 classes the endeavour at self-knowledge and moral self-review as an idle enterprise, because it almost never produces a reformation of practice. Johnson writes:

There is nothing which we estimate so fallaciously as the force of our own resolutions, nor any fallacy which we so unwillingly and tardily detect. He that has resolved a thousand times, and a thousand times deserted his own purpose, yet suffers no abatement of his confidence, but still believes himself his own master. . . .

Custom is commonly too strong for the most resolute resolver though furnished for the assault with all the weapons of philosophy.[47]

Scepticism, having done its worst, traditionally (customarily) ends by endorsing our submission to custom, in the fields of both opinion

---

[46] *Johnson*, ii.316 (*Idler* 103).   [47] Ibid. 84 f.

and practice. Like Hume (in one way) and Sterne (in another), Johnson too observes the overwhelming strength of custom, but he does not endorse it. The essay goes on to deplore the power of 'evil habits', and there is something dynamically paradoxical in Johnson offering these reflections on the inefficacy of self-knowledge as a contribution to our self-knowledge: is this information on which we might, in the teeth of its very content, somehow wish to act? After so much emphasis on the inefficacy of resolution, the essay concludes with the suggestion that those who are not yet in the power of 'evil habits', 'may effectually resolve to escape the tyrant, whom they will very vainly resolve to conquer'.[48] This virtual *non sequitur* in the essay as a whole expresses Johnson's determination to keep in play the desire for resolution and the idea of agency, alongside all the counteracting tendencies of scepticism. But 'determination' is perhaps the wrong term; it better characterizes those *Rambler* situations where the dominion of idleness is held up as something to be resisted. In these *Idler* essays idleness is embraced, or at least accepted, without resistance, and yet a space for the idea of agency still remains: the co-existence itself expresses a kind of sceptical open-endedness.

Even when my other sceptics, Pope, Hume, and Sterne, abandon the purposive self to the stream of things, some crucial shadow of agency likewise still remains. Pope's moral helplessness in the *Epistle to Bolingbroke* is, also, a piece of art; when Hume finds himself 'determined' to live like other people, the word carries the ghost of a pun; and in Tristram's spontaneity and arbitrariness we can—sometimes—glimpse Sterne's design. But the degree to which Johnson insists on keeping space for agency is a quality which distinguishes him from main tendencies in the others' writing. The point of difference is nicely focused in Johnson's opposition to Pope's theory of the 'ruling passion'. This, I have argued, was one way in which Pope figured the sceptical submission to a larger force than that of rational self-determination. Somewhat as Hume speaks of blind submission to the current of nature, so Pope speaks of 'Life's Stream' as moving too fast for self-location or reflection: the only key to our sentiments and actions is the 'ruling passion', something prior to all rationalization or choice. Hume liked this

---

[48] *Johnson*, ii.86.

enough to adopt both the phrase and the idea; in his autobiography, for example, he speaks of the love of literary fame as his 'ruling passion'.[49] And Sterne, also, found much in the idea, which he developed into the notion of the frankly idiosyncratic 'hobbyhorse': 'When a man gives himself up to the government of a ruling passion,——or, in other words, when his HOBBY-HORSE grows head-strong,——farewell cool reason and fair discretion!'[50] It is therefore interesting that Johnson comes down so heavily against the theory; the perceptive Nugaculus ridicules 'the modern dream of the ruling passion' in the *Rambler*,[51] and Johnson goes out of his way to reject it in the *Life of Pope*:

Of any passion thus innate and irresistible the existence may reasonably be doubted. Human characters are by no means constant; men change by change of place, of fortune, of acquaintance; he who is at one time a lover of pleasure is at another a lover of money. Those indeed who attain any excellence commonly spend life in one pursuit, for excellence is not often gained upon easier terms. But to the particular species of excellence, men are directed not by an ascendant planet or predominating humour, but by the first book which they read, some early conversation which they heard, or some accident which excited ardour and emulation. . . .

This doctrine is in itself pernicious as well as false; its tendency is to produce the belief of a kind of moral predestination or overruling principle which cannot be resisted: he that admits it is prepared to comply with every desire that caprice or opportunity shall excite, and to flatter himself that he submits only to the lawful dominion of Nature in obeying the resistless authority of his 'ruling Passion.'[52]

There are two distinct arguments here, one against the truth of the hypothesis, and one against its consequences. What is interesting is that they pull in different directions. In the second argument, Johnson goes to the ethical crux of the matter: 'a kind of moral predestination' is a stern paraphrase of the relaxation of the will that is commonly involved in the sceptical capitulation of the rational to the natural. Pope's *Essay* was plausibly accused of implying determinism in the cosmos; Hume consistently advances a version of psychological determinism; and *Tristram Shandy* everywhere makes the will subject to the power of sentiment, the hobby-horse, and a chain of circumstance leading back to our conception and

---

[49] Pope, *Epistle to Cobham*: pp. 283–8; Hume, *Essays*, ed. Miller, p. xxxiii.
[50] *Tristram Shandy*, ii ch. 5: p. 106.
[51] *Johnson*, iv.188 (*Rambler* 103).   [52] Johnson, *Lives*, iii.174.

beyond. Johnson, as one would expect ('Sir, . . . we *know* our will is free'),[53] insists, against this, on the importance of agency and a measure of self-determination. His terms in the second argument presuppose some element of autonomy: one may choose to comply with desire, or one may choose not to. However, his first argument emphasizes the dependency of motive upon accident and circumstance. The forces which determine how we live are not fixed, he argues, but mutable and arbitrary (which is much more as Pope sees them in the *Epistle to Bolingbroke*). Predestination thus gives way to contingency; but this hardly makes space for the self-determination envisaged in the second argument. Johnson shoots Pope's theory to pieces, but he fires on it from both sides, and thereby reveals the doubleness or tension which it was, perhaps, designed to accommodate, and which certainly characterizes Johnson's own stance. On the one hand there is the sceptic, alert to the way that character, like opinion, is endlessly liable to be in flux, inconclusive, without fixity or certainty. On the other, there is the moralist's voice that speaks of our need not to be altogether abandoned to the vanity of things, but to seek justification, direction, and resolution.

*   *   *

This moralist's attitude is epitomized in the quest of Rasselas. It is perfectly expressed as he sets out to make the choice of life: 'He thought it unsuitable to a reasonable being to act without a plan, and to be sad or chearful only by chance.'[54] He pursues this quest, however, within a fable organized according to an uncompromisingly sceptical intelligence, which famously ends in a 'conclusion, in which nothing is concluded'.[55] *Rasselas*, which was written just a few weeks after the *Idler* paper on Sober, is the key work in this argument: for in it the viewpoints of the sceptic and the moralist most fully interact, and Johnson does, for once, the literary sum (so to speak), with a sustained articulation of the ironic vision which holds the two in play. The only other work where this may be equally true is *The Vanity of Human Wishes*, where the sum comes out very differently. Elsewhere in Johnson's writing, the sceptical working of his intelligence is expressed precisely in the way that different aspects of his understanding of things are urged with

[53] Boswell, *Life*, ii.82 (Oct. 1769).   [54] *Johnson*, xvi.69 (ch. 17).
[55] Ibid. 175 (ch. 49).

different strengths at different moments, without (often) any strong move to resolution. A sentence in the Preface to the *Dictionary* gives the essential *shape* of this intelligence: 'When it shall be found that much is omitted, let it not be forgotten that much likewise is performed.'[56] 'This is true; but that is also true.' We have just seen a miniature example of this in what was called the virtual *non sequitur* of *Idler* 27, and again in his double refutation of the 'ruling passion' hypothesis. Hence selective quotation can always produce a Johnson who is an authoritarian, or a rebel; a Christian moralist, or a classical humanist; a sceptic, or an anti-sceptic—while aggressive interpretation can readily uncover a Johnson who falls into self-contradiction or is divided against himself. Any of these readings may well contain a truth; yet, as Imlac remarks, 'diversity is not inconsistency';[57] and it is when one reads across, from one local assertion to another, that the impressiveness of Johnson's thinking becomes most apparent, as there comes into focus that peculiar combination of definiteness and openness which is itself the expression of sceptical intelligence. In *Rasselas*, however, there is a largeness of ironic vision, an achieved wholeness, that enables it to stand alone: along with a few of the shorter poems, it is, perhaps, the work in which Johnson is most purely the literary artist, and certainly the work in which the thinker and the artist are most intimately connected.

The story records Rasselas's quest to make a rational 'choice of life'. He sets out from a position of privilege and independence, in which all options are in principle open to him, and surveys humanity with the aim of identifying the condition of life most conducive to happiness. His quest is thus for knowledge as well as happiness, moral knowledge of a kind adequate to determine choice and justify action. However, although he observes, consults, and reflects as extensively as may be, this proves to be a quest which cannot be fulfilled, despite the advantages of an apparently limitless travel budget and an adviser, the poet-philosopher Imlac, with wide experience of life. Johnson's analysis establishes two main reasons why Rasselas's quest cannot succeed. One is the inadequacy of the human mind to establish the kind of general truth he

---

[56] *Samuel Johnson: The Major Works*, ed. Donald Greene (Oxford, 2000), p. 327.
[57] Johnson, xvi.33 (*Rasselas*, ch. 8).

seeks about the many-sided complexity of life. As Imlac explains to
Rasselas almost from the start, 'the causes of good and evil . . . are
so various and uncertain, so often entangled with each other, so
diversified by various relations, and so much subject to accidents
which cannot be foreseen, that he who would fix his condition
upon incontestable reasons of preference, must live and die enquir-
ing and deliberating'.[58] Thus when Rasselas and his sister Nekayah
attempt a comparative evaluation of marriage and single life they
cannot conclude which is to be preferred. Nekayah explains to her
brother, who is impatient for some resolution of the question, why
this should be: her apparent self-contradictions, for which he is
inclined to criticize her, are an inevitable consequence of considering such a complex topic in different lights and from different
angles.

Of two systems, of which neither can be surveyed by any human being in
its full compass of magnitude and multiplicity of complication, where is
the wonder, that judging of the whole by parts, I am alternately affected
by one and the other as either presses on my memory or fancy? We differ
from ourselves just as we differ from each other, when we see only part of
the question, as in the multifarious relations of politicks and morality.[59]

The second reason there can be no rational 'choice of life' is that
the same dynamic restlessness of mind which sends Rasselas out of
the Happy Valley on his quest, ensures that none of his intervie-
wees can report themselves as happy or fulfilled, even or especially
if their aims and wishes have been met. Desire being a construction
of the mind, and always involved with the prospect of change, the
achievement of desire never brings the fulfilment it promised. Thus
Imlac explains the likely motive for the construction of the Great
Pyramid, whose cost and labour would seem to have no rational
justification:

It seems to have been erected only in compliance with that hunger of imagination which preys incessantly upon life, and must be always appeased by
some employment. Those who have already all that they can enjoy, must
enlarge their desires. He that has built for use, till use is supplied, must begin
to build for vanity, and extend his plan to the utmost power of human
performance, that he may not be soon reduced to form another wish.

[58] *Johnson*, xvi.67 (*Rasselas*, ch. 16).
[59] Ibid. 105 (ch. 28). Nekayah might have drawn this insight from *Adventurer*
no. 107.

I consider this mighty structure as a monument of the insufficiency of human enjoyments.[60]

For these powerful reasons, Rasselas comes to no conclusions about how best to live. This is reflected in the open-endedness of the narrative, with its 'conclusion, in which nothing is concluded'. This openness, however, is not just a matter of the ending, but pervasive. What Johnson achieves throughout *Rasselas* is an ironic vision that keeps both the voices of sceptic and moralist in play and in relationship, without diminishing either. A simple example comes as early as the second chapter. One common theme of sceptical thought was to question what distinguished the not-so-rational human from the animals. Rasselas, still living in the Happy Valley and suffering from a discontent which he does not as yet understand, compares his dissatisfied condition with that of the animals he sees around him, and draws some firm conclusions about the distinction between them:

'What,' said he, 'makes the difference between man and all the rest of the animal creation? Every beast that strays beside me has the same corporal necessities with myself; he is hungry and crops the grass, he is thirsty and drinks the stream, his thirst and hunger are appeased, he is satisfied and sleeps; he rises again and is hungry, he is again fed and is at rest. I am hungry and thirsty like him, but when thirst and hunger cease I am not at rest; I am, like him, pained with want, but am not, like him, satisfied with fulness. . . . Man has surely some latent sense for which this place affords no gratification, or he has some desires distinct from sense which must be satisfied before he can be happy.'[61]

All this is solid, cogent moral reflection, and clearly carries Johnson's endorsement. His editors helpfully recall his attack on the Rousseauvian ethic of the simple life: 'If a bull could speak, he might as well exclaim,—Here am I with this cow and this grass; what being can enjoy greater felicity?'[62] But as Rasselas develops the thought, we begin to view his philosophizing with a certain irony:

After this he lifted up his head, and seeing the moon rising, walked towards the palace. As he passed through the fields, and saw the animals around him, 'Ye,' said he, 'are happy, and need not envy me that walk thus

---

[60] Ibid. 118 f. (ch. 32).   [61] Ibid. 13 (ch. 2).
[62] Boswell, *Life*, ii.228 (April 1773).

among you, burthened with myself; nor do I, ye gentle beings, envy your felicity; for it is not the felicity of man. I have many distresses from which ye are free; I fear pain when I do not feel it; I sometimes shrink at evils recollected, and sometimes start at evils anticipated: surely the equity of providence has ballanced pecular sufferings with peculiar enjoyments.'

With observations like these the prince amused himself as he returned, uttering them with a plaintive voice, yet with a look that discovered him to feel some complacence in his own perspicacity, and to receive some solace of the miseries of life, from consciousness of the delicacy with which he felt, and the eloquence with which he bewailed them. He mingled cheerfully in the diversions of the evening, and all rejoiced to find that his heart was lightened.[63]

Rasselas's observations are still substantial enough to draw us in, and interest us directly in their content ('burthened with myself' is acute). Yet the combination of a second-person address to the animals with a full-blown theory about the equity of providence, introduced with a 'surely' which, unlike the 'surely' at the end of the previous paragraph, tolerates no alternatives, already reads as a little too much to take altogether seriously; and in the 'Johnsonian' fullness and conclusiveness of 'for it is not the felicity of man', an alert reader may hear the note of something like self-parody. These intimations of irony are then released by the final paragraph, which shows the melancholy on which Rasselas has been congratulating himself to go not quite as deep as he supposes. Yet the generosity of the final sentence renders this irony less corrective than comic in spirit, rather as Imlac, later in the narrative, can be generous toward the illusions with which his young companions protect themselves against the uncomfortable realities which age will bring: 'Imlac, who had no desire to see them depressed, smiled at the comforts which they could so readily procure to themselves . . . . He forbore to force upon them unwelcome knowledge, which time itself would too soon impress.'[64] This generosity is one of the most striking ways in which *Rasselas* differs from *The Vanity of Human Wishes*, with its punitive insistence on unwelcome knowledge and general conclusions: 'Yet hope not life from grief or danger free, | Nor think the doom of man revers'd for thee.'[65] Johnson there piles on the weight. But Rasselas's weighty reflections on the miseries of life lead to a situation where 'all

[63] *Johnson*, xvi.14 (ch. 2).   [64] Ibid. 157 (ch. 45).
[65] Ibid. vi.99 (ll. 155 f.).

rejoiced to find that his heart was lightened': the open quality of the irony plays its part in making light (without making light *of*) something which had seemed heavy ('burthened with myself').

The irony works by allowing the discursive, generalizing voice to expand to the point where it becomes detached from its narrative context, and provokes a shift in perspective, so that one kind of discourse gives way to, or is counterbalanced by, another, and so forfeits any claim to be conclusive or absolute. Another clear example of this comes at the end of Imlac's 'dissertation upon poetry'. After making a number of observations on the qualifications of a true poet, with which Johnson certainly agreed, Imlac rises to a magniloquent conclusion:

His character requires that he estimate the happiness and misery of every condition; observe the power of all the passions in all their combinations, and trace the changes of the human mind as they are modified by various institutions and accidental influences of climate or custom, from the spriteliness of infancy to the despondence of decrepitude. He must divest himself of the prejudices of his age or country; he must consider right and wrong in their abstracted and invariable state; he must disregard present laws and opinions, and rise to general and transcendental truths, which will always be the same: he must therefore content himself with the slow progress of his name; contemn the applause of his own time, and commit his claims to the justice of posterity. He must write as the interpreter of nature, and the legislator of mankind, and consider himself as presiding over the thoughts and manners of future generations; as a being superiour to time and place.[66]

This would be a resounding conclusion, if speech or chapter ended here, but instead Imlac adds a short further paragraph, almost as an afterthought, and this produces some sense of anticlimax. An end is not so easily reached, by the orator or the poet: 'His labour is not yet at an end: he must know many languages and many sciences; and, that his stile may be worthy of his thoughts, must, by incessant practice, familiarize to himself every delicacy of speech and grace of harmony.'[67] At this point Johnson ends the chapter, and begins the next as follows:

Imlac now felt the enthusiastic fit, and was proceeding to aggrandize his own profession, when the prince cried out, 'Enough! Thou hast convinced me, that no human being can ever be a poet. Proceed with thy narration.'

---

[66] Ibid. xvi.44 f. (ch. 10).   [67] Ibid. 45 (ch. 10).

'To be a poet,' said Imlac, 'is indeed very difficult.' 'So difficult,' returned the prince, 'that I will at present hear no more of his labours. Tell me whither you went when you had seen Persia.'[68]

Although Imlac has pitched his rhetoric very high, and has been in no mood to pause for qualifications, what he says about the poet could be supported by what Johnson says in other contexts about Shakespeare, Homer, and Milton. The irony does not *overturn* what has been said, but marks the limit of its duration. There is the aspiration to absolute truth, high generalization, a commanding point of view, like the 'extensive View' which Johnson commands in *The Vanity of Human Wishes*, where he indeed offers 'general and transcendental truths, which will always be the same'[69]—and then, by a kind of necessity, as Imlac's rhetoric begins to call attention to itself, there is the switch into narrative, and the sense of ongoing process which the travelling in *Rasselas* always suggests, with the contingent, rather particular question of where Imlac went after he had seen Persia. *Rasselas* reads as a series of essays set within a narrative, and the irony often turns, as here, on a sense of generic plurality or shift, as discourse forgets, then remembers, its place within the story. It is a form which dramatizes the intellectual's relationship with the wider world, a theme which Johnson had addressed many times in *The Rambler*, and which lies at the heart of eighteenth-century scepticism.

The effect of this is comic, with comedy's familiar smile at the voice of authority. 'To be a poet, said Imlac, is indeed very difficult', picking his way down from the rhetorical heights with a beautifully measured consciousness of the descent required. For although he has many truths about life to tell, none of them are of such a general and transcendental kind as to enable Rasselas to make his choice of life. Imlac enters the story as a figure of intel-

---

[68] *Johnson*, xvi.46 (ch. 11).

[69] The figure in *Rasselas* who offers a similarly extensive view is the engineer who hopes to invent the art of flying; Rasselas's objections have more than literal point:

'You, Sir, whose curiosity is so extensive, will easily conceive with what pleasure a philosopher, furnished with wings, and hovering in the sky, would see the earth, and all its inhabitants, rolling beneath him, and presenting to him successively, by its diurnal motion, all the countries within the same parallel . . .'

'All this,' said the prince, 'is much to be desired, but I am afraid that no man will be able to breathe in these regions of speculation and tranquillity.' *Johnson*, xvi.25 f. (ch. 6).

lectual authority—a 'Doctor Johnson', so to speak, to Rasselas's Boswell—and at first the Rasselas–Imlac relationship dramatizes the relation between naivety and knowledge, question and answer, hopeful inquiry and disabused experience, in a way that subordinates the first term to the second. However, the relationship evolves from being one in which Imlac can simply correct Rasselas's misconceptions, into a more mobile, dialogic rhythm. Imlac's large conclusions about 'the insufficiency of human enjoyments', for example, terminate one kind of inquiry only to initiate another: the formal quest is tacitly set aside as the travellers find themselves drawn into participation in life through contingencies (Pekuah's abduction; the encounter with the astronomer) which none of them, including Imlac, had chosen or foreseen.[70] Imlac's conclusions are also events in a journey, moments in a dynamic process, movements from one place to another. And Imlac (at least when the 'enthusiastic fit' is not upon him) understands this very well: he has nothing that he urgently wants to teach, and functions in dialogue mostly as a counterer, a reactive voice, blocking Rasselas's premature clutches at certainty, opening to his earnest straightforwardness a field of unexpected qualifications and counter-considerations. Even such a 'Johnsonian' aphorism as the much-quoted 'Human life is every where a state in which much is to be endured, and little to be enjoyed', is not, in context, quite so magisterially conclusive as it sounds. Imlac has been expounding the tendency of knowledge to promote happiness and speaking of the very real advantages of life enjoyed by the relatively knowledgeable Europeans. Rasselas then jumps at the hope of a necessary inference from these acknowledged relative goods to the idea of happiness as an achieved state—' "They are surely happy," said the prince, "who have all these conveniences" '—and it is this which elicits Imlac's reply that such happiness as can be met with in practice is not an absolute but a relative condition: ' "The Europeans," answered Imlac, "are less unhappy than we, but they are not happy. Human life is every where . . ." '[71] This undoes Rasselas's

---

[70] I am indebted here to Emrys Jones's attractive suggestion that the forty-nine chapters of the work fall into three sections of sixteen chapters each, with the final chapter as a coda: Rasselas begins his 'experiments upon life' in ch. 17, which are effectively suspended after the visit to the Pyramid in ch. 32. Emrys Jones, 'The Artistic Form of *Rasselas*', in *Review of English Studies*, NS 18 (1967), 387–401.

[71] *Johnson*, xvi.50 (ch. 11).

conclusion about the Europeans, and returns him to the process of ongoing inquiry.

Even when it is the narrator, rather than Imlac, that strikes the note of finality and disillusionment, this Voice of Authority is sustained only with a rhetorical self-consciousness that attracts its own ironies: 'Ye who listen with credulity to the whispers of fancy, and pursue with eagerness the phantoms of hope; who expect that age will perform the promises of youth, and that the deficiencies of the present day will be supplied by the morrow; attend to the history of Rasselas Prince of Abissinia.'[72] That swelling opening to the work is printed immediately beneath one of Johnson's laconic, drily factual chapter-titles: 'Description of a palace in a valley'. Or, as a subtler example, consider Rasselas's response to the stoic philosopher, whose former eloquence now provides him with no comfort on the death of his daughter: 'The prince, whose humanity would not suffer him to insult misery with reproof, went away convinced of the emptiness of rhetorical sound, and the inefficacy of polished periods and studied sentences.'[73] Those final alliterations are just obtrusive enough to register this disenchantment with rhetoric as itself a polished period and a studied sentence. The reflexive turn of the irony here is characteristic of the work; it is like that in chapter 4, for example, when Rasselas 'for a few hours, regretted his regret',[74] or like the splendidly orotund rejoinder of Rasselas to Nekayah in chapter 28: ' "Dear princess," said Rasselas, "you fall into the common errours of exaggeratory declamation, by producing, in a familiar disquisition, examples of national calamities . . ." '[75] or like that pointed up in the title of the final chapter, 'The conclusion, in which nothing is concluded'. What this play of irony confesses—and is unexpectedly at ease with—is the instability even of disillusionment, the impossibility of summing up, of stepping outside the condition of humanity for long enough to draw any final conclusions, of rising to general truths which will always be the same. To be a poet is indeed very difficult.

General truths may always be the same, but the human beings who would rise to them necessarily exist within the flow of time. Rasselas sets out, like a child of the Enlightenment, to establish the

---

[72] *Johnson*, xvi.7 (ch. 1).   [73] Ibid. 76 (ch. 18).
[74] Ibid. 20 (ch. 4).   [75] Ibid. 102 (ch. 28).

permanent truths about life, while the narrative murmurs in the background that time moves on. This is communicated through various comments by Imlac, references to youth and age, characters whose views have changed over time, and, most subtly and effectively, through the image of flowing water: the Nile 'begins his course' in the first chapter, is glimpsed or invoked from time to time, and floods at the end. The desire for permanence is set within the movement of time; this elicits a complex irony, most finely realized in connection with the loss of Pekuah, the maidservant abducted by the Arabs. Nekayah feels the bereavement keenly, so much so that she thinks at first of retiring from the world to a convent; she aspires to an everlasting grief. But time passes.

> Nekayah, seeing that nothing was omitted for the recovery of her favourite, and having, by her promise, set her intention of retirement at a distance, began imperceptibly to return to common cares and common pleasures. She rejoiced without her own consent at the suspension of her sorrows, and sometimes caught herself with indignation in the act of turning away her mind from the remembrance of her, whom yet she resolved never to forget.
>
> She then appointed a certain hour of the day for meditation on the merits and fondness of Pekuah, and for some weeks retired constantly at the time fixed, and returned with her eyes swollen and her countenance clouded. By degrees she grew less scrupulous, and suffered any important and pressing avocation to delay the tribute of daily tears. She then yielded to less occasions; sometimes forgot what she was indeed afraid to remember, and, at last, wholly released herself from the duty of periodical affliction.
>
> Her real love of Pekuah was yet not diminished. A thousand occurrences brought her back to memory . . .[76]

Nekayah believes that she will mourn for Pekuah with a perpetual and undiminishing grief; Imlac, and Johnson, know that she will not. Imlac urges her: 'Do not suffer life to stagnate; it will grow muddy for want of motion: commit yourself again to the current of the world; Pekuah will vanish by degrees.'[77] If this image of surrendering oneself to the current is free from the anxiety which invests it elsewhere in Johnson ('Roll darkling down the torrent of his fate'), this is because the truth which it expresses, and which Imlac knows, does not determine the whole truth about the situation.

---

[76] Ibid. 128 f. (ch. 36).   [77] Ibid. 127 (ch. 35).

The irony that attends upon Nekayah's endeavour to keep her grief
going is itself not conclusive. Our perception that this is a kind of
foolishness interacts with our sense of something proper in such
resolving ('whom yet she resolved never to forget'): for it would be
less than fully human to live only in the immediate moment, as do
the unformed young women Nekayah met on her travels: 'Their
grief, however, like their joy, was transient; every thing floated in
their mind unconnected with the past or future, so that one desire
easily gave way to another, as a second stone cast into the water
effaces and confounds the circles of the first.'[78] When Nekayah
finally releases herself from the duty of periodical affliction, we see
that this is partly because the pain of grief is wearing out with the
passage of time, but also because the pain of grief is still, at
moments, so sharp ('sometimes forgot what she was indeed afraid
to remember'). Indeed, her grief survives her will to grieve: 'her real
love of Pekuah was yet not diminished'. This open quality of the
irony is epitomized in the double implication of 'yet', which gives
us two propositions in one. 'Her real love of Pekuah was *as yet* not
diminished (but would come to be in the course of time)', and 'Her
real love of Pekuah was *however* (despite time's erosion of her will
to grieve) not diminished'. 'Yet not' suggests 'not yet', which looks
towards the end and time's final bleak judgement on the imperma-
nence of love and grief and memory, ideas of the mind by which
human beings invest their experience with the sense of significance
and value: simultaneously, 'yet not' is felt also as a refusal to write
'not yet', a cross-current of resistance to the narrative drift down
the stream of time towards conclusion. These two (theoretically)
opposed attitudes in practice interact with one another, without a
final determination in either's favour. (One might compare 'why do
I yet try to resolve again?', from the *Prayers and Meditations*,
quoted earlier, where 'yet' similarly holds together a logical and a
temporal implication that pull in opposite directions.)

All this helps, I hope, to suggest the importance of the open-
endedness or inconclusiveness of *Rasselas*, which works upon the
mind in a manner quite unlike *The Vanity of Human Wishes*. It is
true that in the visit to the catacombs the travellers confront the
fact of death, and that they there debate the nature of the soul and
the probability of an afterlife. But Johnson's piety here expresses

[78] *Johnson*, xvi.92 (ch. 25).

itself as the reflection that the soul does not seem likely to come to an end, any more than the philosophical argument is able to reach a conclusion. There is no reference to a final judgement. Religious feeling, which hangs in the air rather than being directly invoked as Christian doctrine, here supports, rather than puts an end to, indeterminacy:

'Immateriality seems to imply a natural power of perpetual duration as a consequence of exemption from all causes of decay. . . .'

'But the Being,' said Nekayah, 'whom I fear to name, the Being which made the soul, can destroy it.'

'He, surely, can destroy it,' answered Imlac, 'since, however unperishable, it receives from a superiour nature its power of duration. That it will not perish by any inherent cause of decay, or principle of corruption, may be shown by philosophy; but philosophy can tell no more. That it will not be annihilated by him that made it, we must humbly learn from higher authority.'

The whole assembly stood a while silent and collected. 'Let us return,' said Rasselas, 'from this scene of mortality. How gloomy would be these mansions of the dead to him who did not know that he shall never die; that what now acts shall continue its agency, and what now thinks shall think on for ever.'[79]

Perhaps the most important aspect of Johnson's decision to set *Rasselas* in the East is the way in which this allowed the existence of Christianity in the world without the necessity of invoking it as the supreme authority. Christianity was only partially and imperfectly established in Abyssinia, as Johnson knew from his translation of Lobo's *Voyage to Abyssinia*; Imlac speaks for the most part as a secular sage. The distinction between Christian faith and 'natural religion', which is often treated in this period as a matter of the greatest moment, seems in *Rasselas* to be neither urgent nor absolute. The travellers are aware of Christianity; the visit to the catacombs puts them all into what might be called a religious frame of mind; but religion is felt to be only one part of life, and religious considerations determine neither the characters' actions nor how we think of them. Elsewhere in Johnson's writings Christian truth more often works as a kind of on/off switch, that comes in at the end to cancel or transcend other considerations—as we have seen in the *Vanity*, or *Adventurer* no. 107—but in *Rasselas* the invoca-

79 Ibid. 172–4 (ch. 48).

tion of a religious perspective determines nothing, and it is not a trivial point that this occurs in the *penultimate* chapter.

In the conclusion nothing is concluded. While the Nile is in flood and the travellers are confined to their house, Rasselas, Nekayah, and Pekuah 'divert themselves' with various imaginary and impracticable schemes of happiness: Pekuah desires to be prioress of the convent of St Anthony, Nekayah to found a college of learned women, Rasselas to act as the benevolent dictator of a small kingdom. 'Of these wishes,' we are told, 'they well knew that none could be obtained'.[80] But this does not mean that they are in thrall to the consolations of the unreal. Our feeling for the illusoriness of human expectations and wishes has changed since the beginning of the story. At the beginning, the expectation created by the sonorous opening sentence, and by the juxtaposition in the early chapters of Rasselas's naivety and Imlac's worldly wisdom, is that Rasselas's wishing will come to seem comically naive, a foil for the corrective, disillusioning experience of real life. A pointed irony seems continually about to be released. Yet this expectation in the reader, like Rasselas's own expectations, has itself to be substantially modified in the light of experience. Even such obviously vulnerable flights of the mind as Rasselas's expectation that the laws will deliver perfect justice, or the philosopher's profession of the power of stoicism, or the engineer's expectations of his flying machine, are allowed a tenuous dignity that is not altogether overthrown when such theories, inevitably, collide with practice. It is relevant to recall Johnson's high opinion of *Don Quixote*, which he declared, after the *Iliad*, 'the greatest [book] in the world'.[81] What Johnson found in the madness of Quixote was an extraordinary comic fusion of the dignity, the folly, and the humanity of aspiration:

There would however be few enterprises of great labour or hazard undertaken, if we had not the power of magnifying the advantages which we persuade ourselves to expect from them. When the knight of La Mancha gravely recounts to his companion the adventures by which he is to signalize himself in such a manner that he shall be summoned to the support of empires, solicited to accept the heiress of the crown which he has preserved, have honours and riches to scatter about him, and an island to bestow on his worthy squire, very few readers, amidst their mirth or pity,

---

[80] *Johnson*, xvi.176 (ch. 49).   [81] *Johnsonian Miscellanies*, i. 333.

can deny that they have admitted visions of the same kind . . . When we pity him, we reflect on our own disappointments; and when we laugh, our hearts inform us that he is not more ridiculous than ourselves, except that he tells what we have only thought.[82]

The irony in *Rasselas*, like the irony of Cervantes, is open, not pointed. Rasselas's principle on setting out—'He thought it unsuitable to a reasonable being to act without a plan, and to be sad or chearful only by chance'[83]—turns out to be more nearly quixotic than he could have believed, but it is not therefore to be abandoned. What this means in terms of my larger argument is that the irony in *Rasselas* does not repudiate the 'Johnsonian' impulses to self-determination and to reasoned assertion (the book is full of intelligent reflections on aspects of life), but observes how those impulses cannot come to conclusion; the open-endedness is a way of accommodating both the moralist and the sceptic, of establishing them in relationship with one another.

Thus at the end, the travellers' wishful thinkings co-exist with the realities of circumstance. There is no longer anything here for Imlac to correct, and after we have heard the positive fantasies of Pekuah, Nekayah, and Rasselas, his own milder preference seems to be included within, as much as contradistinguished from, the list of impracticable wishes:

Imlac and the astronomer were contented to be driven along the stream of life without directing their course to any particular port.

Of these wishes that they had formed they well knew that none could be obtained. They deliberated a while what was to be done, and resolved, when the inundation should cease, to return to Abissinia.[84]

Imlac is here allowed no more authority than the others. His wish to have no particular goal is included in the wishes that cannot be obtained—as they all now well know, even while they indulge and cultivate those imaginations. Even the position of wise scepticism is found to stand within, not outside, the human comedy. Imlac, although contented to be driven along the stream of life, will after all direct his course to a particular port: in a powerfully and deliberately open ending to the narrative, they resolve to return to

---

[82] *Johnson*, iii.11 (*Rambler* 2).   [83] Ibid. 69 (ch. 17).
[84] Ibid. 176 (ch. 49).

Abyssinia.[85] What this return implies is that the quest for the choice of life has been recognized as simplistic, and outgrown. The party now understand that the answer to the question, how to live?, is not of a kind to be given by any conceivable encounter with a celebrity moralist or role-model. They understand that in this matter there are no authorities. In that sense, at least, an illusion has been set aside. Resolving (a significant term, as always) to return to Abyssinia implies the impulse to deal in realities; returning to Abyssinia while building ideal kingdoms in imagination, and comparing them with one another, implies a complicated apprehension of what reality is for human beings; and the unstrenuous, constating tone of the final chapter suggests a genial tolerance of such complication. The openness of the ending, like the special openness of *Rasselas* as a whole, does not repudiate the 'Johnsonian' impulse to conclusion and resolution, but includes it within a larger vision, an ironic understanding of the moralist and the sceptic as in necessary, perpetual dialogue.

*   *   *

In the course of his highly favourable review of *Rasselas*, Burke referred to its style as 'peculiar and characteristical of the author'.[86] Another reviewer, Owen Ruffhead, seized on the characteristic quality of Johnson's style as peculiarly inappropriate to a romance narrative like *Rasselas*:

He wants that graceful ease, which is the ornament of romance; and he stalks in the solemn buskin, when he ought to tread in the light sock. His stile is so tumid and pompous, that he sometimes deals in *sesquipedelia*, such as *excogitation, exaggeratory*, &c. with other hard compounds, which it is difficult to pronounce with composed features—as *multifarious, transcendental, indiscerptible*, &c.[87]

'Indiscerptible' may be set aside: it is a technical term that comes

---

[85] This does not imply a return to the Happy Valley; not only would that run counter to Johnson's lifelong insistence on the importance of living in the world, it is hard to imagine any sense in which the Happy Valley could still exist as such for this party.

[86] *Annual Register* (1759), ii.447; quoted in *Johnson: The Critical Heritage*, ed. James T. Boulton (New York, 1971), p. 147; attributed to Burke in the Yale edition, *Johnson*, xvi. p. xlvi.

[87] *Monthly Review*, (May 1759) XX.428; quoted in *Johnson: The Critical Heritage*, p. 141.

into Imlac's philosophical discussion of the nature of the soul. In the case of the other four words that Ruffhead cites, the quality which he calls 'tumid and pompous'—the obtrusively big diction, let us more neutrally call it—does indeed carry a latently comic incongruity, a certain vulnerability to irony. But this is functional in a way that is lost on Ruffhead, who starts out from the prejudice that Johnson is in no sense an ironist: when Johnson uses big language he must be either doing so unconsciously (with the *déformation professionelle* of the dictionary-maker) or aiming at a maximum of sheer dignity and importance (stalking in the solemn buskin). The passages in *Rasselas* that contain three of the four objectionable words have already been quoted earlier in this chapter; the one that remains, *excogitation*, illustrates equally well the principle that applies to all. Imlac is explaining how the intellectual and scholarly astronomer may have begun his fall into the insanity that now holds him, the delusion that he can control the climate:

To indulge the power of fiction, and send imagination out upon the wing, is often the sport of those who delight too much in silent speculation. When we are alone we are not always busy; the labour of excogitation is too violent to last long.[88]

Excogitation, he explains, is a peculiarly vulnerable activity; and we feel this all the more because of the way that the word 'excogitation' belongs to a noticeably intellectualized linguistic register, whose sphere of influence is clearly limited: it is immediately preceded—and endangered—by the simple 'when we are alone we are not always busy', with its sharply contrasting note. The 'tumid' quality of the word recognizes the claim of intellectual speculation to a certain special dignity, while at the same time registering in that claim something provisional and precarious, something open to a potentially ironic questioning from a quite different order of things. This complexity of attitude is pretty much in line with how the narrative presents the astronomer, as a figure both dignified and deranged, and dignified *in* his derangement, since this stands as emblematic of the kind of malfunctioning that is intrinsic to the life of the solitary intellect: the astronomer, we are told, presents only an unusually visible example of a very common condition. So it is not only the speculation of the astronomer that is implicated in

---

[88] *Johnson*, xvi.151 (ch. 44).

the vulnerability of 'excogitation', but intellectual speculation in
general—such as this very piece of speculation about the dangers of
excogitation, and all those other passages in *Rasselas* where the
narrative pauses, and the intellect advances general, quasi-philo-
sophical speculations and conclusions, and terms like *exaggeratory*, *multifarious*, and *transcendental* emerge to crystallize the
processes of thought. These islands of discourse in the stream of
life—such as Imlac's dissertation on poetry, or Nekayah's discussion of marriage and domestic life—have both a real significance,
and a strictly limited application, and the doubleness in our apprehension of them is conveyed, in part, through the big diction with
which Johnson regularly marks the endeavour of thought to establish conclusions. Imlac's analysis of the dangers of solitary 'excogitation' is a strong piece of thinking, but it is not directly
productive: it will be the women's (untheorized) initiative in meeting the astronomer and drawing him into company that will give
him back his sanity.

   Burke referred to the style of *Rasselas* as 'characteristical of the
author'. Although I have been treating *Rasselas* as a special case,
its play of sceptical intelligence expresses something that is
perhaps always implicit in the Johnsonian style. On the one hand,
the characteristic effect of that style is of weight, importance,
deliberateness, authority. Diction with a strong generalizing implication is often preferred, and abstract nouns are regularly chosen
where verbs or adjectival forms would have been more familiar;
syntax is obtrusively complex, with parallelisms and subordina-
tions that permit strong articulations of emphasis, and signal a
determination to achieve a comprehensive view of the topic in all
its complexity. Such a style seems thoroughly unsceptical in its
assertiveness and intellectualism: the style to be expected from the
magisterial 'Doctor Johnson' that we know, or think we know,
from Boswell—or from the caricature of more hostile contemporaries:

> POMPOSO (insolent and loud,
> Vain idol of a *scribbling* crowd,
> Whose very name inspires an awe,
> Whose ev'ry word is Sense and Law
>
>   .   .   .   .   .
>
> Who, to increase his native strength,
> Draws words, six syllables in length,

> With which, assisted with a frown
> By way of Club, he knocks us down) . . .[89]

But there is an implicit sceptical counterbalance. It comes from the very obtrusiveness, the linguistic self-consciousness of a style which, by announcing itself as intellectual construction, opens the question of whether a particular speculation or activity or event can sustain the significance which Johnson's language would attribute to it.[90] This is easiest to notice where Johnson is satirizing pretentiousness, and lends big language to his subject with malicious intent. As with the critical skills of Dick Minim: 'Yet has this diamond lain neglected with common stones, and among the innumerable admirers of *Hudibras* the observation of this superlative passage has been reserved for the sagacity of Minim.'[91] Shenstone's landscape gardening offers a subtler case, and a more nuanced judgement:

Now was excited his delight in rural pleasures, and his ambition of rural elegance; he began from this time to point his prospects, to diversify his surface, to entangle his walks, and to wind his waters, which he did with such judgement and such fancy as made his little domain the envy of the great and the admiration of the skilful: a place to be visited by travellers, and copied by designers.[92]

The reader who suspects that some comedy is lurking in the midst of the praise will find that suspicion confirmed by Johnson's switch into his pointedly plain style: 'The pleasure of Shenstone was all in his eye; he valued what he valued merely for its looks: nothing raised his indignation more than to ask if there were any fishes in his water.'[93] The comedy, though, reaches beyond Shenstone's personal vanity to accommodate a larger sense of the vanity of things. Johnson's dignifying style mimics Shenstone's gardening activities in raising a 'little domain' into something considerable, something of significance: it thereby expresses the fundamental need of the mind for significance, for things not merely to be 'idle':

---

[89] Charles Churchill, *Poetical Works*, ed. D. Grant (Oxford, 1956), pp. 97 f.: *The Ghost*, ii.653–76.

[90] For a fine study of Johnson which shows this sense of the relativity of significance as pervasive in his thinking, see Isobel Grundy, *Samuel Johnson and the Scale of Greatness* (Leicester, 1986).

[91] *Johnson*, ii.189 (*Idler* 60).   [92] Johnson, *Lives*, iii.350.

[93] Ibid. 352.

while it all the time sustains the consciousness that significance is a construction or a function of perspective, dependent on a dignifying linguistic register which may always, in the next paragraph, be withdrawn. Even in so slight a case as this, Johnson's 'characteristical' style enacts one kind of sceptical thinking: significant assertion is grounded in, not embattled against, an understanding of the insignificance of things, or at any rate the recalcitrance of things to support any single line of thought, any movement of excogitation, for very long. This implicit connection of Johnson's style with scepticism is still active (or perhaps *latent*) even when there is no comic target or shift into bathos. The big language by itself draws attention to the audacity of its claim to generalization; the syntactic parallels promote the making of discriminations, heightening consciousness of the different frameworks the mind may bring to the topic; and the marked predilection for abstraction, together with the high level of organization in the syntax, foregrounds the sense of intellectual process, of an unusual predigestion of experience and idea before the moment of utterance. We are made to feel the activity of thinking as a discourse, a power of the mind that may or may not map securely onto the world of object and event; even without the counterpoint of narrative, the Johnsonian style insists upon the gap between the activity of thinking and the object of thought.

Some further implications of this style emerge when one thinks about the canons of taste against which it offends. In his review of *Rasselas*, Ruffhead complained that Johnson's style was deficient in 'graceful ease'; Horace Walpole brought the same criteria to bear on Johnson's style more generally:

The first Criterion that stamps J's works for his, is the loaded Style . . . his words are indiscriminately select, & too forcefull for ordinary occasions. They form a hardness of diction, & a muscular toughness that destroy all ease & simplicity . . . . He is a Standing proof that the Muses leave works unfinished, if they are not embellished by the graces.[94]

The cultured eighteenth-century reader, brought up on Addison's *Spectator*, looked for a stylistic ideal of 'ease' that Johnson's style positively repudiates. In fact, Johnson was in principle no enemy to 'ease and simplicity' in literature; he gave warm praise to Dryden's

[94] *Johnson: The Critical Heritage*, pp. 325 f.

essays for their informality of style—'though all is easy, nothing is feeble'⁹⁵—and wrote appreciatively in the *Idler* about Cowley as a master of 'easy poetry'. But he seems to have thought of this as a quality which, in its best form, belonged to the Restoration period; it went out of poetry after 'the time of *Dryden*', he wrote in the same essay,⁹⁶ and in his praise of Addison's prose-style in the *Lives* there is just audible a note of reservation:

> What he attempted, he performed: he is never feeble, and he did not wish to be energetick; he is never rapid, and he never stagnates. His sentences have neither studied amplitude, nor affected brevity; his periods, though not diligently rounded, are voluble and easy. Whoever wishes to attain an English style, familiar but not coarse, and elegant but not ostentatious, must give his days and nights to the volumes of Addison.⁹⁷

That last sentence echoes a classic formula of praise, applied by Horace to the Greeks, and by Pope to Homer: but the emphasis on diligent labour, given in one of Johnson's diligently rounded periods, seems unlikely to lead to ease. As a quality of style, ease is the suspension of all appearance of effort and striving. It makes one say of a writer what Johnson says of Addison: 'What he attempted, he performed.' Even if, as Pope said in the *Essay on Criticism*, 'True ease in writing comes from art, not chance',⁹⁸ the prior training, the discipline, has become invisible; there is a paradisal continuity between the self and the act of expression, between the mind and the forms of discourse, between consciousness and instinct. Cultivation and spontaneity are one; where easiness reigns, attempt *is* performance.

But the gap between attempt and performance, between the ideas of the mind and realization in the world, is precisely what Johnson's sceptical intelligence everywhere insists on. At the level of language, this manifests itself as an acute awareness of the difference between words and their referents, the almost inevitable possibility of slippage between the two. This is one great theme of the Preface to the *Dictionary*, where the fluidities of language neces-

---

⁹⁵ Johnson, *Lives*, i.418.   ⁹⁶ *Johnson*, ii.242 (*Idler* 77).
⁹⁷ Johnson, *Lives*, ii.149 f. Hester Thrale observed of Addison's prose, that Johnson 'did never like, though he always thought fit to praise it; and his praises resembled those of a man who extols the superior elegance of high painted porcelain, while he himself always chuses to eat off *plate*' (*Johnsonian Miscellanies*, i.283).
⁹⁸ *Pope*, p. 74 (l. 362).

sarily come between the dictionary-maker's own attempt and performance; and it is enacted in the 'loaded' quality of his style, the thickness of linguistic texture which guards against what Soame Jenyns was convicted of, the imposing of 'words for ideas'.[99] At the level of social relations, it involves a principled refusal to be 'polite', to work with terms and meanings as these have been established by social convention. As Walpole and Churchill both implied, Johnson's style is also a question of manners; it involves a rejection of 'the graces', in Walpole's terms, and in Churchill's portrait Johnson's aggressive way with language marks him out as someone 'Who 'bove the Vulgar dares to rise, | And sense of *Decency* defies'[100]—a gate-crasher who does not know his place, with an outsider's disregard of the social decencies.

Johnson's famous clash with Chesterfield over the *Dictionary* has a symbolic significance here, which neatly brings together the issue of language and the issue of manners. Chesterfield was the acknowledged doyen of taste and good breeding, the embodiment of an ideal of high culture understood as the cultivation of the graces. His commendation of Johnson's *Dictionary* in *The World* perfectly expresses this: 'good order and authority' are endorsed as a matter of pure convention, desirable but also arbitrary:

It must be owned that our language is at present in a state of anarchy. . . . Good order and authority are now necessary. But where shall we find them, and at the same time, the obedience due to them? We must have recourse to the old Roman expedient in times of confusion, and chuse a dictator. Upon this principle I give my vote for Mr Johnson to fill that great and arduous post. And I hereby declare that I make a total surrender of all my rights and privileges in the English language, as a free-born British subject, to the said Mr Johnson, during the term of his dictatorship. Nay more; I will not only obey him, like an old Roman, as my dictator, but, like a modern Roman, I will implicitly believe in him as my pope, and hold him to be infallible while in the chair; but no longer.[101]

Chesterfield had been a courtier and diplomat, and his attitude to meaning could be described as diplomatic. In the urbanity of that final conceit which sees Johnson as the Pope, Chesterfield's profes-

[99] *Samuel Johnson*, ed. Greene, p. 534.
[100] Churchill, *Poetical Works*, p. 98: *The Ghost*, ii.677 f.
[101] Adam Fitz-Adam [E. Moore], *The World*, 6 vols. (London, 1755–7), iii.266 f.: no. 100 (28 Nov. 1754).

sion of belief in Johnson's pronouncements offers itself as a public, social gesture, reliable as a guarantee of his social practice and useful as a means of establishing a conventional understanding, but never for a moment to be mistaken for 'real' belief. It is a gracious commendation, and Johnson might graciously have accepted it, and dedicated the *Dictionary* to Chesterfield as an act itself understood to be a convention, a social gesture or transaction. Instead, he replied with the famous letter of rejection, in which his mastery of the forms of politeness makes his refusal of Chesterfield's terms all the more pointed. Politeness becomes ironic, and Johnson, as an 'uncourtly scholar', rudely insists on penetrating the conventional use of such terms as 'patron' and 'servant':

Is not a Patron, My Lord, one who looks with unconcern on a Man struggling for Life in the water and when he has reached ground, encumbers him with help? . . .

Having carried on my work thus far with so little obligation to any favourer of Learning I shall not be disappointed though I should conclude it, if less be possible, with less, for I have been long wakened from that Dream of hope, in which I once boasted myself with so much exultation, My lord, Your Lordship's Most humble,

most obedient Servant,

S. J.[102]

The rejection of Chesterfield has always been recognized as a milestone in the growing independence of the professional writer; it also marks the growing split in eighteenth-century conceptions of culture, as the values of ease and politeness became increasingly hard to reconcile with intellectual seriousness. In *An Essay on Criticism*, the young Pope had imagined the perfect critic as combining the intellectual virtues with the social graces: 'Tho' learn'd, well-bred; and tho' well-bred, sincere.' 'But where's the man?' Pope asks.[103] It is a high ideal, and the force of the double 'though' suggests how nearly oxymoronic this ideal is, even for Pope, even as early as 1711. The triple synthesis of learning, good-breeding, and sincerity could perhaps only ever be an ideal, but to move from the circle of Pope to the circle of Johnson is to feel how the ideal became harder to realize, or perhaps came to seem intrinsically less desirable, as the

---

[102] *The Letters of Samuel Johnson*, ed. Bruce Redford, 5 vols. (Oxford, 1992–4), i.96 f.: to Lord Chesterfield, 7 Feb. 1755.
[103] *Pope*, p. 82 (ll. 635, 631).

century went on. When Johnson expounded the value of good-breeding to his hostess in the Hebrides, he did so with a directness that took no regard of the ordinary forms of courtesy:

Johnson. 'Why, sir, a man grows better humoured as he grows older. He improves by experience. When young, he thinks himself of great consequence, and every thing of importance. As he advances in life, he learns to think himself of no consequence, and little things of little importance; and so he becomes more patient, and better pleased. All good-humour and complaisance are acquired. . . . Common language speaks the truth as to this: we say, a person is well *bred.*' . . .—Lady M'Leod asked, if no man was naturally good?—*Johnson.* 'No, madam, no more than a wolf.'—*Boswell.* 'Nor no woman, sir?'—*Johnson.* 'No, sir.'—Lady M'Leod started at this, saying, in a low voice, 'This is worse than Swift.'[104]

The age of chivalry was certainly dead in this exchange. Johnson's good-breeding, grounded in a rather ruthless perception of the littleness of things, is almost incompatible with eighteenth-century norms of 'politeness'. In another conversation with Boswell, Johnson spells out the rationale for his aggression toward the language of social convention: to succumb to such language is all too easily to forfeit any possibility of real *thinking*. Boswell had declared himself 'vexed' by the turn of contemporary politics; Johnson immediately took him to task for not understanding how little he meant by such a statement:

JOHNSON: 'My dear friend, clear your *mind* of cant. You may *talk* as other people do: you may say to a man, "Sir, I am your most humble servant." You are *not* his most humble servant. You may say, "These are bad times; it is a melancholy thing to be reserved to such times." You don't mind the times. You tell a man, "I am sorry you had such bad weather the last day of your journey, and were so much wet." You don't care six-pence whether he was wet or dry. You may *talk* in this manner; it is a mode of talking in Society: but don't *think* foolishly.'[105]

Although Johnson allows that Boswell 'may *talk* in this manner', it is clearly not a mode of talking that Johnson himself much practises or tolerates. 'It is a mode of talking in Society.' We have seen

---

[104] Boswell, *Life*, v.211 (Sept. 1773). For a stimulating discussion of Johnson's 'impoliteness', see Philip Davis, *In Mind of Johnson: A Study of Johnson the Rambler* (Athens, Ga., 1989), ch. 2: ' "You Tossed and Gored Several Persons" ', pp. 44–96.
[105] Ibid. iv.221 (May 1783).

in Hume how the art of living in society, according to conventions felt to be artificial and in some sense groundless, can express and accommodate a radical scepticism. Hume, after the *Treatise*, announced that his aim was to write and to reason in an 'easy manner', inviting a sociable partnership or collusion with his reader as the most natural, most intelligent outcome of his sceptical analysis. Johnson's scepticism, however, expresses itself in an opposite and indeed oppositional sense, through the continual challenging of conventional terms and the adoption of a 'loaded style' which positively sets itself against 'easy' discourse.

He seemed to take a pleasure in speaking in his own style; for when he had carelessly missed it, he would repeat the thought translated into it. Talking of the Comedy of 'The Rehearsal,' he said, 'It has not wit enough to keep it sweet.' This was easy;—he therefore caught himself, and pronounced a more rounded sentence; 'It has not vitality enough to preserve it from putrefaction.'[106]

This may seem like a case of 'Doctor Johnson' as Pomposo. There is certainly a sense in which the first sentence is better English than the second. But by highlighting Johnson's 'pleasure in speaking in his own style' (a striking idea), Boswell is pointing to a significant underlying habit of mind. By recasting his opinion into the register of self-conscious intellectual discourse—the idiom of an 'uncourtly scholar'—Johnson both claims a greater authority for it, and projects or dramatizes it as 'his own' assertion. It is no longer an easy, natural response, but a deliberated (and hence, of course, debatable) utterance, 'not dogmatically but deliberately'[107] put forward, as he says of his judgements in the *Preface to Shakespeare*. The deliberateness matters, for it expresses that sense of agency in his thinking which was so important to Johnson: the style guarantees that this judgement could not be merely a reflection of 'current opinion', going with the flow: it makes of the judgement a positive act, a conclusive assertion. At the same time, by playing out the conclusiveness so consciously, the style expresses the sceptic's recognition that this formulation inevitably shares in the vulnerability and one-sidedness of all intellectual formulation; the generalizing diction makes us conscious of how simple response (the jokes in *The Rehearsal* aren't funny any more) is grounded in

---

[106] Ibid. 320 (June 1784).   [107] *Johnson*, vii.80.

general principles (the difference between jokes that date and wit that doesn't) that inevitably call for challenge, qualification, or development. The *pleasure* associated with this style has to do with the way in which it allows Johnson to be both sceptical and assertive at once. The assertiveness is shadowed by an ironic intelligence: when he sounds most 'Johnsonian', one can sometimes glimpse, as in the above quotation, Johnson *playing* 'Doctor Johnson'.[108]

Somewhere, Boswell may have understood all this rather acutely. When he first met Johnson he was adrift in London, where he had come hoping, like Rasselas, to make the choice of life: although contemplating a career in the Guards, he felt himself acutely conscious of the ultimate emptiness of aspiration and the difficulty of really committing to any course of action. Like Rasselas, again, he was to engineer a series of encounters with the celebrity moralists of his day—Hume, Voltaire, Rousseau, as well as Johnson—in search of some justifying authority or wisdom in which he could never really believe. In his London journal he wrote:

I see too far into the system of things to be much in earnest. . . . This being the case, I am rather passive than active in life. It is difficult to make my feeling clearly understood. I may say, I act passively. That is, not with my whole heart, and thinking this or that of real consequence, but because so and so things are established and I must submit. . . . Yet I do think it is a happiness to have an object in view which one keenly follows. It gives a lively agitation to the mind which is very pleasurable. I am determined to have a degree of Erskine's indifference, to make me easy when things go cross; and a degree of Macdonald's eagerness for real life, to make me relish things when they go well. . . . The great art I have to study is to balance these two very different ways of thinking properly. It is very difficult to be keen about a thing which in reality you do not regard, and consider as imaginary. But I fancy it may do, as a man is afraid of ghosts in the dark, although he is sure there are none; or pleased with beautiful exhibitions on the stage, although he knows they are not real. Although the Judgment may know that all is vanity, yet Passion may ardently pursue.[109]

---

[108] Cf. Iain McGilchrist, *Against Criticism* (London, 1982), p. 126: referring to the saying that the fox knows many things but the hedgehog knows one big thing, McGilchrist argues that it suited Johnson 'to annex the manner of the hedgehog and apply it to his fox-like interests and opinions'.

[109] *Boswell's London Journal: 1762–1763*, ed. Frederick A. Pottle (London, 1950), pp. 77, 79.

Boswell here associates the suspension of disbelief which happens in the theatre, with the kind of suspension of disbelief seen by a sceptic such as Hume as intrinsic to the art of living. This suggests much about Boswell's fondness for seeing himself as playing a character, so that his daily life in London becomes in his journal entries a series of performances, like an exhibition on the stage; and it is entirely relevant to the way the *Life* projects 'Doctor Johnson' as a quasi-theatrical figure, a stage character. Johnson enters Boswell's life with all the tremendous authority, the life-transforming presence, of the Ghost in *Hamlet*:

Mr Davies having perceived him through the glass-door in the room in which we were sitting, advancing towards us,—he announced his aweful approach to me, somewhat in the manner of an actor in the part of Horatio, when he addresses Hamlet on the appearance of his father's ghost, 'Look, my Lord, it comes.'[110]

In this allusion, which Boswell introduced when he wrote up the original journal entry for publication, one can hear a doubleness which resonates throughout the *Life*: an affirmation of Johnson, certainly, as the great authority-figure and father-substitute whom Boswell was seeking, but also a trace of enjoyable overstatement, of conscious *theatre*, that tinges the Johnson/Ghost identification with comedy. The more vigorously Boswell stages Johnson as a figure of authority and significance, as the panacea for his own sceptical *ennui*, the more that very process of staging brings with it a shadowing comic irony.

In particular, he makes us see Johnson, the proponent of general truths about general nature, as a singular and extraordinary individual. This is epitomized in the epitaph given to Johnson at his death: 'He has made a chasm, which not only nothing can fill up, but which nothing has a tendency to fill up.—Johnson is dead.— Let us go to the next best:—there is nobody;—no man can be said to put you in mind of Johnson.'[111] This uniqueness is not just a matter of Johnson's intellectual distinction. 'Doctor Johnson' can take his place alongside Tristram Shandy or Uncle Toby as one of the supreme 'humorists' or eccentrics of the eighteenth century. Boswell introduced Johnson to his readers as having 'a great deal

---

[110] Boswell, *Life*, i.392 (May 1763).   [111] Ibid. iv.420 f. (Dec. 1784).

of that quality called *humour*',[112] and one large tendency of the
Life was to promote the sense of Johnson as an intensely individual figure, '*Oddity*, as they call him',[113] who although hugely
gregarious was only most precariously and remarkably capable of
living 'in Society' at all. In his review of a new edition of Boswell's
Life Macaulay gathered together, not without malice, many of the
salient images:

Everything about him, his coat, his wig, his figure, his face, his scrofula,
his St Vitus's dance, his rolling walk, his blinking eye, the outward signs
which too clearly marked his approbation of his dinner, his insatiable
appetite for fish-sauce and veal-pie with plums, his inextinguishable thirst
for tea, his trick of touching the posts as he walked, his mysterious practice of treasuring up scraps of orange-peel, his morning slumbers, his
midnight disputations, his contortions, his mutterings, his gruntings, his
puffings, his vigorous, acute, and ready eloquence, his sarcastic wit, his
vehemence, his insolence, his fits of tempestuous rage, his queer inmates,
old Mr Levett and blind Mrs Williams, the cat Hodge and the negro Frank,
all are as familiar to us as the objects by which we have been surrounded
from childhood.[114]

'I inherited . . . a vile melancholy from my father, which has made
me mad all my life, at least not sober', Johnson told Boswell during
their tour of Scotland.[115] It is a sentence which might have come
from Tristram Shandy himself. The remedy for madness, Imlac
explained to the astronomer, is to 'keep this thought always preva-
lent, that you are only one atom of the mass of humanity'; in similar
vein, Johnson counselled Boswell, in the year of their first meeting,
to beware of the 'desire of distinction which inclines every Man first
to hope and then to believe that Nature has given him something
peculiar to himself'.[116] Here, clearly, is the voice of the anti-sceptical
Johnson who insisted on the truth of general nature, and attacked the
theory of a ruling passion and the singularity of Sterne. But what
Boswell's representation of 'Doctor Johnson' does is to suggest something singular and 'peculiar to himself' in that very emphasis on
general truths. It is animated by the paradox that to assert the exis-

---

[112] Boswell, *Life*, v.20 (Aug. 1773).
[113] Ibid. iii.209 (Sept. 1777).
[114] Thomas Babington Macaulay, *Critical and Historical Essays contributed to
the Edinburgh Review* (London, 1878), p. 172.
[115] Boswell, *Life*, v.215 (Sept. 1773).
[116] *Johnson*, xvi.163 (ch. 46); *Letters*, i.239 (to Boswell, 8 Dec. 1763).

tence of general nature and to seek a central, comprehensive point of
view, is a necessarily idiosyncratic enterprise, or at least, in the
person of Johnson, is inextricably bound up with the singular and the
idiosyncratic. It is this tension—between Johnson's centrality and his
eccentricity, between his authority and his peculiarity, between his
domination of Boswell's narrative and his subjection to Boswell's
staging—that gives the *Life* its enduring, and comic, vitality. This
might be developed into a discussion of Boswell's own art. But here
I would rather press the idea of Boswell's *perceptiveness*. Even if
'Doctor Johnson' is a mild travesty or, at best, considerable simplifi-
cation of what Johnson in full intellectual flow was really like,
Boswell's way of staging Johnson may be true to Johnson in a different way—endorsing and admiring the Johnsonian assertiveness,
certainly, but at the same time placing it within the field of an ironic
vision. 'They listened with wonder and pleasure, while Dr Johnson
harangued.'[117] This is somewhat like the quality of irony in *Rasselas*
as a whole, where any assertion of a general truth or position is felt
as a moment in an ongoing process to which the assertion is not
wholly adequate. The pretension to significance, or to the articulation of conclusions, is placed in an open-ended, ongoing dialogue
with events or considerations which offer to undo that claim.

'Dialogue' is here not only a metaphor. If the travellers in
Rasselas do, in some real sense, make progress, one mark of this is
that at the end their wishes and imaginations, however impracticable, are openly exchanged and compared in conversation with each
other. There is a clear contrast here with their earlier reality-flout-
ing daydreams to which they had all confessed, and which could be
indulged only in secret and in solitude. Although all three of their
fantasies at the end are still fantasies of power, it is notable that
they all concern communities—monastic, intellectual, political—
and that the best of them, Nekayah's project to found a college of
learned women, explicitly includes the idea of reciprocal teaching
and learning through conversation.[118] The astronomer's insanity,

---

[117] Boswell, *Life*, v.211 f. (Sept. 1777).
[118] 'The princess thought, that of all sublunary things, knowledge was the best:
She desired first to learn all sciences, and then purposed to found a college of
learned women, in which she would preside, that, by conversing with the old, and
educating the young, she might divide her time between the acquisition and communication of wisdom, and raise up for the next age models of prudence, and patterns
of piety.' *Johnson*, XVI.175 (ch. 49). Although there are ironies enough implanted
here, still Nekayah is, as usual, noticeably more intelligent than her brother.

so significantly placed towards the end of the book, expresses the tendency of any powerful mind left to its own devices: the insanity is dissipated through the effect of company and conversation. And it is a small but striking detail that, of all the social and technological advantages of European civilization, what Rasselas most admires is 'the facility with which separated friends interchange their thoughts'.[119]

Dialogue, or the interchange of thoughts, has been a recurrent theme in this study of scepticism. Two voices which differ, yet where both are cogent, provide scepticism with its simplest, most fundamental case: where those voices find a way of continuing, sustaining a true dialogue, rather than coming to conclusion or conclusions, we have one basic model for scepticism as paradoxically constructive. In *An Essay on Man* and the *Epistle to Bolingbroke*, Pope was in dialogue—literal and imaginative—with Bolingbroke and with the philosophical tendencies which Bolingbroke represented. Hume's scepticism has been understood as inextricably bound up with the relation between author and reader, and most finely expressed in a work of dialogue form. *Tristram Shandy* is writing which aspires, its author tells us, to the condition of conversation, in ways that are responsive to the singularity of the individual and the difficulty of communication. And for Johnson it is dialogue that modulates the drive towards assertion into the play of inquiry, and thereby guarantees its intelligence and, indeed, its sanity. What all four very different writers share is the distinctively eighteenth-century—though also, of course, Socratic—sense that intellectual discussion should never get very far from its roots in oral exchange, and that serious intellectual inquiry is not necessarily trivialized or traduced when understood as a game for voices. This naturally implies a social dimension, and although Johnson's stylistic 'impoliteness', like his impoliteness in manners, repudiates the code of sociability which Hume employed, it does so nonetheless with an intense consciousness of the company of others. The impoliteness is itself a kind of reaching out, a challenging, a provocation to debate. When Johnson wanted his companion's talk to be more *conclusive*, he was surely wishing not for an end to the discussion, but for some-

---

[119] *Johnson*, xvi.50 (ch. 11). On dialogue and *Rasselas*, see Catherine N. Parke, *Samuel Johnson and Biographical Thinking* (Columbia, NY, 1991), pp. 93–102.

thing more definite to query and to challenge; the emphatic conclusiveness of his own writing expresses both the resolution to tell things as they really are, and the hope, in conclusion, of reaction and response.

Select Bibliography and Further Reading

Auerbach, Erich, 'L'Humaine Condition' in *Mimesis: The Representation of Reality in Western Literature*, trans. W. R. Trask (Princeton, 1953).

Bayle, Pierre, *Historical and Critical Dictionary*, trans. Richard H. Popkin (Indianapolis, 1965).

Berkeley, George, *A Treatise Concerning the Principles of Human Knowledge* and *Three Dialogues between Hylas and Philonous* in *The Works of George Berkeley, Bishop of Cloyne*, ed. A. A. Luce and T. E. Jessop, 9 vols. (London, 1948–57; repr. 1964).

Boswell, James, *Boswell's Life of Johnson. Together with Boswell's Journal of a Tour to the Hebrides and Johnson's Diary of a Journey into North Wales*, ed. G. B. Hill, rev. L. F. Powell, 6 vols. (Oxford, 1934–50).

—— *Boswell's London Journal: 1762–1763*, ed. Frederick A. Pottle (London, 1950).

Box, M. A., *The Suasive Art of David Hume* (Princeton, 1990).

Briggs, Peter M., 'Locke's *Essay* and the Tentativeness of *Tristram Shandy*', *Studies in Philology* 82 (1985), 493–520.

Brush, Craig B., *Montaigne and Bayle: Variations on the Theme of Skepticism* (The Hague, 1966).

Burke, Edmund, *Reflections on the Revolution in France*, ed. Conor Cruise O'Brien (Harmondsworth, 1968).

Burnyeat, Myles, ed., *The Skeptical Tradition* (Berkeley, 1983).

Cave, Terence, 'Montaigne' in *The Cornucopian Text: Problems of Writing in the French Renaissance* (Oxford, 1979).

Colie, Rosalie, 'The Essayist in his *Essay*' in *John Locke: Problems and Perspectives*, ed. John W. Yolton (Cambridge, 1969).

Damrosch, Leo, *Fictions of Reality in the Age of Hume and Johnson* (Madison, 1989).

Davis, Philip, *In Mind of Johnson: A Study of Johnson The Rambler* (Athens, Ga., 1989).

Dédéyan, Charles, *Montaigne chez ses amis anglo-saxons*, 2 vols. (Paris, 1944).

Fox, Christopher, *Locke and the Scriblerians: Identity and Consciousness in Early Eighteenth-Century Britain* (Berkeley and Los Angeles, 1988).

Frame, Donald M., *Montaigne's Discovery of Man: The Humanization of a Humanist* (New York, 1955).
—— *Montaigne's Essais: A Study* (Englewood Cliffs, NJ, 1969).
Gibbon, Edward, *Memoirs of My Life*, ed. Georges A. Bonnard (London, 1966).
—— *The History of the Decline and Fall of the Roman Empire*, ed. David Womersley, 3 vols. (Harmondsworth, 1994).
Grundy, Isobel, *Samuel Johnson and the Scale of Greatness* (Leicester, 1986).
—— 'Samuel Johnson: Man of Maxims?' in *Samuel Johnson: New Critical Essays*, ed. Isobel Grundy (London, 1984)
Hammond, Brean, *Pope and Bolingbroke: A Study of Friendship and Influence* (Columbia, NY, 1984).
Hume, David, *A Treatise of Human Nature*, ed. L. A. Selby-Bigge, 2nd ed. rev. P. H. Nidditch (Oxford, 1978).
—— *Enquiries concerning Human Understanding and concerning the Principles of Morals*, ed. L. A. Selby-Bigge, 3rd ed. rev. P. H. Nidditch (Oxford, 1975).
—— *Essays Moral, Political, and Literary*, ed. Eugene F. Miller (Indianapolis, 1985).
—— *The Natural History of Religion and Dialogues concerning Natural Religion*, ed. A. Wayne Colver and John Valdimir Price (Oxford, 1976).
Johnson, Samuel, *The Yale Edition of the Works of Samuel Johnson*, ed. John H. Middendorf *et al.* (New Haven and London, 1958–).
—— *Samuel Johnson: The Major Works*, ed. Donald Greene (Oxford, 2000).
Lamb, Jonathan, 'Sterne's Use of Montaigne', *Comparative Literature* 32 (1980), 1–41.
—— *Sterne's Fiction and the Double Principle* (Cambridge, 1989).
Lanham, Richard A., *Tristram Shandy: The Games of Pleasure* (Berkeley and Los Angeles, 1973).
Leranbaum, Miriam, *Alexander Pope's 'Opus Magnum' 1729–1744* (Oxford, 1977).
Locke, John, *An Essay concerning Human Understanding*, ed. Peter H. Nidditch (Oxford, 1975).
McGilchrist, Iain, *Against Criticism* (London, 1982).
Maclean, Kenneth, *John Locke and English Literature of the Eighteenth Century* (Princeton, 1936; reissued New York, 1962).
Marchi, Dudley M., *Montaigne among the Moderns: Receptions of the Essais* (Providence, RI, 1994).
Maskell, Duke, 'Locke and Sterne, or Can Philosophy Influence Literature?', *Essays in Criticism* 23 (1973), 22–40.

Montaigne, Michel de, *Essays of Michael Seigneur de Montaigne*, trans. Charles Cotton, 2nd ed., 3 vols. (London, 1693). A good and readily available modern translation is that by M. A. Screech, *The Essays of Michel de Montaigne* (London, 1991).

Mullan, John, 'Laurence Sterne and the "Sociality" of the Novel', in *Sentiment and Sociability: The Language of Feeling in the Eighteenth Century* (Oxford, 1988).

Norton, David Fate, *David Hume: Common-Sense Moralist, Sceptical Metaphysician* (Princeton, 1982).

—— (ed), *The Cambridge Companion to Hume* (Cambridge, 1993).

Nussbaum, Martha C., *Love's Knowledge: Essays on Philosophy and Literature* (Oxford, 1990).

Nuttall, A. D., *A Common Sky: Philosophy and the Literary Imagination* (London, 1974).

—— *Pope's 'Essay on Man'* (London, 1984).

Parker, Fred, 'Johnson and the Lives of Poets', *The Cambridge Quarterly* 29 (2000), 323–37.

Pascal, Blaise, 'A Conversation with Monsieur de Saci', trans. G. F. Pullen, in *The Essential Pascal*, ed. Robert W. Gleason (New York, 1966).

—— *Pensées*, trans. Martin Turnell (London, 1962).

Pope, Alexander, *Poetical Works*, ed. Herbert Davis (Oxford, 1966).

Popkin, Richard H., *The High Road to Pyrrhonism* (San Diego, 1980).

—— *The History of Scepticism from Erasmus to Spinoza* (Berkeley and Los Angeles, 1979).

Potkay, Adam, *The Passion for Happiness: Samuel Johnson and David Hume* (Ithaca, NY, 2000).

Prince, Michael, *Philosophical Dialogue in the British Enlightenment: Theology, aesthetics and the novel* (Cambridge, 1996).

Prior, Matthew, 'Dialogue between Mr John Lock and Seigneur de Montaigne' in *The Literary Works of Matthew Prior*, ed. H. Bunker Wright and Monroe K. Spears, 2 vols. (Oxford, 1959).

Richetti, John J., *Philosophical Writing: Locke, Berkeley, Hume* (Cambridge, Mass., 1983).

Rorty, Richard, *Contingency, Irony, and Solidarity* (Cambridge, 1989).

Screech, M. A., *Montaigne and Melancholy: The Wisdom of the Essays* (London, 1983).

Simpson, David, 'Hume's Intimate Voices and the Method of Dialogue', in *Texas Studies in Literature and Language* 21 (1979), 68–92.

Sitter, John, 'Hume's Stylistic Emergence' in *Literary Loneliness in Mid-Eighteenth-Century England* (Ithaca, NY, 1982).

Solomon, Harry M., *The Rape of the Text: Reading and Misreading Pope's Essay on Man* (Tuscaloosa, Ala., 1993).

Stack, Frank, *Pope and Horace: Studies in Imitation* (Cambridge, 1985).

Starobinski, Jean, *Montaigne in Motion*, trans. A. Goldhammar (Chicago, 1985).

Sterne, Laurence, *The Florida Edition of the Works of Laurence Sterne*, ed. Melvyn New *et al.* (Gainesville, Fla., 1978–).

Swift, Jonathan, *A Tale of a Tub*, ed. Herbert Davis (Oxford, 1939).

Tave, Stuart, *The Amiable Humorist* (Chicago, 1960).

Traugott, John, *Tristram Shandy's World: Sterne's Philosophical Rhetoric* (Berkeley and Los Angeles, 1954).

Yolton, John W., *John Locke and the Way of Ideas* (Oxford, 1956).

Index

Addison, Joseph 122–3, 164–5, 167, 270–1
  on Locke 84–5
  on Montaigne 44 n. 93, 45–6
Aristotle 164

Bacon, Francis 45, 108
Bayle, Pierre 16–20, 25, 53, 123
Beckett, Samuel 248–9
Bell, Michael 26 n. 52
Bergson, Henri 206 n. 35
Berkeley, George 9, 58–9, 61, 71–2, 78, 106, 211
Biro, John 149
Blake, William 56 n. 3, 126–7
Boileau Despréaux, Nicolas 246 n. 38
Bolingbroke, Henry St John, Viscount 6, 86, 90, 105–11, 114–16, 123, 130–4
  and Locke 57, 71, 73, 106–8, 132–3
  and Montaigne 110, 131–3
Boswell, James 151, 166, 233, 268, 274–9
Box, M. A. 164 n. 53
Briggs, Peter 206 n. 35
Browne, Thomas 46
Burke, Edmund 7–8, 28–9, 49, 53, 133 n. 90, 266, 268
Burnet, Thomas 73–4
Butler, Joseph 77–8, 179
Byron, George Gordon, Lord 46 n. 104

Cervantes, Miguel de 264–5
Charron, Pierre 43 n. 88, 97, 131, 208 n. 39
Chesterfield, Philip Stanhope, 4th Earl of 272–3
Churchill, Charles 268–9, 272
Cibber, Colley 45
Cicero 161–2, 164, 187
Coste, Pierre 42
Cotton, Charles 37, 42
Cowley, Abraham 46, 271
Craig, Edward 148 n. 22

Crousaz, J. P. de 87

Dancy, Jonathan 185 n. 103
Davis, Philip 274 n. 104
Deporte, Michael 218 n. 65
Dryden, John 44, 46, 246 n. 38, 270–1

Epictetus 225–7
Epicurus 177
Erasmus, Desiderius 130, 228 n. 83

Fielding, Henry 44, 133 n. 90
Fogelin, Robert 149

Gibbon, Edward 8, 13, 16–17, 20–2, 45, 65, 177, 186
Goldsmith, Oliver 123
Grundy, Isobel 269 n. 90

Halifax, George Savile, 1st Marquis of 43
Hammond, Brean 102, 111 n. 48
Hazlitt, William 47
Hobbes, Thomas 120, 169
Horace 89–91, 98–101, 136, 271
Horne, George 154 n. 33
Hume, David 30, 58, 138–89, 244, 277, 280
  on Berkeley 9, 211
  Dialogues concerning Natural Religion 15–16, 180–8
  dying 150–1
  Enquiry concerning Human Understanding 172–89
  Enquiry concerning the Principles of Morals 167–72
  on instinct 123, 125
  and Johnson 139–40, 165–7, 171, 176, 179, 181–2, 232, 235–6, 244, 248, 250–1, 275
  and Locke 65, 78–9, 141, 164
  and Montaigne 153–4, 158–60
  philosophical commentators on 148–50
  political theory 144

Hume, David (*cont.*):
  and Pope 125, 147, 154, 156, 189,
    251
  on Rousseau 212
  and sociability 160–7
  and Sterne 150, 154, 189, 191, 193
  Treatise of Human Nature 23–8,
    41, 50, 141–8, 153–8
  on the will 157–9, 165

Jacobson, Anne 148 n. 22
Jenyns, Soame 7, 11, 14–15, 115, 125,
    272
Johnson, Samuel 5–6,13, 46, 232–81
  on Addison 271
  Beckett on 248
  on Bolingbroke 133 n. 90
  on Burke 29
  on *Don Quixote* 264–5
  as 'Dr Johnson' 233, 268, 276–9
  and ease 270–2, 275
  and Hume 139–40, 165–7, 171,
    176, 179, 181–2, 232, 235–6,
    244, 248, 250–1, 275
  and idleness 245–50
  on Jenyns 7, 14–16, 115, 176
  and language 11–13, 30, 65,
    266–72, 275–6
  on man as machine 204
  on Montaigne 45, 232
  on mortality 217, 239–40, 244–5
  and Pope 30–1, 112, 136–7, 232,
    236–7, 248, 250–2
  Prayers and Meditations 240, 249,
    262
  Rasselas 252–68, 279–80
  on religion 22–3, 179, 238–40,
    242, 263–4
  against scepticism 8–9, 232–6
  on Shakespeare 233–5
  singularity and generality 234–7,
    241, 277–9
  and sociability 51–2, 271–5,
    279–81
  and Sterne 194, 204, 210–11,
    217–18, 232, 234–6, 248,
    250–1, 277–8
  Vanity of Human Wishes 240–4,
    252, 256, 258, 261–2
  on the will 249–52
  on wit 5, 29
Jones, Emrys 259 n. 70
Juvenal 242

Kant, Immanuel 4
Keats, John 138
Kenshur, Oscar 20 n.

La Bruyère, Jean de 34 n. 66
La Mettrie, Julien de 204
La Rochefoucauld, Duc de 120, 235–6
Lamb, Jonathan 219 n. 68
Lanham, Richard 218–19
Lee, Henry 59
Leibniz, Gottfried 57
Locke, John 5, 6, 10–11, 16, 34–5, 46,
    50, 53, 54–85, 106–8, 123,
    132–3
  on general ideas 64, 71–2, 80, 211
  on language 64–8, 82–4, 132–3
  on materialism 76
  on moral knowledge 70–4
  on personal identity 76–8
  in Pope 91–7
  in Prior 34–5, 68–9, 92–5
  in the *Spectator* 84–5
  and Sterne 204–6, 214
  on substance 63, 74–8, 81
  and supposing 81–4
Lucretius 44 n. 94, 110
Luther, Martin 130

Macaulay, Thomas 278
McGilchrist, Iain 219 n. 67, 276 n.
    108
Mack, Maynard 95
Mandeville, Bernard 120, 169
Montaigne, Michel de 32–50, 53,
    129–37, 153–4, 158–60, 208,
    219–27, 232
  and Pope 91–8, 118, 127–37
  and Sterne 208, 219–27
Mullan, John 214 n. 52

New, Melvyn 228 n. 83
Newton, Isaac 63
Nietzsche, Friedrich 4
Norris, John 59, 228 n. 83
Norton, David Fate 148
Nuttall, A. D. 88, 127 n. 73

Paine, Thomas 29
Parke, Catherine 280 n. 119
Pascal, Blaise 43, 44 n. 93, 129
Plato 4, 41–2, 103, 108, 131–3
Pope, Alexander 7–8, 86–137, 273,
    280

and Bolingbroke 86, 98–111,
  114–16, 130–4
To Bolingbroke 89–96, 98–105,
  134–5
To Cobham 117–20
and 'easy' writing 165, 271
Eloisa to Abelard 112
Essay on Man 30–2, 46, 57, 87–9,
  103–5, 109–30, 137
and Hume 125, 147, 154, 156,
  189, 251
Iliad 112
on instinct 122–7
and Locke 91–7
and Montaigne 91–8, 118,
  127–37
'Opus Magnum' 96–7
on passion 117–22, 250–2
and Prior 92–5
The Rape of the Lock 112
and Sterne 191–2, 251
Unfortunate Lady 112
on words 11, 65
Popkin, Richard 8 n. 11
Prior, Matthew 34–5, 37, 45, 68–9,
  92–5
Pyrrho 13–14

Richetti, John 140 n. 6, 165 n. 56
Rorty, Richard 3–4
Rousseau, Jean-Jacques 47–9, 53, 212,
  229
Ruffhead, Owen 266–7, 270

scepticism:
  and (belief in) illusion 81–5, 161–3,
    220–1, 224–5, 229–31, 246–8,
    276–7
  and irony 2–4, 29–32, 40–2,
    49–50, 103, 132–4, 147–9,
    177–87, 256–62
  and language 11–13, 82–4, 64–9,
    195–6, 214–16, 266–75
  and religion 9–10, 14–23, 73–4,
    114–16, 129–30, 175–87, 190,
    238–40, 262–3
  and singularity 68–9, 210–14,
    222–3, 235, 277–9
  and society 46–53, 125–6, 159–67,
    186–9, 271–5
  and the will 40–2, 91, 98–101,
    153–9, 244–52, 270–1
Scott, Walter 140

Shaftesbury, Anthony Cooper, 3rd Earl
  of 50, 72
Shenstone, William 269
Simpson, David 140 n. 6, 185 n. 103
Sitter, John 160 n. 42, 164 n. 53
Smith, Adam 139–40, 150, 174, 179
Socrates 3, 24, 39–42, 103, 133, 162
  n. 48, 220
Solomon, Harry 88 n. 2, 111 n. 48
Spectator, The 84–5, 164, 270–1
Stack, Frank 101–2
Steele, Richard 211–12
Sterne, Laurence 27–30, 46, 189–231,
  280
  the Bastille 200–2
  Bobby's death 193–8
  end of *Sentimental Journey* 230–1
  hobby-horses 192, 210, 213–14,
    217
  and Hume 150, 154, 189, 191, 193
  Jenny 228, 230
  and Johnson 194, 204, 210–11,
    217–18, 232, 234–6, 248,
    250–1, 277–8
  Journal to Eliza 228–30
  and Locke 68, 83, 204–6, 211, 214
  mechanism and psychology 204–7
  and Montaigne 44, 208, 219–27
  and Pope 191–2, 251
  sermon: on conscience 227–8
  sermon: 'Philanthropy
    Recommended' 198–200
  singularity 210–14, 222–3
  stoicism 223–6
  Toby's amours 207–10, 215–16
  Toby and the fly 213
  Trim 202–9
  Walter 191–4
Stillingfleet, Edward 60 n. 17, 64, 72,
  75–6, 79–80, 93 n. 12
Strawson, Galen 148 n. 21
Swift, Jonathan:
  'Digression concerning Madness'
    52–3, 152–3, 167, 171
  on language 67, 196
  on Locke 59–61, 67
  and Pope 120, 123–4
  spider and bee 93 n. 12

Tave, Stuart 211
Temple, William 46
Thrale, Hester 235, 240, 271 n. 97
Tindal, Matthew 110

Toland, John 60, 110
Traugott, John 227 n.

Voltaire (François Arouet) 57, 115, 204

Walpole, Horace 270, 272

Warburton, William 87, 89, 91–2, 102
Watts, Isaac 9, 73, 75, 77
Wehrs, Donald 219 n. 68
Wesley, John 9–10

Young, Edward 132

Lightning Source UK Ltd.
Milton Keynes UK
UKHW012359240223
417644UK00001B/27

9 780199 253180